Family Consecration
Prayer & Meditation Book™

Divine Mercy Edition

Compiled by Jerome F. Coniker

D0862419

Apostolate for Family Consecration®

ii

NIHIL OBSTAT: Rev. Msgr. Socrates Villegas
    Vicar General, Archdiocese of Manila

IMPRIMATUR: His Eminence Jaime Cardinal Sin
    Archbishop of Manila

January 18, 1998

© MCMXCVIII *Apostolate for Family Consecration,* Inc.
All Rights Reserved in All Media.

Apostolate for Family Consecration®
John Paul II Holy Family Center, known as
Catholic Familyland®, 3375 County Road 36
Bloomingdale, OH 43910-7903 U.S.A.
Phone: 740-765-4301 or 1-800-FOR-MARY
Fax: 740-765-5561 • www.familyland.org
e-mail: info@familyland.org   **U.S.A.**

In the Philippines:
Apostolate for Family Consecration®
St. Joseph Center, P.O. Box 0026
Las Piñas City, PHILIPPINES
Philippines' Phone: (632) 800-4440 or 800-4439
Phil. Fax: (632) 800-4438 • email: st_paul@mozcom.com

Library of Congress Catalog Card Number: 94-80245
ISBN: 0-932406-31-9

Scripture quotations are taken from the Revised Standard
Version of the Bible (unless otherwise indicated), © 1946, 1952,
1971 by the Division of Christian Education of the National
Council of the Churches of Christ in the USA and used by permission. Illustrations are by Charles Jaskiewicz and are taken
from *The Apostolate's (Vatican Approved) Family Catechism.*
The pictures on pages 10, 41, 316, 347, and 511 are used by
permission of the Apostleship of Prayer.

Founded in 1975

APOSTOLATE
for family consecration®
Helping you nourish families through the Catholic Faith

Canonical Global Center — Archdiocese of New York

FOREWORD

THE STRATEGIC VISION of Jesus Christ is clear: "That all may be one" (Jn 17:11). His mission is equally clear: "to bring glad tidings to the poor, to proclaim liberty to captives, recovery of sight to the blind and release to prisoners" (Lk 4:18). His objectives are manifold, but His strategy is to effect the adoption of every person as a child of God. This means that Jesus strategically uses the temporal reality of the *human family* as a model for the Church. In other words, the Church was founded by our Lord to be the *Family of God*. He Himself deliberately entered the world through a mother and was educated in a family setting. He introduced God as Father, Himself as the Son, named those who did the will of His Father as His brothers and sisters, and gave us His mother to be our own.

This is why Church communion must always be seen in a family context. The "People of God" are not just "people," they are more precisely *children*, and unless we become so, we cannot enter His kingdom. In order for us to be of God, we are to be "a people set apart" or consecrated; and applying the same argument, the Church must therefore become "a universal family set apart"—composed of families consecrated to the one God, restored and united in Christ, by the healing power of the Holy Spirit.

We must be set apart from the world before we can be united into the Church. But while these truths are somewhat difficult to understand, we must continue pondering them in our hearts with the *simplicity* of children. Simple prayer is the key to progressive simplicity, which in turn leads us to a deeper faith. This is why I am so thankful to the Lord and Our Lady for the Apostolate for Family Consecration, a ministry to the family undertaken by families themselves! The AFC now offers us this *Family Consecration Prayer & Meditation Book* which contains volumes of truths "in a few precise words." More than a compendium of prayers and lists, it includes a way of looking at Christian life that is precisely and unerringly in a family context.

We must compliment the AFC for its transparent openness to reveal itself, share its gifts and in the process, enrich itself with the gifts of others. Cardinal Francis Arinze's contribution to this book [see section 68], needless to say, is particularly uplifting, for it is a veritable personal retreat guide. The good Cardinal himself is a statement of simplicity. The Coniker family has acknowledged and responded to a call beyond their own family's; and because of this, they have become a real treasure to the Universal Family. The Apostolate for Family Consecration is no longer theirs alone; it effectively belongs to the whole Church.

I fully endorse and encourage married couples to avail of this manual of family spirituality. It will clarify greatly their grasp of the "true and proper ministry" that is theirs to undertake. It is a great outline for the clergy's ministry to families. Let us not mistake the overall goal of this book: to effect a consecration — a "setting apart" for God — of all families, as a preparation for ecclesial communion. Let us avail of its spiritual wealth to prepare for the "year of favor from the Lord."

✝ Jaime Cardinal L. Sin
Archbishop of Manila

Jaime Card. Sin

Villa San Miguel, 18 January 1998
Feast of the Santo Niño

CONTENTS

53. **Examination of Conscience Exercises***

Family Consecration Prayer & Meditation Book codes:

FCPB = All Family Consecration Prayer & Meditation Books
FCPB-DM = Divine Mercy Edition
FCPB-MC = Marian Consecration Edition
FCPB-JS = St. Joseph & the Communion of Saints Edition
FCCI = Family Consecration Classics I Edition

THE FAMILY APOSTOLATE™

The Apostolate for Family Consecration was founded on June 18, the month of the Sacred Heart, during the Holy Year of 1975, and was officially approved by the Catholic Church in the month of Our Lady, October 3, 1975.

On March 25, 1986, the Feast of the Annunciation, the founder of the Family Apostolate was inspired to adopt the Marian and Family centered spirituality of Pope John Paul II as the spirituality of the AFC. On the following day, it was officially approved for the entire work.

The mission of the Apostolate for Family Consecration is to nourish families through the Catholic Faith and to simultaneously consecrate families and parishes in the Truth as found in Sacred Scripture (especially Mt. 5-7, Lk. 1, Jn. 6 & 17, and 1 Cor. 13), the *Catechism of the Catholic Church*, *The Splendor of Truth*, *The Gospel of Life*, and other works of Pope John Paul II; and St. Louis de Montfort's Marian consecration, which Pope John Paul II has made and proclaimed.

This mission is accomplished by providing parents, bishops, pastors, and spiritual associations with on-going tri-media evangelization and catechetical systems designed to transform families, neighborhoods, and parishes into truly God-centered communities by creatively sharing and proclaiming the timeless truths of the Catholic Faith as embodied in the Eucharistic, Marian, and family-centered spirituality of Pope John Paul II. This transformation is accomplished primarily through a structured outreach program known as

The Apostolate's *Lay Ecclesial Team Evangelization System,*™ which is open to individuals of diverse Church-approved spiritualities and associations.

The Family Apostolate's motto is:

*All for the Sacred and
Eucharistic Heart of Jesus;
all through the Sorrowful and
Immaculate Heart of Mary;
all in union with St. Joseph.*

See section 800 for suggestions on how to pray and use this prayer and meditation book. We suggest that you first reflectively read the following key sections: 68, 77, 42a, 53c, 73, 67a, 69, and 102, respectively.

THE APOSTOLATE'S CREDO

The "Credo" and positive attitude of the Apostolate for Family Consecration is taken from Pope John Paul II's statement recorded in his newspaper, *L'Osservatore Romano,* on July 1, 1985. We are not to criticize, but to overcome evil with good.

"We must not deny or forget these negative facts. But neither must we dwell upon this shadowy area. It is not a problem of pointing an accusing finger at others, at this or that individual, when many are involved, perhaps even ourselves. **We must seek the deeper reasons, the spiritual causes**.

"In order to change the world you are asked to live in a different way. Not on the superficial level, a prey to the many pressures that our consumer society puts on to you, but profoundly. Find a pause for prayer, for reflection, for silence, in order to discover your true selves in a true relationship with God and with others.

"**It is not possible to live and grow in the faith without the support of a group, of a Christian community.** It is here that you will learn together to build a better world.

"**These groups must not be closed in upon themselves.**"

THE APOSTOLATE'S MANDATE

The mandate for the Apostolate for Family Consecration is set forth very clearly in the documents of the Second Vatican Council, of which Pope John Paul II, as Archbishop Karol Wojtyla, was a key participant.

"The laity...are given this special vocation: to make the Church present and fruitful in those places and circumstances where it is only through them that she can become the salt of the earth. Thus, every lay person, through those gifts given to him, is at once the witness and the living instrument of the mission of the Church itself 'according to the measure of Christ's bestowal' (Eph. 4:7)." (Vatican II document, *Lumen Gentium,* 33)

"All the laity, then, have the exalted duty of working for the ever greater spread of the divine plan of salvation to all men, of every epoch and all over the earth. Therefore may the way be clear for them to share diligently in the salvific work of the Church according to their ability and the needs of the times." (*ibid.*)

"Organizations created for group apostolate afford support to their members, train them for the apostolate, carefully assign and direct their apostolic activities; and as a result a much richer harvest can be hoped for from them than if each one were to act on his own." (Vatican II document, *Apostolicam Actuositatem,* 18)

LETTER FROM POPE JOHN PAUL II

*read by his United States
Ambassador, Archbishop
Cacciavillan, at The
Apostolate's annual Totus Tuus
"Consecrate Them in Truth"
Conference:*

I have learned with pleasure that on October 22-24, 1993, the Apostolate for Family Consecration will sponsor a Conference in Pittsburgh on the theme "Consecrate Them in Truth." I ask you kindly to convey to all associated with this worthy initiative my greetings and the assurance of my closeness in prayer.

Since the Conference aims to support and implement the message of the recent World Youth Day, I renew the invitation which I made in Denver: "I ask you to have the courage to commit yourselves **to the truth**. Have the courage **to believe the Good News about Life** which Jesus teaches in the Gospel. Open your minds and hearts to the beauty of all that God has made and to his special, personal love for each one of you" (Vigil, August 14, 1993, No.4).

It is my hope that the Conference will inspire many Christian families to become ever more authentic "domestic Churches," in which the word of God is received with joy, bears fruit in lives of holiness and love, and shines forth with new brilliance as a beacon of hope for all to see. The faith-filled witness of Christian families is an essential element in the new evangelization to which the Holy Spirit is calling the Church in our time.

I am pleased that the Conference will seek to develop effective means of passing on to families and parishes the rich deposit of the Church's faith as presented in the *Catechism of the Catholic Church*. **Because "family catechesis precedes, accompanies and enriches all other forms of catechesis"** *(Catechesi Tradendae, 68)*, **I encourage the Apostolate for Family Consecration in its efforts to promote an effective catechesis in homes and parishes.**

With these sentiments, I commend the work of the Conference to the intercession of Mary, Mother of the Church. To the organizers, speakers and participants I cordially impart my Apostolic Blessing, which I willingly extend to all the members of their families.

From the Vatican, October 10, 1993

Joannes Paulus PP. II

Pope John Paul II blesses AFC founders Gwen and Jerry Coniker—parents of 13 and grandparents of 35.

SPIRITUAL SUPPORT OF MOTHER TERESA

On May 1, 1976, the Feast of St. Joseph, Mother Teresa of Calcutta joined the Advisory Council of the Apostolate for Family Consecration. She said that our work was the most important work in the world, that the most devastating starvation in the western world today is the spiritual undernourishment of the family.

On April 22, 1978, Mother Teresa wrote:

"Dear Mr. Coniker, Let every member of our community be a Sacri-State Member for the work of the Apostolate for Family Consecration. I wholeheartedly pray for the success of The Apostolate and its marvelous work in renewing the family through systematic transformation of neighborhoods into God-centered communities. God bless you."

The Offering of Suffering for our Work

Our spiritual support comes from our Sacri-State Members, who are suffering for our work. Mother Teresa told us to find a suffering (Sacri-State) member for every active member in The Apostolate. This suffering member, she advised, should offer all his/her suffering to God, through Mary, for a specific active member.

This union, she said, would be a great spiritual power that would make our active member's work more fruitful. An active member, in turn, offers his/her work to the Holy Family in union with his suffering Sacri-State member—called by Mother Teresa, one's "second-self."

Mother Teresa with the Coniker family of 13 children. Mother Teresa visited The Apostolate's center to produce a series of videotapes on family consecration.

"As long as you did it to one of these My least brethren, you did it to Me."

LDM+
7th October, 1994

Dear Jerry and Gwen Coniker

God love you for the beautiful work that you are doing for family Consecration, and especially for all that you are doing to save and protect the little unborn babies. Let us pray now that the "Be Not Afraid Family Hours" [on video] will touch the hearts of people, bring them closer to God, and help them to see that the child is the most beautiful gift of God to the family.

I know that you have both given of yourselves wholeheartedly to serve God through this special apostolate of yours, and I am praying for you, that you receive the help that you need and the necessary Graces for you to continue.

Keep the joy of loving Jesus in your hearts, and share this joy with all you meet, especially your own family.

God bless you
Mr Teresa mc

Mother Teresa

THE APOSTOLATE'S UNIQUE "FAMILY WISDOM CURRICULUM™"
A Means of Consecrating Families and Parishes in the Truth

The *Family Wisdom Curriculum* is a formation and teaching method which creatively uses an integrated system of three forms of media—video, audio, and the printed word—to draw families more deeply into Sacred Scripture, Vatican II documents, the *Catechism of the Catholic Church*, *The Splendor of Truth*, *Gospel of Life*, and other papal documents, and spiritual classics such as Dietrich von Hildebrand's *Transformation in Christ*.

Videotapes are used in a controlled environment such as the church or home. **Audiotapes** can be used to sanctify time while around the home, on vacation, driving, exercising, or cleaning. Common **books** are used in family, group, school, and parish settings.

The *Family Wisdom Curriculum* is designed by parents, yet it is taught by experts through video, audio, and the written word. It effectively links Catholic parents, children, teachers, and pastors in a parish or diocesan catechetical and evangelization process. The resources are interwoven to maximize comprehension and retention of Catholic truths, and most importantly, to facilitate family-to-family evangelization and the blending of the Catholic faith with Catholic family values.

The *Family Wisdom Curriculum* faculty is comprised of some of the greatest spiritual personalities in the Church, such as Pope John Paul II; Roman Curia members (the Pope's direct staff) such as Cardinal Alfonso Lopez Trujillo, Cardinal Francis Arinze, Cardinal Pio Laghi, Cardinal Jozef Tomko, Cardinal

Jose Sánchez, Cardinal Edouard Gagnon, Cardinal J. Francis Stafford, and Archbishop John Foley; prominent Church leaders of Asia such as Cardinal Jaime Sin, Bishop Ramón Arguelles, and Msgr. Josefino Ramirez; prominent Church leaders of the United States such as Archbishop Agostino Cacciavillan, Cardinals John O'Connor, Bernard Law, and Anthony Bevilacqua; and Bishops Gilbert Sheldon, Thomas Daily, and Thomas Welsh; as well as internationally known figures such as Mother Teresa and Fr. Patrick Peyton.

In this on-going formation and teaching method, the *Family Wisdom Curriculum* systematically consecrates people in the Truth and continually creates windows of opportunities for them to delve more deeply into Sacred Scripture, Vatican II, the *Catechism of the Catholic Church* and *The Splendor of Truth*. See pages 546–579.

FAMILY WISDOM CURRICULUM™

Evangelize with
Be Not Afraid Family Hours®
72 weekly videos—start them in the home and pray them into the parish church!

Family Catechism on Tape
Dialogue with Cardinal Arinze

interviewed by Jerry Coniker on 22 audio or video tapes

The Apostolate's Family Catechism™ is cross-referenced with the Catechism of the Catholic Church and with Veritatis Splendor

Catechize with the Vatican-approved
Apostolate's Family Catechism™
Includes quotes from Sacred Scripture & Vatican Council II documents. Contains over 600 pictures.

 *Live your consecration by joyfully fulfilling the responsibilities of each present moment for Jesus, through His Immaculate Mother, in union with St. Joseph.*
(*Reflectively read sections 42a and 77.*)

1a. Consecration to Jesus through the Immaculate Conception
A prayer for special occasions

Immaculate Mother, you are the masterpiece of God's creation. You are the Immaculate Conception and mirror His likeness and Will. Mother, the source of your power is your Divine Maternity, and therefore, all generations will call you blessed. You are the perfect model for the members of the Church to imitate, because you always seek to form others into the image of your Divine Son, so that they can become one spirit with Him (cf. 1 Corinthians 6:17).

I, (name), a poor sinner, solemnly consecrate myself, my family, the Apostolate for Family Consecration, and my country to you, the Immaculate Conception. I ask you, as our Patroness, to enable us to transform our country into a God-centered nation, thus helping us to fulfill our destiny.

Mother of Sorrows, you manifested your motherhood at Calvary for us, and through your maternal Immaculate Heart, your Mystical Spouse, the Holy Spirit, dispenses His life-giving graces. Please obtain for me the grace of a tender love for your Divine Son in the Most Holy Eucharist, for St. Joseph, and for my family and community.

Through you, most Immaculate Heart of Mary, in union with St. Joseph, I unconditionally give to the Sacred Heart of Jesus all my spiritual and material possessions.

Most pleasing Daughter of the Father, I ask you to apply all my indulgences to the Poor Souls of my loved ones and others in Purgatory and ask them, along with the angels and saints, to pray to the Lord, our God, that I, my family, and the members of my community and country, may die to our selfishness and have the desire always to truly do His Will, no matter what the cost. Amen.

2. The Magnificat (cf. Luke 1:46-55)
Saturday Meditation

My soul magnifies the Lord, and my spirit rejoices in God my Savior:

Because He has regarded the lowliness of His handmaid; for behold, henceforth all generations shall call me blessed;

Because He who is mighty has done great things for me, and holy is His Name;

And His mercy is from generation to generation on those who fear Him.

He has shown might with His arm, He has scattered the proud in the conceit of their hearts.

He has put down the mighty from their thrones, and has exalted the lowly.

He has filled the hungry with good things, and the rich He has sent away empty.

He has given help to Israel, His servant, mindful of His mercy, even as He spoke to our fathers, to Abraham and to his posterity for ever. Amen.

2a. The Family Apostolate's Morning Offering *(daily)*

Most Holy Trinity, Father, Son, and Holy Spirit, I adore You profoundly. Help me and all the members of my family, parish, and The Apostolate to take up our crosses this day and to be strengthened and guided by the Most Holy Family.

Give us the grace to fulfill our destinies and to have total trust in You. Help us not to be disturbed about the past *(provided that we are in the state of grace)* or worried about the future, but to realize that we are secure in Your Will when we fulfill the responsibilities of each present moment as perfectly and as mercifully as we can for the unique mission of the Apostolate for Family Consecration. Let The Apostolate fulfill its destiny while always abiding in Christ and remaining an obedient and fruitful branch of the Catholic Church.

Help us to gratefully offer our prayers, works, joys, and sufferings, along with our interior and exterior possessions, including the value of our good actions, past, present, and future, all for the Sacred and Eucharistic Heart of Jesus, all through the Sorrowful and Immaculate Heart of Mary, all in union with St. Joseph. Amen.

2b. Hail Holy Queen

Daily prayer of the Archconfraternity of
Our Lady of Guadalupe Shrine & the AFC

Hail Holy Queen, Mother of mercy; our life, our sweetness, and our hope. To thee do we cry, poor banished children of Eve. To thee do we send up our sighs, mourning, and weeping in this valley of tears.

Turn then, most gracious advocate, thine eyes of mercy toward us; and after this our exile, show unto us the blessed fruit of thy womb, Jesus. O clement, O loving, O sweet Virgin Mary.

Pray for us, O holy Mother of God, that we may be made worthy of the promises of Christ. Amen.

2c. The Angelus *(3 times daily)*

V. The angel of the Lord declared unto Mary,

R. And she conceived by the Holy Spirit.

Hail Mary...

V. Behold the Handmaid of the Lord,

R. Be it done unto me according to thy word.

Hail Mary...

V. And the Word was made flesh,
R. And dwelt among us.

Hail Mary...

V. Pray for us, O holy Mother of God,

R. That we may be made worthy of the promises of Christ.

Let us pray: Pour forth, we beseech Thee, O Lord, Thy grace into our hearts; that we, to whom the Incarnation of Christ Thy Son was made known by the message of an angel, may by His Passion and Cross be brought to the glory of His Resurrection. Through the same Christ our Lord. Amen.

2d. Daily Prayer to the Holy Spirit

Most Holy Spirit, source of all holiness, we pray that humanity will soon recognize and embrace the Catholic Church's timeless teachings so that we will see, in our age, the public reign of Christ through Mary, in union with St. Joseph, for which we should be working and sacrificing.

Be our Union of Love with the Father, the Holy Family, and all of the people in our lives, especially with our families and community.

Mary our Mother please show us how to draw closer to your Spouse, the Holy Spirit. We ask all of this in your Son's Name, Jesus Christ. Amen.

2e. Immaculate Conception Prayer for The Apostolate *(daily)*

O Immaculate Conception, Mary, my Mother, live in me, my family, and all the members, benefactors, and candidates of The Apostolate; act in us; speak in and through us. Think your thoughts in our minds, love through our hearts. Give us your own dispositions and feelings. Teach, lead, and guide us to Jesus. Correct, enlighten, and expand our thoughts and behavior. Possess our souls; take over our entire personalities and lives. Replace us with yourself. Incline us to constant adoration and thanksgiving; pray in and through us. Let us live in you and keep us in this union always. Amen.

2f. St. Joseph Prayer for The Apostolate *(daily)*

St. Joseph, unite my prayers with those of the other members and friends of the society of the Apostolate for Family Consecration throughout the world.

We know, St. Joseph, that Our Lord will refuse you nothing. Please ask God to bless The Apostolate and all of its members and friends. Ask Our Lord to help The Apostolate and its Lay Ecclesial Teams to make the best use of the modern means of communications to consecrate families, parishes, and movements in the Truth and to help families understand and imitate the Eucharistic, Marian, and family-centered spirituality of Pope John Paul II.

St. Joseph, we are confident that you will remove all obstacles in the path of this spiritual renewal program so that our society may be transformed through a chain reaction which will renew our families, neighborhoods, parishes, schools, country, and the entire world.

Form the society of the Apostolate for Family Consecration into a useful instrument of the Holy Family, and never let its members and leaders lose their holy zeal for souls or fall into the sin of spiritual pride like that of the Pharisees, which is so fatal to the work of God. Use The Apostolate as an instrument to bring about the social reign of the Most Holy Family in our age. Amen.

2g. St. Michael the Archangel *(daily)*

St. Michael the Archangel, defend us in battle; be our safeguard against the wickedness and snares of the devil. May God rebuke him, we humbly pray, and do you, O prince of the heavenly host, by the power of God, cast into hell, satan and all the other evil spirits who prowl through the world seeking the ruin of souls. Amen.

2h. Guardian Angel *(daily)*

Angel of God, my guardian dear, to whom God's love commits me here, ever this day be at my side, to light, to guard, to rule, and to guide. Amen.

2i. First Corinthians 13
Try to read frequently

If I speak in the tongues of men and of angels, but have not love, I am a noisy gong or a clanging cymbal. 2 And if I have prophetic powers, and understand all mysteries and all knowledge, and if I have all faith, so as to remove mountains, but have not love, I am nothing. 3 If I give away all I have, and if I deliver my body to be burned, but have not love, I gain nothing.

4 Love is patient and kind; love is not jealous or boastful; 5 it is not arrogant or rude. Love does not insist on its own way; it is not irritable or resentful; 6 it does not rejoice at wrong, but rejoices in the right. 7 Love bears all things, believes all things, hopes all things, endures all things.

8 Love never ends; as for prophecies, they will pass away; as for tongues, they will cease; as for knowledge, it will pass away. 9 For our knowledge is imperfect and our prophecy is imperfect; 10 but when the perfect comes, the imperfect will pass away. 11 When I was a child, I spoke like a child, I thought like a child, I reasoned like a child; when I became a man, I gave up childish ways. 12 For now we see in a mirror dimly, but then face to face. Now I know in part; then I shall understand fully, even as I have been fully understood. 13 So faith, hope, love abide, these three; but the greatest of these is love.

4. Apostolate's Act of Consecration
Try to say this prayer after Mass

Heavenly Father, grant that we, who are nourished by the Body and Blood of Your Divine Son, may die to our own selfishness and be one spirit with Christ, as we seek to fulfill Your distinctive plan for our lives. *(pause)*

Form me and all the members of my family, community, and The Apostolate into instruments of atonement. Unite our entire lives with the Holy Sacrifice of Jesus in the Mass of Calvary, and accept our seed sacrifice offering of all of our spiritual and material possessions, for the Sacred and Eucharistic Heart of Jesus, through the Sorrowful and Immaculate Heart of Mary, in union with St. Joseph. *(pause)*

Our Father, let Sacred Scripture's Four "C's" of Confidence, Conscience, seed-Charity, and Constancy be our guide for living our consecration as peaceful children, and purified instruments of the Most Holy Family. *(pause)*

Let us live our consecration by remaining perpetually confident, calm, cheerful, and compassionate, especially with the members of our own family and community. *(pause)*

Please protect our loved ones and ourselves from the temptations of the world, the flesh, and the devil. Help us to become more sensitive to the inspirations of Your Holy Spirit, the Holy Family, our Patron Saints and Guardian Angels. *(pause)*

And now, Most Heavenly Father, inspire us to establish the right priorities for Your precious gift of time. And most of all, help us to be more sensitive to the needs and feelings of our loved ones. *(pause)*

Never let us forget the souls in Purgatory who are dependent upon us for help. Enable us to gain, for the Poor Souls of our loved ones and others, as many indulgences as possible. We ask You this, Our Father, in the Name of Our Lord and Savior Jesus Christ, Your Son and the Son of Mary. Amen.

5. Short Form
Consecration Prayer

Most Holy Family, unite my daily life with the Holy Sacrifice of the Mass. Accept all of my spiritual and material possessions as my seed of sacrifice offered to the Sacred and Eucharistic Heart of Jesus, through the Sorrowful and Immaculate Heart of Mary, in union with St. Joseph. This shall be my commitment in life, in death, and in eternity. Amen.

6a-9. The Holy Rosary
*Five decades of the Rosary
should be prayed daily*

For the Church's teachings on the Rosary, see the Catechism of the Catholic Church, paragraphs 971, 2678, and 2708.

How to pray the Rosary:

Pray the Apostles' Creed (#6a) on the Crucifix. Then offer one Our Father (#6b) on the large bead, and three Hail Marys (#6c) on each of the three small beads for the Holy Father, the Pope. After the three Hail Marys, pray the Glory Be (#7a), the Fatima Rosary Prayer (#7b), and the Consecration Prayer (#7c).

Announce the Mystery for the decade (see #7d) and meditate on it while praying. Pray one Our Father on the large bead. Pray the Hail Mary on each of the ten small beads. On the next large bead, pray the Glory Be, the Rosary Prayer, and the Consecration Prayer. Then, on the same large bead, announce the next Mystery and begin again with the Our Father. Continue until you have prayed all five decades.

After the Rosary, pray #8, 8a, 9, 10 & 11a. (Note: Pope Leo XIII asked for a prayer to St. Joseph to be recited at the end of the Rosary.) Please see pages 582, 616, and 649 for Rosary meditation resources.

6a. Apostles' Creed

I believe in God, the Father Almighty, Creator of Heaven and earth; and in Jesus Christ, His only Son, our Lord; Who was conceived by the Holy Spirit, born of the Virgin Mary, suffered under Pontius Pilate, was crucified, died and was buried; He descended into hell, the third day He rose again from the dead, He ascended into Heaven, and is seated at the right hand of God, the Father Almighty. From thence He shall come to judge the living and the dead. I believe in the Holy Spirit, the Holy Catholic Church, the Communion of Saints, the forgiveness of sins, the resurrection of the body, and life everlasting. Amen.

For an explanation of the term "descended into hell," see paragraphs 631-637 of the Catechism of the Catholic Church. For a complete explanation of the Apostles' Creed, see paragraphs 198-1065.

6b. Our Father

In the Philippines:

Our Father, Who art in Heaven; hallowed be Thy name; Thy Kingdom come; Thy will be done on earth as it is in Heaven. Give us this day our daily bread; and forgive us our trespasses, as we forgive those who trespass against us; and lead us not into temptation; but deliver us from evil. Amen.

Our Father in Heaven, holy be Your Name. Your Kingdom come. Your Will be done on earth as it is in Heaven. Give us this day our daily bread; and forgive us our sins, as we forgive those who sin against us. Do not bring us to the test, but deliver us from evil. Amen.

For a detailed explanation of the Our Father, see paragraphs 2759–2865 of the Catechism of the Catholic Church.

6c. Hail Mary

In the Philippines:

Hail Mary, full of grace; the Lord is with thee; blessed art thou among women and blessed is the fruit of thy womb, Jesus. Holy Mary, Mother of God, pray for us sinners, now and at the hour of our death. Amen.

Hail Mary, full of grace; the Lord is with you; blessed are you among women and blessed is the fruit of your womb, Jesus. Holy Mary, Mother of God, pray for us sinners, now and at the hour of our death. Amen.

To learn about the Church's teachings on Mary, see the Catechism of the Catholic Church, paragraphs 411, 487–511, 721–726, 773, 829, 963–975, 2617–2619, and 2622.

7a. Glory Be

Glory be to the Father, and to the Son, and to the Holy Spirit. As it was in the beginning, is now, and ever shall be, world without end. Amen.

For more on the Holy Trinity, see the Catechism of the Catholic Church's index, under "Trinity." Some key paragraphs are: 232-234, 238-246, 253-255, 683 and 687.

7b. Fatima Rosary Prayer

The prayer Our Lady of Fatima requested to be said after each decade of the Rosary.

O My Jesus, forgive us our sins; save us from the fires of hell; lead all souls to Heaven, especially those who are in most need of Your mercy.

7c. The Apostolate's Motto and Short Form Consecration Prayer
Said after every decade of the Rosary following 7b

All for the Sacred and Eucharistic Heart of Jesus, all through the Sorrowful and Immaculate Heart of Mary, all in union with St. Joseph.

After the Rosary, pray #8, 8a, 9, 10 & 11a.

7d. Mysteries of the Rosary

FIRST JOYFUL MYSTERY

The Annunciation of the Archangel Gabriel to the Virgin Mary.

We ask for the gifts of the Holy Spirit and an increase in the virtue of humility.

(Read St. Luke 1:28–38 and the Catechism of the Catholic Church, paragraphs 456–486.)

Hail Mary full of grace.

Let it be done unto me according to Thy word.

SECOND JOYFUL MYSTERY

The Visitation of the Virgin Mary to Elizabeth, the Mother of St. John the Baptist.

We ask for the gifts of the Holy Spirit and an increase in the virtue of generosity.

(Read St. Luke 1:39–56.)

My soul magnifies the Lord.

His mercy is from generation to generation.

THIRD JOYFUL MYSTERY

The Birth of Our Lord at Bethlehem.

*We ask for the gifts of the Holy Spirit and
an increase in the virtue of detachment
from the things of this world.*

(Read St. Luke 2:4–20 and the Catechism of the Catholic
Church, paragraphs 437, 487–511, and 525.)

There was no room for Him at the inn.

The Word was made flesh and He dwelt among us.

Fourth Joyful Mystery

The Presentation of Our Lord in the Temple.

*We ask for the gifts of the Holy Spirit and
an increase in the virtue of obedience.*

*(Read St. Luke 2:22–40 and the Catechism of the Catholic
Church, paragraphs 144–152 and 527–530.)*

Every first-born male must be consecrated to the Lord.

*This Child is set for the fall and rising of
many in Israel...a sign of contradiction.*

FIFTH JOYFUL MYSTERY

The Finding of Our Lord in the Temple.

*We ask for the gifts of the Holy Spirit and
an increase in the virtue of fear of the Lord—
fear of ever losing God because of our sins.*

*(Read St. Luke 2:41–52 and the Catechism of the Catholic
Church, paragraphs 531–534.)*

They looked for Him with great anxiety.

Did you not know that I must be in My Father's house?

FIRST SORROWFUL MYSTERY

The Agony of Our Lord in the Garden of Gethsemane.

We ask for the gifts of the Holy Spirit and the grace of abandonment to the will of the Father.

(Read St. Luke 22:39–46 and the Catechism of the Catholic Church, paragraph 612.)

Father if You are willing, remove this cup from Me...but not My will, but Yours be done.

SECOND SORROWFUL MYSTERY

The Scourging of Our Lord at the Pillar.

We ask for the gifts of the Holy Spirit and an increase in the virtue of purity to spread throughout the world.

(Read St. Mark 14:55–15:20 and the Catechism of the Catholic Church, paragraphs 2517–2533.)

Anxious to satisfy the mob, Pilate ordered Jesus to be brutally scourged.

THIRD SORROWFUL MYSTERY

The Crowning of Our Lord with Thorns.

We ask for the gifts of the Holy Spirit and an increase in the virtue of moral courage, by not striking back at those who hurt us.

(Read St. Mark 15:16–20, St. John 18:28-46 and 19:1-16; and the Catechism of the Catholic Church, paragraphs 2838–2845.)

They crowned Him with thorns and called out, "Crucify Him! Crucify Him!"

FOURTH SORROWFUL MYSTERY

The Carrying of the Cross by Our Lord to Calvary.

We ask for the gifts of the Holy Spirit and an increase in the virtue of constancy.

(Read St. Luke 23:26–31 and St. Mark 15:21-22.)

Our Mother of Sorrows is with Our Lord on His way to Calvary

Fifth Sorrowful Mystery

The Crucifixion and Death of Our Lord.

*We ask for the gifts of the Holy Spirit and
the grace to die to our own selfishness so that
we can be one spirit with Christ.*

*(Read St. John 19:23–30, St. Matthew 27:32-56, and the
Catechism of the Catholic Church, paragraphs 613–630.)*

*My God, My God, why have You abandoned Me!
(Our Lord is feeling the deep pain of rejected love.)*

FIRST GLORIOUS MYSTERY

The Resurrection of Our Lord from the Dead.

*We ask for the gifts of the Holy Spirit and
an increase in the virtue of faith.*

*(Read St. John 20:19–31, St. Luke 24:1-49, and the Catechism
of the Catholic Church, paragraphs 631–658.)*

*Peace be with you...as My Father has
sent Me, I am sending you.*

SECOND GLORIOUS MYSTERY

The Ascension of Our Lord into Heaven.

*We ask for the gifts of the Holy Spirit and
an increase in the virtue of hope.*

*(Read St. Mark 16:15–20, St. Matthew 28:16-20, and the
Catechism of the Catholic Church, paragraphs 659–664.)*

*Go and teach...make diciples of all nations...remember,
I am with you always, until the end of time.*

THIRD GLORIOUS MYSTERY

The Descent of the Holy Spirit upon Mary and the Apostles.

We ask for the gifts of the Holy Spirit and an increase in the virtue of charity.

(Read Acts 2:1–38 and the Catechism of the Catholic Church, paragraphs 731–747.)

I will pour out My Spirit upon all mankind.

FOURTH GLORIOUS MYSTERY

The Assumption of Our Blessed Mother into Heaven.

We ask for the gifts of the Holy Spirit and the grace of a happy death for all the members of our family and The Apostolate.

(Read Wisdom 7:22–30 and 8:1–21; and the Catechism of the Catholic Church, paragraphs. 964–966.)

She is a reflection of the eternal light, pure mirror of God's active power.

FIFTH GLORIOUS MYSTERY

The Coronation of Our Blessed Lady as Queen of Heaven and Earth.

We ask for the gifts of the Holy Spirit and an increase in true devotion to Mary to spread throughout the world.

(Read Revelation 12, Genesis 3:15, and the Catechism of the Catholic Church, paragraphs 966–975.)

Note: The seven gifts of the Holy Spirit are Wisdom, Understanding, Knowledge, Fortitude, Counsel, Piety, and Fear of the Lord. Also see 53L of this book.

8. St. Joseph Prayer after the Rosary

Glorious St. Joseph, spouse of the Immaculate Virgin, obtain for me and all the members of my family and loved ones, a confident, sinless, generous, and patient heart, and perfect resignation to the Divine Will.

Be our guide, father, and model throughout life, that we may merit a death like yours, in the arms of Jesus and Mary.

Help us, St. Joseph, in our earthly strife, to fulfill our responsibilities and ever to lead a pure and blameless life.

Heavenly Father, please ask the Holy Spirit, Who resides in the innermost recesses of my soul, to help me to call to mind all of my sins and faults. Help me to detach myself from these faults and sins so that I can be a useful instrument in the hands of the Most Holy Family, to achieve Your distinctive plan for my life.

Let me now pause for a few moments to think of my sins, faults, and omissions.

8a. Examination of Conscience Prayer

Reflectively read your "key card" and part of the Examination of Conscience in section 53a–53m.

Mother Mary, please obtain for me, my family, and the members and families of The Apostolate the Gifts of the Holy Spirit and the grace to live the virtues which will help us overcome our primary faults. Let us be caught up in the Holy Spirit's love for the Father and the Holy Family.

9. Act of Contrition
Recited daily

O my God! I am heartily sorry for having offended Thee, and I detest all of my sins, because I dread the loss of Heaven and the pains of hell, but most of all because they have offended Thee, my God, Who art all-good and deserving of all my love. I firmly resolve with the help of Thy grace, to confess my sins, to do penance, and to amend my life. Amen.

Let us pray: Heavenly Father, in the Name of Our Lord Jesus Christ, we ask You to release a Poor Soul of one of our loved ones from Purgatory for each of us who have received Your Son in Holy Communion this day, and we ask these souls being released to pray continually that our families and the members and families of The Apostolate do Your will.

10. Seed-Charity Prayer in the Spirit of St. Francis
Try to reflect on one part each day

Lord, make me an instrument of Your peace;
Where there is hatred,
let me sow seeds of love;
Where there is injury,
let me sow seeds of pardon;
Where there is discord,
let me sow seeds of union;
Where there is doubt,
let me sow seeds of faith;
Where there is despair,
let me sow seeds of hope;
Where there is darkness,
let me sow seeds of light;
And where there is sadness,
let me sow seeds of joy.

O Divine Master, grant that I may not so much seek

to be consoled as to console You in others, to be loved, as to love You in others,

For it is in giving that we receive. It is in pardoning that we are pardoned, and it is in dying as a seed to our selfishness that we are born to eternal life. Amen.

11a. Act of Spiritual Communion
May be said throughout the day,
especially on Thursdays

My Jesus, I believe that You are in the Blessed Sacrament. I love You above all things, and I long for You in my soul. Since I cannot now receive You sacramentally, come at least spiritually into my heart. As though You have already come, I embrace You and unite myself entirely to You; never permit me to be separated from You. Amen.

11b. Mother Teresa's Nazareth Prayer for the Family
Recommended after the family Rosary

Heavenly Father, You have given us a model of life in the Holy Family of Nazareth. Help us, O loving Father, to make our family another Nazareth where love, peace, and joy reign.

May it be deeply contemplative, intensely Eucharistic, and vibrant with joy. Help us to stay together in joy and sorrow through family prayer. Teach us to see Jesus in the members of our family, especially in their distressing disguise.

May the Eucharistic Heart of Jesus make our hearts meek and humble like His and help us to carry out our family duties in a holy way.

May we love one another as God loves each one of us more and more each day, and forgive each others' faults as You forgive our sins.

Help us, O loving Father, to take whatever You give and to give whatever You take with a big smile.

Immaculate Heart of Mary, cause of our joy, pray for us. St. Joseph, pray for us. Holy Guardian Angels, be always with us, guide and protect us. Amen.

14. Act of Consecration to St. Joseph
Recited on Wednesdays

St. Joseph, I consecrate myself, my entire family and all of my loved ones to you, that you may ever be our father, our patron, and our guide in the way of salvation. Obtain for us purity of heart and a fervent devotion to the spiritual life. Grant that, following your example, we may direct all our actions to the greater glory of God, in union with the Sacred Heart of Jesus, the Immaculate Heart of Mary, and in union with you.

Finally, St. Joseph, pray for my family, my loved ones, and the members of the Apostolate, that we may be partakers in the peace and joy which were yours throughout your life and at the hour of your death. Amen.

14a. Seven Sorrows and Joys of St. Joseph Chaplet

*Recommended devotion for
Wednesdays in place of the Rosary*

1. Prayer

(All) Jesus and Mary, Saint Joseph loved you without bounds. He achieved a union with you that no other soul has been privileged to achieve. Use me as your earthly instrument to honor St. Joseph. I am reciting these prayers in union with You and the Holy Spirit.

2. Petition

(All) Glorious St. Joseph, accept this novena as our seed of faith in your powerful intercession with Almighty God and His Immaculate Mother. We are confident that God will multiply this seed of faith by helping us to fulfill the responsibilities we have taken upon ourselves. We pray that all the members of our families and loved ones will be spiritually and physically protected and guided to fulfill the vocations that God has predestined for them. We pray that all of our enterprises will be successful, and that our parish, diocese, and all apostolates flourish and be protected from error. And particularly we pray that God will grant us the favor we now ask of you, or if it is His will, one that is better for us.

(Pause and silently make your request.)

Pray the Apostles' Creed (#6a), one Our Father (#6b), three Hail Marys (#6c), and one Glory Be (#7a) for the Holy Father's intentions.

The Seven Sorrows and Joys of St. Joseph

First Sorrow and Joy

(Leader) St. Joseph, chaste spouse of the Immacu-

late Mother of God, by the deep SORROW which pierced your heart at the thought of quietly leaving Mary so that she would not be punished by the law when found to be with child; by the deep JOY that you felt when the angel revealed to you in a dream the mystery of the Incarnation of Jesus through the power of the Holy Spirit, and your vital role as the guardian of the Holy Family,

(All) St. Joseph, obtain for me, my family, and all the members and families of The Apostolate, from the Hearts of Jesus and Mary, the grace for surmounting all anxiety and the grace of total and absolute trust in God. Win for us from the Sacred Heart of Jesus the indestructible peace of which He is the eternal source.

Pray one Our Father, Seven Hail Marys, and one Glory Be.

(All) O My Jesus, forgive us our sins; save us from the fires of hell; lead all souls to Heaven, especially those who are in most need of Your mercy.

(All) All for the Sacred and Eucharistic Heart of Jesus, all through the Sorrowful and Immaculate Heart of Mary, all in union with St. Joseph.

Second Sorrow and Joy

(Leader) St. Joseph, faithful guardian of Jesus, by the bitter SORROW which your heart experienced in seeing the Child Jesus lying in a manger, and by the deep JOY which you did feel at seeing the Wise Men recognize and adore Him as their God,

(All) Grant through your prayers that my conscience and the consciences of all the members of my family and all the members and families of The Apostolate, purified by your protection, may become sinless cribs, where the Savior of the world may be received with love and respect.

Pray one Our Father, Seven Hail Marys, and one Glory Be.

(All) O My Jesus, forgive us our sins, save us from the fires of hell; lead all souls to Heaven, especially those who are in most need of Your mercy.

(All) All for the Sacred and Eucharistic Heart of Jesus, all through the Sorrowful and Immaculate Heart of Mary, all in union with St. Joseph.

Third Sorrow and Joy

(Leader) St. Joseph, by the SORROW with which your heart was pierced at the sight of the blood which flowed from the infant Jesus in the circumcision, and by the JOY that filled your soul at the privilege of bestowing the sacred and mysterious Name of Jesus,

(All) Intercede for us, that the merits of this Precious Blood, poured out as a Seed-Sacrifice offering for our salvation, may be applied to my family and all the members and families of The Apostolate, so that the Divine Name of Jesus may be engraved forever in our hearts.

Pray one Our Father, Seven Hail Marys, and one Glory Be.

(All) O My Jesus, forgive us our sins; save us from the fires of hell; lead all souls to Heaven, especially those who are in most need of Your mercy.

(All) All for the Sacred and Eucharistic Heart of Jesus, all through the Sorrowful and Immaculate Heart of Mary, all in union with St. Joseph.

Fourth Sorrow and Joy

(Leader) St. Joseph, by your deep SORROW when Simeon declared that the heart of Mary would be pierced with the sword of sorrow at the time that her Divine Son generously sacrificed Himself for our sins, and by your JOY when Simeon added that the Seed-Sacrifice offering of Jesus was to bear an abundant harvest of redeemed souls,

(All) Obtain for me, my family, and all the members and families of The Apostolate, the grace to unite ourselves with the sorrows of Mary and to share in the salvation which Jesus brought to the earth.

Pray one Our Father, Seven Hail Marys, and one Glory Be.

(All) O My Jesus, forgive us our sins; save us from the fires of hell; lead all souls to Heaven, especially those who are in most need of Your mercy.

(All) All for the Sacred and Eucharistic Heart of Jesus, all through the Sorrowful and Immaculate Heart of Mary, all in union with St. Joseph.

Fifth Sorrow and Joy

(Leader) St. Joseph, by your SORROW when told to flee into the foreign and hostile land of Egypt, and by your JOY in seeing their satanic idols fall to the ground as the Living God passed by,

(All) Grant that I, the members of my family, and all the members and families of The Apostolate will not fear to do God's will, which is distinct for each one of us, and will always trust in Him as the total source of both

our spiritual and material security.

Pray one Our Father, Seven Hail Marys, and one Glory Be.

(All) O My Jesus, forgive us our sins; save us from the fires of hell; lead all souls to Heaven, especially those who are in most need of Your mercy.

(All) All for the Sacred and Eucharistic Heart of Jesus, all through the Sorrowful and Immaculate Heart of Mary, all in union with St. Joseph.

Sixth Sorrow and Joy

(Leader) St. Joseph, by the SORROW of your heart caused by the fear of the son of Herod after your obedient return from Egypt, and by your JOY in sharing the company of Jesus and Mary at Nazareth,

(All) Grant for us that, freed from all fear, we may enjoy the peace of a good conscience, live securely in union with Jesus and Mary, and experience your assistance at the hour of our death.

Pray one Our Father, Seven Hail Marys, and one Glory Be.

(All) O My Jesus, forgive us our sins; save us from the fires of hell; lead all souls to Heaven, especially those who are in most need of Your mercy.

(All) All for the Sacred and Eucharistic Heart of Jesus, all through the Sorrowful and Immaculate Heart of Mary, all in union with St. Joseph.

Seventh Sorrow and Joy

(Leader) St. Joseph, by the bitter SORROW with which the loss of the Child Jesus crushed your heart, and by the holy JOY which filled your soul in recovering your treasure when you re-entered the Temple,

(All) I beg you not to permit me, any member of my family, or any member or family of The Apostolate to lose our Savior Jesus through sin. Yet, should this mis-

38

fortune befall any of us, grant that we may share your eagerness in seeking him, and obtain for us the grace of finding Him, and never losing Him again.

Pray one Our Father, Seven Hail Marys, and one Glory Be.

(All) O My Jesus, forgive us our sins; save us from the fires of hell; lead all souls to Heaven, especially those who are in most need of Your mercy.

(All) All for the Sacred and Eucharistic Heart of Jesus, all through the Sorrowful and Immaculate Heart of Mary, all in union with St. Joseph.

(Leader) Behold the faithful and prudent servant,

(All) Whom the Lord set over His house.

Conclude the chaplet by praying the Prayer to St. Joseph after the Rosary (#8), making an examination of conscience (#8a), and praying an Act of Contrition (#9).

17. The Chaplet of the Holy Family

It is important to invoke the Holy Spirit:

Come, O Holy Spirit, fill the hearts of Thy faithful and enkindle in them the fire of Thy love.

V. Send forth Thy Spirit, and they shall be created.

R. And thou shall renew the face of the earth.

Let us pray: O God, who by the light of the Holy Spirit, did instruct the hearts of the faithful, grant that in the same Holy Spirit, we may be truly wise, and ever rejoice in His consolation. Through Christ Our Lord. Amen.

St. Joseph, Patron, guardian of Jesus and protector of the Holy Family, we invoke you to pray for all families to be renewed and united in the love of Jesus and to bring healing and wholeness to all families. May you assist us to imitate the example of your Holy Family so that we may share with them their eternal happiness, who now lives and rules with God the Father. Amen.

Recite this chaplet on the beads of the Rosary as follows:

On the large bead: O Divine Infant Jesus, who will reign over the whole world, have mercy on us.

On the small beads: Our Lady of Divine love, pray for us.

In conclusion say three times: Jesus, Mary, and Joseph, I love you, save souls.

18. St. Ignatius Prayer

Take, O Lord, my liberty. Receive my memory, my understanding, my imagination, my entire will. All that I am and have You have bestowed on me. I want to give it back to You, to be entirely subject to Your Divine Will. Only grant me Your love and Your grace. With these I am rich enough, and I desire nothing more. Amen.

19. The 12 Promises of the Sacred Heart to Saint Margaret Mary

1. I will give them the graces necessary in their state of life.

2. I will establish peace in their houses.

3. I will comfort them in all of their afflictions.

4. I will be their secure refuge during life, and above all in death.

5. I will bestow a large blessing upon all their undertakings.

6. Sinners shall find in My Heart the source and the infinite ocean of mercy.

7. Tepid souls shall grow fervent.

8. Fervent souls shall quickly mount to high perfection.

9. I will bless every place where a picture of My Heart shall be set up and honored.

10. I will give to the priests the gift of touching the most hardened hearts.

11. Those who shall promote this devotion shall have their names written in My Heart, never to be blotted out.

12. I promise you in the excessive mercy of My Heart that My all-powerful love will grant to all those who communicate on the First Friday in nine consecutive months the grace of final penitence; they shall not

die in my disgrace nor without receiving the Sacraments; My Divine Heart shall be their safe refuge in this last moment.

20. Divine Mercy

For the Divine Mercy Chaplet, see #20f.

The entire section 20 is printed with the permission of The Congregation of the Sisters of Our Lady of Mercy – the same order as Blessed Sr. Faustina in Krakow, Poland, with the imprimatur from:

*Nihil Obstat: Rev. Tomasz Chmura
Krakow, July 25, 1994
†Imprimatur: Franciszek Cardinal Macharski
Archbishop of Krakow
The Metropolitan Curia
Krakow, August 1, 1994*

"The Church must consider it one of her principle duties – at every stage of history and especially in our modern age – to proclaim and to introduce into life the mystery of mercy, supremely revealed in Jesus Christ. Not only for the Church herself as the community of believers but also in a certain sense for all humanity, this mystery is the source of a life different from the life which can be built by man, who is exposed to the oppressive forces of the threefold concupiscence active within him...

"The Church proclaims the truth of God's mercy revealed in the crucified and Risen Christ, and she professes it in various ways. Furthermore, she seeks to practice mercy towards people through people, and she sees in this an indispensable condition for solicitude for a better and "more human" world, today and tomorrow. However, at no time and in no historical period – especially at a moment as critical as our own – can the Church forget the prayer that is a cry for the mercy of God amid the many forms of evil which weigh upon humanity and threaten it. Precisely this is the fundamental right and duty of the Church in Christ Jesus, her right and duty towards God and towards humanity."

Pope John Paul II *(Dives in Misericordia 14.15)*

20a. Blessed Sister Faustina

The task of "proclaiming and introducing into life" the mystery of God's mercy, and imploring that mercy for the world, which the Holy Father, Pope John Paul II places before the entire Church, was entrusted to Blessed Sister Faustina as her life's witness and mission.

Sister Faustina was born in 1905 in the village of Glogowiec, near Lodz in Poland as the third of ten children in the family of Marianna and Stanislaw Kowalska. From her childhood she was distinguished by a love for prayer, diligence at work, obedience and a sensitivity for the poor. She attended not quite three years of elementary schooling, and later, as a teenager, left her family home to work as a domestic servant.

At the age of twenty she entered the Congregation of the Sisters of Our Lady of Mercy in which, as Sister Maria Faustina, she spent thirteen years of her life performing the duties of cook, gardener, and doorkeeper. Her life, though seemingly very ordinary, monotonous and drab, concealed in itself an exceptionally profound union with God. From her childhood she desired to become a great saint, and she consistently strove toward that goal, working together with Jesus for the salvation of lost souls, even to the extent of offering her life as a sacrifice for sinners. Therefore, her life as a religious was marked with the stigma of suffering, but also with extraordinary mystical graces.

It was to this religious, who though simple, had boundless trust in God, that Jesus directed that amazing declaration, *In the Old Covenant I sent prophets wielding thunderbolts to My people. Today I am sending you with My mercy to the people of the whole world. I do not want to punish aching mankind, but I desire to heal it, pressing it to My Merciful Heart* (Diary, 1588).*

The mission of Blessed Sister Faustina consists in:

- reminding the world of the truth of our faith revealed in Holy Scripture about the merciful love of God towards every human being, even the greatest sinner;

- conveying new forms of devotion to Divine Mercy; and

- initiating a great movement of devotees and apostles of Divine Mercy; who would lead people toward the renewal of Christian life in the spirit of this devotion; in other words, in the evangelical spirit of a childlike confidence in God and an active love of neighbor.

Worn out and weakened by tuberculosis and the sufferings she bore in sacrifice for sinners, Sister Faustina died in the odor of sanctity in Krakow on October 5, 1938, at the age of 33. On the first Sunday after Easter, April 18, 1993, in St. Peter's Square in Rome, Pope John Paul II declared her one of the community of the blessed. On the following day during his general audience he said, "God has spoken to us through the spiritual wealth of Blessed Sister Faustina Kowalska. She left to the world the great message of Divine Mercy and an incentive to complete self-surrender to the Creator. God endowed her with a singular grace that enabled her to experience His mercy through mystical encounter and by a special gift of contemplative prayer.

"Blessed Sister Faustina, thank you for reminding the world of that great mystery of Divine Mercy; that 'startling mystery', that inexpressible mystery of the Father, which today every individual and the whole world need so very much."

---

* *The numbers shown in parentheses after each quote refer to passages from Sr. Faustina's diary, Divine Mercy in My Soul.*

The Devotion to the Divine Mercy
According to the forms given to
Blessed Sister Faustina

20b. The Essence of the Divine Mercy Devotion

1. Trust expresses the disposition we should have toward God. It includes not only the virtue of hope, but also a lively faith, humility, perseverance and remorse for sins-committed. It is simply the attitude of a child who trusts boundlessly in the merciful love and omnipotence of the Heavenly Father in every situation.

Trust is so essential to the Divine Mercy devotion that without it the devotion cannot exist; this is because our worship of the Divine Mercy is first and foremost an expression of trust. An attitude of trust alone (even without the practice of other forms of the devotion) already assures the trusting soul of grace that it will receive God's mercy. *I desire,* Jesus promised, *to grant unimaginable graces to those souls who trust in My mercy* (687). *Let them approach this sea of mercy with great trust. Sinners will attain justification, and the just will be confirmed in good. Whoever places his trust in My mercy will be filled with My divine peace at the hour of death* (1520).

Trust is not only the essence or soul of this devotion, but also the condition for obtaining graces. *The graces of My mercy,* Jesus told Sister Faustina, *are drawn by means of one vessel only, and that is — trust. The more a soul trusts, the more it will receive. Souls that trust boundlessly are a great comfort to Me, because I pour all the treasures of My graces into them. I rejoice that they ask for much, because it is my desire to give much, very much* (1578). *The soul which will trust in My mercy is most fortunate, because I Myself take care of it* (1273). *No soul that has called upon My mercy has been disappointed or brought to shame. I delight particularly in a soul which has placed its trust in My goodness (1541).*

2. Mercy expresses the disposition we should have towards every human being. Jesus told Sister Faustina, *I demand...deeds of mercy, which are to arise out of love for Me. You are to show mercy to your neighbors always and everywhere. You must not shrink from this or try to excuse or absolve yourself from it. I am giving you three ways of exercising mercy toward your neighbor: the first – by deed, the second – by word, the third – by prayer. In these three degrees is contained the fullness of mercy and it is an unquestionable proof of love for Me. By this means a soul glorifies and pays reverence to My mercy (742).*

This attitude of an active love of neighbor is also a condition for obtaining graces. Jesus recalled the Gospel maxim when He said, *If a soul does not exercise mercy somehow or other, it will not obtain My mercy on the day of judgement. Oh, if only souls knew how to gather eternal treasure for themselves, they would not be judged, for they would forestall My judgement with their mercy (1317).*

The Lord desires that those who worship Him perform at least one act of mercy every day. *My daughter,* Jesus told Sister Faustina, *know that My Heart is mercy itself. From this sea of mercy, graces flow out upon the*

*whole world...I desire that your heart be an abiding
place of My mercy. I desire that this mercy flow out upon
the whole world through your heart. Let no one who
approaches you go away without that trust in My mercy
which I so ardently desire for souls* (1777).

20c. The Image of the Divine Mercy

The image of the Divine Mercy originates from a
vision that Sister Faustina had in Plock on February 22,
1931. In that vision Christ expressed His desire to have
such an image painted and that the words in the signature beneath it be: "Jesus, I trust in you".

The image represents the risen Christ, whose
hands and feet bear the marks of the crucifixion. From
His pierced Heart, not visible in the image, two rays
issue forth: red and pale. When asked about their meaning Jesus explained, *the pale ray stands for the Water
which makes souls righteous. The red ray stands for the
Blood which is the life of souls. These two rays issued
forth from the very depths of My tender mercy when My
agonized Heart was opened by a lance on the Cross*
(299). In other words, these two rays signify the
Sacraments, and also the Holy Church born of the
pierced side of Christ, as well as the gifts of the Holy
Spirit, of which water is a symbol in Scripture. *Happy is
the one who will dwell in their shelter,* said Jesus, *for the
just hand of God shall not lay hold of him* (299).

The image then, portrays the great mercy of God,
which was fully revealed in the Paschal Mystery of
Christ, and is manifested in the Church most effectively through the Holy Sacraments. The purpose of this
image is to serve as a vessel for obtaining graces, and to
be a sign which is to remind the world of the need to
trust in God and to show mercy toward our neighbor.
The words found in the signature beneath the image,
Jesus, I trust in you, speak of an attitude of trust. The

image, Jesus said, *is to be a reminder of the demands of My mercy, because even the strongest faith is of no avail without works* (742).

Jesus, I Trust in You.

The veneration of this image is based on confident prayer joined with deeds of mercy. Jesus attached the following promises to the veneration of the image thus understood: the grace of salvation, great progress on the road to Christian perfection, the grace of a happy death, and all other graces and temporal blessings which people who practice mercy will ask Him for with trust.

I am offering people a vessel, Jesus told Sister Faustina, *with which they are to keep coming for graces*

*to the fountain of mercy. That vessel is this image with
the signature: ~Jesus, I trust in You~ (327). By means of
this image I shall be granting many graces to souls; so
let every soul have access to it (570). I promise that the
soul that will venerate this image will not perish. I also
promise victory over (its) enemies already here on earth,
especially at the hour of death. I Myself will defend it as
My own glory (48).*

*The flames of mercy are burning Me. I desire to pour
them out upon human souls. Oh, what pain they cause
Me when they do not want to accept them!...Tell aching
mankind to snuggle close to My merciful Heart, and I
will fill it with peace (1074). Mankind will not have
peace until it turns with trust to My mercy (300).*

*Speak to the world about My mercy; let all mankind
recognize My unfathomable mercy. It is a sign for the
end times; after it will come the day of justice. While
there is still time, let them have recourse to the fount of
My mercy; let them profit from the Blood and Water
which gushed forth for them (848). Before I come as a
just Judge, I first open wide the doors of My mercy. He
who refuses to pass through the doors of My mercy must
pass through the doors of My justice (1146).*

20d. Act of Entrustment to the Divine Mercy

O Most Merciful Jesus, Your goodness is infinite,
and the treasures of Your grace inexhaustible. I trust
boundlessly in Your mercy, which is above all Your
works. I consecrate myself to You completely and unre-
servedly, so as to live and strive for Christian perfection.

I want to spread Your mercy by performing works
of mercy, both spiritual and corporal, laboring especially for the conversion of sinners, bringing consolation to
those in need, to the sick and the suffering.

Guard me then, O Jesus, as Your own possession and Your own glory. Though I sometimes tremble with fear, aware of my weakness, at the same time I have boundless trust in Your mercy. Oh, that all people would come to know the infinite depths of Your mercy, while there is still time, so that they may place their trust in Your merciful love and glorify You forever. Amen.

20e. The Feast of Divine Mercy

According to Jesus' wish, the Feast of Mercy is to be celebrated on the first Sunday after Easter. Jesus is showing us the close connection between the Easter mystery of man's Redemption and this feast. The liturgy for this day extols God most fully in the mystery of His mercy.

The Feast of Mercy is to be not only a day designated for the singular worship of God's Mercy, but also a day of grace for all people, particularly for sinners. Jesus attached great promises to this feast, the greatest of which is connected with the reception of Holy Communion on that day. It is the promise of *complete forgiveness of sins and punishment*. In other words, this grace is equal only to the one we receive in the Sacrament of Holy Baptism. The greatness of this feast lies also in the fact that everyone, even those who are converted that very day, may obtain any grace for the asking, if what they ask for be compatible with God's will. *I want this image,* Jesus told Sister Faustina,...*to be solemnly blessed on the first Sunday after Easter; that Sunday is to be the Feast of Mercy* (49). *I desire that the Feast of Mercy be a refuge and shelter for all souls, and especially for poor sinners. On that day the very depths of My tender mercy are open. I pour out a whole ocean of graces upon those souls who approach the fount of My mercy. The soul that will go to Confession and receive Holy Communion shall obtain complete forgiveness of sins and punishment. On that day are open all the divine floodgates through which graces flow. Let no soul fear to draw near to Me, even though its sins be as scarlet* (699).

The Feast of My Mercy has issued forth from My very depths for the consolation of the whole world, (1517) *and is confirmed in the vast depths of My tender mercies* (420).

See 20f for the Chaplet of Divine Mercy, and see page 584 for the Day of Grace Parish Mission program.

20e.1 The preparation for this feast is to be a novena consisting of the recitation of the Divine Mercy Chaplet for nine days, beginning on Good Friday. Sister Faustina's Diary also contains another novena which Jesus dictated for her own personal use and attached to it a promise regarding her person alone. All Christians may likewise make this novena with fervor and that is why we have included it in this prayer book.

20e.2 Novena before the Feast of Mercy

I desire, Jesus told Sister Faustina, *that during these nine days you bring souls to the fount of My mercy, that they may draw therefrom strength and refreshment and whatever graces they need in the hardships of life and, especially, at the hour of death. On each day you will bring to My Heart a different group of souls, and you will immerse them in this ocean of My mercy, and I will bring all these souls into the house of My Father... On each day you will beg My Father, on the strength of My bitter Passion, for graces for these souls (1209).*

(For the Divine Mercy novena videotapes, ask for Resource #133-310VK. Also see page 574, Resource #133-410VK.)

FIRST DAY

Today, bring to Me all mankind, especially all sinners, and immerse them in the ocean of My mercy. In this way you will console Me in the bitter grief into which the loss of souls plunges Me.

Most Merciful Jesus, whose very nature it is to have compassion on us and to forgive us, do not look upon our sins, but upon the trust which we place in Your infinite goodness. Receive us all into the abode of Your Most Compassionate Heart, and never let us escape from It. We beg this of You by Your love which unites You to the Father and the Holy Spirit.

Eternal Father, turn Your merciful gaze upon all mankind and especially upon poor sinners, all enfolded in the Most Compassionate Heart of Jesus. For the sake of His sorrowful Passion, show us Your mercy, that we may praise the omnipotence of Your mercy forever and ever. Amen.

The Chaplet of Divine Mercy (see 20f for chaplet)

SECOND DAY

Today bring to Me the souls of priests and religious, and immerse them in My unfathomable mercy. It was they who gave Me the strength to endure My bitter Passion. Through them, as through channels, My mercy flows out upon mankind.

Most Merciful Jesus, from whom comes all that is good, increase Your grace in us, that we may perform worthy works of mercy, and that all who see us may glorify the Father of Mercy who is in heaven.

Eternal Father, turn Your merciful gaze upon the company (of chosen ones) in Your vineyard — upon the souls of priests and religious; and endow them with the strength of Your blessing. For the love of the Heart of Your Son, in which they are enfolded, impart to them Your power and light, that they may be able to guide others in the way of salvation, and with one voice sing praise to Your boundless mercy for ages without end. Amen.

The Chaplet of Divine Mercy (#20f).

THIRD DAY

Today bring to Me all devout and faithful souls, and immerse them in the ocean of My mercy. These souls brought Me consolation on the Way of the Cross. They were that drop of consolation in the midst of an ocean of bitterness.

Most Merciful Jesus, from the treasury of Your mercy, You impart Your graces in great abundance to each and all. Receive us into the abode of Your Most Compassionate Heart and never let us escape from It. We beg this of You by that most wondrous love for the heavenly Father with which Your Heart burns so fiercely.

Eternal Father, turn Your merciful gaze upon faithful souls, as upon the inheritance of Your Son. For the sake of His sorrowful Passion, grant them Your blessing and surround them with Your constant protection. Thus may they never fail in love or lose the treasure of the holy faith, but rather, with all the hosts of Angels and Saints, may they glorify Your boundless mercy for endless ages. Amen.

The Chaplet of Divine Mercy (#20f)

FOURTH DAY

Today bring to Me the pagans and those who do not yet know me. I was thinking also of them during My bitter Passion, and their future zeal comforted My Heart. Immerse them in the ocean of My mercy.

Most Compassionate Jesus, You are the Light of the whole world. Receive into the abode of Your Most Compassionate Heart the souls of pagans who as yet do not know You. Let the rays of Your grace enlighten them that they, too, together with us, may extol Your wonderful mercy; and do not let them escape from the abode which is Your Most Compassionate Heart.

Eternal Father, turn Your merciful gaze upon the souls of pagans and of those who as yet do not know You, but who are enclosed in the Most Compassionate Heart of Jesus. Draw them to the light of the Gospel. These souls do not know what great happiness it is to love You. Grant that they, too, may extol the generosity of Your mercy for endless ages. Amen.

The Chaplet of Divine Mercy (#20f).

FIFTH DAY

Today bring to Me the souls of heretics and schismatics, and immerse them in the ocean of My mercy. During My bitter Passion they tore at My Body and

Heart; that is, My Church. As they return to unity with the Church, My wounds heal, and in this way they alleviate My Passion.

Most Merciful Jesus, Goodness Itself, You do not refuse light to those who seek it of You. Receive into the abode of Your Most Compassionate Heart the souls of heretics and schismatics. Draw them by Your light into the unity of the Church, and do not let them escape from the abode of Your Most Compassionate Heart; but bring it about that they, too, come to adore the generosity of Your mercy.

Eternal Father, turn Your merciful gaze upon the souls of heretics and schismatics, who have squandered Your blessings and misused Your graces by obstinately persisting in their errors. Do not look upon their errors, but upon the love of Your own Son and upon His bitter Passion, which He underwent for their sake, since they, too, are enclosed in the Most Compassionate Heart of Jesus. Bring it about that they also may glorify Your great mercy for endless ages. Amen.

The Chaplet of Divine Mercy (#20f).

SIXTH DAY

Today bring to Me the meek and humble souls and the souls of little children, and immerse them in My mercy. These souls most closely resemble My Heart. They strengthened Me during My bitter agony. I saw them as earthly Angels, who would keep vigil at My altars. I pour out upon them whole torrents of grace. Only the humble soul is able to receive My grace. I favor humble souls with My confidence.

Most Merciful Jesus, You Yourself have said, "Learn from Me for I am meek and humble of heart." Receive into the abode of Your Most Compassionate Heart all meek and humble souls and the souls of little children. These souls send all heaven into ecstasy, and they are the heavenly Father's favorites. They are a

56

sweet smelling bouquet before the throne of God; God Himself takes delight in their fragrance. These souls have a permanent abode in Your Most Compassionate Heart, O Jesus, and they unceasingly sing out a hymn of love and mercy.

Eternal Father, turn Your merciful gaze upon meek and humble souls, and upon the souls of little children, who are enfolded in the abode which is the Most Compassionate Heart of Jesus. These souls bear the closest resemblance to Your Son. Their fragrance rises from the earth and reaches Your very throne. Father of mercy and of all goodness, I beg You by the love You bear these souls and by the delight You take in them: bless the whole world, that all souls together may sing out the praises of Your mercy for endless ages. Amen.

The Chaplet of Divine Mercy (#20f).

SEVENTH DAY

Today bring to Me the souls who especially venerate and glorify My mercy, and immerse them in My mercy. These souls sorrowed most over My Passion and entered most deeply into my spirit. They are living images of My

Compassionate Heart. These souls will shine with a special brightness in the next life. Not one of them will go into the fire of hell. I shall particularly defend each one of them at the hour of death.

Most Merciful Jesus, whose Heart is Love Itself, receive into the abode of Your Most Compassionate Heart the souls of those who particularly extol and venerate the greatness of Your mercy. These souls are mighty with the very power of God Himself. In the midst of all afflictions and adversities they go forward, confident of Your mercy. These souls are united to Jesus and carry all mankind on their shoulders. These souls will not be judged severely, but Your mercy will embrace them as they depart from this life.

Eternal Father, turn Your merciful gaze upon the souls who glorify and venerate Your greatest attribute, that of Your fathomless mercy, and who are enclosed in the Most Compassionate Heart of Jesus. These souls are a living Gospel; their hands are full of deeds of mercy, and their spirit, overflowing with joy, sings a canticle of mercy to You, O Most High! I beg You O God: Show them Your mercy according to the hope and trust they have placed in You. Let there be accomplished in them the promise of Jesus, who said to them, I Myself will defend as My own glory, during their lifetime, and especially at the hour of their death, those souls who will venerate My fathomless mercy.

The Chaplet of Divine Mercy (#20f).

EIGHTH DAY

Today bring to Me the souls who are in the prison of Purgatory, and immerse them in the abyss of My mercy. Let the torrents of My Blood cool down their scorching flames. All these souls are greatly loved by Me. They are making retribution to My justice. It is in your power to bring them relief. Draw all the indulgences from the treasury of My Church and offer them the alms of the spirit and pay off their debt to My justice.

Most Merciful Jesus, You Yourself have said that You desire mercy; so I bring into the abode of Your Most Compassionate Heart the souls in Purgatory, souls who are very dear to You, and yet, who must make retribution to Your justice. May the streams of Blood and Water which gushed forth from Your Heart put out the flames of the purifying fire, that in that place, too, the power of Your mercy may be praised.

Eternal Father, turn Your merciful gaze upon the souls suffering in Purgatory, who are enfolded in the Most Compassionate Heart of Jesus. I beg You, by the sorrowful Passion of Jesus Your Son, and by all the bitterness with which His most sacred Soul was flooded, manifest Your mercy to the souls who are under Your just scrutiny. Look upon them in no other way than through the Wounds of Jesus, Your dearly beloved Son; for we firmly believe that there is no limit to Your goodness and compassion.

The Chaplet of Divine Mercy (#20f).

NINTH DAY

Today bring to Me souls who have become luke-warm, and immerse them in the abyss of My mercy. These souls wound My Heart most painfully. My soul suffered the most dreadful loathing in the Garden of Olives because of lukewarm souls. They were the reason I cried out: "Father, take this cup away from Me, if it be Your will." For them, the last hope of salvation is to flee to My mercy.

Most compassionate Jesus, You are Compassion Itself. I bring lukewarm souls into the abode of Your Most Compassionate Heart. In this fire of Your pure love let these tepid souls, who, like corpses, filled You with such deep loathing, be once again set aflame. O Most Compassionate Jesus, exercise the omnipotence of Your mercy and draw them into the very ardor of Your love; and bestow upon them the gift of holy love, for nothing is beyond Your power.

Eternal Father, turn Your merciful gaze upon luke-warm souls, who are nonetheless enfolded in the Most Compassionate Heart of Jesus. Father of Mercy, I beg You by the bitter Passion of Your son and by His three-hour agony on the Cross: Let them, too, glorify the abyss of Your mercy... (1209-1229)

The Chaplet of Divine Mercy (#20f).

20e.3 Celebrating the Feast of Mercy

It is Jesus' express desire that the image of Divine Mercy be solemnly blessed and given public (meaning liturgical) veneration, so that priests may tell souls of this great and unfathomable mercy of God.

In order for people to benefit from these great gifts which the Lord wishes to give to every person and all humanity, they should be in the state of grace (i.e., having made a good Holy Confession); they should fulfill the conditions of the Divine Mercy devotion (that of trust and active love of neighbor) and on that day approach the *Source of Life*; in other words, receive Holy Communion.

(See pages 584–586 for the Day of Grace Parish Mission program.)

20e.4 The Sacrament of Reconciliation and Penance

Jesus' words to Sister Faustina

When you go to Confession, to this fountain of My mercy, the Blood and Water which came forth from My Heart always flow down upon your soul and ennoble it. Every time you go to Confession, immerse yourself entirely in My mercy, with great trust, so that I may pour the bounty of My grace upon your soul. When you approach the confessional, know this, that I Myself am waiting there for you. I am only hidden by the priest, but I Myself act in your soul. Here the misery of the soul meets the God of mercy. Tell souls that from this fount of mercy souls draw graces solely with the vessel of trust. If their trust is great, there is no limit to My generosity. The torrents of grace inundate humble souls. The proud remain always in poverty and misery because My grace turns away from them to humble souls (1602).

Tell souls where they are to look for solace; that is, in the Tribunal of Mercy. There the greatest miracles take place (and) are incessantly repeated. To avail oneself of this miracle, it is not necessary to go on a great pilgrimage or to carry out some external ceremony; it suffices to come with faith to the feet of My representative and to reveal to him one's misery and the miracle of Divine Mercy will be fully demonstrated. Were a soul like a decaying corpse so that from a human standpoint, there would be no (hope of) restoration and everything would already be lost, it is not so with God. The miracle of Divine Mercy restores that soul in full. Oh, how miserable are those who do not take advantage of the miracle of God's mercy! You will call out in vain, but it will be too late (1448).

20e.5 Holy Communion

The graces Our Lord has prepared for the Feast of Mercy are connected with full participation in Holy Mass. This includes receiving Holy Communion, to which the promise of *complete forgiveness of sins and punishment* is attached.

Jesus' words to Sister Faustina

I desire to unite Myself with human souls...When I come to a human heart in Holy Communion, My hands are full of all kinds of graces which I want to give to the soul. But souls do not even pay any attention to Me; they leave Me to Myself and busy themselves with other things. Oh, how sad I am that souls do not recognize Love! (1385).

Oh, how painful it is to Me that souls so seldom unite themselves to Me in Holy Communion. I wait for souls, and they are indifferent toward Me. I love them tenderly and sincerely, and they distrust Me. I want to lavish My graces on them, and they do not want to accept them. They treat Me as a dead object, whereas My Heart is full of love and mercy (1447).

Holy Communion in the Life of Sister Faustina

The most solemn moment of my life is the moment when I receive Holy Communion. I long for each Holy Communion, and for every Holy Communion I give thanks to the Most Holy Trinity (1804).

Today, I prepare for the coming of the King.

What am I, and who are You, O Lord, King of eternal glory? O my heart, are you aware of who is coming to you today? Yes, I know, but – strangely – I am not able to grasp it. Oh, if He were just a king, but He is the King of kings, the Lord of lords. Before Him, all power and dominion tremble. He is coming to my heart today.

I hear Him approaching. I go out to meet Him and invite Him. When He entered the dwelling of my heart, it was filled with such reverence that it fainted with fear, falling at His feet. Jesus gives her His hand and graciously permits her to take her place beside Him. He reassures her saying, See, I have left My heavenly throne to become united with you. What you see is just a tiny part and already your soul swoons with love. How amazed will your heart be when you see Me in all My glory. But I want to tell you that eternal life must begin already here on earth through Holy Communion. Each Holy Communion makes you more capable of communing with God throughout eternity (1810).

20f. The Chaplet of Divine Mercy

Jesus dictated the Chaplet of Divine Mercy to Sister Faustina in Vilnius in 1935. In the revelations that followed He disclosed to her its value and efficacy, as well as the promises He attached to it.

In this prayer we are offering the *Body and Blood, Soul and Divinity* of Jesus Christ to God the Father. We are uniting ourselves with His sacrifice offered on the Cross for the salvation of the world. By offering God the Father His *most dearly beloved Son,* we are using the most convincing argument with which to be heard. We are asking for mercy *for us and for the whole world*. The word "us" refers to the person reciting the chaplet and those for whom he desires to offer it or for whom he should pray. The "whole world" indicates all people living on earth and the souls in Purgatory. By praying the words of this chaplet we are performing an act of love toward our neighbor, which along with trust, is the indispensable condition for obtaining the graces.

Jesus promised, *It pleases Me to grant everything they ask of Me by saying the chaplet* (1541), and He added, *if (it)...be compatible with My will* (1731). The special promises pertain to the hour of death; that is, the grace of a happy and peaceful death. This grace may be obtained not only by those who recite the chaplet with confidence and perseverance but also by the dying, at whose bedside others will pray it. *Priests,* Jesus said, *will recommend it to sinners as their last hope of salvation, even if there were a sinner most hardened, if he were to recite this chaplet only once, he would receive grace from My infinite mercy* (687). Jesus promised to grant grace to those who recite this prayer at least once in their lifetime, providing it is said with an attitude of complete trust, humility, and a sincere, deep sorrow for sin.

The Chaplet of Divine Mercy
on ordinary rosary beads

Begin with:

Our Father, Who art in heaven, hallowed be Thy name; Thy kingdom come; Thy will be done on earth as it is in heaven. Give us this day our daily bread; and forgive us our trespasses as we forgive those who trespass against us; and lead us not into temptation, but deliver us from evil. Amen.

Hail Mary, full of grace. The Lord is with Thee. Blessed art Thou among women, and blessed is the fruit of Thy womb, Jesus. Holy Mary, Mother of God, pray for us sinners, now and at the hour of our death. Amen.

I believe in God, the Father almighty, creator of heaven and earth.

I believe in Jesus Christ, His only Son, our Lord. He was conceived by the power of the Holy Spirit, and born of the Virgin Mary. He suffered under Pontius Pilate, was crucified, died and was buried. He descended to the dead. On the third day He rose again. He ascended into heaven, and is seated at the right hand of the Father. He will come again to judge the living and the dead.

I believe in the Holy Spirit, the holy Catholic Church, the communion of saints, the forgiveness of sins, the resurrection of the body, and the life everlasting. Amen.

On the large bead before each decade:

Eternal Father, I offer you the Body and Blood, Soul and Divinity of Your dearly beloved Son, Our Lord Jesus Christ, in atonement for our sins and those of the whole world.

On the 10 small beads of each decade:

For the sake of His sorrowful Passion, have mercy on us and on the whole world.

Conclude with: (after five decades)

Holy God, Holy Mighty One, Holy Immortal One, have mercy on us and on the whole world *(3 times)*.

(See p. 587 for the Chaplet on audio & video, Resource #147-58VK.)

20g. The Hour of Mercy

As often as you hear the clock strike the third hour, immerse yourself completely in My mercy, adoring and glorifying it; invoke its omnipotence for the whole world, and particularly for poor sinners; for at that moment mercy was opened wide for every soul (1320).

It is Jesus' desire that the moment of His Death on the Cross (3:00 p.m.) be venerated every day; the hour which He said *was the hour of grace for the whole world — mercy triumphed over justice* (1572). At this hour, He wants us to meditate upon His sorrowful Passion because it reveals most distinctly the love God has for His people. At this time Jesus wants us to worship and glorify the Mercy of God, and, by the merits of His passion, to implore the necessary graces for ourselves and the whole world, especially for sinners.

Try your best, Jesus instructed Sister Faustina, *to make the Stations of the Cross in this hour, provided that your duties permit it; and if you are not able to make the Stations of the Cross, then at least step into the chapel for a moment and adore, in the Blessed Sacrament, My heart, which is full of mercy; and should you be unable to step into the chapel, immerse yourself in prayer there where you happen to be, if only for a very brief instant* (1572).

This is the hour, as Jesus promised, in which *you can obtain everything for yourself and for others for the asking* (1572). *I will refuse nothing to the soul that makes a request of Me in virtue of My Passion* (1320).

The Hour of Mercy is associated explicitly with three o'clock in the afternoon. Our prayers at this time should be directed to Jesus, and our petitions should appeal to the merits of His sorrowful Passion.

Prayers at the Hour of Mercy

20g.1   O Blood and Water, which gushed forth from the Heart of Jesus as a fount of Mercy for us, I trust in You (187).

20g.2   You Yourself, Jesus, surely out of love for us, underwent such a terrible Passion. Your Father's justice would have been propitiated with a single sigh from You, and all Your self-abasement is solely the work of Your mercy and Your inconceivable love...At the moment of Your death on the Cross, You bestowed upon us eternal life; allowing Your most holy side to be opened, You opened an inexhaustible spring of mercy for us, giving us Your dearest possession, the Blood and Water from Your Heart. Such is the omnipotence of Your mercy. From it all grace flows to us (1747).

20g.3   O Jesus, eternal Truth, our Life, I call upon You and beg Your mercy for poor sinners. O sweetest Heart of my Lord, full of pity and unfathomable mercy, I plead with you for poor sinners. O Most Sacred Heart, Fount of Mercy from which gush forth rays of inconceivable graces upon the entire human race, I beg of You light for poor sinners. O Jesus, be mindful of Your own bitter Passion and do not permit the loss of souls redeemed at so dear a price of Your most precious Blood.

O Jesus, stretched out upon the cross, I implore You, give me the grace of doing faithfully the most holy will of Your Father, in all things, always and everywhere. And when this will of God will seem to me very harsh and difficult to fulfill, it is then I beg You, Jesus, may power and strength flow upon me from your wounds, and may my lips keep repeating, "Your will be done, O Lord."

O Savior of the world, Lover of man's salvation, who in such terrible torment and pain, forgot Yourself to think only of the salvation of souls, O most compassionate Jesus, grant me the grace to forget myself that I may live totally for souls, helping You in the work of salvation, according to the most holy will of Your Father (1265).

20g.4 You expired, Jesus, but the source of life gushed forth for souls, and the ocean of mercy opened up for the whole world. O Fount of Life, unfathomable Divine Mercy, envelop the whole world and empty Yourself out upon us (1319).

20h. Spreading the Divine Mercy Devotion

Souls who spread the honor of My mercy I shield through their entire life as a tender mother her infant, and at the hour of death I will not be a Judge for them, but the Merciful Savior (1075). By these words, Jesus is encouraging us to spread the worship of Divine Mercy; He has promised maternal care to those who do so by shielding them throughout their entire life and at the hour of death. He made a singular promise to priests saying, *Hardened sinners will repent on hearing their words, when they will speak about My unfathomable mercy, about the compassion I have for them in My Heart. To priests who will proclaim and extol My mercy, I will give wondrous power, and I will anoint their words and touch the hearts of those to whom they will speak* (1521).

The foundation for the worship and apostolate of Divine Mercy is the testimony of one's own life according to the spirit of this devotion; namely, the spirit of childlike confidence in the goodness and omnipotence of God, accompanied by an active love of one's neighbor.

All those souls, Jesus said, *who will glorify My mercy and spread its worship, encouraging others to trust in My mercy, will not experience terror at the hour of death. My mercy will shield them in that final battle* (1540).

***

O Eternal Love, I want all the souls You have created to come to know You. I would like to be a priest, for then I would speak without cease about Your mercy to sinful souls drowned in despair. I would like to be a missionary and carry the light of faith to savage nations in order to make You known to souls, and to be completely consumed for them and to die a martyr's death by completely emptying myself and denying myself for love of You, O Jesus, and of immortal souls. Great love can change small things into great ones (302).

It is my greatest desire that souls should recognize You as their eternal happiness, that they should come to believe in Your goodness and glorify Your infinite mercy (305).

20i. Selected Prayers from Sister Faustina's Diary

20i.1 The Praises of the Divine Mercy

The Love of God is the flower – Mercy the fruit. Let the doubting soul read these considerations on Divine Mercy and become trusting.

Divine Mercy, gushing forth from the bosom of the Father, I trust in You.

Divine Mercy, greatest attribute of God, I trust in You.

Divine Mercy, incomprehensible mystery, I trust in You.

Divine Mercy, fount gushing forth from the mystery of the Most Blessed Trinity, I trust in You.

Divine Mercy, unfathomed by any intellect, human or angelic, I trust in You.

Divine Mercy, from which wells forth all life and happiness, I trust in You.

Divine Mercy, better than the heavens, I trust in You.

Divine Mercy, source of miracles and wonders, I trust in You.

Divine Mercy, encompassing the whole universe, I trust in You.

Divine Mercy, descending to earth in the Person of the Incarnate Word, I trust in You.

Divine Mercy, which flowed out from the open wound of the Heart of Jesus, I trust in You.

Divine Mercy, enclosed in the Heart of Jesus for us, and especially for sinners, I trust in You.

Divine Mercy, unfathomed in the institution of the Sacred Host, I trust in You.

Divine Mercy, in the founding of Holy Church, I trust in You.

Divine Mercy, in the Sacrament of Holy Baptism, I trust in You.

Divine Mercy, in our justification through Jesus Christ, I trust in You.

Divine Mercy, accompanying us through our whole life, I trust in You.

Divine Mercy, embracing us especially at the hour of death, I trust in You.

Divine Mercy, endowing us with immortal life, I trust in You.

Divine Mercy, accompanying us at every moment of our life, I trust in You.

Divine Mercy, shielding us from the fire of hell, I trust in You.

Divine Mercy, in the conversion of hardened sinners, I trust in You.

Divine Mercy, astonishment for Angels, incomprehensible to Saints, I trust in You.

Divine Mercy, unfathomed in all the mysteries of God, I trust in You.

Divine Mercy, lifting us out of every misery, I trust in You.

Divine Mercy, source of our happiness and joy, I trust in You.

Divine Mercy, in calling us forth from nothingness to existence, I trust in You.

Divine Mercy, embracing all the works of His hands, I trust in You.

Divine Mercy, crown of all of God's handiwork, I trust in You.

Divine Mercy, in which we are all immersed, I trust in You.

Divine Mercy, sweet relief for anguished hearts, I trust in You.

Divine Mercy, only hope of despairing souls, I trust in You.

Divine Mercy, repose of hearts, peace amidst fear, I trust in You.

Divine Mercy, delight and ecstasy of holy souls, I trust in You.

Divine Mercy, inspiring hope against all hope, I trust in You (949).

Eternal God, in whom mercy is endless and the treasury of compassion inexhaustible, look kindly upon us and increase Your mercy in us, that in difficult moments we might not despair nor become despondent, but with great confidence submit ourselves to Your holy will, which is Love and Mercy itself (950).

O incomprehensible and limitless Mercy Divine, to extol and adore You worthily, who can? Supreme attribute of Almighty God, You are the sweet hope for sinful man (951).

(For the Divine Mercy in My Soul Diary, see page 587, Resource #522-6.)

20i.2 Before the Blessed Sacrament

I adore You, Lord and Creator, hidden in the Blessed Sacrament. I adore You for all the works of Your hands, that reveal to me so much wisdom, goodness and mercy, O Lord. You have spread so much beauty over the earth, and it tells me about Your beauty, even though these beautiful things are but a faint reflection of You, Incomprehensible Beauty. And although You have hidden Yourself and concealed Your beauty, my eye, enlightened by faith, reaches You, and my soul recognizes its Creator, its Highest Good; and my heart is completely immersed in prayer of adoration.

My Lord and Creator, Your goodness encourages me to converse with You. Your mercy abolishes the chasm which separates the Creator from the creature. To converse with You, O Lord, is the delight of my heart. In You I find everything that my heart could desire. Here Your light illumines my mind, enabling it to know You more and more deeply. Here streams of graces flow down upon my heart. Here my soul draws eternal life.

O my Lord and Creator, You alone, beyond all these gifts, give Your own self to me and unite Yourself intimately with Your miserable creature. Here, without searching for words, our hearts understand each other. Here, no one is able to interrupt our conversation. What I talk to You about, Jesus, is our secret, which creatures shall not know...These are secret acts of forgiveness, known only to Jesus and me; this is the mystery of His mercy, which embraces each soul separately. For this incomprehensible goodness of Yours, I adore You, O Lord and Creator, with all my heart and all my soul. And, although my worship is so little and poor, I am at peace because I know that You know it is sincere, however inadequate... (1692).

20i.3 In Thanksgiving

O Jesus, eternal God, thank You for Your countless graces and blessings. Let every beat of my heart be a new hymn of thanksgiving to You, O God. Let every drop of my blood circulate for You, Lord. My soul is one hymn in adoration of Your mercy. I love You, God, for Yourself alone (1794).

20i.4 For Divine Mercy for the World

O Greatly Merciful God, Infinite Goodness, today all mankind calls out from the abyss of its misery to

Your mercy – to Your compassion, O God, and it is with its mighty voice of misery that it cries out. Gracious God, do not reject the prayer of this earth's exiles! O Lord, Goodness beyond our understanding, Who are acquainted with our misery through and through, and know that by our own power we cannot ascend to You, we implore You: anticipate us with Your grace and keep on increasing Your mercy in us, that we may faithfully do Your holy will all through our life and at death's hour. Let the omnipotence of Your mercy shield us from the darts of our salvation's enemies, that we may with confidence, as Your children, await Your final coming – that day known to You alone. And we expect to obtain everything promised us by Jesus in spite of all our wretchedness. For Jesus is our hope: Through His merciful Heart, as through an open gate, we pass through to heaven (1570).

20i.5 For the Holy Church and Priests

O my Jesus, I beg You on behalf of the whole Church: Grant [her] love and the light of Your Spirit, and give power to the words of priests so that hardened hearts might be brought to repentance and return to You, O Lord. Lord, give us holy priests; You yourself maintain them in holiness. O Divine and Great High Priest, may the power of Your mercy accompany them everywhere and protect them from the devil's traps and snares which are continually being set for the souls of priests. May the power of Your mercy, O Lord, shatter and bring to naught all that might tarnish the sanctity of priests, for You can do all things (1052).

Jesus, my most beloved, I beg You for the triumph of the Church, for blessings on the Holy Father, and on all the clergy; for the grace of conversion for impenitent sinners. And I ask You for a special blessing and for light, O Jesus, for the priests before whom I will make my confessions throughout my lifetime (240).

20i.6 For One's Country

Most merciful Jesus, I beseech You through the intercession of Your Saints, and especially the intercession of Your dearest Mother who nurtured You from childhood, bless my native land. I beg You, Jesus, look not on our sins, but on the tears of little children, on the hunger and cold they suffer. Jesus, for the sake of these innocent ones, grant me the grace that I am asking of You for my country (286).

20i.7 To Obtain Love of God

Most sweet Jesus, set on fire my Love for You and transform me into Yourself. Divinize me that my deeds may be pleasing to You. May this be accomplished by the power of the Holy Communion which I receive daily (1289).

20i.8 To Obtain an Understanding of God

I often ask the Lord Jesus for an intellect enlightened by faith. I express this to the Lord in these words: Jesus, give me an intellect, a great intellect, for this only, that I may understand You better; because the better I get to know You, the more ardently will I love You. Jesus, I ask You for a powerful intellect, that I may understand divine and lofty matters. Jesus, give me a keen intellect with which I will get to know Your Divine Essence and Your indwelling, Triune life. Give my intellect these capacities and aptitudes by means of Your special grace. Although I know that there is a capability through grace which the Church gives me, there is still a treasure of graces which You give us, O Lord, when we ask You for them. But if my request is not pleasing to You, then I beg You, do not give me the inclination to pray thus (1474).

20i.9 Invocations of Trust

O my God, my only hope, I have placed all my trust in You, and I know I shall not be disappointed (317).

***

I know the full power of Your mercy, and I trust that You will give me everything Your feeble child needs (898).

***

O Jesus, concealed in the Blessed Sacrament of the Altar, my only love and mercy, I commend to You all the needs of my body and soul. You can help me, because You are Mercy itself. In You lies all my hope (1751).

20i.10 Prayer of Trust

I fly to Your mercy, Compassionate God, who alone are good. Although my misery is great, and my offenses are many, I trust in Your mercy, because You are the God of mercy; and, from time immemorial, it has never been heard of, nor do heaven or earth remember, that a soul trusting in Your mercy has been disappointed.

O God of compassion, You alone can justify me, and You will never reject me when I, contrite, approach Your merciful Heart, where no one has ever been refused, even if he were the greatest sinner (1730)

20i.11 For the Grace to be Merciful to Others

I want to be completely transformed into Your Mercy and to be Your living reflection, O Lord. May the greatest of all divine attributes, that of Your unfathomable mercy, pass through my heart and soul to my neighbor.

Help me, O Lord, that my eyes may be merciful, so that I may never suspect or judge from appearances, but look for what is beautiful in my neighbors' souls and come to their rescue.

Help me, that my ears may be merciful, so that I may give heed to my neighbors' needs and not be indifferent to their pains and moanings.

Help me, O Lord, that my tongue may be merciful, so that I should never speak negatively of my neighbor, but have a word of comfort and forgiveness for all.

Help me, O Lord, that my hands may be merciful and filled with good deeds, so that I may do only good to my neighbors and take upon myself the more difficult and toilsome tasks.

Help me, that my feet may be merciful, so that I may hurry to assist my neighbor, overcoming my own fatigue and weariness. My true rest is in the service of my neighbor.

Help me, O Lord, that my heart may be merciful so that I myself may feel all the sufferings of my neighbor. I will refuse my heart to no one, I will be sincere even with those who, I know, will abuse my kindness. And I will lock myself up in the most merciful Heart of Jesus. I will bear my own suffering in silence. May Your Mercy, O Lord, rest upon me (163).

20i.12 For the Conversion of Sinners

God of great mercy, who deigned to send us Your only-begotten Son as the greatest proof of Your fathomless love and mercy, You do not reject sinners; but in Your boundless mercy You have opened for them also Your treasures, treasures from which they can draw abundantly, not only justification, but also all the sanctity that a soul can attain. Father of great mercy, I desire that all hearts turn with confidence to Your infinite mercy. No one will be justified before You if he is not accompanied by Your unfathomable mercy. When You reveal the mystery of Your mercy to us, there will not be enough of eternity to properly thank You for it (1122).

***

O Jesus, how sorry I feel for poor sinners. Jesus, grant them contrition and repentance. Remember Your own sorrowful Passion. I know Your infinite mercy and cannot bear it that a soul that has cost You so much should perish. Jesus, give me the souls of sinners; let Your mercy rest upon them. Take everything away from me, but give me souls. I want to become a sacrificial host for sinners. Let the shell of my body conceal my offering, for Your Most Sacred Heart is also hidden in a Host, and certainly You are a living sacrifice. Transform me into Yourself, O Jesus, that I may be a living sacrifice and pleasing to You. I desire to atone at each moment for poor sinners... O my Creator and Father of great mercy, I trust in You, for You are Goodness Itself (908).

20i.13 In Times of Suffering

O Living Host, support me in this exile, that I may be empowered to walk faithfully in the footsteps of the Savior. I do not ask, Lord, that You take me down from the cross, but I implore You to give me the strength to remain steadfast upon it. I want to be stretched out upon the cross as You were, Jesus. I want all the tortures and pains that You suffered. I want to drink the cup of bitterness to the dregs (1484).

***

O my Jesus, give me strength to endure suffering so that I may not make a wry face when I drink the cup of bitterness. Help me Yourself to make my sacrifice pleasing to You. May it not be tainted by my self-love ... may everything that is in me, both my misery and my strength, give praise to You, O Lord (1740).

20i.14 For a Happy Death

O merciful Jesus, stretched on the cross, be mindful of the hour of our death. O most merciful Heart of Jesus, opened with a lance, shelter me at the last moment of my life. O Blood and Water, which gushed forth from the Heart of Jesus as a fount of unfathomable mercy for me (cleanse me of my sins and offenses). O dying Jesus, Hostage of mercy, avert the Divine wrath at the hour of my death (813).

***

O my Jesus, may the last days of my exile be spent totally according to Your most holy will. I unite my sufferings, my bitterness and my last agony itself to Your

Sacred Passion; and I offer myself for the whole world to implore an abundance of God's mercy for souls, and in particular for the souls (of sinners). I firmly trust and commit myself entirely to Your holy will, which is mercy itself. Your mercy will be everything for me at the last hour (1574).

20i.15 To the Mother of God

O Mary, my Mother and my Lady, I offer You my soul, my body, my life and my death, and all that will follow it. I place everything in Your hands. O my Mother, cover my soul with Your virginal mantle and grant me the grace of purity of heart, soul and body. Defend me with Your power against all enemies...O lovely lily! You are for me a mirror, O my Mother! (79)

***

Mother of God, Your soul was plunged into a sea of bitterness; look upon Your child and teach it to suffer and to love while suffering. Fortify my soul that pain will not break it. Mother of grace, teach me to live by (the power of) God (315).

***

O sweet Mother of God, I model my life on You; You are for me the bright dawn; in You I lose myself, enraptured. O Mother, Immaculate Virgin, in You the divine ray is reflected, midst storms, 'tis You who teach me to love the Lord, O my shield and defense from the foe (1232).

80

20i.16 Prayer to Obtain Graces Through the Intercession of Blessed Sister Faustina

O Jesus, who filled Blessed Faustina with profound veneration for Your boundless Mercy, deign, if it be Your holy will, to grant me, through her intercession, the grace for which I fervently pray...

My sins render me unworthy of Your Mercy, but be mindful of Sister Faustina's spirit of sacrifice and self-denial, and reward her virtue by granting the petition which, with childlike trust, I present to You through her intercession.

Our Father..., Hail Mary..., Glory Be...

Blessed Faustina, pray for us.

20i.17 Prayer for the Canonization of Blessed Sister Faustina

Heavenly Father, You made Blessed Faustina a great apostle of Your infinite mercy. Grant that she may be counted among the community of saints so that by following her example and supported by her intercession we may, with complete confidence, fulfill Your holy will in all things. Through Christ Our Lord. Amen.

Whoever receives a grace through the intercession of Blessed Faustina is asked to write to:

The Congregation of the Sisters of
Our Lady of Mercy
ul. Siostry Faustyny 3/9
30-420 Krakow
Poland

20j. The Congregation of the Sisters of Our Lady of Mercy

The Congregation of the Sisters of Our Lady of Mercy to which Blessed Faustina belonged, is dedicated, in collaboration with the infinite mercy of God, to the task of saving souls. Special care is directed toward girls and women in need of moral assistance. It also carries out Blessed Sister Faustina's mission by proclaiming the message Jesus entrusted to her and by imploring God's mercy for the whole world.

21. Holy Trinity Prayer in the Spirit of Fatima
Also an adoration prayer.
Recommended for Sundays.

Most Holy Trinity, Father, Son, and Holy Spirit, I adore You profoundly. I offer you the most precious Body, Blood, Soul, and Divinity of Jesus Christ, present in all the tabernacles of the world, in reparation for the outrages, sacrileges, and indifferences by which he is offended. By the infinite merits of His Most Sacred Heart and through the Immaculate Heart of Mary, in union with St. Joseph, I beg the conversion of poor sinners. Amen.

21a. O Sacrament Most Holy

O Sacrament Most Holy, O Sacrament Divine, All praise and all thanksgiving be every moment Thine.

22. Act of Reparation to the Sacred Heart of Jesus
In the Spirit of Mother Teresa
Recommended for Fridays.

Sacred Heart of Jesus, humbly prostrate before You, we come to renew our consecration, with the resolution of repairing, by an increase of love and fidelity to You, all the outrages unceasingly offered You. We firmly resolve that:

The more your mysteries are blasphemed, the more firmly we shall believe in them, O Sacred Heart of Jesus!

The more impiety endeavors to extinguish our hopes of immortality, the more we shall trust in Your Heart, sole Hope of mortals!

The more hearts resist Your divine attractions, the more we shall love You, O infinitely amiable Heart of Jesus!

The more Your divinity is attacked, the more we shall adore it, O Divine Heart of Jesus!

The more Your holy Laws are forgotten and transgressed, the more we shall observe them, O most Holy Heart of Jesus.

The more Your sacraments are despised and abandoned, the more we shall receive them with love and respect, O Most Liberal Heart of Jesus.

The more Your adorable virtues are forgotten, the more we shall endeavor to practice them, O Heart, Model of every virtue!

The more Your holy vows of Marriage are neglected and broken, the more we shall observe them with love and fidelity, O Heart most faithful.

The more the demon labors to destroy the life of prayer and purity in consecrated souls, the more we will try to keep Purity – pure, Chastity – chaste, Virginity – virginal, O most pure Heart of Jesus.

The more mothers destroy the presence and image of God through abortion, the more we shall save them by caring for them or by giving them in adoption, O tender Heart of Jesus.

O Sacred Heart, give us so strong and powerful a grace that we may be Your apostles in the midst of the world, and Your crown in a happy eternity. Amen.

84

23. Consecration to the Sacred Heart of Jesus

(Read the "Catechism of the Catholic Church," sections 478 and 2669.)

Most Sweet Jesus, humbly at your feet, we renew the consecration of our family to Your Divine Heart. Be our King forever! In you we have full and entire confidence. May Your spirit penetrate our thoughts, our desires, our words, and our works. Bless our undertakings, share in our joys, in our trials, and in our labors. Grant us to know You better, to love You more, to serve You without faltering.

By the Immaculate Heart of Mary, Queen of Peace, set up Your Kingdom in our country. Enter closely into the midst of our families and make them Your own through the solemn enthronement of Your Sacred Heart, so that soon one cry may resound from home to home: *May the triumphant Heart of Jesus be everywhere loved, blessed, and glorified forever!* Honor and glory be to the Sacred Heart of Jesus and Mary in union with St. Joseph! Sacred Heart of Jesus, protect our families.

23a. Litany of the Sacred Heart of Jesus

Leader: Lord, have mercy on us.
All: Christ, have mercy on us

Leader: Lord, have mercy on us; Christ hear us.
All: Christ, graciously hear us

Leader   **Response**

God, the Father of Heaven,
God the Son, Redeemer of the world,
God the Holy Spirit,

Have mercy on us

Holy Trinity, one God,
Heart of Jesus, Son of the Eternal Father,
Heart of Jesus, formed by the Holy Spirit in the
    Virgin Mother's womb,
Heart of Jesus, substantially united to the Word
    of God,
Heart of Jesus, of infinite majesty,
Heart of Jesus, holy temple of God,
Heart of Jesus, rich unto all who call upon You,
Heart of Jesus, fount of life and holiness,
Heart of Jesus, propitiation for our offenses,
Heart of Jesus, overwhelmed with reproaches,
Heart of Jesus, bruised for our iniquities,
Heart of Jesus, obedient even unto death,
Heart of Jesus, pierced with a lance,
Heart of Jesus, source of all consolation,
Heart of Jesus, our life and resurrection,
Heart of Jesus, our peace and reconciliation,
Heart of Jesus, victim for our sins,
Heart of Jesus, salvation of those who hope in You,
Heart of Jesus, hope of those who die in You,
Heart of Jesus, delight of all saints,

Have mercy on us

Leader: Lamb of God, Who takes away the sins of the
    world,
All: *Spare us, O Lord*

Leader: Lamb of God, Who takes away the sins of the
    world,
All: *Graciously hear us, O Lord*

Leader: Lamb of God, Who takes away the sins of the
    world,
All: *Have mercy on us*

Leader: Jesus, meek and humble of Heart,
All: *Please make our hearts like Your own*

Leader: Let us pray:

Almighty and everlasting God, look upon the Heart

of Your well beloved Son and upon the praise and satisfaction which He offers you in the name of sinners; and in Your goodness, grant them pardon when they seek your mercy, in the Name of Your Son, Jesus Christ, Who lives and reigns with You forever and ever. Amen.

23b. Litany of the Holy Name of Jesus

Leader: Lord, have mercy on us.
All: Christ, have mercy on us

Leader: Lord, have mercy on us; Jesus hear us.
All: Jesus, graciously hear us

Leader

God the Father of heaven,
God the Son, Redeemer of the world,
God the Holy Spirit,
Holy Trinity, one God,
Jesus, Son of the living God,
Jesus, splendor of the Father,
Jesus, brightness of eternal light,
Jesus, King of glory,
Jesus, sun of justice,
Jesus, Son of the Virgin Mary,
Jesus, most amiable
Jesus, most admirable,

Response

Have mercy on us

Jesus, mighty God,
Jesus, Father of the world to come,
Jesus, angel of the great counsel,
Jesus, most powerful,
Jesus, most patient,
Jesus, most obedient,
Jesus, meek and humble of heart,
Jesus, lover of chastity,
Jesus, lover of us
Jesus, God of peace,
Jesus, author of life,
Jesus, model of virtues,
Jesus, lover of souls,
Jesus, our God,
Jesus, our refuge,
Jesus, Father of the poor,
Jesus, treasure of the faithful,
Jesus, Good Shepherd,
Jesus, true light,
Jesus, eternal wisdom,
Jesus, infinite goodness,
Jesus, our way and our life,
Jesus, joy of angels
Jesus, King of patriarchs
Jesus, master of Apostles,
Jesus, teacher of Evangelists,
Jesus, strength of martyrs,
Jesus, light of confessors,
Jesus, purity of virgins,
Jesus, crown of all saints,

Have mercy on us

Be merciful,   *Spare us, O Jesus*
Be merciful,   *Graciously hear us, O Jesus*

From all evil,
From all sin,
From Your wrath,
From the snares of the devil,
From the spirit of fornication,
From everlasting death,

Jesus, deliver us

From the neglect of Your inspirations,
Through the mystery of Your holy Incarnation,
Through Your nativity,
Through Your infancy,
Through Your most divine life,
Through Your labors,
Through Your agony and Passion,
Through Your cross and dereliction,
Through Your sufferings,
Through Your death and burial,
Through Your Resurrection,
Through Your Ascension,
Through Your institution of the most Holy
    Eucharist,
Through Your joys,
Through Your glory,

Jesus, deliver us

Leader: Lamb of God, Who takes away the sins of the
    world,
All: *Spare us, O Jesus*

Leader: Lamb of God, Who takes away the sins of the
    world,
All: *Graciously hear us, O Jesus*

Leader: Lamb of God, Who takes away the sins of the
    world,
All: *Have mercy on us, O Jesus*

Leader: Jesus, hear us
All: *Jesus, graciously hear us*

Leader: Let us pray:

O Lord Jesus Christ, Who has said: Ask and you
shall receive; seek and you shall find; knock and it shall
be opened unto you; grant, we beseech You, to us who
ask the gift of Your divine love, that we may ever love
You with all our hearts, and in all our words and
actions, and never cease praising You.

Give us, O Lord, a perpetual fear and love of Your
holy Name; for You never fail to govern those whom You

do solidly establish in Your love. Who lives and reigns world without end. Amen.

24. Scripture Passages for the Enthronement of the Sacred Heart and the Holy Family in the Home

John 17:15-19	Luke 19:1-10
1 Corinthians 13:4-7	Ephesians 6:10-17
Galatians 4:1-2 & 6	Luke 1:26-33

Exodus 24:7 *All that the Lord has spoken we will do.*

Psalm 29:10 *The Lord sits enthroned as King for ever.*

Matthew 6:33-34 *But seek first His Kingdom and His righteousness, and all these things shall be yours as well. Therefore do not be anxious about tomorrow, for tomorrow will be anxious for itself.*

John 18:37 *Pilate said to Him "So you are a king?" Jesus answered, "You say that I am a king."*

Luke 19:5 *I must stay in your house today.*

Revelation 3:20 *I stand at the door and knock.*

Revelation 22:20 *Surely I am coming soon.*

See pages 580–581 for Consecration & Enthronement program.

25. Scripture Passages for Consecrating a Business

1 Corinthians 9:24-27	Luke 12:15-21
Philippians 4:4-7	John 4:34-38
Mark 12:13-17	Matthew 18:20
2 Peter 1:2-7	Matthew 11:28-29
Matthew 7:12-14	John 2:13-17
Philippians 4:12-13	Matthew 21:13

29a. Daily Offering

O My Jesus, I offer this for love of You, for the conversion of poor sinners and in reparation for all the sins committed against the Immaculate Heart of Mary. *(Fatima Prayer)*

29b. Act of Faith & Intercession
Said during Mass at the Consecration

My Jesus, I believe, I adore, I trust, and I love You. I ask pardon for those who do not believe, do not adore, do not trust, and do not love You. *(Fatima Prayer)*

31a. Immaculate Conception Prayer for All

O Immaculate Conception, Mary, my Mother, live in me, act in me, speak in and through me. Think your thoughts in my mind, love through my heart. Give me your dispositions and feelings. Teach, lead, and guide me to Jesus. Correct, enlighten, and expand my thoughts and behavior. Possess my soul; take over my entire personality and life. Replace me with yourself. Incline me to constant adoration and thanksgiving. Pray in and through me. Let me live in you and keep me in this union always. Amen.

34. Litany of Thanksgiving

Before retiring, thank God for something specific and
possibly reflect on one of the following points
(try to recite on Sundays)

Jesus, help us now to pause for a few moments and to think of all the spiritual and material gifts that You have showered upon us, our families, and the entire human race.

- Lord, You have given us an immortal life.

- Lord, You took upon Yourself our nature, and have made us members of your royal family and heirs of the thrones in Heaven.

- Lord, You loved us so, that You died for us on Calvary, so that we could be with you for all eternity.

- You created Your Mother immaculate and You loved her above all creation, yet You shared Mary with us by making her our Mother as well.

- You created St. Joseph and allowed him to be the guardian of Your children on earth.

- You created the billions of angels and saints and allowed them to help us in our earthly pilgrimage.

- You allow us to be present at Your sacrificial offering to the Father at Mass every day.

- You humble yourself in the Holy Eucharist to become our daily bread. Your Eucharistic Presence in all the tabernacles of the world continually intercedes for us with our Father.

- You instituted the other sacraments to give us strength, while Your Church guides us on the narrow path to eternal paradise.

- You have given us many sacramentals, such as the Brown Scapular of Our Lady of Mount Carmel, to remind us of the spiritual realities that affect our lives, and to properly dispose us for the reception of special graces You want to confer on us.

- And most of all, Jesus, You sent Your Most Holy Spirit to dwell within us. Through Baptism, You have made an interior heaven within us. You have truly made us a temple of the Holy Spirit of the Father and Yourself. You daily give us opportunities to become one spirit with You by interiorly uniting ourselves with Your Spirit who dwells within us closer than our very breath (cf. 1 Corinthians 3:16-17).

- Indeed Lord, what else can You do for us that You have not already done?

Pause and thank God for His specific blessings. You may want to reflect on just one of these gifts each day.

34a. The Blessing Before Meals (daily)

Bless us, O Lord, and these thy gifts, which we are about to receive from thy bounty, through Christ our Lord. Amen

We pray, Father, for all those families who do not have enough food this day, and may the souls of the faithfully departed, through the mercy of God, rest in peace. Amen. (try to say the Angelus, #2c, before meals)

34b. Grace After Meals (daily)

We give thee thanks, almighty God, for these and all thy benefits, which we have received from thy bounty, through Christ our Lord. Amen.

35. Plea to the Everliving God for the Unborn

Lord God, our Eternal Father, we come to Your throne full of awe and reverence at Your saving power. Through Our Brother and Savior Jesus Christ, we beg You to help us stop the widespread slaughter of unborn life in our land. May our love for our innocent brothers and sisters closely resemble the love that exists in the Holy Family. Help us to provide all human  life with protection under our civil laws. We know that through the intercession of our Mother Mary, chosen Spouse of the Holy Spirit, our request will be granted. Through Christ our Lord. Amen.

40. Litany of the Patrons of the Apostolate for Family Consecration

Try to recite on Tuesdays

Petition-Leader

Response

God the Father, Our Creator,
God the Son, our Redeemer,
God the Holy Spirit, our Consoler,
Holy Trinity, One God,
Most Sacred and Eucharistic Heart of Jesus,

Have mercy on my family and The Apostolate

Most Sorrowful and Immaculate Heart of Mary,
St. Joseph, our Guardian,
Most Holy Family, our Example,
St. Anne and St. Joachim,
St. John the Baptist,

Form my family and The Apostolate

St. Michael, Prince of Angels,

St. Raphael, Guardian of married couples,

St. Gabriel, Guardian of those consecrated to
Mary,

Holy Choir of the Seraphim, Standard for a
God-centered life,

Holy Choir of the Cherubim, Pillar of Faith
and Purity,

Holy Choir of the Thrones, Mainstay for higher
units of authority,

Holy Choir of the Dominions, Pillar of spiritual
authority,

Holy Choir of the Virtues, Advocate of the spiritual life,

Holy Choir of the Powers, Mainstay against
the demons,

Holy Choir of the Principalities, Protectors of
parishes and spiritual associations,

Holy Choir of the Archangels, Advocate of religious and lay apostles,

Holy Choir of the Angels, Guardians of the
people of God,

Our own guardian angels,

St. Peter, our first Holy Father,

St. Paul the Evangelist,

St. John the Evangelist,

St. James the Apostle,

St. Andrew the Apostle,

St. Philip the Apostle,

St. Bartholomew the Apostle,

St. Thomas the Apostle,

St. Matthew the Apostle,

St. James the Less,

St. Simon the Apostle,

St. Jude the Apostle, and Patron of desperate
cases,

St. Matthias the Apostle,

Protect my family and The Apostolate

Intercede for my family and The Apostolate

St. Tarsicius, Standard for Eucharistic
Devotion,
St. Maria Goretti, Patroness of purity,
St. Francis of Assisi, Standard for Christian
Renewal,
St. Dominic, Patron of the Holy Rosary,
St. Thomas Aquinas, Patron of Catholic educa-
tion,
St. John Neumann, Patron of catechists,
St. Ignatius Loyola, Defender of the Faith,
St. Jerome, Patron of Scripture studies,
St. Patrick, Patron of God-centered countries,
St. Teresa of Avila, Model for the interior life
and devotion to St. Joseph,
St. Therese, the Little Flower, Patroness of the
active apostolate,
St. Margaret Mary, Patroness of Devotion to
the Sacred Heart,
St. Catherine of Sienna, Model for lay celi-
bates,
St. Louis de Montfort, Patron of total consecra-
tion,
St. Martin de Porres, Patron of the suffering,
St. John Bosco, Patron of youth,
St. Nicholas, Patron of those in financial need,
St. Dominic Savio, Patron of youthful deaths,
St. Maximilian Kolbe, Model for Marian devo-
tion,
St. Vincent Pallotti, Patron of the lay aposto-
late,
St. Elizabeth Ann Seton, Patroness of Catholic
schools,
St. Thomas Moore, Patron of fidelity to the
Holy Father,
Our own Patron Saints,

Amen.

*Privately ask Blessed Kateri Tekakwitha and Blessed Juan
Diego to pray for vocations in the Apostolate's Catholic Corps,
and ask August Mauge for interior peace.*

40a. Prayer for the Canonization of August Mauge

September 15, 1910 - November 4, 1980

Dear Lord, through the Immaculate Heart of Mary, You granted Your servant, August Mauge, countless graces to use quietly his professional skills to help those in need. He was truly a person for others. He was a model of peaceful and humble acceptance of one's responsibility at each present moment to serve God and neighbor.

Like August, may we joyfully work in Christ to strengthen family and parish community life. Help us, as You helped him, to have peace of heart in times of personal tribulation. Grant us the grace to strive with tranquil courage for the upbuilding of the Church through parish evangelization and family consecration.

Glorify August, Your faithful servant, O Lord. May his cause for canonization come speedily to a happy conclusion for the spread of true family values and for the deepening of parish and family life in the Sacred Hearts of Jesus and Mary.

We make our prayer and petition (*make your specific request*) through Christ Our Lord. Amen.

With Ecclesiastical permission

Biographical Sketch

August Mauge was a native of Chicago. After his military service in World War II, he worked as an accountant. He was ever ready to assist poor families who needed his professional services. He was one of the founding members of the Apostolate for Family Consecration. He was a source of quiet strength for all in intensifying their prayer life and their awareness of being a pilgrim people. He was a dedicated member of St. Frances of Rome parish in suburban Chicago, Illinois, joyfully accepting the responsibilities of the parish ministries asked of him. At his funeral many people gave a remarkable tribute to his outstanding virtues. He is buried in St. Adalbert Cemetery in Niles, Illinois.

Those who receive favors through the intercession of August (his friends addressed him as "Augie") or have any personal knowledge of him, are asked to communicate with: August Mauge Guild, P.O. Box 182, Winthrop Harbor, IL 60096 or call 1-800-FOR-MARY.

40b. Prayer to One's Patron Saints

My Patron Saints, (mention them by name), please help me to imitate your virtues and assist me as I strive to fulfill God's distinctive plan for my life. Amen.

42. Reparation for Sin
Excerpts from the Apostolic Constitution on the Revision of Indulgences, Pope Paul VI, January 1, 1967

The numbers found at the end of the paragraphs refer to section numbers in Pope Paul VI's document.

Sins Must be Expiated

The truth has been divinely revealed that sins are followed by punishments. God's holiness and justice inflict them. Sins must be expiated...

In fact, every sin upsets the universal order God, in his indescribable wisdom and limitless love, has established. Further, every sin does immense harm to the sinner himself and to the community of men. (2)

What Expiation Involves

The full taking away and, as it is called, reparation

for sin requires two things. Firstly, friendship with God must be restored. Amends must be made for offending his wisdom and goodness. This is done by a sincere conversion of mind. Secondly, all the personal and social values, as well as those that are universal, which sin has lessened or destroyed must be fully made good....

The very fact that punishment for sin exists and that it is so severe make it possible for us to understand how foolish and malicious sin is and how harmful its consequences are.

The doctrine of Purgatory clearly demonstrates that even when the guilt of sin has been taken away, punishment for it or the consequences of it may remain to be expiated or cleansed. (3)

The Communion of Saints

By the hidden and kindly mystery of God's will a supernatural solidarity reigns among men. A consequence of this is that the sin of one person harms other people just as one person's holiness helps others. (4)

Following in Christ's steps, those who believe in Him have always tried to help one another along the path which leads to the heavenly Father, through

Pope Paul VI

prayer, the exchange of spiritual goods and penitential expiation. The more they have been immersed in the fervor of love, the more they have imitated Christ in His sufferings. They have carried their crosses to make expiation for their own sins and the sins of others. They were convinced that they could help their brothers to obtain salvation from God, Who is the Father of mercies. This is the very ancient dogma called the Communion of Saints. It means that the life of each individual son of God is joined in Christ and through Christ by a wonderful link to the life of all his other Christian brethren. Together they form the supernatural unity of Christ's Mystical Body so that, as it were, a single mystical person is formed. (5) [Also see section 42a.]

What Indulgences Are: The Church's Authoritative Intervention

The taking away of the temporal punishment due to sins when their guilt has already been forgiven has been called specifically "indulgences…"

In fact, in granting an indulgence, the Church uses its powers as minister of Christ's Redemption…

The authorities of the Church have two aims in granting indulgences. The first is to help the faithful to expiate their sins. The second is to encourage them to do works of piety, penitence and charity, particularly those which lead to growth in faith and which help the common good.

Further, if the faithful offer indulgences by way of intercession for the dead they cultivate charity in an excellent way. (8)

42a. Reparation and the Dual Dimension of Pope John Paul II's Consecration
by Jerome F. Coniker

1.   Pope John Paul II has taught us how to enter into that era of peace promised by Our Lady of Fatima. While in New York in 1995, the Holy Father asked families to do two things: pray the Rosary and study the *Catechism of the Catholic Church.* He continues to tell us, "Take the Gospel to your neighbors!" By vigorously learning the Faith and teaching it to our children and our neighbors, we can truly renew family life and society.

If those of us who have been given the light of the Catholic faith do not make heroic sacrifices now to do what the Holy Father is telling us to do, our society will continue on its "free-fall" into the abyss of immorality, and we will see, before our very eyes, the fulfillment of the "conditional" prophecies of the approved apparitions of Our Lady in Fatima and Akita (Japan). I say "conditional" because that is what they are—conditional to the degree of how we sacrificially respond to Our Lady's requests.

First, let's reflect on what Pope John Paul II wrote in his book, *Crossing the Threshold of Hope,* with reference to Fatima:

"Perhaps this is also why the Pope was called from a faraway country, perhaps this is why it was necessary for the assassination attempt to be made in St. Peter's Square precisely on May 13, 1981, the anniversary of the first apparition at Fatima—so that all could become more transparent and comprehensible, so that the voice of God which speaks in human history through the 'signs of the times' could be more easily heard and understood." (p.131)

The Holy Father went on to write:

"On this universal level, if victory comes it will be brought by Mary. *Christ will conquer through her because he wants the Church's victories now and in the future to be linked to her....*

"I held this conviction even though I did not yet know very much about Fatima. I could see, however, that there was a certain continuity among La Salette, Lourdes, and Fatima—and, in the distant past, our Polish Jasna Gora." (p. 221)

When the Pope was shot

2. "And thus we come to May 13, 1981, when I was wounded by gunshots fired in St. Peter's Square. At first, I did not pay attention to the fact that the assassination attempt had occurred on the exact anniversary of the day Mary appeared to the three children at Fatima in Portugal and spoke to them the words that **now, at the end of this century, seem to be close to their fulfillment.**

"With this event, didn't Christ perhaps say, once again, 'Be not afraid'? Did he repeat this Easter exhortation to the Pope, to the Church, and indirectly, to the entire human family?"

The Pope went on to say:

"At the end of the second millennium, we need, perhaps more than ever, the words of the Risen Christ: 'Be not afraid!' Man who, even after the fall of Communism, has not stopped being afraid and who truly has many reasons for feeling this way, needs to hear these words.

"Nations need to hear them, especially those nations that have been reborn after the fall of the Communist empire, as well as those that witnessed this event from the outside. Peoples and nations of the entire world need to hear these words.

"Their conscience needs to grow in the certainty that Someone exists who holds in His hands the destiny of this passing world; Someone who holds the keys to death and the netherworld (cf. Rev 1:18); Someone who is the Alpha and the Omega of human history (cf. Rev. 22:13)—be it the individual or collective history. And this Someone is Love (cf. 1 Jn 4:8,16)—Love that became man, Love crucified and risen, Love unceasingly present among men. It is Eucharistic Love. It is the infinite source of communion. He alone can give the ultimate assurance when He says 'Be not afraid!'" (pp. 221-222)

Fatima

3.   When our family lived in Portugal from 1971–1973, we obtained a copy of a letter that Sister Lucia wrote to the Bishop of the Diocese of Leiria (where Fatima is located) about Our Lady's apparition on July

13, 1917. Sister Lucia is the only living seer of Fatima since Jacinta (age 7 at the time of the apparition) and Francisco (age 9) died shortly after they told Our Lady that they would

be willing to offer their lives up for the conversion of sinners—for your family and my family.

The vision of hell

4. Lucia's words:

"Our Lady showed us a large sea of fire which seemed to be beneath the earth. Plunged in this fire were the demons and the souls, who were like embers, transparent and black or bronze-colored, with human forms which floated about in the conflagration, borne by the flames which issued from it with clouds of smoke, falling on all sides as sparks fall in great conflagrations, without weight or equilibrium, among shrieks and groans of sorrow and despair which horrified us and caused us to quake with fear.

"The demons were distinguished by horrible and loathsome forms of animals, frightful and unknown, but transparent and black. This vision vanished in a moment. Providentially, our good Heavenly Mother had promised us in the first apparition to take us to Heaven. Otherwise, I think we would have died of fright and horror..." (Letter dated August 31, 1941 from Sr. Lucia to the Bishop of Leiria.)

The great Fatima prophecies

5.   The following are Sister Lucia's words, published by the Bishop of Leiria. I have organized them in an outline with an *asterisk (*) to indicate the prophecies that have already been fulfilled*:

"Shortly afterwards, we raised our eyes to Our Lady, who said with goodness and sadness: 'You have seen hell, where the souls of poor sinners go.

- To save them, God wishes to establish in the world devotion to my Immaculate Heart.* [However, more should be done.]

- If they do what I will tell you, many souls will be saved, and there will be peace. The war is going to end.* [World War I]

- But if they don't stop offending God, another and worse one [World War II] will begin in the reign of Pius XI.*

- When you shall see a night illuminated by an unknown light [Jan 25-26, 1938]*, know that this is the great sign that God will give you, that He is going to punish the world by means of war, hunger and persecutions of the Church, and of the Holy Father.*

- To prevent this, I shall come to ask for the consecration of Russia to my Immaculate Heart; and for the Communion of Reparation on the First Saturdays.*

- If they listen to my request, Russia will be converted, and there will be peace.

- If not:

    Russia will scatter her errors throughout the world,*

    She will provoke wars and persecutions of the Church,*

    The good will be martyred* [Note: there have been more martyrs in this century than in the entire 2000 year history of the Church],

The Holy Father will have much to suffer,*

And various nations will be annihilated. [This has not happened and does not have to happen if we consecrate ourselves in the dual dimension of Pope John Paul II's consecration.]

• In the end, my Immaculate Heart will triumph.

The Holy Father will consecrate Russia to me,* [Pope John Paul II did this on May 13, 1982, in Fatima and on March 25, 1984, in Rome]

And she will be converted,

And a certain period of peace will be granted to the world.'"

The miracle of the sun

6.   Our Lady's final apparition at Fatima took place on October 13, 1917. This was the great "Miracle of the Sun." Cardinal Joseph Carberry once told me that never before in the history of the world has a public miracle, such as this, ever occurred, one that was prophesied in advance to occur on a specific day, at a specific place, and which was witnessed by over 70,000 people. *It was also documented as an historic fact by an atheistic press that was controlled by an atheistic government.*

When we lived near Fatima for two years, I had the privilege to study the Fatima message under the instruction of Father Gabriel Pausback, O'Carm., who was the assistant general of the Carmelite Order and author of *Saints of Carmel*. He introduced me to the Marto's (Jacinta's and Francisco's family) and others who had witnessed the miracle of the Sun.

The "Miracle of the Sun" was not like many other reported apparitions, where some could see the phenomenon and others could not. On October 13, 1917, everyone within a 20 mile radius saw the entire plateau of Fatima bathed in light-shafts of blue, red, yellow and green. Then they saw the sun spinning in the sky, and they ran for their lives when they saw it plummet towards the earth. The fire ball that appeared to be the sun stopped at the tree tops, hovered there for a few minutes and slowly went back into the heavens, leaving everyone present completely dry, when before the event they had been drenched from the rainfall.

Cardinal Carberry also told me that since there has never been a miracle such as this before, the message — which the miracle confirmed — must be of the greatest significance!

Approved Apparitions of Akita

7.   Now let's consider the prophecies of the approved apparitions of Our Lady in Akita, Japan. Let me first give some background on these apparitions.

They started in 1975 and were approved, on April 22, 1984, by Bishop John Shojiro Ito, who at the time was Bishop of Niigata.

The current Ordinary of the Niigata diocese, Bishop Francis Sato, has also approved the apparitions. This approval was documented when our chaplain, Father Kevin Barrett, interviewed Bishop Sato on videotape in March of 1995 at his residence in Japan.

Fr. Kevin Barrett, Family Apostolate Chaplain, interviewing Bishop Francis Sato of Akita.

The seer, Sister Agnes Sasagawa, like Sr. Lucia of Fatima, submitted in total obedience to the bishop of the diocese where the apparitions occurred. It is important to note that this is the way of the Church, *that we are protected from deception by humbly submitting to Church authority.*

In the letter of approval issued by Bishop Ito, he quoted Our Blessed Mother as saying:

"As I told you, if men do not repent and better themselves, the Father will inflict a terrible punishment on all humanity. ***It will be a punishment greater than the deluge, such as one will never have been seen before.*** Fire will fall from the sky and will wipe out a great part of humanity, the good as well as the bad, sparing neither priests nor faithful. The survivors will find themselves so desolate that they will envy the dead. The only arms which will remain for you will be the Rosary and the Sign left by my Son. Each day recite the prayers of the Rosary. With the Rosary, pray for the Pope, the Bishops and the priests...

"...In order that the world might know His anger, the *Heavenly Father is preparing to inflict a great chastisement on all mankind.* With my Son, I have intervened so many times to appease the wrath of the Father. *I have prevented the coming of calamities by offering Him the sufferings of the Son on the Cross, His*

*Precious Blood, and beloved souls who console Him and form a cohort of victim souls. **Prayer, penance, and courageous sacrifices can soften the Father's anger...***" (taken from the letter of approval by Bishop John Shojiro Ito of April 22, 1984).

St. Kolbe on Obedience

8.   What is meant by the "penance" and "courageous sacrifices" which are necessary to prevent chastisement? **I believe that the penance and courageous sacrifices that God is asking of us is obedience to the Holy Father, the Pope.** The most difficult thing for man to do is to bend his will to lawful authority. This is the greatest reparation for sin we can offer.

The great Polish Marian saint and martyr of Auschwitz, St. Maximilian Kolbe, who started the Knights of the Immaculata movement shortly after he had a vision of Our Lady of Fatima standing over Moscow, said:

"Not in mortification, not in great prayer, not in labor, not in rest, but in *obedience is the essence and merit of holiness*" (*Aim Higher*, p. 84).

Obedience is the key. Doing penance and making sacrifices does not just mean praying and fasting. Although there are norms established by the Church for prayer and fasting, they are not the only thing we are supposed to do. ***Obedience to lawful authority represents the most pleasing penance and constitutes the most heroic sacrifices in order to repair for sin.***

As Catholics, we need to humble ourselves and bend our wills to the Holy Father if we want to be holy and receive an outpouring of God's mercy. ***Obedience is the key to drawing down God's mercy upon the*** *families of the world*.

Our Lord said in Matthew 7:21:

"It is not those who say, 'Lord, Lord,' that will enter the kingdom of Heaven, *but those who do the will of My Father*."

The Key to Hope and Mercy

9.   Obedience to the Pope and reparation for sin gives us hope.

The messages of both Fatima and Akita have underscored the fact that reparation for sin is the formula for drawing down God's mercy upon our world. At the Apostolate's Catholic Familyland, we are seeking to teach families about reparation: what it means and how it should be effected in our daily lives. We have summarized what we call the Marian Multiplier "formula" for bringing down God's mercy.

The Marian Multiplier

10. First Point: **Sin** is the cause of all unhappiness. Every sin affects not only the sinner, but the entire world.

Second Point: **Grace** is more powerful than sin; the Redemption is greater than the Fall. Jesus has conquered satan. We have nothing to fear from the devil if we follow Christ (which also means following His Vicar on earth, the Pope, and the Teaching Magisterium of the Church), love God and neighbor and strive to grow in the grace Jesus won for us on Calvary.

Third Point: **Personal holiness** is essential for salvation. But our personal holiness alone is not enough to offset the effects of the sins of mankind and bring about a healing of families and world peace.

Fourth Point: **Consecration** to Jesus through Mary. When enough of us give the little holiness we have to Jesus through Mary, she will be able to purify and multiply it by her incalculable merits to most effectively repair for sins in our age and obtain grace from her Son to convert poor sinners and bring peace and healing into families and the world.

Every sin affects society

11. Reflecting on the First Point, let's look at what Pope John Paul II said in Section 16 of his document *On Reconciliation and Penance*:

"In other words, there is no sin, not even the most intimate and secret one, the most strictly individual one that exclusively concerns the person committing it.

"With greater or lesser violence, with greater or lesser harm, *every sin has repercussions on the entire ecclesial body and on the whole human family."*

In Section 2 of the Apostolic Constitution on indulgences (*Indulgentiarum doctrina*), dated January 1, 1967, Pope Paul VI states:

"In fact, every sin upsets the universal order God, in His indescribable wisdom and limitless love, has established. Further, every sin does immense harm to the sinner himself and to the community of men."

This means that when someone sins, it not only hurts the sinner but the entire Mystical Body of Christ. It gives the devil more power to tempt us and to draw us away from God's will into venial sin, and eventually into mortal sin.

When we think about this, it can be very discouraging. We look around and see sin everywhere, and it seems that so few people are trying to do God's will. But there is hope.

Reparation—Repairing for Sin

12. If sin is the "bad news" then the Second Point (grace) is truly the heart of the "Good News" of the Gospel. Jesus, by his redemptive sacrifice, has won for us the grace to overcome and to repair for the sin in our lives and in our world.

I believe that the best definition of reparation for sin is from Pope Paul VI's Apostolic Constitution on indulgences. Providentially, former President Ronald Reagan quoted this definition in his welcoming address to Pope John Paul II when His Holiness visited the United States in 1987. In Section 4, Pope Paul VI says:

"By the hidden and kindly mystery of God's will, a supernatural solidarity reigns among men. A consequence of this is that the sin of one person harms other people just as one person's holiness helps others."

In this same document, Pope Paul VI presents a more detailed explanation on reparation and what we must do to repair for sin. His Holiness states:

"The truth has been divinely revealed that sins are followed by punishments. God's holiness and justice inflict them. Sins must be expiated...

"The full taking away and, as it is called, reparation of sin requires two things:

"Firstly, friendship with God must be restored. Amends must be made for offending His wisdom and goodness. This is done by a sincere conversion of mind [repentance and formation].

"Secondly, all the personal and social values as well as those that are universal, which sin has lessened or destroyed, must be fully made good...[evangelization and catechesis]" (Apostolic Constitution *Indulgentiarum doctrina*, sections 2–3).

Like the current of a river

13. You can compare the concept of reparation to a river in which people are swimming upstream, against the current, in order to get to Heaven. The more sin there is in the world, the stronger the current becomes (temptation), making it harder for everyone to reach Heaven.

However, when people grow in grace, they are repairing for their own sins and the sins of the whole world. They are helping to make the current run more slowly so that everyone in the family and in the world is able to swim more easily upstream (actual graces) and reach their heavenly goal if they truly will it.

Like a magnetic field

14. Another analogy can be made. Reparation may be compared with magnetic fields. God seeks to attract our free wills by His love and truth (actual grace). The devil seeks to seduce us by his lies and the empty pleasures

of evil (temptation). By choosing to sin, man repels God and allows himself to be seduced by the devil. When many people sin, all society feels less attraction to God, and more and more people succumb to the corrupting seduction of the devil (temptation).

However, as more people renounce sin and allow themselves to be drawn to God, gaining grace and merit for their souls and the whole Mystical Body of Christ through their prayers and good works, they help to increase the attraction (actual grace) felt by all to God and His goodness.

In order for us to grow in grace (Second Point) and offset the effects of sin, we have to develop a prayer life, receive the sacraments and practice the virtues (Third Point). Naturally, the fervor and the love we have for God determines the amount of grace that we receive and therefore, determines the amount of reparation that is made for our own sins and for the sins of the world.

Consecration to Jesus through Mary

15. Now, if the devil is always actively trying to seduce souls away from God by his perverse influence, the Mother of Jesus, the woman of Genesis (cf. 3:15) and of Revelation (chapter 12), is ever more so attracting her children to God. She is the chosen vessel through whom God wishes to crush the head of satan.

The late Cardinal Luigi Ciappi, who served the last five popes as personal theologian and was the primary theological advisor for The Apostolate, explained to us how, in the Fourth Point, our Blessed Mother's singular holiness helps us to more effectively repair for sin, especially through the power of consecration. In his letter of August 24, 1989, he said:

"How true it is when we give all of our merits to Mary, she multiplies them by her incalculable merits. This puts into motion positive spiritual forces to repair the damage due to sin and significantly change the course of history, if enough make this commitment.

"Mary's merits can multiply the effects of one person's holiness and help countless souls. Only heaven knows the depth of holiness a soul must achieve to tip the scales for world peace."

Mary never ceases to dispense the precious graces of Jesus, her Son, upon her children. And when we entrust to her our prayers, merits, and good works, through consecration, she purifies and multiplies their power to repair for sin and presents them to Jesus on our behalf.

Restoring Order through Reparation

16. When we live a life of reparation for sin, we are growing in union with God. Soon after founding the Apostolate for Family Consecration in 1975, I wrote the following explanation about the effects of "planting seeds" of prayer, charity, and sacrifice, accompanied by the "water and sunshine" of our devout reception of the sacraments in our lives:

"Our meritorious actions help to bring back the spiritual balance in the universe by lessening the control of the forces of evil over our lives and those of our families, our neighborhoods, our schools, our parishes, our dioceses, and indeed, the entire world.

"Every supernaturally good act performed in the state of grace gives us a reward or merit, increasing our capacity for peace and our capacity to know, love and serve God for all eternity. In addition to, and through total consecration to Jesus through Mary, our merits are purified, multiplied and preserved for us throughout our entire pilgrimage on earth.

"Through consecration, we give to our Blessed Mother the privilege of directing our prayers. We more humbly acknowledge the reality that we are God's children, confident that Our Heavenly Mother knows better than we what we need in order to more perfectly accomplish God's will.

"Finally, because of the Church's intercessory power, many of our meritorious acts can be enriched by the Church through indulgences. Thus we have the power to help release a soul from Purgatory everyday through our plenary (full) indulgences, and relieve the suffering of the Holy Souls through our partial indulgences."

We need to better understand that indulgences are an added satisfactory effect given to our prayers and good works by the Church as part of the power of the "keys" entrusted to her by Christ in the person of the Apostle Peter (cf. Matt 16:19 and Jn. 20:34). If we are in the state of grace and fulfill one of the norms laid down by the Church, we can continually earn plenary (no more than one a day) and partial indulgences for ourselves and for the souls in Purgatory. Please read #45a for a summary of the norms for indulgences.

The Dual Dimensions of Pope John Paul II's Consecration

17. The Third and Fourth Points are incorporated into the dual dimensions of Pope John Paul II's consecration, which can bring the light of the truth into our dark

world so that our families can live in the greatest era of peace and religion the world has ever known.

The dual dimensions of Pope John Paul II's consecration is *Totus Tuus* and *Consecrate them in Truth*.

The first dimension

18. *Totus Tuus* (Latin for 'Totally yours') refers to giving everything to Jesus through Mary, according to the formula of St. Louis de Montfort which the Holy Father wrote about in his book, *Crossing the Threshold of Hope* (p. 213).

If we follow this formula of consecration, which Pope John Paul proclaims and lives, we give the few merits that we have to our Blessed Mother who then takes them and multiplies them by her incalculable merits and presents them to Jesus on our behalf.

St. Louis de Montfort's formula

19. In his treatise, *True Devotion to the Blessed Virgin*, St. Louis wrote:

"For by it (this devotion) we show love for our neighbor in an outstanding way, since we give Him through Mary's hands all that we prize most highly—that is, the satisfactory and prayer value of all our good works, down to the least good thought and the least little suffering. We give our consent that all we have already acquired or will acquire until death should be used in accordance with our Lady's will for the conversion of sinners or the deliverance of souls from Purgatory" (section 171).

"It must be noted that our good works, passing through Mary's hands, are progressively purified. Consequently, their merit and their satisfactory

and prayer value is also increased. That is why they become much more effective in relieving the souls in Purgatory and in converting sinners than if they did not pass through the virginal and liberal hands of Mary.

"Stripped of self-will and clothed with disinterested love, the little that we give to the Blessed Virgin is truly powerful enough to appease the anger of God and draw down His mercy. It may well be that at the hour of death a person who has been faithful to this devotion will find that he has freed many souls from Purgatory and converted many sinners, even though he performed only the ordinary actions of his state of life. Great will be his joy at the judgment. Great will be his glory throughout eternity" (section 172).

"Mary amassed such a multitude of merits and graces during her sojourn on earth that it would be easier to count the stars in heaven, the drops of water in the ocean or the sands of the seashore than count her merits and graces. She thus gave more glory to God than all the angels and saints have given or will ever give Him. Mary, wonder of God, when souls abandon themselves to you, you cannot but work wonders in them (section 222)!

"Our Blessed Lady, in her immense love for us, is eager to receive into her virginal hands the gift of our actions, imparting to them a marvelous beauty and splendor, presenting them herself to Jesus most willingly" (section 223).

Apostolate's celibate Catholic Corps member, Jomelia, renewing her consecration and commitment to the Asian missions.
(see pages 622–626)

St. Maximilian Kolbe's prophecy for modern times

20. "Modern times are dominated by satan and will be more so in the future. The conflict with hell cannot be engaged by men, even the most clever. The Immaculata alone has from God the promise of victory over satan. However, assumed into Heaven, the Mother of God now requires our cooperation. She seeks souls who will consecrate themselves entirely to her, who will become in her hands effective instruments for the defeat of satan and the spreading of God's kingdom upon earth."

The second dimension

21. Let's now consider the second dimension of Pope John Paul II's consecration, Consecrate Them in Truth or evangelization and catechesis, which represents his highest priority. Our Lord, in effect, defined "consecration" in John 17 when he said:

Verse 3: "Eternal life is this—to know You." [catechesis]

Verse 4: "I have glorified You on earth by finishing the work You gave me to do." [evangelization]

Verse 15: "Protect them from the evil one."

Verse 17: "Consecrate them in truth. Your word is truth."

Verse 19: "I consecrate Myself so that they too may be consecrated in the truth.

Verse 21: "That they may be one as We are one."

When we steep ourselves in the truth, as put forth in Sacred Scripture, the Second Vatican Council documents, the Catechism of the Catholic Church, papal documents, etc., we are better disposed to pray, to receive the sacraments and practice virtue—in short, to be holy, gaining ever more grace and merit. Then we can give Our Blessed Mother many more of our graces and merits to multiply by her incalculable merits, putting into motion a tremendous spiritual power that can defeat satan and bring about the era of peace which she promised at Fatima.

The Holy Father referred to this era in the last page of his book, *Crossing the Threshold of Hope*, when he wrote:

"André Malraux was certainly right when he said that the twenty-first century would be the century of religion or it would not be at all."

I believe that our Holy Father is telling us that if we do God's will and repair for sin, we will see a century of great religion and evangelization for our children and grandchildren to grow up in. But if we don't enter into a life of vigorous evangelization, catechesis and prayer, we will see, because of the evil use of modern technology, the darkest age of purification that the world has ever experienced.

Let's walk with His Holiness over the threshold of hope into the greatest period of light, evangelization, and peace that the world has ever known—that era of peace that Our Lady promised at Fatima.

A Summary —
Cardinal Mario Luigi Ciappi, O.P.

22. The following article from the Pope's newspaper about the late papal theologian, Mario Luigi Cardinal Ciappi, gives you an idea of His Eminence's relationship with the papacy and his competency at reading the signs of the times.

Cardinal Ciappi was the master of the papal palace and papal theologian for the last five popes and was our primary theological advisor from 1979 until his death on April 22, 1996. Please read the following with great care.

St. Dominic was the first papal theologian;
St. Thomas Aquinas was the fourth; and Cardinal Luigi
Ciappi was the eighty-fourth Dominican Theologian
of the Papal Household. His Eminence was also the
primary theological advisor of the Apostolate
for Family Consecration.

Excerpts from Pope John Paul II's homily at Cardinal Ciappi's funeral, April 25, 1996

23. "Dear brothers and sisters, today in St. Peter's Basilica we are celebrating the funeral of beloved Cardinal Mario Luigi Ciappi, whom God called to himself last Monday evening after a long life spent in service to the Church and, in particular, to the Holy See. I have felt a personal bond with him since my studies, and I am pleased to honor his memory at this moment, so full of emotion, by my testimony of sincere esteem and deep gratitude.

"His brilliant and keen capacity for theological investigation grew and was quickly noticed.

"With a profound knowledge of the theological thought, he was himself a capable theologian who was able to serve the Church generously, first by teaching dogmatic theology and Thomistic aesthetics. The results he achieved in this task brought him to the attention of Pope Pius XII, who in 1955 wanted him at his side as Master of the Sacred Palace. He was confirmed in this office by Pope John XXIII and Pope Paul VI, who spelled out his duties in the Motu Proprio Pontificalis Domus, and appointed him Theologian of the Papal Household.

"His clear thinking, the soundness of his teaching and his undisputed fidelity to the Apostolic See, as well as his ability to interpret the signs of the times according to God, were qualities that made him a valued collaborator during the intense period of the Second Vatican Council to which he made a significant and balanced contribution.

"His careful scholarly work was always accompanied by an intense spiritual life and prayer, the first and fundamental nourishment of his whole life."

(Used by permission of L'Osservatore Romano)

Greatest miracle in the history of the world

24. Luigi Cardinal Ciappi's letter of October 9, 1994, on the next page, is a good summary of this entire treatise. His Eminence talks about the greatest miracle in the history of the world as he addressed our annual Totus Tuus Conference.

Cardinal Ciappi, O.P., and Fr. Thomas Morrison, O.P., our first staff Theologian, celebrating Mass at the Apostolate's Sacred Hearts Chapel

Vatican City
October 9, 1994

*Il Teologo Emerito
della Casa Pontificia*

Dear Jerry and Gwen:

Once again, your Totus Tuus – "Consecrate Them in Truth" Conference will be serving the Church in a very timely way.

25.   Your use of the social communications and the way in which you are using audio and video tape is **a 'fail-safe method' of teaching** and will allow families of today's media culture, which the Holy Father frequently mentions, to become powerful instruments of the Immaculata to bring about the era of peace she promised at Fatima.

26.   *Yes, a miracle was promised at Fatima, the greatest miracle in the history of the world, second only to the Resurrection. And that miracle will be an era of peace which has never really been granted before to the world.*

27.   *I believe that this peace will begin in the domestic church, the family, and go out to the parishes and into the diocese, the country, and the world. This lasting peace will be the fruit of a life of service and of evangelizing one's family and neighbors with the truth that will set them free!*

28.   Our Blessed Mother promised us this era of peace if we say the daily Rosary, practice the First Saturday Communion of Reparation, and live lives consecrated in the truth. This consecration includes giving all of our possessions, both interior and exterior, to Jesus through the Immaculate Heart of Mary, and, as you know, in the Apostolate for Family Consecration, we like to add, "in union with St. Joseph."

29.   As primary theological advisor to the Apostolate for Family Consecration since 1979, I have reminded its members frequently that **consecration is not just a prayer or a devotion but a commitment to a way of life which must be nourished through continuous formation in the eternal truths of our Faith**.

Yours in the Hearts of Jesus and Mary,

Mario Luigi Card. Ciappi, O.P.

Mario Luigi Cardinal Ciappi, O.P.
Papal Theologian Emeritus for Popes Pius XII, John XXIII,
Paul VI, John Paul I, and John Paul II

45a. Summary of Norms for Gaining Indulgences for the Poor Souls in Purgatory or Oneself

Issued by Pope Paul VI on January 1, 1967

(Try to partially review or think about on Mondays)

A **plenary indulgence** is a complete release from the temporal punishment due for sins already forgiven (as far as their guilt is concerned). Only one plenary indulgence may be obtained a day.

Conditions for a plenary indulgence:

A. One must be baptized and in the state of grace.

B. One must receive Holy Communion each time a plenary indulgence is sought.

C. One must go to Confession several days preceding or following the indulgenced action. A single sacramental Confession suffices for gaining several plenary indulgences.

D. One must have a disposition of mind and heart which totally excludes all attachment to sin, even venial sin, otherwise one can only gain a partial indulgence.

E. One must pray for the intentions of the Holy Father, the Pope, preferably one "Our Father" and one "Hail Mary," however, any other pious prayer may be substituted.

F. One must have at least a general intention to gain a plenary indulgence.

G. One must perform the indulgenced work.

A plenary indulgence may be obtained every day by completing *one* of the following works, provided the conditions mentioned above have been fulfilled:

- At least a half hour of adoration of the Blessed Sacrament.
- The private recitation of the Rosary before the Blessed Sacrament or with others in your family,

religious community, or pious association.

- At least a half hour of pious reading of Sacred Scripture.

- Walking the Stations of the Cross in a church or with a properly erected display of the Stations.

A partial indulgence removes part of the temporal punishment due for sins already forgiven. Several partial indulgences may be obtained each day.

Conditions for a partial indulgence:

A. One must be baptized and in the state of grace.

B. One must be inwardly contrite [have at least a striving intention to cut oneself off from all attachment to sin].

C. One must have a general intention to gain an indulgence.

D. One must fulfill the action prescribed in *one* of the following three general grants of indulgences:

- Raise one's mind in humble prayer to God while fulfilling one's responsibilities and enduring the trials of life.

- Give of one's time or goods as a charitable act to assist people who are in need of spiritual comfort or instruction or who are in need of material assistance (donation of time and resources to the work of the Church are, therefore, indulgenced).

- Voluntarily deprive oneself of what is lawful and pleasing, such as fasting or giving up dessert or a favorite TV program.

For more information on indulgences, see section 45 in FCPB–JS or read the "The Handbook of Indulgences: Norms and Grants," published by authority of the National Conference of Catholic Bishops. Also see the "Catechism of the Catholic Church," sections 1032, 1471-1479, and 1498.

46. Veni Creator
Try to recite on Mondays.

Come, O Creator Spirit blest,
And in our souls take up Thy rest;
Come with Thy grace and heavenly aid
To fill the hearts which Thou hast made.

Great Paraclete, to Thee we cry,
O highest gift of God most high!
O font of life! O fire of love!
And sweet anointing from above.

Thou in Thy sevenfold gifts art known,
The finger of God's hand we own;
The promise of the Father, Thou!
Who dost the tongue with power endow.

Kindle our senses from above,
And make our hearts o'erflow with love;
With patience firm and virtue high
The weakness of our flesh supply.

Far from us drive the foe we dread,
And grant us Thy true peace instead;
So shall we not, with Thee for guide,
Turn from the path of life aside.

O may Thy grace on us bestow
The Father and the Son to know,

And Thee through endless times confessed
Of both the eternal Spirit blest.

All glory while the ages run
Be to the Father and the Son,
Who rose from death; the same to Thee,
O Holy Ghost, eternally. Amen.

46a. Come Holy Spirit

V. Come, Holy Spirit, fill the hearts of Your faithful and kindle in them the fire of Your divine love.

R. Send forth Your Spirit and they shall be created: And You will renew the face of the earth.

Let us pray: O God, Who by the light of the Holy Spirit instructs the hearts of the faithful, grant we beseech You to be truly wise and ever rejoice in His presence, through Jesus Christ Our Lord. Amen.

46e. The Holy Spirit:
Secret to Sanctity and Happiness
by Cardinal Mercier

Five minutes every day keep your imagination quiet. Shut your eyes to all things of sense and close your ears to all the sounds of earth, so as to be able to withdraw into the sanctuary of your baptized soul, the temple of the Holy Spirit. Speak there to that Holy Spirit, saying:

O Holy Spirit, Soul of my soul, I adore You. Enlighten, guide, strengthen and console me. Tell me what I ought to do and command me to do it. I promise to be submissive to everything that You permit to happen to me. Show me only what is Your will.

If you do this, your life will be happy and at peace. Consolation will abound, even in the midst of troubles. Grace will be given in proportion to the trial as well as strength to bear it, bringing you to the Gates of Paradise.

46f. Prayers for the Seven Gifts of the Holy Spirit

Sunday—Wisdom

Come Holy Spirit:

Grant me the *Spirit of Wisdom*, that I may despise the perishable things of this world, and aspire only after the things that are eternal.

Monday—Understanding

Come Holy Spirit:

Grant me the *Spirit of Understanding*, to enlighten my mind with the light of Your divine truth.

Tuesday—Counsel

Come Holy Spirit:

Grant me the *Spirit of Counsel*, that I may ever choose the surest ways of pleasing God and gaining heaven.

Wednesday—Fortitude

Come Holy Spirit:

Grant me the *Spirit of Fortitude*, that I may overcome with courage all the obstacles that oppose my salvation.

Thursday—Knowledge

Come Holy Spirit:

Grant me the *Spirit of Knowledge*, that I may know God and know myself, and grow perfect in the science of the Saints.

Friday—Piety

Come Holy Spirit:

Grant me the *Spirit of Piety*, that I may find the service of God sweet and amiable.

Saturday—Fear of the Lord

Come Holy Spirit:

Grant me the *Spirit of Fear of the Lord*, that I may be filled with a loving reverence towards God, and may dread in any way to displease Him.

Daily

Now let us pause for a few moments of silent prayer to reflect on our needs and to formulate our own petitions under the guidance and inspiration of the Holy Spirit.

Concluding Prayer

Let us pray:

O God, grant that our constant prayers may make us deserving of the Holy Spirit. We are grateful for all the graces and lights we have received. With His continued assistance may we attain the perfection in the state of life to which You have called us. This we ask, through the merits of Jesus Christ, Your Son, Amen.

49. Consecration to Jesus Christ, the Incarnate Wisdom, through the Blessed Virgin Mary

by St. Louis de Montfort
(Try to meditatively recite on First Saturdays)

O Eternal and Incarnate Wisdom! O sweet and most adorable Jesus! True God and true man, only Son of the eternal Father, and of Mary, always Virgin!

I adore You profoundly in the bosom and splendor of Your Father throughout eternity; and I adore You also in the virginal bosom of Mary, Your most worthy Mother, in the time of Your Incarnation.

I give You thanks for emptying Yourself, taking the form of a slave in order to rescue me from the cruel slavery of the devil. I praise and glorify You for being pleased to submit Yourself to Mary, Your holy Mother, in all things, in order to make me Your faithful slave (consecrated child) through her.

But alas! Ungrateful and faithless as I have been, I have not kept the promises which I made so solemnly to You in my Baptism; I have not fulfilled my obligations; I do not deserve to be called Your child, nor yet Your slave; and as there is nothing in me which does not merit Your anger and Your repulsion, I dare not come by myself before Your most holy and august majesty.

It is on this account that I have recourse to the intercession of Your most holy Mother, whom You have given me for a mediatrix with You. It is through her that I hope to obtain from You contrition, the pardon of my sins, and the acquisition and preservation of wisdom.

Hail, then, O Immaculate Mary, living tabernacle of the Divinity, where the Eternal Wisdom willed to be hidden and to be adored by angels and by men! Hail, O Queen of Heaven and earth, to whose empire everything is subject which is under God.

Hail, O sure refuge of sinners, whose mercy fails no one. Hear the desires which I have of the Divine Wisdom; and for that end receive the vows and offerings which in my lowliness I present to you.

I, N., a faithless sinner, renew and ratify today in your hands the vows of my Baptism; I renounce forever satan, his pomps and works, and I give myself entirely to Jesus Christ, the Incarnate Wisdom, to carry my cross after Him all the days of my life, and to be more faithful to Him than I have ever been before.

In the presence of all the heavenly court I choose you this day for my Mother and Queen. I deliver and consecrate to you, as your slave (child), my body and soul, my goods, both interior and exterior and even the value of all my good actions, past, present, and future; leaving to you the entire and full right of disposing of me, and all that belongs to me, without exception, according to your good pleasure, for the greater glory of God in time and in eternity.

Receive, O most kind Virgin, this little offering of my slavery (spiritual childhood), in honor of, and in union with, that subjection which the Eternal Wisdom willed to your maternal guidance, in homage to the power which both of You have over this poor sinner, and in thanksgiving for the privileges with which the Holy Trinity has favored you. I declare that I wish henceforth, as your true slave (child), to seek your honor and to obey you in all things.

O Admirable Mother, present me to your dear Son as His eternal slave (loyal child) so that as He has redeemed me through you, by you He may receive me!

O Mother of mercy, grant me the grace to obtain the true Wisdom of God; and for that end receive me among those whom you love, lead, nourish, and protect as your children and your slaves.

O faithful Virgin, make me in all things so perfect a disciple, imitator, and slave (spiritual child) of the Incarnate Wisdom, Jesus Christ your Son, that I may attain, through your intercession and by your example, to the fullness of His age on earth and of His glory in Heaven. Amen.

A plenary indulgence, under the usual conditions, on the feast of the Immaculate Conception and April 28. — Preces et Pia Opera, 75.

50b. Act of Consecration to Jesus through Mary
by St. Maximilian Kolbe

O Immaculata, Queen of Heaven and earth, refuge of sinners and our most loving Mother, God has willed to entrust the entire order of mercy to you.

I, N., a repentant sinner, cast myself at your feet humbly imploring you to take me with all that I am and have, wholly to yourself as your possession and property. Please make of me, of all my powers of soul and body, of my whole life, death, and eternity, whatever most pleases you.

If it pleases you, use all that I am and have without reserve, wholly to accomplish what was said of you: "She will crush your head," and, "You alone have destroyed all heresies in the whole world."

Let me be a fit instrument in your immaculate and merciful hands for introducing and increasing your glory to the maximum in all the many strayed and indifferent souls, and thus help extend as far as possible the blessed kingdom of the most Sacred Heart of Jesus.

For wherever you enter you obtain the grace of conversion and growth in holiness, since it is through your hands that all graces come to us from the most Sacred Heart of Jesus. Amen.

50f. Jesus Defines Consecration
John 17

Jesus raised His eyes to Heaven and said:

"Father, the hour has come:
glorify Your Son
so that Your Son may glorify You;
2 and, through the power over all mankind that You have given Him,
let Him give eternal life to all those you have entrusted to Him.

3 **And eternal life is this:**
to know You, the only true God,
and Jesus Christ whom You have sent.
4 **I have glorified You on earth**
by finishing the work
that You gave Me to do.
5 Now, Father, it is time for you to glorify Me
with that glory I had with You
before ever the world was.

6 **I have made Your name known**
to the men You took from the world to give Me.

They were Yours and You gave them to Me,
and they have kept Your word.
[7] Now at last they know
that all You have given Me comes indeed from You;
[8] for I have given them
the teaching You gave to Me,
and they have truly accepted this,
that I came from You,
and have believed that it was You who sent Me.

[9] I pray for them;
I am not praying for the world
but for those You have given Me,
because they belong to You:
[10] all I have is Yours
and all You have is mine,
and in them I am glorified.
[11] I am not in the world any longer,
but they are in the world,
and I am coming to You.
Holy Father,
keep those You have given Me true to Your name,
so that they may be one like us.
[12] While I was with them,
I kept those You had given Me true to Your name.
I have watched over them and not one is lost
except the one who chose to be lost,
and this was to fulfill the scriptures.

[13] But now I am coming to You
and while still in the world I say these things
to share my joy with them to the full.
[14] I passed Your word on to them,
and the world hated them,
because they belong to the world
no more than I belong to the world.
[15] **I am not asking You to remove them from the
world, but to protect them from the evil one.**
[16] They do not belong to the world
any more than I belong to the world.

¹⁷ **Consecrate them in the truth;**
Your word is truth.

¹⁸ **As You sent Me into the world,**
I have sent them into the world,
¹⁹ **and for their sake I consecrate myself**
so that they too may be consecrated in truth.
²⁰ **I pray not only for these,**
but for those also
who through their words will believe in Me.
²¹ **May they all be one.**
Father, may they be one in us,
as You are in Me and I am in You,
so that the world may believe it was You who sent Me.
²² **I have given them the glory You gave to Me,**
that they may be one as we are one.
²³ With Me in them and You in Me,
may they be so completely one
that the world will realize that it was You who sent Me
and that I have loved them as much as You loved Me.

²⁴ Father,
I want those You have given Me
to be with Me where I am,
so that they may always see the glory
You have given Me
because You loved Me
before the foundation of the world.

²⁵ Father, Righteous One,
the world has not known You,
but I have known You,
and these have known
that You have sent Me.
²⁶ I have made Your name known to them
and will continue to make it known,
so that the love with which You loved Me may be in
them,
and so that I may be in them."

(Consecrate your family in the Truth with the Vatican-approved Family Wisdom Curriculum. See pages 578-579 and the inside back cover.)

50h. Act of Faith

O my God, I firmly believe that You are one God in three Divine Persons, Father, Son, and Holy Spirit; I believe that Your Divine Son became man and died for our sins, and that He will come to judge the living and the dead. I believe these and all the truths which the Holy Catholic Church teaches, because You have revealed them, who can neither deceive nor be deceived.

50i. Act of Hope

O my God, relying on Your infinite goodness and promises, I hope to obtain pardon of my sins, the help of Your grace, and life everlasting, through the merits of Jesus Christ, my Lord and Redeemer.

50j. Act of Charity

O my God, I love You above all things, with my whole heart and soul, because You are all-good and worthy of all love. I love my neighbor as myself for the love of You. I forgive all who have injured me, and I ask pardon of all whom I have injured.

53. Examination of Conscience Exercises

We suggest that you use one of the following sections to help you examine your conscience each day.

53a. Scripture's Four C's

Confidence:

— How well have I trusted God?

— Have my fears and worries betrayed my trust in God?

— *Humble yourselves therefore under the mighty hand of God, that in due time he may exalt you. Cast all your anxieties on him, for he cares about you.* (1 Pet. 5:6-7)

Conscience:

— How well have I prayed, practiced silence, and listened to God?

— Have I used my spiritual, material, and emotional goods as God has called me to do?

— Have I thanked God for all that He has given me?

— Have I obeyed my superiors, which is a true test of my willingness to surrender my will to God?

— *He himself bore our sins in his body on the tree, that we might die to sin and live to righteousness.* (1 Pet. 2:24)

— Have I fallen from grace by using artificial contraceptives? (All contraceptives are forbidden.)

— Have I sought spiritual counsel from someone who fully subscribes to the teachings of *Humane Vitae* (the document which outlines clearly the Church's teaching on marriage) before using natural family planning?

Charity:

— How well have I treated others, particularly those in my family?

— Have I taught by good example and loving authori-

ty, or have I abused my authority by not being charitable or just? Do I try too hard to change others
rather than change myself?

— Have I been a hypocrite by talking about others or
looking down on others? The only people with whom
Christ really grew angry were the Pharisees when
they judged others, St. Peter when he tried to talk
Him out of carrying the Cross, and those who made
irreverent use of God's house!

— How well have I lived my total self-giving (i.e., total
consecration)?

— *Clothe yourselves, all of you, with humility toward
one another, for "God opposes the proud, but gives
grace to the humble."* (1 Pet. 5:5)

— *If I speak in the tongues of men and of angels, but
have not love, I am a noisy gong or a clanging cymbal. And if I have prophetic powers, and understand
all mysteries and all knowledge, and if I have all
faith, so as to remove mountains, but have not love, I
am nothing. If I give away all I have, and if I deliver
my body to be burned, but have not love, I gain nothing. Love is patient and kind; love is not jealous or
boastful; it is not arrogant or rude. Love does not
insist on its own way; it is not irritable or resentful;
it does not rejoice at wrong, but rejoices in the right.
Love bears all things, believes all things, hopes all
things, endures all things.* (1 Cor. 13:1-7)

Constancy:

— How well have I applied myself to my tasks and
responsibilities? Have I gone the extra mile for God?

— Have I stayed in God's presence by turning my mind
to Him frequently during the day?

— Have I maintained a positive and patient attitude,
looking for the harvest of graces which will enable
me to do God's will in His due season?

— Have I used the grace offered to me in each present moment to say "yes" to God, or do I allow the world, the flesh, or the devil to distract me and therefore offend God by regretting the past or feeling sorry for myself?

— Do I offend God by worrying about the future? I must remember that the only moment over which I have control is the present moment; which should be offered with great intensity to God!

— *Be sober, be watchful. Your adversary the devil prowls around like a roaring lion, seeking some one to devour.* (1 Pet. 5:8)

53b. The Seven Capital Virtues and Seven Capital Sins

In our prayer we ask for the grace to overcome our faults by practicing the virtue that is the opposite of each of our faults.

1. Let the virtue of humility (acknowledgment of my total dependence on God for what is good) overcome my tendency toward pride and egoism and my desire for fullness and recognition.

2. Let the virtue of liberality overcome my tendency toward spiritual and material avarice and my desire for security and prosperity.

3. Let the virtue of temperance overcome my tendency toward gluttony and uncontrolled self-indulgence in food, television, and other forms of normally licit pleasures.

4. Let the virtues of chastity and self-control overcome my tendency toward mental and physical lust.

5. Let the virtue of meekness overcome my tendency toward anger, which manifests itself when my human plans (no matter how good they may be) are upset. Often I may fail to use trials as stepping stones toward that total detachment which, as Pope John Paul II has

said, purifies our feelings and lifts our spirits so that we can hear the voice of God and train our consciences.

6. Let the virtue of brotherly love overcome my tendency toward envy. Let me understand that the vision of The Apostolate promotes the truth with great intensity so that authentic brotherly love will be manifested through the systematic transformation of neighborhoods into strong God-centered communities, in the joyful spirit of Pope John Paul II.

7. Let the virtue of diligence overcome my tendency toward sloth (laziness). Let me not fall into the trap of feeling sorry for myself when others appear to be doing less work than myself; rather, let me go the extra mile and fulfill my responsibilities better than I have to, because I do it for God, not for man.

53c. The Spiritual Works of Mercy

The spiritual works of mercy are a form of Christian charity in favor of the soul or spirit of one's neighbor. Let's check ourselves to see how we have been following these norms through our work in The Apostolate:

1. Converting the sinner (clothing the spiritually naked with grace)

2. Instructing the ignorant (feeding the spiritually hungry and thirsty)

3. Counseling the doubtful

4. Comforting the sorrowful

5. Bearing wrongs patiently

6. Forgiving injury

7. Praying for the living and the dead

53d. The Corporal Works of Mercy

Christ taught us the corporal works of mercy, which will be His standards for salvation at the Last Judgment. (cf. Mt. 25:34-46 and the *Catechism of the Catholic Church*, section 2447)

1. Feeding the hungry

2. Giving drink to the thirsty

3. Clothing the naked

4. Giving shelter to the homeless

5. Visiting the sick

6. Visiting those in prison

7. Burying the dead

53e. The Precepts of the Church
What is Expected of Catholic Christians, as found in the Catechism of the Catholic Church

2041 The precepts of the Church are set in the context of a moral life bound to and nourished by liturgical life. The obligatory character of these positive laws decreed by the pastoral authorities is meant to guarantee to the faithful the indispensable minimum in the spirit of prayer and moral effort, in the growth in love of God and neighbor:

2042 The first precept ("You shall attend Mass on Sundays and holy days of obligation.") requires the faithful to participate in the Eucharistic celebration when the Christian community gathers together on the day commemorating the Resurrection of the Lord.

The second precept ("You shall confess your sins at least once a year.") ensures preparation for the Eucharist by the reception of the sacrament of reconciliation, which continues Baptism's work of conversion and forgiveness.

The third precept ("You shall humbly receive your Creator in Holy Communion at least during the Easter season.") guarantees as a minimum the reception of the Lord's Body and Blood in connection with the Paschal feasts, the origin and center of the Christian liturgy.

2043 The fourth precept ("You shall keep holy the holy days of obligation.") completes the Sunday observance by participation in the principal liturgical feasts which honor the mysteries of the Lord, the Virgin Mary, and the saints.

The fifth precept ("You shall observe the prescribed days of fasting and abstinence.") ensures the times of ascesis and penance which prepare us for the liturgical feasts; they help us acquire mastery over our instincts and freedom of heart.

The faithful also have the duty of providing for the material needs of the Church, each according to his abilities.

53f. The Seven Gifts of the Holy Spirit

Father John Hardon, S.J., writes that the seven gifts of the Holy Spirit are "the seven forms of supernatural initiative conferred with the reception of sanctifying grace. They are in the nature of supernatural reflexes or reactive instincts that spontaneously answer to divine impulses of grace, almost without reflection but always with full consent."

Wisdom

Most Holy Spirit, help me, my family, and all the members of The Apostolate to respond well to Your will by judging all things according to Your spiritual standards. Help us to contemplate Your truths and to apply them, in a practical manner, to our daily lives.

Understanding

Most Holy Spirit, help me, my family, and all the members of The Apostolate to go beyond faith and to penetrate the very core of revealed truths by giving us insights into their meaning. Confirm us in our faith by giving us great confidence in the revealed word of God.

Knowledge

Most Holy Spirit, give me, my family, and all the members of The Apostolate the ability to judge everything from a supernatural point of view. Help us to see the providential purpose of whatever enters our lives and to discern clearly between impulses of temptation and inspirations of grace.

Fortitude

Most Holy Spirit, help me, my family, and all the members of The Apostolate to persevere in carrying out Your distinctive plan for our lives. Make us ready to sacrifice whatever is truly necessary in order to do Your will.

Counsel

Most Holy Spirit, help me, my family, and all the members of The Apostolate to judge properly and rightly, by a sort of supernatural intuition, what should be done, especially in difficult situations. Please speak to our hearts and enlighten us as to what we should do in each present moment. Help us to think of Mat. 10:19-20: *When they deliver you up, do not be anxious how you are to speak or what you are to say; for what you are to say will be given to you in that hour; for it is not you who speak, but the Spirit of your Father speaking through you.*

Help us to understand that counsel refers to conducting ourselves, primarily, prudently and, secondarily, to the advice we might give to others about their conduct. Enlightened by the Holy Spirit, a person will know what to do in a specific case, what advice to give someone when he is consulted, or what command to make when he is in authority.

Piety

Most Holy Spirit, infuse into my soul, and into the souls of all of my family members and the members of The Apostolate, a profound respect for God, a generous love for Him, and an affectionate obedience to legitimate authority; thus I may show others the most perfect way to please God.

Fear of the Lord

Most Holy Spirit, confirm in me, my family, and all of the members of The Apostolate a profound respect for the majesty of God, a loving sorrow for the least fault committed, and a vigilant love in order that we may avoid all occasions of sin.

53g. The Eight Beatitudes
Catechism of the Catholic Church, Section 1716

(cf. Mt. 5:3-12 and Lk. 6:20-23)

Lord, help me, my family, and all of the members of The Apostolate to practice the Beatitudes and to realize that they are expressions of the New Covenant, where happiness is assured already in this life, provided that a person totally gives himself to the imitation of Christ.

The Beatitudes are:

1. Blessed are the poor in spirit, for theirs is the Kingdom of Heaven.

2. Blessed are those who mourn, for they shall be comforted.

3. Blessed are the meek, for they shall inherit the earth.

4. Blessed are those who hunger and thirst for righteousness, for they shall be satisfied.

5. Blessed are the merciful, for they shall obtain mercy.

6. Blessed are the pure in heart, for they shall see God.

7. Blessed are the peacemakers, for they shall be called sons of God.

8. Blessed are those who are persecuted for righteousness' sake, for theirs is the Kingdom of Heaven. Blessed are you when men revile you and persecute you and utter all kinds of evil against you falsely on My account. Rejoice and be glad, for your reward is great in Heaven, for so men persecuted the prophets who were before you.

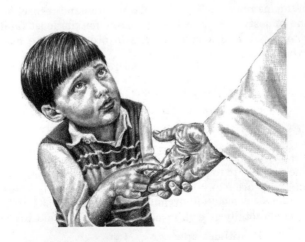

53h. An Examination of Conscience in Light of the Ten Commandments

Refer to Exodus 20:1-17, Deuteronomy 5:6-21

THE FIRST COMMANDMENT

1. I am the Lord your God: you shall not have strange gods before me.

- Have I received Holy Communion in the state of mortal sin?

- Have I neglected to confess a mortal sin in a previous confession to a priest, when I was aware of having committed one?

- Have I practiced superstition?

- Have I been engaged in occult practices such as consulting horoscopes, tarot cards, or ouija boards?

- Have I participated in seances, or in satanic or demonic services and/or prayers?

- Have I refused to accept any teaching of the Church?

- Have I put my soul in danger by reading, viewing, or listening to material that attacks the teachings of the Catholic Church in matters of faith or morals?

- Do I belong to any anti-Catholic organizations?

- Have I attended the meetings or gatherings of any anti-Catholic organizations?

- Have I profaned (desecrated) or spoken sinfully against a sacred person, place, or thing?

- Have I been slow or reluctant to perform my duties toward God?

- Have I neglected to pray?

- Have I neglected to prepare myself properly for Holy Communion?

THE SECOND COMMANDMENT

2. You shall not take the Name of the Lord your God in vain.

- Have I taken the Holy Name of God in vain?
- Have I spoken His Name in anger?
- Have I jokingly or irreverently spoken about God?
- Have I been a baptismal or confirmation sponsor in a non-Catholic ceremony?
- Have I broken any promises (oaths) in which I invoked God's Name?

THE THIRD COMMANDMENT

3. Remember to keep holy the Lord's Day.

- Have I failed to attend Mass on Sundays or holy days of obligation without just cause (for example, serious illness or impassible roads or pathways)?
- Have I arrived at Mass on Sundays or holy days of obligation after the Liturgy of the Word without just cause?
- Have I worn improper attire to Mass, or have I otherwise distracted others from paying attention at Mass?
- Do I fast and practice abstinence on the days or at times which are appointed by the Church?
- Have I fulfilled my yearly Easter duty of receiving Holy Communion (and Confession, if necessary)?
- Have I fulfilled the Church's precept to confess my sins at least once a year? *(Catechism of the Catholic Church, 2042)*
- Have I performed (or required others to perform) servile or manual labor on Sundays (not including work to save souls or work required by your employer, enjoyable gardening, or acts of mercy such as helping a neighbor in need or milking cows and feeding

livestock)?

- Have I deliberately failed to pay attention at Mass?
- Am I generous in helping the Church in her necessities as much as I can?

THE FOURTH COMMANDMENT

4. Honor your father and your mother.

For Parents:

- Have I set a bad example for my children?
- When I do correct my children's faults, is it done with charity?
- Have I made sure that my children make their First Confession and First Communion at about the age of seven?
- Have I failed to take my children to Mass on Sundays and holy days of obligation; or neglected to provide them with an orthodox Catholic education; or neglected to teach them how to pray; or failed to lead them to the sacraments?
- Have I failed to supervise my children with respect to the friends they choose and the entertainment they pursue?
- Do I monitor my children in their choice of reading material, in the shows they watch on television, or in the movies they attend?
- Have I separated from or divorced my spouse civilly without consultation of a priest who follows the mind of the Church?
- Do I seek God's help every day to fulfill my duties as a parent?

For Children:

- Have I disobeyed my parents, or been disrespectful to

them in other ways?

- Do I nurse angry feelings or show resentment when I am corrected by my parents?

- Have I been moody, sour, or bad-tempered towards other people?

- Do I desire to leave my parents' household when I am too young or for other improper reasons?

- Am I a financial burden to my parents when I can take care of my own financial needs and am old enough to help support the household?

- Do I fight and/or quarrel with my brothers and sisters?

- Have I failed to express my love for my parents?

- Have I failed to help my parents when they were unable to meet their basic needs?

- Do I faithfully perform — without complaining — the household and outdoor chores my parents give me to do?

THE FIFTH COMMANDMENT

5. You shall not kill.

- Have I lost my temper or become unjustly angry at others?

- Have I murdered or otherwise unjustly injured (no matter how slight) anyone?

- Have I been a reckless driver?

- Have I tempted others to sin by my bad example or sinful conversation?

- Have I encouraged others to read or watch sinful materials or programs or to otherwise do sinful things?

- Have I tried to make up for, or repair for, the bad example I may have given others?

- Have I been jealous of others? Have I been envious of the possessions of others?

- How many people have I led into sin? What type of sins were they?

- Have I tried to commit suicide?

- Have I failed to take proper care of my health?

- Have I mutilated myself or someone else?

- Have I been drunk or intoxicated on alcohol or other substances?

- Have I intentionally overindulged in food or drink (gluttony)?

- Have I participated in gang fights or other illegal gang activities?

- Have I picked fights with others?

- Have I been a bully?

- Have I consented to a sterilization or encouraged others to do so, or actively taken part in someone else's sterilization?

- Have I practiced contraception or encouraged others to do so?

- Have I recommended, consented to, advised, or actively taken part in an abortion?

- Am I aware of the Church's teaching that abortion is a mortal sin, and that those who actively take part (for example, doctor, nurse, and mother) in an abortion are automatically excommunicated? (However, most priests have the authority to lift that excommunication.)

- Have I harmed anyone's reputation by my speech or actions?

- Have I desired to take revenge of anyone who offended me?

- Have I hated or nursed bad feelings toward any person?

- Have I maliciously teased or insulted others?

- Have I refused to forgive anyone who may have offended me?

- Have I sought pardon of those whom I have offended?

THE SIXTH AND NINTH COMMANDMENTS

6. You shall not commit adultery.
9. You shall not covet your neighbor's wife.

- Have I entertained impure thoughts? Have I deliberately recalled impure thoughts or images? Do I watch soap operas or other impure programs?

- Have I had sexual relations with a member of the opposite sex when we weren't married to each other (fornication)?

- Have I had sexual relations with a married person who is not my spouse (adultery)?

- Although I may never have fully carried them out, have I consented to impure desires?

- Were any circumstances present to make the sin of impurity even more serious, for example, having impure relations with someone who is consecrated to God by vows (sacrilege), or who is married to someone other than myself (adultery), or who is a member of my family (other than my spouse if I am married) (incest)?

- Have I engaged in impure conversations? Did I begin them?

- Have I sought to have a good time by engaging in entertainment which placed me in proximate [close] occasions of sin, such as sensual dances; sexually suggestive movies, plays, and reading material; evil company; houses of prostitution; and massage parlors?

- Am I aware of the fact that I might already be sinning by simply placing myself in a proximate occasion of sin? Such circumstances can include sharing of a room with a member of the opposite sex, being alone with a member of the opposite sex with whom I have continually sinned with, or deliberately taking such a person to a secluded place.

- Have I neglected to dress modestly or to otherwise safeguard purity?

- Have I willfully looked at immodest pictures?

- Have I displayed immodest looks or glances at others?

- Did I do any of the above things, knowing that they involved gravely sinful matter?

- Have I led others to commit the sins of immodesty or impurity? Specifically speaking, what were they?

- Have I committed impure acts by myself (masturbation)? Did I do so deliberately and freely, knowing that serious matter was involved? Did I know that masturbation freely and willfully performed is a mortal sin?

- Have I committed impure acts with someone else either of the opposite or the same sex (homosexual acts)? How many times did I do so? Were there any circumstances (such as impure acts with members of my family other than my spouse, or with persons consecrated to God by vows or promises) which could have made the sin especially serious?

- Did these sinful acts have any consequences?

- Did I do anything to prevent possible consequences (artificial contraception) or to eliminate actual consequences after the conception of new life (abortion)?

- Do I have evil or immoral friendships? Have I taken steps to break these friendships?

- Have I been engaged in immodest conduct or conversation with someone I am seriously thinking of marrying?

- Have I tended to use this person as an object for my pleasure, rather than a person created in God's image and likeness whom God has placed in my life to respect and reverence?

- Have I been involved in acts which arouse lustful desires (such as prolonged embraces, petting, and passionate kissing)?

- Have I failed to protect my spouse, fiance, or friend from sinning?

- Have I failed to investigate beforehand the sinful potentials of watching a particular show or reading a particular book or magazine?

For Married People:

- Have I made improper use of marriage?
- Have I denied my spouse of her or his marital right?
- Have I engaged in adulterous acts or desires?
- Have I used or consented to the use of artificial contraceptives?
- Have I suggested that others do so? (On sterilization, abortion, etc., refer to the Fifth Commandment)
- Do I practice natural means of conception control without justifiable reasons before God for doing so?

THE SEVENTH AND TENTH COMMANDMENTS

7. You shall not steal.

10. You shall not covet your neighbor's goods.

- Have I stolen anything? What was it worth?
- Have I returned the stolen item, or do I intend to return it?
- Have I damaged or been responsible for the damage of another person's property? What would be the cost of repairing or replacing it?
- Have I caused harm to anyone in business dealings by means of fraud, deception, or coercion?
- Have I spent beyond my means?
- Have I deprived others of their needs by spending too little?
- Have I supported the Church and charitable organizations according to my means?
- Have I honored my debts?
- Have I taken stolen property or refused to seek the owner of property that I have found?
- Have I seriously entertained temptations to steal?
- Have I been lazy with respect to my employment,

household chores, work, or studies?

- Have I been greedy?
- Have I placed too high a value on material goods?
- Have I failed to help those whom I know are truly needy?
- Have I been irresponsible with money or other means of wealth which God has entrusted to me?
- Have I been envious of the wealth or material goods of another person?

THE EIGHTH COMMANDMENT

8. You shall not bear false witness against your neighbor.

- Have I lied?
- Have I sought to make up for the damage caused by my lies?
- Have I accused others of wrongdoing without sufficient evidence?
- Have I been guilty of detraction (that is, speaking about the faults of others without having a good reason for doing so)?
- Have I been guilty of calumny (that is, to falsely accuse someone of sinful conduct)?
- Have I gossiped about another person?
- Have I too hastily judged someone of improper conduct?
- Have I, without sufficient cause, suspected someone to be guilty of misconduct?
- Have I been excessively critical, negative, or uncharitable in my speech?
- Have I failed to honor the confidences or secrets entrusted to me by another? Have I revealed them to someone else without permission or without due or

serious cause?

- Have I used the technique of binding others to secrecy about something that should be revealed to lawful authority? Do I realize that this practice is very divisive if it is outside of Confession?

- Have I failed to defend the good name or honor of others?

53i. Examination of Conscience Reflections
by Jerome F. Coniker

Most Holy Family, help me to call to mind the instances in the past few hours or days when I sowed bad seeds and lost my peaceful union with God, and when I did not make full use of Scriptures Four C's for Peaceful Seed Living (Confidence, Conscience, Seed-Charity, and Constancy) as part of my daily life.

Please uproot these negative seeds and help me to purify my conscience, which is the seedbed for the growth of grace in my soul.

Purify me so that my virtuous acts and sacrifices will be used to atone for sin. Allow me to peacefully rise above my problems and grow into a worthy instrument by becoming one spirit with the Lord and the Holy Family.

Help me, Most Holy Family, to forgive others. Inspire me to be respectful to those over whom I have authority and to praise their good points more than I point out their faults (cf. 2 Cor. 10:8).

Enable me to see the causes of my daily sins and faults, and to give them to Jesus so that He can wash them in His Precious Blood and transform them into virtues.

Never let me forget that it is God's power of grace combined with my good works that will overpower my sinful nature. Help me to see that without God as my Source, salvation would be impossible (cf. Lk. 18:26-27).

(Pause to reflect)

Inspire me, Most Holy Family, to make and to keep practical resolutions for the amendment of my life. Never let me forget that I primarily teach others by the example of my daily life, and that I will be held accountable for every thought, word, and action during my test on earth (cf. Mat. 12:36-37).

Help me to be as good to all the members of my family as I am to those whom I meet outside my home. Now, Most Holy Family, please let me picture myself as the person I want to become, a person who mirrors your virtues.

Help me to visualize how you would act if you were in my place at this time; and how you would treat the members of my family or community, especially those who need my time and undivided attention; *(pause)* and those who have hurt me. *(pause)*

Help me to show affection rather than anger to all whom you bring into my life, especially those in my own family or community. *(pause)*

...put on the new nature, which is being renewed in knowledge after the image of its creator. (Col. 3:10)

Pause and imagine Jesus, Mary, or Joseph living your life. Visualize yourself as a virtuous person who is perpetually confident, calm, cheerful, and compassionate, especially under pressure and with the members of your own family and community.

Visualize how you should have handled yourself the last time you lost your peaceful union with God by your faults, willful sins, and selfishness.

Let everyone who names the name of the Lord depart from iniquity. (2 Tim. 2:19)

...do not let the sun go down on your anger, and give no opportunity to the devil. (Eph. 4:26-27)

Most Holy Spirit of the Father and the Son, dwelling deep within the innermost recesses of my soul (cf. 1 Cor. 2:10-16), help me to realize that sin is the cause of all unhappiness because it gives the forces of evil more power over my life and over the entire world.

Inspire me to encourage others to help those who suffer. We can do this, not only by our much needed almsgiving which represents a true sacrifice of the fruits of our work and security, but also by our supernaturally good acts of prayer and charity and by the fervent reception of the sacraments.

Help me to unite the trials I encounter in the faithful fulfillment of the responsibilities of my state in life with the Holy Sacrifice of the Mass, which is continually being offered throughout the world.

Never let me forget, Most Holy Spirit, that You dwell within me. If I unite every act of my daily life with You and the Holy Family, I become a useful instrument to counteract the unhappy effects of sin. This can help to bring true peace and happiness not only into my life, but into the lives of the people in my family, my community, my school, my parish, and the entire Mystical Body of Christ on earth.

Because there is one bread, we who are many are one body, for we all partake of the one bread. (1 Cor.10:17)

Most Holy Spirit, You are the Source of truth and enlightenment. Teach me the truths of my Faith, and then give me the grace to believe and live them.

These things I have spoken to you, while I am still with you. But the Counselor, the Holy Spirit, whom the Father will send in my name, He will teach you all things, and bring to your remembrance all that I have said to you. (Jn. 14:25-26)

For just as the body is one and has many members, and all the members of the body, though many, are one body, so it is with Christ. For by one Spirit we were all baptized into one body — Jews or Greeks, slaves or free

— and all were made to drink of one Spirit. (1 Cor. 12:12-13)

He is the head of the body, the church. (Col. 1:18)

Remember those who are in prison, as though in prison with them; and those who are ill-treated, since you also are in the body. (Heb. 13:3)

He has put all things under his feet and has made him the head over all things for the church, which is his body, the fullness of him who fills all in all. (Eph. 1:22-23)

...that is, how the Gentiles are fellow heirs, members of the same body, and partakers of the promise in Christ Jesus through the gospel. (Eph. 3:6)

Therefore, putting away falsehood, let every one speak the truth with his neighbor, for we are members one of another. (Eph. 4:25)

For no man ever hates his own flesh, but nourishes and cherishes it, as Christ does the church, because we are members of his body. (Eph. 5:29-30)

53j. Excerpt from Veritatis Splendor
by Pope John Paul II

26. In the *moral catechesis of the Apostles*, besides exhortations and directions connected to specific historical and cultural situations, we find an ethical teaching with precise rules of behavior. This is seen in their Letters, which contain the interpretation, made under the guidance of the Holy Spirit, of the Lord's precepts as they are to be lived in different cultural circumstances (cf. Rom. 12-15; 1 Cor. 11-14; Gal. 5-6; Eph. 4-6; Col. 3-4; 1 Pt. and Jas.).

Note: See Volume II of our 2-volume Apostolate's Family Catechism for the unabridged text of Veritatis Splendor.

531. Gifts of the Holy Spirit and Infused Virtues

© MCMXCVI (Used with permission)
Rev. Bernard M. Geiger, O.F.M., Conv.

The Gifts of the Holy Spirit supply, as it were, the forms and paths which our spiritual development and our service of God will take, while the Infused Virtues drive and bring about that development and service. If we choose to give in to the Capital Sins, they will block or kill the life of the Gifts and Virtues. If we choose to develop the habits of the Gifts and Virtues, they will put to death the seven capital tendencies to sin in us.

Gifts of the Holy Spirit — permanent capacities to receive and use particular lights from Jesus' fullness of Truth

Infused Virtues — permanent capacities to receive and use particular powers from Jesus' fullness of Grace

Capital Sins and their Effects — tendencies in us which lead to sin and bondage to Satan if not curbed

PART I: THEOLOGICAL VIRTUES
Unite us directly to God

1. Gift of Knowledge

Permanent capacity to receive the light of Jesus' knowledge, so that we can use it to make acts of, and develop habits of, supernatural knowledge. We need these acts and habits to become informed and conscious of God's call, His plan for our salvation and divine adoption, and the New Covenant which activates the plan.

Virtue of Faith

Permanent capacity to receive the power of Jesus' absolute adherence and obedience to the Truth, so that we can use it to make acts of, and develop habits of, supernatural faith. We need these acts and habits to believe firmly that God's revelation of Himself and of His Kingdom of Love are true, that God is infinite goodness; faith enables us to grow in our consciousness and celebration of the truth about God.

Capital Sins: Covetousness & Avarice

Darkens the mind, produces indifference to God, which leads to ignorance of God, God's call, His plan for our salvation, our divine adoption, and the New Covenant. Covetousness addicts us to worldly treasures as cheap substitutes for the treasure of God's Kingdom of Love.

Read the Catechism of the Catholic Church, paragraphs 31–38, 153–165, 2087–2089, 2535–2536, 2541, and 2552.

2. Gift of Understanding

Permanent capacity to receive the light of Jesus' understanding, so that we can use it to make acts of, and develop habits of, supernatural understanding. We need these acts and habits to understand our relationships with the Divine Persons, Mary, the Angels, the Saints, and each other in His Kingdom of Love, and what it means for each of us personally.

Virtue of Hope

Permanent capacity to receive the power of Jesus' commitment to His Father's Will and plan, so that we can use it to make acts of, and develop habits of, supernatural hope. We need these acts and habits to resolutely and perseveringly commit ourselves to God and His Kingdom of Love. This commitment incorporates us into the Kingdom.

Capital Sin: Gluttony

Numbs the mind and prevents understanding of God's plan and Covenant, and so forestalls commitment to them. Gluttony addicts us to pleasures of food and drink as cheap substitutes for the true meaning of life and for commitment to God.

Read the Catechism of the Catholic Church, paragraphs 84–95, 1817–1821, 2090– 2092, 2548–2549, and 2705.

3. Gift of Piety

Permanent capacity to receive the light of Jesus' piety — His habit of mentally identifying with the Father and with each of us — so that we can use it to make acts of, and develop habits of, supernatural piety. These acts and habits enable us to identity with God and each of our neighbors in God's Kingdom of Love — to see God as my Father and myself as His son or daughter; Jesus as my Brother and Redeemer; and Mary as my Mother, etc.

Virtue of Charity/Love

Permanent capacity to receive the power of Jesus' love and self-giving, so that we can use it to make acts of, and develop habits of, supernatural charity. By these acts and habits we can always say "yes" to Him and to all He wants to give us and ask of us. This "yes" allows Jesus to begin living in us and allows us to live in Him.

Capital Sin: Lust

Lust is a kind of false love. It causes alienation and isolation from others, and prevents real love of God, self, and neighbor. Lust addicts us to illicit sexual gratification as a cheap substitute for authentic Christian friendship and unselfish affectionate love.

Read the Catechism of the Catholic Church, paragraphs 1822–1829, 1889, 2093–2094, and 2514–2533.

PART II: CARDINAL VIRTUES
*Enable us to express, prove, and grow in our
love of God by implementing His plan and
Covenant in a practical way*

4. Gift of Wisdom

Permanent capacity to receive the light of Jesus'
wisdom, so that we can use it to make acts of, and develop habits of, supernatural wisdom. They enable us to
see where we have come from, where we are going in
God's plan, and how to get there; and how to discern the
potential, the means, and the opportunities which God
gives us to achieve our destiny.

Virtue of Prudence

Permanent capacity to receive Jesus' power of prudence, so that we can use it to make acts of, and develop habits of, supernatural prudence. These acts and
habits enable us to set and prioritize goals for implementing God's plan for us, and to plan or choose projects
and programs which help us achieve these goals.

Capital Sin: Pride (Self-Worship)

Produces false self-image and delusions, refusal to
serve God. Addicts us to lying, empty boasting, possess-
ing power over others and dominating them, and doing
whatever we please as perverse substitutes for true wisdom and prudence.

*Read the Catechism of the Catholic Church, paragraphs
1786–1789, 1806, 1950, 2094, and 2779.*

5. Gift of Counsel

Permanent capacity to receive the light of Jesus'
counsel, so that we can use it to make acts of, and develop habits of, supernatural counsel. These acts and
habits enable us to discern what God wants us to think,
say, or do at each moment; and to plan a daily agenda,

along with the ways and means to carry it out.

Virtue of Justice

Permanent capacity to receive Jesus' power of justice, so that we can use it to make acts of, and develop habits of, supernatural justice. These acts and habits enable us to always do the right thing, consistently giving ourselves firm, effective self-commands to always do God's Will, and keep our New Covenant with Him.

Capital Sin: Envy

Tendency to sadness at others' good fortune, success, talents, etc. — inspired by pride. Envy produces cunning in efforts to cut others down, spoil their success, manipulate them, and exalt self. It addicts us to cunning and hypocrisy as perverse substitutes for true counsel and justice.

Read the Catechism of the Catholic Church, paragraphs 1807, 2479, 2484–2487, 2538–2540, and 2846–2849.

6. Gift of Fear of the Lord

Permanent capacity to receive the light of Jesus' sensitivity to what pleases or displeases God and of his reverence for God and his compassion for others; so that we can use it to make acts of, and develop habits of, this gift. These acts and habits enable us to control our imaginations with images of Jesus, Mary, and the Saints which turn on or turn off the emotions of delight, desire, joy, dismay, aversion, and sorrow.

Virtue of Temperance

Permanent capacity to receive Jesus' power of temperance, so that we can use it to make acts of, and develop habits of, supernatural temperance. These acts and habits enable us to toughen our wills and commitments by focusing the power of Jesus' or Mary's own delight, desire, and joy on them; and their dismay or disgust, aversion, and sorrow on any temptation to neglect or abandon these commitments.

Capital Sin: Sloth

Unwillingness to make the effort to develop fear of the Lord and temperance. Sloth produces insensitivity to what pleases and displeases God; insensitivity to our neighbor's feelings, needs, and condition. It addicts us to avoiding difficulties, suffering, and sacrifice, and leads to cynicism as a perverse substitute for sensitivity, compassion, and healthy toughness of will regarding what is good.

Read the Catechism of the Catholic Church, paragraphs 1453, 1809, 2094, 2341, and 2427.

7. Gift of Fortitude

Permanent capacity to receive the light of Jesus' mental fortitude (fortitude of mind), so that we can use it to make acts of, and develop habits of, this gift. They enable us to use our imagination and memories to produce or recall images of Jesus which turn on or turn off emotions of courage, confident commitment, enthusiasm, fear, despair, and anger.

Virtue of Fortitude

Permanent capacity to receive Jesus' power of "intestinal" fortitude (fortitude of heart), so that we can use it to make acts of, and develop habits of, supernatural fortitude. These acts and habits enable us to focus Jesus' and Mary's emotions of courage, confident commitment, and enthusiasm on doing God's Will; and their emotions of fear, despair, and anger on sin, false hopes, Satan, etc.

Capital Sin: Anger (cruel/vicious/uncontrolled)

Produces a false conscience and moral weakness. Addicts us to murderous, insane, vindictive, and vengeful thoughts, speech, and actions as perverse substitutes for fortitude of mind and heart.

Read the "Catechism of the Catholic Church," sections 1808, 2262, 2302, 2473, and 2848–2849.

53m. Five Steps to Confession

1. Examine your conscience.

2. Be sorry for your sins; try to have perfect sorrow. Try to make an act of contrition (#9) before going to Confession.

3. Make a firm resolution not to sin again and to avoid the occasions of sin.

4. Tell your sins to a priest and receive absolution (all mortal sins must be confessed).

5. Perform your penance promptly.

You can begin your confession by saying "Bless me Father for I have sinned, my last confession was _____ (weeks/months/years) ago." Then tell your sins. Say an "Act of Contrition" (#9) when asked by the Priest before the absolution.

We need to rid ourselves of our desires for possessions, power, and pleasure.

59. The Way of the Cross with Reflections on Divine Mercy

Begin by offering one Our Father (#6b), one Hail Mary (#6c), and The Apostles' Creed (#6a) for the intentions of our Holy Father in order to partially fulfill the Church's requirements for obtaining a plenary indulgence.

All:

Eternal Father, I offer You the Body and Blood, Soul, and Divinity of Your dearly beloved Son, Our Lord Jesus Christ, in atonement for our sins and those of the whole world.

Leader:

For the sake of His sorrowful Passion,

All:

Have mercy on us and on the whole world. *(One time)*

All: *(Stand and sing)*

At the Cross her sta-tion keep-ing, stood the mourn-ful

Mo - ther weep - ing, close to Je- sus to the last.

FIRST STATION

Jesus is Condemned to Death

Leader:

We adore You, O Christ, and we praise You:
(All genuflect)

All:

Because by Your holy Cross You have redeemed the world.

Leader: *(All stand)*

Consider how Jesus, after having been scourged and crowned with thorns, was unjustly condemned by Pilate to die on the Cross.

All:

My adorable Jesus, it was not Pilate, no, it was my sins that condemned You to die. * I beg You, by the merits of this sorrowful journey, * to assist my soul and the souls of all the members of my family and of The Apostolate in our journey towards eternity. * We love You, our beloved Jesus; * we ask for the grace to love You more than ourselves; * we repent with our whole heart for ever having offended You. * Never permit us to separate ourselves from You again. * Grant that we may love You always, and then do with us what You will. *

All: *(Kneel)*

Eternal Father, I offer You the Body and Blood, Soul, and Divinity of Your dearly beloved Son, our Lord Jesus Christ, in atonement for our sins and those of the whole world.

Leader:

For the sake of His sorrowful Passion, *(Four times with response below)*

All:

Have mercy on us and on the whole world. *(Four times)*

All: Jesus, I trust in You.

All: *(Stand and sing)*

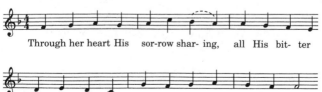

Through her heart His sor-row shar-ing, all His bit-ter an-guish bear-ing; now at length the sword had passed.

SECOND STATION

Jesus Bears His Cross

Leader:

We adore You, O Christ, and we praise You:
(All genuflect)

All:

Because by Your holy Cross You have redeemed the
world.

Leader: *(All stand)*

Consider how Jesus, in making this journey with the
Cross on His shoulders, thought of us, and for us offered
to His Father the death He was about to undergo.

All:

My most beloved Jesus, * I embrace all the tribulations You have destined for me until death. * I beseech You, by the merits of the pain You did suffer in carrying Your Cross, * to give me and all the members of my family and of The Apostolate the necessary help to carry our crosses with perfect patience and resignation. * We love You, our beloved Jesus; * we ask for the grace to love You more than ourselves; * we repent with our whole heart for ever having offended You. * Never permit us to separate ourselves from You again. * Grant that we may love You always, * and then do with us what You will.

All: *(Kneel)*

Eternal Father, I offer You the Body and Blood, Soul, and Divinity of Your dearly beloved Son, our Lord Jesus Christ, in atonement for our sins and those of the whole world.

Leader:

For the sake of His sorrowful Passion, *(Four times with response below)*

All:

Have mercy on us and on the whole world. *(Four times)*

All: Jesus, I trust in You.

All: *(Stand and sing)*

Oh, how sad and sore di- stressed was that Mo- ther

high- ly blest__ of the sole be- got- ten One.

THIRD STATION

Jesus Falls the First Time

Leader:

We adore You, O Christ, and we praise You:
(All genuflect)

All:

Because by Your holy Cross You have redeemed the
world.

Leader: *(All stand)*

Consider this first fall of Jesus under His Cross. His
flesh was torn by scourges, His head was crowned with
thorns, and He had lost a great quantity of blood. He
was so weakened that He could scarcely walk, and yet
He had to carry this great load upon His shoulders. The

soldiers struck Him rudely, and thus He fell several times in His journey.

All:

My beloved Jesus, it is not the weight of the Cross but my sins which have made You suffer so much pain. * By the merits of this first fall, deliver me, my family, and all of the members of The Apostolate from the misfortune of falling into mortal sin. * We love You, our beloved Jesus; * we ask for the grace to love You more than ourselves; * we repent with our whole heart for ever having offended You. * Never permit us to separate ourselves from You again. * Grant that we may love You always, and then do with us what You will.

All: *(Kneel)*

Eternal Father, I offer You the Body and Blood, Soul, and Divinity of Your dearly beloved Son, our Lord Jesus Christ, in atonement for our sins and those of the whole world.

Leader:

For the sake of His sorrowful Passion, *(Four times with response below)*

All:

Have mercy on us and on the whole world. *(Four times)*

All: Jesus, I trust in You.

All: *(Stand and sing)*

Christ a- bove in tor-ment hangs; She be- neath be-

holds the pangs__, of Her dy- ing glor- ious Son.

FOURTH STATION

Jesus Meets His Mother

Leader:

We adore You, O Christ, and we praise You:
(All genuflect)

All:

Because by Your holy Cross You have redeemed the world.

Leader: *(All stand)*

Consider the meeting of the Son and the Mother which took place on this journey, Jesus and Mary looked at each other, and their looks became as so many arrows to wound those hearts which loved each other so tenderly.

All:

My most loving Jesus, * by the sorrow You experienced in this meeting, * grant me and all the members of my family and of The Apostolate the grace of a truly devoted love for your Most Holy Mother. * And you our Queen, * who was overwhelmed with sorrow, obtain for us, by your intercession, a continual and tender remembrance of the Passion of your Son. * We love You, our beloved Jesus; * we ask for the grace to love You more than ourselves; * we repent with our whole heart for ever having offended You. * Never permit us to separate ourselves from You again. * Grant that we may love You always, and then do with us what You will.

All: *(Kneel)*

Eternal Father, I offer You the Body and Blood, Soul, and Divinity of Your dearly beloved Son, our Lord Jesus Christ, in atonement for our sins and those of the whole world.

Leader:

For the sake of His sorrowful Passion, *(Four times with response below)*

All:

Have mercy on us and on the whole world. *(Four times)*

All: Jesus, I trust in You.

All: *(Stand and sing)*

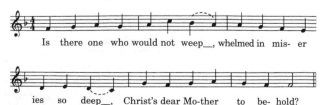

Is there one who would not weep__, whelmed in mis- er

ies so deep__, Christ's dear Mo-ther to be- hold?

FIFTH STATION

Jesus is Helped by Simon

Leader:

We adore You, O Christ, and we praise You:
(All genuflect)

All:

Because by Your holy Cross You have redeemed the
world.

Leader: *(All stand)*

Consider how the executioners, seeing that at each step
Jesus from weakness was on the point of expiring, and
fearing that He would die on the way, when they wished
Him to die the ignominious death of the Cross, con-
strained Simon the Cyrenian to carry the Cross behind
Our Lord.

All:

My most sweet Jesus, * I pray for the grace not to draw back from the cross as the Cyrenian did, * and for the grace to accept it and embrace it. * I pray to accept in particular the death You have destined for me, with all the pains that may accompany it; * I unite it to Your death, I offer it to You. * You have died for love of me; I will die for love of You, and to please You. * Help me and all the members of my family and of The Apostolate by Your grace. * We love You, our beloved Jesus; we ask for the grace to love You more than ourselves; * we repent with our whole heart for ever having offended You. * Never permit us to separate ourselves from You again. * Grant that we may love You always, and then do with us what You will.

All: *(Kneel)*

Eternal Father, I offer You the Body and Blood, Soul, and Divinity of Your dearly beloved Son, our Lord Jesus Christ, in atonement for our sins and those of the whole world.

Leader:

For the sake of His sorrowful Passion, *(Four times with response below)*

All:

Have mercy on us and on the whole world. *(Four times)*

All: Jesus, I trust in You.

All: *(Stand and sing)*

Can the hu- man heart re- frain__ from par- tak- ing

in her pain__, in that Mo- ther's pain un- told?

SIXTH STATION

Jesus is Consoled by Veronica

Leader:

We adore You, O Christ, and we praise You:
(All genuflect)

All:

Because by Your holy Cross You have redeemed the world.

Leader: *(All stand)*

Consider how the holy woman named Veronica, seeing Jesus so afflicted and His face bathed in sweat and blood, presented Him with a towel, with which He wiped His adorable face, leaving on it the impression of His holy countenance.

All:

My most beloved Jesus, * Your face was beautiful before, but in this journey it has lost all its beauty, * and wounds and blood have disfigured it. * Alas, our souls were once beautiful when we received Your grace in Baptism, * but we have disfigured them since by our sins. * You alone, our Redeemer, can restore our souls to their former beauty by Your Passion. * We love You, our beloved Jesus; * we ask for the grace to love You more than ourselves; * we repent with our whole heart for ever having offended You. * Never permit us to separate ourselves from You again. * Grant that we may love You always, and then do with us what You will.

All: *(Kneel)*

Eternal Father, I offer You the Body and Blood, Soul, and Divinity of Your dearly beloved Son, our Lord Jesus Christ, in atonement for our sins and those of the whole world.

Leader:

For the sake of His sorrowful Passion, *(Four times with response below)*

All:

Have mercy on us and on the whole world. *(Four times)*

All: Jesus, I trust in you.

All: *(Stand and sing)*

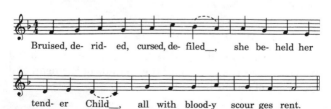

Bruised, de- rid- ed, cursed, de- filed__, she be- held her

tend- er Child__, all with blood-y scour ges rent.

SEVENTH STATION

Jesus Falls the Second Time

Leader:

We adore You, O Christ, and we praise You:
(All genuflect)

All:

Because by Your holy Cross You have redeemed the world.

Leader: *(All stand)*

Consider the second fall of Jesus under the Cross, a fall which renews the pain of all the wounds of the head and members of our afflicted Lord.

All:

My most gentle Jesus, * how many times You have pardoned me, and how many times have I fallen again and begun again to offend You! * By the merits of this new fall, * give me and all the members of my family and of The Apostolate the necessary help to persevere in Your grace until death. * Grant that, in all temptations which assail us, we may always commend ourselves to You. * We love You, our beloved Jesus; * we ask for the grace to love You more than ourselves; * we repent with our whole heart for ever having offended You. * Never permit us to separate ourselves from You again. * Grant that we may love You always, and then do with us what You will.

All: *(Kneel)*

Eternal Father, I offer You the Body and Blood, Soul, and Divinity of Your dearly beloved Son, our Lord Jesus Christ, in atonement for our sins and those of the whole world.

Leader:

For the sake of His sorrowful Passion, *(Four times with response below)*

All:

Have mercy on us and on the whole world. *(Four times)*

All: Jesus, I trust in You.

All: *(Stand and sing)*

O thou Mo-ther, fount of love__, touch my spir-it

from a-bove__; make my heart with thine ac-cord.

EIGHTH STATION

Jesus Meets the Women of Jerusalem

Leader:

We adore You, O Christ, and we praise You:
(All genuflect)

All:

Because by Your holy Cross You have redeemed the world.

Leader: *(All stand)*

Consider how those women wept with compassion at seeing Jesus in such a pitiable state, streaming with blood as He walked along; but Jesus said to them: *Weep not for Me, but for your children.* (Lk. 23:28)

All:

My Jesus, laden with sorrows, * I weep for the offenses I have committed against You, * because of the pains they have deserved, * and still more because of the displeasure they have caused You, Who have loved me so much. * It is Your love, more than the fear of hell, * which causes me to weep for my sins and the sins of all the members of my family and of The Apostolate. * We love You, our beloved Jesus; * we ask for the grace to love You more than ourselves; * we repent with our whole heart for ever having offended You. * Never permit us to separate ourselves from You again. Grant that we may love You always, and then do with us what You will.

All: *(Kneel)*

Eternal Father, I offer You the Body and Blood, Soul, and Divinity of Your dearly beloved Son, our Lord Jesus Christ, in atonement for our sins and those of the whole world.

Leader:

For the sake of His sorrowful Passion, *(Four times with response below)*

All:

Have mercy on us and on the whole world. *(Four times)*

All: Jesus, I trust in You.

All: *(Stand and sing)*

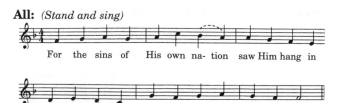

For the sins of His own na- tion saw Him hang in de- so la- tion, till His spir- it forth He sent.

NINTH STATION

Jesus Falls the Third Time

Leader:

We adore You, O Christ, and we praise You:
(All genuflect)

All:

Because by Your holy Cross You have redeemed the world.

Leader: *(All stand)*

Consider the third fall of Jesus Christ. His weakness was extreme, and the cruelty of His executioners excessive, who tried to hasten His steps when He had scarcely strength to move.

All:

My outraged Jesus, * by the merits of the weakness You suffered in going to Calvary, * give me and all the members of my family and of The Apostolate strength sufficient to conquer all human respect * and all our wicked passions, which have led us to despise Your friendship. * We love You, our beloved Jesus; * we ask for the grace to love You more than ourselves; * we repent with our whole heart for ever having offended You. * Never permit us to separate ourselves from You again. * Grant that we may love You always, and then do with us what You will.

All: *(Kneel)*

Eternal Father, I offer You the Body and Blood, Soul, and Divinity of Your dearly beloved Son, our Lord Jesus Christ, in atonement for our sins and those of the whole world.

Leader:

For the sake of His sorrowful Passion, *(Four times with response below)*

All:

Have mercy on us and on the whole world. *(Four times)*

All: Jesus, I trust in You.

All: *(Stand and sing)*

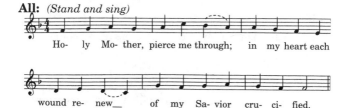

Ho- ly Mo- ther, pierce me through; in my heart each wound re- new__ of my Sa- vior cru- ci- fied.

TENTH STATION

Jesus is Stripped of His Garments

Leader:

We adore You, O Christ, and we praise You:
(All genuflect)

All:

Because by Your holy Cross You have redeemed the world.

Leader: *(All stand)*

Consider the violence with which the executioners stripped Jesus. His inner garments adhered to His torn flesh, and they dragged them off so roughly that the skin came with them. Compassionate your Savior thus

cruelly treated, and say to Him,

All:

My innocent Jesus, * by the merits of the torment You have felt, * help me and all the members of my family and of The Apostolate to strip ourselves of all affection to things of earth, * in order that we may place all our love in You, Who are so worthy of our love. * We love You, our beloved Jesus; * we ask for the grace to love You more than ourselves; * we repent with our whole heart for ever having offended You. * Never permit us to separate ourselves from You again. * Grant that we may love You always, and then do with us what You will.

All: *(Kneel)*

Eternal Father, I offer You the Body and Blood, Soul, and Divinity of Your dearly beloved Son, our Lord Jesus Christ, in atonement for our sins and those of the whole world.

Leader:

For the sake of His sorrowful Passion, *(Four times with response below)*

All:

Have mercy on us and on the whole world. *(Four times)*

All: Jesus, I trust in You.

All: *(Stand and sing)*

Make me feel as thou hast felt__, make my soul to glow and melt__ with the love of Christ my Lord.

ELEVENTH STATION

Jesus is Nailed to the Cross

Leader:

We adore You, O Christ, and we praise You:
(All genuflect)

All:

Because by Your holy Cross You have redeemed the world.

Leader: *(All stand)*

Consider how Jesus, after being thrown on the Cross, extended His hands and offered to His Eternal Father the sacrifice of His death for our salvation. These barbarians fastened Him with nails, and then, raising the

Cross, allowed Him to die with anguish on this infamous tree.

All:

My Jesus, filled with rejection, * nail my heart and the hearts of all the members of my family and of The Apostolate to Your feet, * that they may ever remain there to love You and never leave You again. * We love You, our beloved Jesus; * we ask for the grace to love You more than ourselves; * we repent with our whole heart for ever having offended You. * Never permit us to separate ourselves from You again. * Grant that we may love You always, * and then do with us what You will.

All: *(Kneel)*

Eternal Father, I offer You the Body and Blood, Soul, and Divinity of Your dearly beloved Son, our Lord Jesus Christ, in atonement for our sins and those of the whole world.

Leader:

For the sake of His sorrowful Passion, *(Four times with response below)*

All:

Have mercy on us and on the whole world. *(Four times)*

All: Jesus, I trust in You.

All: *(Stand and sing)*

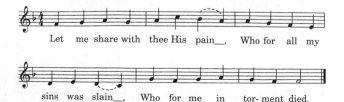

Let me share with thee His pain__, Who for all my sins was slain__, Who for me in tor- ment died.

TWELFTH STATION

Jesus Dies on the Cross

Leader:

We adore You, O Christ, and we praise You:
(All genuflect)

All:

Because by Your holy Cross You have redeemed the world.

Leader: *(All stand)*

Consider how Jesus, after three hours' agony on the Cross, consumed at length with anguish, abandons Himself to the weight of His body, bows His head, and dies.

All:

O my dying Jesus, * I kiss devoutly the Cross on which You died for love of me, and for all the members of my family and of The Apostolate. * We have merited by our sins to die a miserable death; * but Your death is our hope. * Ah, by the merits of Your death, * give us grace to die embracing Your feet and burning with love for You. * We yield our souls into Your hands. * We love You, our beloved Jesus; * we ask for the grace to love You more than ourselves; * we repent with our whole heart for ever having offended You. * Never permit us to separate ourselves from You again. * Grant that we may love You always, * and then do with us what You will.

All: *(Kneel)*

Eternal Father, I offer You the Body and Blood, Soul, and Divinity of Your dearly beloved Son, our Lord Jesus Christ, in atonement for our sins and those of the whole world.

Leader:

For the sake of His sorrowful Passion, *(Four times with response below)*

All:

Have mercy on us and on the whole world. *(Four times)*

All: Jesus, I trust in You.

All: *(Stand and sing)*

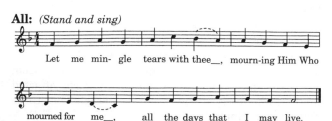

Let me min-gle tears with thee__, mourn-ing Him Who mourned for me__, all the days that I may live.

THIRTEENTH STATION

Jesus is Laid in the Arms of His Mother

Leader:

We adore You, O Christ, and we praise You:
(All genuflect)

All:

Because by Your holy Cross You have redeemed the world.

Leader: *(All stand)*

Consider how, after the death of Our Lord, two of His disciples, Joseph and Nicodemus, took Him down from the Cross and placed Him in the arms of His afflicted Mother, who received Him with unutterable tenderness and pressed Him to her bosom.

All:

O Mother of Sorrows, * for the love of this Son, accept me and all the members of my family and of The Apostolate as your obedient children, * and pray to Him for us. * And You, our Redeemer, * since You have died for us, permit us to love You; * for we wish but You, and nothing more. * We love You, our beloved Jesus; * we ask for the grace to love You more than ourselves; * we repent with our whole heart for ever having offended You. * Never permit us to separate ourselves from You again. * Grant that we may love You always, * and then do with us what You will.

All: *(Kneel)*

Eternal Father, I offer You the Body and Blood, Soul, and Divinity of Your dearly beloved Son, our Lord Jesus Christ, in atonement for our sins and those of the whole world.

Leader:

For the sake of His sorrowful Passion, *(Four times with response below)*

All:

Have mercy on us and on the whole world. *(Four times)*

All: Jesus, I trust in You.

All: *(Stand and sing)*

By the Cross with thee to- stay__, there with thee to weep and pray__, is all I ask of thee to give.

FOURTEENTH STATION

Jesus is Laid in the Tomb

Leader:

We adore You, O Christ, and we praise You:
(All genuflect)

All:

Because by Your holy Cross You have redeemed the world.

Leader: *(All stand)*

Consider how the disciples carried the body of Jesus to bury it, accompanied by His holy Mother, who arranged it in the sepulcher with Her own hands. They then closed the tomb and all withdrew.

All: Oh, my buried Jesus, * I kiss the stone that enclosed You; * but You rose again on the third day. * I beseech You by Your Resurrection, * make me and the members of my family and of The Apostolate rise gloriously with You on the last day, * to be always united with You in Heaven, * to praise You, and love You forever. * We love You, our beloved Jesus; * we ask for the grace to love You more than ourselves; * we repent with our whole heart for ever having offended You. * Never permit us to separate ourselves from You again. * Grant that we may love You always, * and then do with us what You will.

All: *(Kneel)*
Eternal Father, I offer You the Body and Blood, Soul, and Divinity of Your dearly beloved Son, our Lord Jesus Christ, in atonement for our sins and those of the whole world.

Leader: For the sake of His sorrowful Passion, *(Four times with response below)*

All: Have mercy on us and on the whole world. *(Four times)*

All: Jesus, I trust in You.

All: *(Kneel and sing)*

Vir- gin of all vir-gins blest__, li- sten to my fond re- quest__: let me share thy grief di- vine.

All: *(Remain kneeling)*
Holy God, Holy Mighty One, Holy Immortal One, have mercy on us and on the whole world. *(Three times)*

Jesus, I trust in You.

64. Excerpt from the Encyclical
The Redeemer of Man
by Pope John Paul II

On the Eucharist

20. The Church lives by the Eucharist, by the fullness of this sacrament, the stupendous content and meaning of which have often been expressed in the Church's magisterium from the most distant times down to our own days. However, we can say with certainty that, although this teaching is sustained by the acuteness of theologians, by men of deep faith and prayer, and by ascetics and mystics, in complete fidelity to the Eucharistic mystery, it still reaches no more than the threshold, since it is incapable of grasping and translating into words what the Eucharist is in all its fullness, what is expressed by it and what is actuated by it. Indeed, the Eucharist is the ineffable sacrament! The essential commitment and, above all, the visible grace and source of supernatural strength for the Church as the People of God is to persevere and advance constantly in Eucharistic life and Eucharistic piety and to develop spiritually in the climate of the Eucharist. With all the greater reason, then, it is not permissible for us, in thought, life, or action, to take away from this truly most holy sacrament its full magnitude and its essential meaning. **It is at one and the same time a sacrifice-sacrament, a communion-sacrament, and a presence-sacrament.** And, although it is true that the Eucharist always was and must continue to be the most profound revelation of the human brotherhood of Christ's disciples and confessors, it cannot be treated merely as an "occasion" for manifesting this brotherhood. When celebrating the sacrament of the body and blood of the Lord, the full magnitude of the divine mystery must be respected, as must the full meaning of this sacramental sign in which Christ is really present and

is received, the soul is filled with grace, and the pledge of future glory is given. This is the source of the duty to carry out rigorously the liturgical rules and everything that is a manifestation of community worship offered to God Himself, all the more so because in this sacramental sign He entrusts Himself to us with limitless trust, as if not taking into consideration our human weakness, our unworthiness, the force of habit, routine, or even the possibility of insult. Every member of the Church, especially bishops and priests, must be vigilant in seeing that this sacrament of love shall be at the center of the life of the People of God, so that through all the manifestations of worship due to it Christ shall be given back "love for love" and truly become "the life of our souls." Nor can we, on the other hand, ever forget the following words of St. Paul: "Let a man examine himself, and so eat of the bread and drink of the Cup."

© *L'Osservatore Romano. Printed with permission.*

64a. Privilege of Receiving Holy Communion Twice a Day

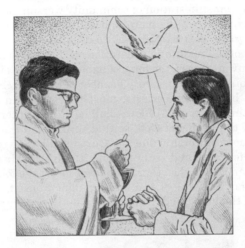

"Canon 917 — **A person who has received the Most Holy Eucharist may receive it again on the same day only during the celebration of the Eucharist in which the person participates, with due regard for the prescription of can. 921, §2.**

"The purpose of this canon is twofold: on the one hand, to promote active participation in the Eucharist [Mass] including the full sacramental sharing in the Lord's Body and Blood; on the other hand, to prevent the abuse of receiving multiple Communions out of superstition, ignorance, or misguided devotion.

"The 1917 Code (*CIC* 857) forbade the reception of Communion more than once a day except in danger of death or in need of impeding irreverence. The law was mitigated repeatedly after Vatican II to allow more frequent opportunities to receive twice on the same day. This canon greatly simplifies the post-conciliar legislation by permitting the reception of Communion twice in a day for any reason, provided the second reception occurs in the context of the Eucharist [Mass] at which one is actually participating. Such participation implies minimally one's physical presence at the Eucharist [Mass]. It excludes a second Communion outside of Mass except as Viaticum, and it also excludes a second Communion during a Mass at which one is not participating, such as when one enters in the course of the Mass only to receive Communion." (*The Code of Canon Law: A Text and Commentary*, Study Edition, commissioned by the Canon Law Society of America, 1985)

The following is an excerpt from a talk given by Rev. John Hardon, S.J., world renowned theologian, at the Sacred Heart Conference held in Detroit, Michigan on September 10, 1994.

Every person in the state of grace has the virtue of charity. When we're baptized, we receive three theological virtues: faith, hope, and charity. Anyone who loses the state of grace always, always loses the virtue of charity.

One reason, by the way, and a fundamental one, why Holy Communion must be received in the state of grace is found when one beholds its very purpose: Holy Communion is to deepen, strengthen, enliven, and develop that virtue of charity that was infused into our souls when we were baptized.

I come now to my second recommendation, which follows logically on the first, to receive Holy Communion, I add, if at all possible, everyday. Many things I don't know. One thing I do know: I would not be now here speaking to you as a priest and of all subjects, on the Holy Eucharist, except for my widowed mother. I never remember—never—from childhood, that she did not assist at Mass and receive Holy Communion everyday.

Pope St. Pius X, in restoring frequent Communion to the Catholic Church, explained the primary meaning of the petition of the Lord's prayer, "Give us this day our daily bread." The primary object of that petition—we beg that every human being eventually, every Catholic now, receive Holy Communion everyday. I'm not quite finished with part two. For the first time, in 2000 years of the Church's history, not only does the Church encourage the faithful to receive Holy Communion daily, **she now not only allows or reluctantly permits, I mean it, she encourages receiving Holy Communion even twice a day, provided the second Communion is received in the Sacrifice of the Mass.**

We are living in the most homicidal century of human history. Never in our wildest dreams...and to think I should now be speaking, while in Egypt, the leaders of nations are dividing, debating, whether they should not require murder as a condition for political and financial support from wealthy nations like our own. How we need, how desperately we need, the grace that only Jesus can give, the grace of generosity through the Sacrament of Holy Communion.

Finally, Christ our Lord instituted—beyond the Sacrifice-Sacrament of the Mass, beyond the Communion-Sacrament of Holy Communion—the Presence-Sacrament of the Holy Eucharist, Who is the same Jesus now here who had His Heart pierced on Calvary; it is the same Jesus with the same flesh and blood that His Mother gave Him. As Augustine tells us: the body of Jesus is the body of Mary; the blood of Jesus is the blood of Mary; the Heart of Jesus comes from the Heart of Mary.

What is, finally, the distinctive grace that we receive in worshipping Our Lord really present in the Blessed Sacrament? It is—listen—it is the grace of seeing Jesus Christ present in those whom God puts into our lives. On the last day, as Christ foretold, we shall be judged. We shall be judged on whether or not we have seen Jesus in those who are in need. As Christ tells us,

"Whatever you have done to the least of those who are My brethren, you have done to Me." How we need—how we need to see Jesus Christ in those whom God puts into our lives and the source of that vision, born of faith, is our Baptism, of course, but nourished and strengthened by our praying before Our Lord in the Holy Eucharist. Jesus Christ, in the fullness of His humanity, is in our midst.

Except for Mary, there would be no Jesus. Except for Jesus, there would be no Christianity. Except for Christianity, there would be no selfless love. Except for selfless love, there would be no Christian family.

We close with a prayer:

Mary, Mother of Jesus, it was from you that your Divine Son received His flesh and blood and His human heart. Except for you, we would not have Him in the Blessed Sacrament. But dear Mother, you know how weak our faith is. We beg you, dear Mother, to obtain from your Divine Son, the miracle of converting hardened, selfish, stubborn human hearts to the Heart of your Son, so that believing in Him now, seeing Him in those whom Jesus puts into our lives, we may enjoy Him and you, our Mother, in that everlasting Holy Eucharist for which we were made. Amen.

67a. The Friends of the Cross
by Saint Louis Marie de Montfort

Imprimi Potest
S. Laurentii ad Separim die 3a Maii, 1950.
A. Josselin, S.M.M., Superior General

Nihil Obstat
Martinus J. Healy, S.T.D., Censor Liborum

Imprimatur
Thomas Edmundus Molloy, S.T.D., Episcopus
Brooklyniensis.
Brooklynii, XX mensis Octobris 1950

Printed with permission from: The Montfort Publications, Montfort Missionaries, Bay Shore, NY.

Apostolate for Family Consecration's
Peace of Heart Forum

Please obtain the video series #126-3774VK (set of 8 half-hour programs), which guides you through this section. We suggest that you gather a group of people to meet weekly to play the corresponding videotape and to discuss the material that you prayed and meditated on for the past week. You can use one of the following video/reading plans. See pages 588–613 for more details about the Peace of Heart Forums.

4-Week Video/Reading Plan

Session 1
Video 126-3760V *(show 126-3761 & 126-3762)*.
Read the Preface through section 17 before the next session.

Session 2
Video 126-3763V *(show 126-3764 & 126-3765)*.
Read sections 18–40 before the next session.

Session 3
Video 126-3767V *(show 126-3768 & 127-3769)*.
Read section 41–end before the next session.

Session 4
Video 126-3770V *(show 126-3771 & 126-3772)*.
Complete video set #126-3774VK

8-Week Video/Reading Plan

Session 1
Video 126-3760V *(show 126-3761)*.
Read Preface–section 10 before the next session.

Session 2
Video 126-3760V *(show 126-3762)*.
Read sections 11–17 before the next session.

Session 3
Video 126-3763V *(show 126-3764)*.
Read sections 18–28 before the next session.

Session 4
Video 126-3763V *(show 126-3765)*.
Read sections 29–40 before the next session.

Session 5
Video 126-3767V *(show 126-3768)*.
Read sections 41–49 before the next session.

Session 6
Video 126-3767V *(show 126-3769)*.
Read sections 50–62 before the next session.

Session 7
Video 126-3770V *(show 126-3771)*.
Read "The Triumph of the Cross" before the next session.

Session 8
Video 126-3770V *(show 126-3772)*.
Complete set #126-3774VK

Preface

St. Louis Marie Grignon de Montfort (1673-1716), author of this "Letter," is widely known through his treatise on *The True Devotion to the Blessed Virgin Mary* and its abridgment *The Secret of Mary.* Well has he merited the title of "Apostle of Mary" and deservedly he is called "Tutor of the Legion of Mary."

Addressing the many pilgrims at the canonization of St. de Montfort, July 1947, the Holy Father calls him "the guide who leads you to Mary and from Mary to Jesus." Speaking of St. Louis' "Prayer for Missionaries," Father Faber says: "Since the Apostolical Epistles, it would be hard to find words that burn so marvelously." He has founded two religious congregations: the priests and the brothers of the Company of Mary (Montfort Fathers) and the Daughters of Wisdom. To his sons and daughters he has left a rich heritage of doctrinal writings.

In this "Letter" St. Louis manifests his passionate love for the Cross and pours forth the noble sentiments of his ardent soul. Like St. Paul, he is "determined to know nothing... except Jesus Christ, and Him crucified" (1 Cor. 2: 2); "indeed a stumbling block to the Jews and foolishness to the Gentiles, but to those who are called...the Wisdom of God" (1 Cor 1: 23, 24).

While giving missions in the city of Nantes in 1708, this eloquent preacher of the Cross and devout slave of Jesus in Mary formed, from the most fervent souls among his audiences, an association of "The Friends of the Cross." This fraternity or association was established in the localities evangelized by the holy Missionary to fight against the many disorders and vices of the times and to make reparation for the outrages perpetrated against the Sacred Heart of Jesus. Each time he visited these places he exhorted the members to persevere in their first fervor. Alas! Suddenly he was forbidden to preach to them. Through intrigues, machinations and calumny his arch enemies, the Jansenists, prevailed to have their redoubtable adversary silenced.

During the summer of 1714 Father de Montfort stopped at Rennes. Here, too, with diabolical hate and fury, the Jansenists succeeded in having the saintly Missionary silenced. Welcoming this added humiliation — for his heaviest cross was to be without a cross — he took refuge at his *alma mater*, the Jesuit College at Rennes, where he was warmly received. Here he buried himself in an eight day retreat meditating on the mystery of Calvary. From an incessant heart-to-heart talk with the Man of Sorrows and His Blessed Mother he received a new light and a more ardent love for the Crucified Savior.

On the last day of the retreat St. Louis, always eager to lead the faithful souls on the Royal Road of the Cross, desired to communicate to his fervent followers the fruits of his sublime meditation and poured forth the burning sentiments of his apostolic soul in the following "Letter."

In this epistle he gives us a holy doctrine which he preached and lived all his life, thus imitating his Divine Master, Jesus Christ. It is believed that as a seminarian he wrote those two wonderful poems: "The Strength of Patience" (39 stanzas) and the "Triumph of the Cross" (31 stanzas) in which we find the elements contained in this "Letter." As a young priest he wrote his first book, "Love of Eternal Wisdom," and in its beautiful fourteenth chapter, "The Triumph of Eternal Wisdom in the

Cross and by the Cross," is demonstrated the author's great love for the Folly of the Cross. In his allocution on St. de Montfort, quoted above, the Holy Father said: "Being crucified himself, he has a perfect right to speak with authority on Christ Crucified.... He gives a sketch of his own life when drawing up a plan of life in his 'Letter to the Friends of the Cross' "(cf. "Letter," No. 4, paragraph 2).

When this "Letter" appeared, St. Louis had already written *The Secret of Mary* and most probably had finished its lucid development *True Devotion to the Blessed Virgin Mary* to which this "Letter" is very closely related and is, as it were, the development and completion of the saintly author's "plan of forming a true client of Mary and a true disciple of Jesus Christ" (True Devotion no. 111).

Although written more than two centuries ago to fight against the evils and vices of those days, this "Letter" retains all its usefulness and freshness. It wages a holy war on the evils, vices, pagan materialism, and secularism of the present day. St. Louis gives us a panacea for all these ills: Christian mortification, prayer and a total consecration of ourselves to the Immaculate Heart of Mary. In a strong staccato tone he tells us "to suffer, to weep, to fast, to pray, to hide ourselves, to humiliate ourselves, to impoverish ourselves, to mortify ourselves. He who has not the spirit of Christ, which is the spirit of the Cross, does not belong to Him, but they who belong to Him have crucified their flesh and their concupiscences."

Is this not the message Our Lady of Fatima gave to the world—penance, mortification, sacrifice, prayer and consecration to her Immaculate Heart— in 1917. Is it not Our Blessed Mother who guided and inspired her faithful Apostle to write it!

Thus imbued with a burning love for Christ Crucified, a love born of humiliation, suffering, persecution and contempt, like his Divine Master, St. Louis gives us, at the close of his "Letter," some wise, prudent rules that teach us how to suffer and bear our crosses patiently, willingly and joyfully in the footsteps of Our Lord and Crucified Savior. Thus convinced of the necessity of the Cross, stimulated by the happy effects it produces in our souls, and guided by these same rules laid down by St. Louis de Montfort we will more readily renounce Satan, the world and the flesh; we will more patiently bear our trials, crosses and tribulations and we will more carefully heed Christ's admonition: "If any one wishes to come after Me let him deny himself, and take up his cross daily and follow Me" (Luke 8-23).

The Editor

Contents

Introduction

Dear Friends of the Cross:

1. Since the divine Cross keeps me hidden and prevents me from speaking, I cannot, and do not even wish to express to you by word of mouth the feelings of my heart on the divine *excellence* and *practices* of your Association in the adorable Cross of Jesus Christ.

However, on this last day of my retreat, I come out, as it were, from the sweet retirement of my interior, to trace upon paper a few little arrows from the Cross with which to pierce your noble hearts. God grant that I could point them with the blood of my veins and not with the ink of my pen. Even if blood were required, mine, alas!, would be unworthy. May the spirit of the living God, then, be the life, vigor and tenor of this letter. May His unction be my ink, His divine Cross my pen, and your hearts my paper.

Part I
Excellence of the Association of the Friends of the Cross

I. Grandeur of the Name, Friends of the Cross

2. Friends of the Cross, you are a group of crusaders united to fight against the world, not like those religious, men and women, who leave the world for fear of being overcome, but like brave, intrepid warriors on the battlefront, refusing to retreat or even to yield an inch. Be brave. Fight with all your might.

Bind yourselves together in that strong union of heart and mind which is far superior, far more terrifying to the world and hell than the armed forces of a well-organized kingdom are to its enemies. Demons are united for your destruction, but you, be united for their overthrow; the avaricious are united to barter and hoard up gold and silver, combine your efforts in the pursuit of the eternal treasures hidden in the Cross; reprobates unite to make merry, but you, be united to suffer.

3. You call yourselves "Friends of the Cross." What a wonderful name! I must admit that it charms and fascinates me. It is brighter than the sun, higher than the heavens, more imposing and resplendent than any title given to king or emperor. It is the great name of Christ Himself, true God and true Man at one and the same time. It is the unmistakable title of a Christian.

4. Its splendor dazzles me but the weight of it frightens me. For this title implies that you have taken upon yourselves difficult and inescapable obligations, which are summed up in the words of the Holy Spirit: "A chosen generation, a kingly priesthood, a holy nation, a purchased people" (1 Peter 2:9).

A Friend of the Cross is one chosen by God from among ten thousand who have reason and sense for their only guide. He is truly divine, raised above reason and thoroughly opposed to the things of sense, for he lives in the light of true faith and burns with love for the Cross.

A Friend of the Cross is a mighty king, a hero who triumphs over the devil, the world and the flesh and their three-fold concupiscence. He overthrows the pride of Satan by his love for humiliation, he triumphs over the world's greed by his love for poverty, and he restrains the sensuality of the flesh by his love for suffering.

A Friend of the Cross is a holy man, separated from visible things. His heart is lifted high above all that is frail and perishable; "his conversation is in heaven" (Phil. 3: 20); he journeys here below like a stranger and pilgrim. He keeps his heart free from the world, looks upon it with an unconcerned glance of his left eye and disdainfully tramples it under foot.

A Friend of the Cross is a trophy which the crucified Christ won on Calvary, in union with His Blessed Mother. He is another Benoni (Gen. 35:18) or Benjamin, a son of sorrow, a son of the right hand. Conceived in the sorrowful heart of Christ, he comes into this world through the gash in the Savior's right side and is all empurpled in His blood. True to this heritage, he breathes forth only crosses and blood, death to the world, the flesh, and sin; and hides himself here below with Jesus Christ in God (Col. 3:3).

Thus, a perfect Friend of the Cross is a true Christ-bearer, or rather another Christ, so much so that he can say with truth: "I live, now not I, but Christ lives in me" (Gal. 2:20).

5. My dear Friends of the Cross, does every act of yours justify what the eminent name you bear implies? Or at least are you, with the grace of God, in the shadow of Calvary's Cross and of Our Lady of Pity, really eager and truly striving to attain this goal? Is the way you follow the one that leads to this goal? Is it the true way of life, the narrow way, the thorn-strewn way to Calvary? Or are you unconsciously traveling the world's broad road the road to perdition? Do you realize that there is a highroad which to all appearances is straight and safe for man to travel, but which in reality leads to death?

6. Do you really know the voice of God and grace from the voice of the world and human nature? Do you distinctly hear the voice of God, our kind Father, pronouncing His three-fold curse upon every one who fol-

lows the world in its concupiscence: "Woe, woe, woe to the inhabitants of the earth" (Apoc. 8:13) and then appealing to you with outstretched arms: "Be separated, My chosen people (Is. 48:20; 52:11; Jer. 50:8; 51:6), beloved Friends of the Cross of My Son, be separated from those worldlings, for they are accursed by My Majesty, repudiated by My Son (John 17:9) and condemned by My Holy Spirit (John 16:8-12). Do not sit in their chair of pestilence; take no part in their gatherings; do not even step along their highways (Ps. 1:1). Hurry away from this great and infamous Babylon (Is. 48:20; Jer. 51:6); listen only to the voice of My Beloved Son; follow only in His footprints; for He is the One I have given to be your Way, Truth, Life (John 14:6) and Model: hear Him"(Matt. 17:5; Luke 9:35; Mark 9:6; 2 Pet. 1:17).

Is your ear attentive to the pleadings of the lovable and cross-burdened Jesus, "Come, follow Me; he that follows Me will never walk in darkness (John 8:12); have confidence, I have conquered the world" (John 16:33)?

II. The Two Groups

A. The Followers of Christ and the Followers of the World

7. Dear Brothers, these are the two groups that appear before you each day, the followers of Christ and the followers of the world.

Our loving Savior's group is to the right, scaling a narrow path made all the narrower by the world's corruption. Our kind Master is in the lead, barefooted, thorn-crowned, robed in His blood and weighed down by a heavy cross. There is only a handful of people who follow Him, but they are the bravest of the brave. His gentle voice is not heard above the tumult of the world, or men do not have the courage to follow Him in poverty, suffering, humiliation and in the other crosses His servants must bear all the days of their life.

B. The Opposing Spirit of the Groups

8. To the left is the world's group, the devil's in fact, which is far superior in number, and seemingly far more colorful and splendid in array. Fashionable folk are all in a hurry to enlist, the highways are overcrowded, although they are broad and ever broadening with the crowds that flow through in a torrent. These roads are strewn with flowers, bordered with all kinds of amusements and attractions, and paved with gold and silver (Matt. 7:13-14).

9. To the right, the little flock that follows Jesus can speak only of tears, penance, prayer, and contempt for worldly things. Sobbing in their grief, they can be heard repeating: "Let us suffer, let us weep, let us fast, let us pray, let us hide, let us humble ourselves, let us be poor, let us mortify ourselves, for he who has not the spirit of Christ, the spirit of the Cross, is not Christ's. Those who are Christ's have crucified their flesh with its concupiscence. We must be conformed to the image of Jesus Christ or else be damned!" "Be brave," they keep saying to each other, "be brave, for if God is for us, in us, and leading us, who dare be against us? The One Who is dwelling within us is stronger than the one who is in the world; no servant is above his master; one moment of light tribulation wins an eternal weight of glory; there are fewer elect than man may think; only the brave and daring take heaven by storm; the crown is given only to those who strive lawfully according to the Gospel, not according to the fashion of the world. Let us put all our strength into the fight, and run very fast to reach the goal and win the crown." Friends of the Cross spur each other on with such divine words.

10. Worldlings, on the contrary, rouse one another to persist in their unscrupulous depravity. "Enjoy life, peace, and pleasure," they shout, "Enjoy life, peace and

pleasure. Let us eat, let us drink, let us sing, let us dance, let us play. God is good, He did not make us to damn us; God does not forbid us to enjoy ourselves; we shall not be damned for that; away with scruples; we shall not die." And so they continue.

C. Loving Appeal of Jesus

11. Dear Brothers, remember that our beloved Jesus has His eyes upon you at this moment, address- ing you individually: "See how almost everybody leaves Me practically alone on the royal road of the Cross. Blind idol-worshippers sneer at My Cross and brand it folly. Obstinate Jews are scandalized at the sight of it as if it were some monstrosity (1 Cor. 1:23). Heretics tear it down and break it to pieces out of sheer contempt. But one thing I cannot say without My eyes filling with tears and My heart being pierced with grief is that the very children I nourished in My bosom and trained in My school, the very members I quickened with My spirit have turned against Me, forsaken Me, and joined the ranks of the enemies of My Cross (Is. 1:2; Phil. 3:18). Would you also leave Me? (John 6:68). Would you also forsake me and flee from My Cross, like the worldlings, who are acting as so many Anti-Christs? (1 John 2:12). Would you subscribe to the standards of the day (Rom. 12:2); despise the poverty of My Cross, and go in quest of riches; shun the sufferings connected with My Cross to run after pleasure; spurn the humiliations that must be borne with My Cross, and pursue worldly honors? There are many who pretend that they are friends of Mine and love Me, but in reality they hate Me because they have no love for My Cross. I have many friends of My table, but few indeed of My Cross." (*Imitation of Jesus Christ*, Book 2, Chap. 11.)

12. In answer to the gracious invitation which Jesus extends, let us rise above ourselves. Let us not, like Eve, listen to the insidious suggestions of sense. Let us look up to the unique Author and Finisher of our

faith, Jesus crucified (Heb. 12:2). Let us fly from the corrupting concupiscence and enticements of a corrupt world (2 Pet. 1:4). Let us love Jesus in the right way, standing by Him through the heaviest of crosses. Let us meditate seriously on these remarkable words of our beloved Master which sum up the Christian life in its perfection: "If any man will come after Me, let him deny himself, and take up his cross, and follow Me" (Matt. 16:24).

Part II
Practices of Christian Perfection

The Divine Master's Program

13. Christian perfection consists:

1. in willing to become a saint: "If any man will come after Me";

2. in self-denial: "Let him deny himself";

3. in suffering: "Let him take up his cross";

4. in doing: "Let him follow Me."

14. If *anyone*, not *many a one*, shows that the elect who are willing to be made conformable to the crucified Christ by carrying their cross are few in number, it would cause us to faint away from grief to learn how surprisingly small is their number.

It is so small that among ten thousand people there is scarcely one to be found, as was revealed to several Saints, among whom was St. Simon Stylita, referred to by the holy Abbot Nilus, followed by St. Basil, St. Ephrem, and others. So small, indeed, that if God willed to gather them together, He would have to cry out as He did of old through the voice of a prophet: "Come together one by one" (Is. 27:12), one from this province and one from that kingdom.*

I. The Desire to Become a Saint

15. If anyone *wills*: if a person has a real and definite determination and is prompted not by natural feelings, habit, self-love, personal interest, or human respect, but by an all-masterful grace of the Holy Spirit which is not communicated indiscriminately: "It is not given to all men to understand this mystery" (Matt. 13:11). In fact, only a privileged number of men receive this practical knowledge of the mystery of the Cross. For that man who climbs up to Calvary and lets himself be nailed on the Cross with Jesus, in the heart of his own country, must be a brave man, a hero, a resolute man, one who is lifted up in God, who treats as muck both the world and hell, as well as his very body and his own will. He must be resolved to relinquish all things, to undertake anything and to suffer everything for Jesus.

Understand this, dear Friends of the Cross, if there should be anyone among you who has not this firm resolve, he is just limping along on one foot, flying with one wing, and undeserving of your company, since he is not worthy to be called a Friend of the Cross, for we must love the Cross as Jesus Christ loved it "with a great heart and a willing mind" (2 Macc. 1: 3). That kind of half-hearted will is enough to spoil the whole flock,

---

*St. Louis de Montfort here speaks of that small group of saintly souls who carry their cross more perfectly. He does not, however, exclude from salvation that vast multitude of less perfect Christians which the mercy of God wills to save.

like a sheep with the scurvy. If any such one has slipped into your fold through the contaminated door of the world, then in the name of the crucified Christ, drive him out as you would a wolf from your sheepfold.

16. "If anyone will come *after Me*": for I have humbled Myself and reduced Myself to mere nothingness in such a way that I made Myself a worm rather than a man: "I am a worm and no man" (Ps. 21:7). After Me: for if I came into the world, it was only to espouse the Cross: "Behold I am come" (Ps. 39:8; Heb. 10:7-9); to set the cross in My heart of hearts: "In the midst of my heart" (Ps. 39:9); to love it from the days of my youth: "I have loved it from my youth" (Wisdom 8:2); only to long for it all the days of my life: "how straitened I am" (Luke 12:50); only to bear it with a joy I preferred even to the joys and delights that heaven and earth could offer: "Who, having joy set before him, endured the cross" (Heb. 12:2); and, finally, not to be satisfied until I had expired in its divine embrace.

II. Self-Denial

17. Therefore, if anyone wants to come after Me, annihilated and crucified, he must glory as I did, only in the poverty, humiliation and suffering of My Cross: "let him deny himself" (Matt. 16:24).

Far be from the Company of the Friends of the Cross those who pride themselves in suffering, the worldly-wise, elated geniuses and self-conceited individuals who are stubborn and puffed-up with their lights and talents. Far be they from us, those endless talkers who make plenty of noise but bring forth no other fruit than vainglory. Far from us those high-browed devotees everywhere displaying the self-sufficient pride of Lucifer: "I am not like the rest!"(Luke 18:11). Far be from us those who must always justify themselves when blamed, resist when attacked, and exalt themselves when humbled.

Be careful not to admit into your fellowship those

frail, sensitive persons who are afraid of the slightest pin-prick, who sob and sigh when faced with the lightest suffering, who have never experienced a hair-shirt, a discipline, or any other penitential instrument, and who, with their fashionable devotions, mingle the most artful delicacy and the most refined lack of mortification.

III. Suffering

18. *Let him take up his cross*, the one that is *his*. Let this man or this woman, rarely to be found and worth more than the entire world (Prov. 31:10-31), take up with joy, fervently clasp in his arms, and bravely set upon his shoulders this cross that is his own and not that of another; his own cross, the one that My Wisdom designed for him in every detail of number, weight, and measurement; his own cross whose four dimensions, its length, breadth, thickness, and height (Eph. 3:18), I very accurately gauged with My own hands; his own cross which, all out of love for him, I carved from a section of the very Cross I bore on Calvary; his cross, the grandest of all the gifts I have for My chosen ones on earth; his cross, made up in its thickness of temporal loss, humiliation, disdain, sorrow, illness and spiritual trial which My Providence will not fail to supply him with every day of his life; his cross, made up in its length of a definite period of days or months when he will have to bear with slander or be helplessly stretched out on a bed of pain, or forced to beg, or else a prey to temptation, dryness, desolation, and many another mental anguish; his cross, made up in its breadth of hard and bitter situations stirred up for him by his relatives, friends, or servants; his cross, finally, made up in its depth of secret sufferings which I will have him endure, nor will I allow him any comfort from created beings, for by My order they will turn from him too and even join Me in making him suffer.

19. Let him *carry* it, and not drag it, not shoulder

it off, not lighten it, nor hide it. Let him hold it high in hand, without impatience or peevishness, without voluntary complaint or grumbling, without dividing or softening, without shame or human respect.

Let him place it on his forehead and say with St. Paul: "God forbid that I should glory save in the Cross of Our Lord Jesus Christ" (Gal. 6:14).

Let him carry it on his shoulders, after the example of Jesus Christ, and make it his weapon to victory and the scepter of his empire (Is. 9:16).

Let him root it in his heart and there change it into a fiery bush, burning day and night with the pure love of God, without being consumed.

20. The cross: it is the cross he must carry, for there is nothing more necessary, more useful, more agreeable and more glorious than suffering for Jesus Christ.

21. All of you are sinners and there is not a single one who is not deserving of hell; I myself deserve it the most. These sins of ours must be punished either here or hereafter. If they are punished in this world, they will not be punished in the world to come.

If we agree to God's punishing here below, this punishment will be dictated by love. For mercy, which holds sway in this world, will mete out the punishment, and not strict justice. This punishment will be light and momentary, blended with merit and sweetness and followed up with reward both in time and eternity.

22. But if the punishment due to our sins is held over for the next world, then God's avenging justice, which means fire and blood, will see to the punishing. What horrible punishment! How incomprehensible, how unspeakable! "Who knows the power of Your anger?" (Ps. 89:11). Punishment devoid of mercy (James 2:13), pity, mitigation or merit; without limit and without end. Yes, without end! That mortal sin of a moment that you committed, that deliberate evil thought which now escapes your memory, the word that is gone with the wind, that act of such short duration against God's law — they shall all be punished for an eternity, punished with the devils of hell, as long as God is God! The God of vengeance will have no pity on your torments or your sobs and tears, violent enough to cleave the rocks. Suffering and still more suffering, without merit, without mercy, and without end!

23. Do we think of this, my dear Brothers and Sisters, when we have some trial to undergo here below? Blessed indeed are we who have the privilege of exchanging an eternal and fruitless penalty for a temporary and meritorious suffering, just by patiently carrying our crosses. What debts we still have to pay! How many sins we have committed which, despite a sincere confession and heartfelt contrition, will have to be atoned for in Purgatory for many a century, simply because in this world we were satisfied with a few insignificant penances! Let us settle our debts with good grace here below in cheerfully bearing our crosses, for in the world to come everything must be expiated, even the idle word (Matt. 12:36), even to the last farthing. If we could lay hands on the devil's death-register in which he has noted down all our sins and the penalty to be paid, what a heavy debt we would find, and how joyfully we would suffer many years here on earth rather than a single day in the world to come.

24. Don't you flatter yourselves, Friends of the

Cross, that you are, or that you want to be, the friends of God? Be firmly resolved then to drink of the chalice which you must necessarily drink if you wish to enjoy the friendship of God. "They drank the chalice of the Lord and became the friends of God" (Common of Apostles, Lesson 7). The beloved Benjamin had the chalice while his brothers had only the wheat (Gen. 44:1-4). The disciple whom Jesus preferred had his Master's heart, went up with Him to Calvary, and drank of His chalice. "Can you drink my chalice?" (Matt. 20:22). To desire God's glory is good, indeed, but to desire it and pray for it without being resolved to suffer all things is mere folly and senseless asking. "You know not what you ask (Matt. 20:22)...you must undergo much suffering" (Acts 14:21): you must; it is necessary, it is indispensable! We can enter the kingdom of heaven only at the price of many crosses and tribulations.

25. You take pride in being God's children and you do well; but you should also rejoice in the lashes your good Father has given you and in those He still means to give you; for He scourges every one of His children (Prov. 3: 11; Heb. 13:5-6; Apoc. 3:19). If you are not of the household of His beloved sons, then — how unfortunate! what a calamity! — you are, as St. Augustine says, listed with the reprobates. Augustine also says: "The one that does not mourn like a stranger and wayfarer in this world cannot rejoice in the world to come as a citizen of heaven" (Sermon 31, 5 and 6). If God the Father does not send you worth-while crosses from time to time, that is because He no longer cares for you and is angry at you. He considers you a stranger, an outsider undeserving of His hospitality, or an unlawful child who has no right to share in his father's estate and no title to his father's supervision and discipline.

26. Friends of the Cross, disciples of a crucified God, the mystery of the Cross is a mystery unknown to the Gentiles, repudiated by the Jews and spurned by both heretics and bad Catholics, yet it is the great mystery

which you must learn to practice at the school of Jesus Christ and which you can learn only at His School. You would look in vain for any philosopher who taught it in the Academies of ancient times; you would ask in vain either the senses or reason to throw any light on it, for Jesus alone, through His triumphant grace, is able to teach you this mystery and make you relish it.

Become proficient, therefore, in this super-eminent branch of learning under such a skillful Master. Having this knowledge, you will be possessed of all other branches of learning, for it surpassingly comprises them all. The Cross is our natural as well as our supernatural philosophy. It is our divine and mysterious theology. It is our philosopher-stone which, by dint of patience, is able to transmute the grossest of metals into precious ones, the sharpest pain into delight, poverty into wealth and the deepest humiliation into glory. He amongst you who knows how to carry his cross, though he know not A from B, towers above all others in learning.

Listen to the great St. Paul, after his return from the third heaven, where he was initiated into mysteries which even the Angels had not learned. He proclaims that he knows nothing, and wants to know nothing but Jesus Christ crucified (1 Cor. 2:2). You can rejoice, then, if you happen to be a poor man without any schooling or a poor woman deprived of intellectual attainments, for if you know how to suffer with joy you are far more learned than a doctor of the Sorbonne who is unable to suffer as you do.

27. You are members of Jesus Christ (1 Cor. 6:15; 12:27; Eph. 5:30). What an honor! But, also, what need for suffering this entails! When the Head is crowned with thorns, should the members be wearing a laurel of roses? When the Head is jeered at and covered with mud from Calvary's road, should its members be enthroned and sprayed with perfume? When the Head has no pillow on which to rest, should its members be reclining on soft feathers? What an unheard of monster

such a one would be! No, no, dear companions of the Cross make no mistake. The Christians you see around you, fashionably attired, super-sensitive, excessively haughty and sedate, are neither true disciples nor true members of the crucified Jesus. To think otherwise would be an insult to your thorn-crowned Head and His Gospel truth. My God! How many would-be Christians there are who imagine they are members of the Savior when in reality they are His most insidious persecutors, for while blessing themselves with the sign of the Cross, they crucify Him in their hearts.

If you are led by the spirit of Jesus and are living the same life with Him, your thorn-crowned Head, then you must look forward to nothing but thorns, nails, and lashes — in a word, to nothing but a cross. A real disciple needs to be treated as his Master was, as a member as its Head. And if the Head should offer you, as He offered St. Catherine of Siena, the choice between a crown of thorns and a crown of roses, do as she did and grasp the crown of thorns, fastening it tightly to your brow in the likeness of Jesus.

St. Maximilian Kolbe also chose the crown of thorns.

28. You are aware of the fact that you are living temples of the Holy Spirit (1 Cor. 6:19) and that, like living stones (1 Pet. 2: 5), you are to be placed by the God of love in the heavenly Jerusalem He is building. You must expect then to be shaped, cut, and chiseled under the hammer of the Cross, otherwise you would remain unpolished stone, of no value at all, to be disregarded and cast aside. Do not cause the hammer to recoil when

it strikes you. Yield to the chisel that is carving you and the hand that is shaping you. It may be that this skillful and loving Architect wants to make you a cornerstone in His eternal edifice, one of His most faithful portraits in the heavenly kingdom. So let Him see to it. He loves you, He really loves you; He knows what He is doing, He has experience. Love is behind every one of His effective strokes; nor will a single stroke miscarry unless your impatience deflects it.

29. At times the Holy Spirit compares the cross to a winnowing that clears the good grain from the chaff and dust (Matt. 3:13; Luke 3:17). Like grain in the winnowing, then, let yourself be shaken up and tossed about without resistance, for the Father of the household is winnowing you and will soon have you in His harvest. He also likens the cross to a fire whose intense heat burns rust off iron. God is a devouring fire (Deut. 4:24; 9:3; Heb. 13:29) dwelling in our souls through His Cross, purifying them yet not consuming them, exemplified in the past as a burning bush (Ex. 3:2-3). He likens it at times to the crucible of a forge where gold is refined (Prov. 17:3; Eccl. 2:5) and dross vanishes in smoke, but, in the processing, the precious metal must be tried by fire, while the baser constituents go up in smoke and flame. So, too, in the crucible of tribulation and temptation, true Friends of the Cross are purified by their constancy in suffering while the enemies of the Cross vanish in smoke by their impatience and murmurings.

30. Behold, dear Friends of the Cross, before you a great cloud of witnesses (Heb. 12:1-2) who silently testify that what I assert is the truth. For instance, consider Abel, a righteous man, who was slain by his own brother; then Abraham, a righteous man, who journeyed on the earth like a wanderer; Lot, a righteous man, who was driven from his own country; Jacob, a righteous man, who was persecuted by his own brother; Tobias, a righteous man, who was stricken with blindness; Job, a righteous man, who was pauperized, humiliated, and

covered with sores from the crown of his head to the soles of his feet.

31. Consider the countless Apostles and Martyrs who were bathed in their own blood; the countless Virgins and Confessors who were pauperized, humiliated, exiled, and cast aside. Like St. Paul they fervently proclaim: Behold our beloved Jesus, "Author and Finisher of the faith" (Heb. 12:2) we put in Him and in His Cross; it was necessary for Him to suffer and so to enter through the Cross into His glory (Luke 24:26)."

There at the side of Jesus consider Mary, who had never known either original or actual sin, yet whose tender, immaculate Heart was pierced with a sharp sword even to its very depths. If I had time to dwell on the Passion of Jesus and Mary, I could prove that our sufferings are naught compared to theirs.

32. Who, then, would dare claim exemption from the cross? Who would refuse to rush to the very place where he knows he will find a cross awaiting him? Who would refuse to borrow the words of the martyr, St. Ignatius: "Let fire and gallows, wild beasts, and all the torments of the devil assail me, so that I may rejoice in the possession of Jesus Christ."

33. If you have not the patience to suffer and the generosity to bear your cross like the chosen ones of God, then you will have to trudge under its weight, grumbling and fretting like the reprobates; like the two animals that dragged the Ark of the Covenant, lowing as they went (1 Kings 6:12); like Simon the Cyrenaean who unwillingly put his hand to the very Cross of Christ (Matt. 27:32; Mark 15:21), complaining while he carried it. You will be like the impenitent thief who, from the summit of his cross, plunged headlong into the depths of the abyss.

No, the cursed earth on which we live cannot give us happiness. We can see none too clearly in this benighted land. We are never perfectly calm on this troubled sea. We are never without warfare in a world of temptation and battlefields. We cannot escape scratches on a thorn-covered earth. Both elect and reprobate must bear their cross here, either willingly or unwillingly. Remember these words:

"Three crosses stand on Calvary's height
One must be chosen, so choose aright;
Like a saint you must suffer, or a penitent thief,
Or like a reprobate, in endless grief."

This means that if you will not suffer gladly as Jesus did, or patiently like the penitent thief, then you must suffer despite yourself like the impenitent thief. You will have to drain the bitterest chalice even to the dregs, and with no hope of relief through grace. You will have to bear the entire weight of your cross, and without the powerful help of Jesus Christ. Then, too, you will have that awful weight to bear which the devil will add to your cross, by means of the impatience the cross will cause you. After sharing the impenitent thief's unhappiness here on earth, you will meet him again in the fires of hell.

34. But if you suffer as you should, your cross will be a sweet yoke (Matt. 11:30), for Christ will share it with you. Your soul will be borne on it as on a pair of wings to the portals of Heaven. It will be the mast on your ship guiding you happily and easily to the harbor of salvation.

Carry your cross with patience: a cross patiently borne will be your light in spiritual darkness, for he knows naught who knows not how to suffer (Eccl. 34:9).

Carry your cross with joy and you will be inflamed with divine love, for only in suffering can we dwell in the pure love of Christ.

Roses are only gathered from among thorns. As wood is fuel for the fire, so too is the Cross the only fuel for God's love. Remember that saying we read in the "Following of Christ": "Inasmuch as you do violence to yourself," suffering patiently, "insofar do you advance" in divine love (Bk. 1, Chap. 15, 11). Do not expect anything great from those fastidious, slothful souls who refuse the Cross when it approaches and who do not go in search of any, when discretion allows. What are they but untilled soil, which can produce only thorns because it has not been turned up, harrowed, and furrowed by a judicious laborer. They are like stagnant water which is unfit for either washing or drinking.

Carry your cross joyfully and none of your enemies will be able to resist its conquering strength (Luke 21:15), while you yourself will enjoy its relish beyond compare. Yes, indeed, Brethren, remember that the real Paradise here on earth is to be found in suffering for Jesus. Ask the saints. They will tell you that they never tasted a banquet as delicious to the soul as when they underwent the severest torments. St. Ignatius the Martyr said: "Let all of the torments of the devil come upon me!" "Either suffering or death!" said St. Theresa, and St. Magdalen de Pazzi: "Not death but suffering!" "May I suffer and be despised for Thy sake," said St.

John of the Cross. In reading the lives of the saints we find many others speaking in identical terms.

Dear Brethren, believe the Word of God, for the Holy Spirit says: The Cross affords all kinds of joy to anyone without exception who suffers cheerfully for God (Jas. 1: 2). The joy that springs from the cross is keener than the joy which a poor person would experience if overladen with an abundance of riches, than the joy of a peasant who is made ruler of his country, than the joy of a commander-in-chief over the victories he has won, than the joy of a prisoner released from his fetters. In conclusion, let us picture the greatest joys to be found here below: the joy of a crucified person who knows how to suffer not only equals them but even surpasses them all.

35. Be glad, therefore, and rejoice when God favors you with one of His choicest crosses, for without realizing it you are being blessed with the greatest gift that Heaven has, the greatest gift of God. Yes, the cross is God's greatest gift. If you could only understand this, you would have Masses said, you would make novenas at the tombs of the saints; you would undertake long pilgrimages, as did the saints, to obtain this divine gift from Heaven.

36. The world claims it is madness on your part, degrading and stupid, rash and reckless. Let the world, in its blindness, say what it likes. This blindness, which is responsible for a merely human and distorted view of the cross, is a source of glory for us. For every time they provide us with crosses by mocking and persecuting us, they are simply offering us jewels, setting us upon a throne, and crowning us with laurels.

37. What I say is but little. Take all of the wealth and honors and scepters and brilliant diadems of monarchs and princes, says St. John Chrysostom, they are all insignificant compared with the glory of the Cross; it is greater even than the glory of the Apostles and the Sacred Writers. Enlightened by the Holy Spirit, this

saintly man goes as far as to say: "If I were given the preference, I would gladly leave Heaven to suffer for the God of Heaven. I would prefer the darkness of a dungeon to the thrones of the highest heaven and the heaviest of crosses to the glory of the Seraphim. Suffering for me is of greater value than the gift of miracles, the power to command the infernal spirits, to master the physical universe, to stop the sun in its course, and to raise the dead to life. Peter and Paul are more glorious in the shackles of a dungeon than in being lifted to the third heaven and presented with the keys to Paradise."

38. In fact, was it not the Cross that gave Jesus Christ "a name which is above all names; that in the name of Jesus every knee should bow of those that are in heaven, on earth, and under the earth" (Phil. 2:9-10). The glory of the one who knows how to suffer is so great that the radiance of his splendor rejoices heaven, angels, and men, and even the God of Heaven. If the saints in Heaven could still wish for something, they would want to return to earth so as to have the privilege of bearing a cross.

39. If the cross is covered with such glory on earth, how magnificent it must be in Heaven. Who could ever understand and tell the eternal weight of glory we are given when, even for a single instant, we bear a cross as a cross should be borne (2 Cor. 4:17)! Who could ever collate the glory that will be given in Heaven for the crosses and sufferings we carried for a year, perhaps even for a lifetime?

40. Evidently, my dear Friends of the Cross, heaven is preparing something grand for you, as you are told by a great Saint, since the Holy Ghost has united you so intimately to an object which the whole world so carefully avoids. Evidently, God wishes to make of you as many saints as you are Friends of the Cross, if you are faithful to your calling and dutifully carry your cross as Jesus Christ has carried His.

IV. In Christ-like Fashion

41. But mere suffering is not enough. For even the devil and the world have their martyrs. We must suffer and bear our crosses in the footsteps of Jesus. *Let him follow Me*: this means that we must bear our crosses as Jesus bore His. To help you do this, I suggest the following rules:

Fourteen Rules To Follow in Carrying One's Cross

42. First. Do not, deliberately and through your own fault, procure crosses for yourself. You must not do evil in order to bring about good. You should never try to bring discredit upon yourself by doing things improperly, unless you have a special inspiration from on high. Strive rather to imitate Jesus Christ, who did all things well (Mark 7:37), not out of self-love or vainglory, but to please God and to win over His fellow man. Even though you do the best you can in the performance of your duty, you will still have to contend with contradiction, persecution, and contempt, which Divine Providence will send you against your will and without your choice.

43. Second. Should your neighbor be scandalized, although without reason, at any action of yours which in itself is neither good nor bad, then, for the sake of charity, refrain from it, to avoid the scandal of the weak. This heroic act of charity will be of much greater worth than the thing you were doing or intended to do.

If, however, you are doing some beneficial or necessary thing for others and were unreasonably disapproved by a hypocrite or prejudiced person, then refer the matter to a prudent adviser, letting him judge of its expediency and necessity. Should his decision be favorable, you have only to continue and let these others talk, provided they take no means to prevent you. Under such circumstances, you have our Lord's answer to His disciples when they informed Him that Scribes and

Pharisees were scandalized at His words and deeds: "Let them alone; they are blind." (Matt. 15:14).

44. Third. Certain holy and distinguished persons have been asking for and seeking, or even, by eccentricities, bringing upon themselves crosses, disdain, and humiliation. Let us simply adore and admire the extraordinary workings of the Holy Spirit in these souls. Let us humble ourselves in the presence of this sublime virtue, without making any attempt to reach such heights, for compared with these racing eagles and roaring lions, we are simply fledglings and cubs.

45. Fourth. You can nevertheless and even should ask for the wisdom of the Cross, that sapid, experimental knowledge of the truth which, in the light of faith, shows us the deepest mysteries, among  others the mystery of the Cross. But this can be had only by dint of hard toil, profound humiliation, and fervent prayer. If you need that perfect spirit (Ps. 50:14) which enables us to bear the heaviest crosses with courage — that sweet, kindly spirit (Luke 11:13) which enables us to relish in the higher part of the soul things that are bitter and repulsive — that wholesome, upright spirit (Ps. 50:12) which seeks God and God alone — that all-embracing knowledge of the Cross — briefly that infinite treasure which gives the soul that knows how to make good use of it a share in the friendship of God (Wisdom 7:14). Ask for this wisdom, ask for it constantly, fervently, without hesitation or fear of not obtaining it. You will certainly obtain it and then see clearly, in the light of your own experience, how it is possible to desire, seek, and relish the Cross.

46. Fifth. If, inadvertently, you blunder into a cross, or even if you do so through your own fault, then hum-

ble yourselves interiorly under the mighty hand of God (1 Pet. 5:6), but do not worry over it. You might say to yourself: "Lord, there is another trick of my trade." If the mistake you made was sinful, accept the humiliation you suffer as punishment. But if it was not sinful, then humbly accept it in expiation of your pride. Often, actually very often, God allows His greatest servants, those who are far advanced in grace, to make the most humiliating mistakes. This humbles them in their own eyes and in the eyes of their fellow men. It prevents them from seeing and taking pride in the graces God bestows on them or in the good deeds they do, so that, as the Holy Spirit declares: "No flesh should glory in the sight of God" (1 Cor. 1:29).

47. Sixth. Be fully persuaded that, through the sin of Adam and through our own actual sins, everything within ourselves is vitiated, not only the senses of the body but even the powers of the soul. So much so that as soon as the mind, thus vitiated, takes delight in poring over some gift received from God, then the gift itself, or the act or the grace is tarnished and vitiated and God no longer favors it with His divine regard. Since looks and thoughts of the human mind can spoil man's best actions and God's choicest gifts, what about the acts which proceed from man's own will and which are more corrupt than the acts of the mind?

So we need not wonder, when God hides His own within the shadow of His countenance (Ps. 30:21), that they may not be defiled by the regards of their fellow men or by their own self-consciousness. What does not this jealous God allow and do to keep them hidden! How often He humiliates them! Into how many faults He permits them to fall! How often He allows them to be tempted as St. Paul was tempted (2 Cor. 12:7)! In what a state of uncertainty, perplexity, and darkness he leaves them! How wonderful God is in His saints, and in the means He takes to lead them to humility and holiness!

48. Seventh. Be careful not to imitate proud, self-centered zealots. Do not think that your crosses are tremendous, that they are tests of your fidelity to God and tokens of God's extraordinary love for you. This gesture has its source in spiritual pride. It is a snare quite subtle and beguiling, but full of venom. You ought to acknowledge, first, that you are so proud and sensitive that you magnify straws into rafters; scratches into deep wounds; rats into elephants; a meaningless word, a mere nothing, in truth, into an outrageous, treasonable insult. Second, you should acknowledge that the crosses God sends you are really and truly loving punishments for your sins, and not special marks of God's benevolence. Third, you must admit that He is infinitely lenient when He sends you some cross or humiliation, in comparison with the number and atrocity of your sins. For these sins should be considered in the light of the holiness of a God Whom you have offended and Who can tolerate nothing which is defiled; in the light of a God dying and weighted down with sorrow at the sight of your sins; in the light of an everlasting hell which you have deserved a thousand times, perhaps a hundred thousand times. Fourth, you should admit that the patience you put into suffering is more tinged than you think with natural human motives. You have only to note your little self-indulgences, your skillful seeking for sympathy, those confidences you so naturally make to friends or perhaps to your spiritual director, your quick, clever excuses, the murmurings, or rather the detractions so neatly worded, so charitably spoken against those who have injured you, the exquisite delight you take in dwelling on your misfortunes and that belief so characteristic of Lucifer, that you are somebody (Acts 8:9), and so forth. Why, I should never finish if I were to point out all the ways and by-ways human nature takes, even in its sufferings.

49. Eighth. Take advantage of your sufferings, and more so of the small ones than of the great. God consid-

ers not so much what we suffer as how we suffer. To suffer much, yet badly, is to suffer like reprobates. To suffer much, even bravely, but for a wicked cause, is to suffer as a martyr of the devil. To suffer much or little for the sake of God is to suffer like saints.

If it be right to say that we can choose our crosses, this is particularly true of the little and obscure ones as compared with the huge, conspicuous ones, for proud human nature would likely ask and seek for the huge, conspicuous crosses, even to the point of preferring them and embracing them. But to choose small, unnoticeable crosses and to carry them cheerfully requires the power of a special grace and unshakable fidelity to God. Do then as the storekeeper does with his merchandise: make a profit on every article; suffer not the loss of the tiniest fragment of the true Cross. It may be only the sting of a fly or the point of a pin that annoys you, it may be the little eccentricities of a neighbor, some unintentional slight, the insignificant loss of a penny, some little restlessness of soul, a slight physical weakness, a light pain in your limbs. Make a profit on every article as the grocer does, and you will soon become wealthy in God, as the grocer does in money, by adding penny to penny in his till. When you meet with the least contradiction, simply say: "Blessed be God! My God I thank you." Then treasure up in the till of God's memory the cross which has just given you a profit. Think no more of it, except to say: "Many thanks!" or, "Be merciful!"

50. Ninth. The love you are told to have for the Cross is not sensible love, for this would be impossible to human nature. It is important to note the three kinds of love: sensible love, rational love, and love that is faithful and supreme; in other words, the love that springs from the lower part of man, the flesh; the love that springs from the superior part, his reason; and the love that springs from the supreme part of man, from the summit of his soul, which is the intellect enlightened by faith.

51. God does not ask you to love the Cross with the will of the flesh. Since the flesh is the subject of evil and corruption, all that proceeds from it is evil and it cannot, of itself, submit to the will of God and His crucifying law. It was this aspect of His human nature which Our Lord referred to when He cried out, in the Garden of Olives: "Father,...not My will but Thine be done." (Luke 22:42). If the lower powers of Our Lord's human nature, though holy, could not love the Cross without interruption, then, with still greater reason, will our human nature, which is very much vitiated, repel it. At times, like many of the saints, we too may experience a feeling of even sensible joy in our sufferings, but that joy does not come from the flesh, though it is in the flesh. It flows from our superior powers, so completely filled with the divine joy of the Holy Spirit, that it spreads to our lower powers. Thus a person who is undergoing the most unbearable torture is able to say: "My heart and my flesh have rejoiced in the living God" (Ps. 83:3).

52. There is another love for the Cross which I call rational, since it springs from the higher part of man, his reason. This love is wholly spiritual. Since it arises from the knowledge of the happiness there is in suffering for God, it can be and really is perceived by the soul. It also gives the soul inward strength and joy. Though this rational and perceptible joy is beneficial, even very beneficial, it is not an indispensable part of joyous, divine suffering.

53. This is why there is another love, which the masters of the spiritual life call the love of the summit and highest point of the soul, and which the philosophers call the love of the intellect. When we possess this love, even though we experience no sensible joy or rational pleasure, we love and relish, in the light of pure faith, the cross we must bear, even though the lower part of our nature may often be in a state of warfare and alarm and may moan and groan, weep and sigh for relief; and thus we repeat with Jesus Christ: "Father,...

not My will but Yours be done" (Luke 22:42), or with the
Blessed Virgin: "Behold the handmaid of the Lord, be it
done to me according to Thy word" (Luke 1:38).

It is with one of these two higher loves that we
should accept and love our cross.

54. Tenth. Be resolved then, dear Friends of the
Cross, to suffer every kind of cross without excepting or
choosing any: all poverty, all injustice, all temporal loss,
all illness, all humiliation, all contradiction, all calumny, all spiritual dryness, all desolation, all interior and
exterior trials. Keep saying: "My heart is ready, O God,
my heart is ready" (Ps. 56:8). Be ready to be forsaken by
men and angels, and, seemingly, by God Himself. Be
ready to be persecuted, envied, betrayed, calumniated,
discredited, and forsaken by everyone. Be ready to
undergo hunger, thirst, poverty, nakedness, exile,
imprisonment, the gallows, and all kinds of torture,
even though you are innocent of everything with which
you may be charged. What if you were cast out of your
own home like Job and Saint Elizabeth of Hungary;
thrown, like this saint, into the mire; or dragged upon a
manure pile like Job, malodorous and covered with
ulcers, without anyone to bandage your wounds, without a morsel of bread, never refused to a horse or a dog?
Add to these dreadful misfortunes all of the temptations
which God allows the devil to prey upon you, without
pouring into your soul the least feeling of consolation.

Firmly believe that this is the summit of divine glory and real happiness for a true, perfect Friend of the Cross.

55. Eleventh. For proper suffering, form the pious habit of considering four things:

First, the Eye of God. God is like a great king, who from the height of a tower observes with satisfaction his soldier in the midst of the battle and praises his valor. What is it on earth that attracts God's attention? Kings and emperors on their thrones? He often looks at them with nothing but contempt. Brilliant victories of a nation's armies, precious stones, any such things that are great in the sight of men? "What is great to men is an abomination before God" (Luke 16:15). What then does God look upon with pleasure and delight? What is He asking the Angels about, and even the devils? It is about the man who is fighting for Him against riches, against the world, hell and himself; the man who is cheerfully carrying his cross. Hast thou not seen upon earth that great wonder which the heavens consider with admiration? said the Lord to Satan; "hast thou considered My servant Job" (Job 2:3), "who is suffering for Me?

56. Second, the Hand of God. Every disorder in nature, from the greatest to the smallest, is the work of His almighty Hand. The Hand that devastates an army of a hundred thousand (4 Kings 19:35) will make a leaf drop from a tree, and a hair fall from your head (Luke 21:18). The Hand that was laid so heavily upon Job is particularly light when it touches you with some little trial. This Hand fashions day and night, sun and darkness, good and evil. God permits the sin which provokes you; He is not the cause of its malice, although He does allow the act.

If anyone, then, treats you as Semei treated King David (2 Kings 16:5-11), loading you with insults and casting stones at you, say to yourself: "I must not mind; I must not take revenge, for this is an ordinance of God.

I know that I have deserved every abuse and it is only right that God punish me. Desist, my hands, and strike not; desist, my tongue, and speak not; the person who injures me by word or deed is an ambassador, mercifully sent by God to punish me as His love alone knows how. Let us not incur His justice by assuming His right to vengeance. Let us not despise His mercy by resisting the affectionate strokes of His lash, lest, for His vengeance, He should remand us to the rigorous justice of eternity."

Consider how God bears you up with one Hand, of infinite power and wisdom, while with the other He chastises you. With the one He deals out death, while with the other He dispenses life. He humbles you and raises you up. With both arms, He reaches sweetly and mightily (Wisdom 8:1) from the beginning of your life to its end. Sweetly: by not allowing you to be tempted or afflicted beyond your strength. Mightily: by favoring you with a powerful grace, proportioned to the vehemence and duration of your temptation or affliction. Mightily: — and the spirit of His holy Church bears witness — "He is your stay on the brink of a precipice, your guide along a misleading road, your shade in the scorching heat, your raiment in the pouring rain or the biting cold. He is your conveyance when you are utterly exhausted, your help in adversity, your staff on the slippery way. He is your port of refuge when, in the throes of a tempest, you are threatened with ruin and shipwreck."

57. Third, consider the Wounds and Sorrows of our crucified Jesus. Hear what He Himself has to say: "All ye that pass along the thorny and crucifying way I had to follow, look and see. Look with the eyes of your body; look with the eye of contemplation, and see if your poverty, nakedness, disgrace, sorrow, and desolation are like unto Mine. Behold Me, innocent as I am, then will you complain, you who are guilty?" (Lam. 1:12).

The Holy Spirit tells us, by the mouth of the

Apostles, that we should keep our eyes on Jesus Crucified (Gal. 3:1), and arm ourselves with this thought of Him (1 Pet. 4:1), which is our most powerful and most penetrating weapon against all our enemies. When you are assailed by poverty, disrepute, sorrow, temptation, or any other cross, arm yourselves with this shield, this breastplate, this helmet, this two-edged sword (Eph. 6:12-18), that is, with the thought of Jesus crucified. There is the solution to your every problem, the means you have to vanquish all your enemies.

58. Fourth, lift up your eyes, behold the beautiful crown that awaits you in Heaven if you carry your cross as you should. That was the reward which kept patriarchs and prophets strong in faith under persecution. It gave heart to the Apostles and martyrs in their labors and torments. Patriarchs used to say as Moses had said: "We would rather be afflicted with the people of God," so as to enjoy eternal happiness with Him, "than to have the pleasure of sin for a short time" (Heb. 11:25-26). The prophets repeated David's words: "We suffer great persecutions on account of the reward" (Ps. 68: 8; 118:112). The Apostles and martyrs voiced the sentiments of St. Paul: "We are, as it were, men appointed to death: we are made a spectacle to the world, and to angels, and to men," by our sufferings "being made the offscouring of the world," (1 Cor. 4:9-13), "by reason of the exceeding and eternal weight of glory, which this momentary and light tribulation worketh in us" (2 Cor. 4:17).

Let us see and listen to the angels right above us: "Be careful not to forfeit the crown that is set aside for you if you bravely bear the cross which is given you. If you do not bear it well, someone will bear it in your stead and will take your crown. All the saints warn us: fight courageously, suffer patiently, and you will be given an everlasting kingdom." Let us hear Jesus: "To him only will I give My reward who shall suffer and overcome through patience" (Apoc. 2,6; 11,17; 3,5; 21,7).

Let us lower our eyes and see the place we deserve, the place that awaits us in hell, in the company of the wicked thief and the reprobate, if we go through suffering as they did, resentful and bent on revenge. Let us exclaim after St. Augustine: "Burn, O Lord, cut, carve, and divide me in this world, in punishment for my sins, provided You pardon them in eternity."

59. Twelfth. Never murmur or deliberately complain about any created thing that God may use to afflict you. It is important to note the three kinds of complaints that may arise when misfortune assails you. The first is natural and involuntary. This happens when the human body moans and groans, sobs and sighs and weeps. If, as I said, the higher point of the soul submits to the will of God, there is no sin. The second is rational. Such is the case when we complain and disclose our hardship to some superior or physician who is able to remedy it. This complaint may be an imperfection, if too eagerly made, but it is no sin. The third is sinful. This happens when a person complains of others either to rid himself of the suffering they cause him, or to take revenge. Or else when he wilfully complains about the sorrow he must bear and shows signs of grief and impatience.

60. Thirteenth. Whenever you are given a cross, be sure to embrace it with humility and gratitude. If God, in His infinite goodness, favors you with a cross of some

importance, be sure to thank him in a special way and have others join you in thanking him. Do as that poor woman did who, through an unjust lawsuit, lost everything she owned. She immediately offered the last few pennies she had, to have a Mass said in thanksgiving to Almighty God for the good fortune that had come to her.

61. Fourteenth. If you wish to be worthy of the best crosses, those that are not of your choice, then, with the help of a prudent director, take on some that are voluntary.

Suppose you have a piece of furniture that you do not need but prize. Give it to some poor person, and say to yourself: "Why should I have things I do not need, when Jesus is destitute?"

Do you dislike certain kinds of food, the practice of some particular virtue, or some offensive odor? Taste this food, practice this virtue, endure this odor, conquer yourself.

Is your affection for some person or thing too ardent and tender? Keep away, deprive yourself, break away from things that appeal to you.

Have you that natural tendency to see and be seen, to be doing things or going some place? Mind your eyes and hold your tongue, stop right where you are and keep to yourself.

Do you feel a natural aversion to some person or thing? Rise above yourself by keeping near them.

62. If you are truly Friends of the Cross, then, without your knowing it, love, which is always ingenious, will discover thousands of little crosses to enrich you. Then you need not fear self-conceit which often accompanies the patient endurance of conspicuous crosses, and since you have been faithful in a few things, the Lord will keep His promise and set you over many things (Matt. 25:21, 23): over many graces He will grant you; over many crosses He will send you; over much glory He will prepare for you...

The Triumph of the Cross

I

The Cross in mystery
Is veiled for us below;
Without great light to see,
Who shall its splendor know?
Alone the lofty mind
Shall this high secret trace;
And none shall heaven find
Who grasps it not by grace.

II

Nature the Cross abhors;
Reason gives it a frown;
The learned man ignores
It. Satan tears it down.
Despite a pious art,
Even the fervent soul
Oft takes it not to heart,
But plays the liar's role.

III

Essential is the Tree,
And we who know its cost
Must mount to Calvary
Or languish and be lost.
As Saint Augustine states
With outcry ominous,
We all are reprobates
Unless God chastens us.

IV
Its Necessity

One road to heaven runs:
The highway of the Cross.

It was the royal Son's,
His road to life from loss.
And every stone of it
That guides the pilgrim's feet
Is chiseled fair to fit
In Zion's holy street.

V

Vain is the victory
Of him who, conquering
The world, lacks mastery
Of self through suffering;
Vain if he has not Christ,
Slain Christ, for exemplar,
Or spurns the Sacrificed
For dread of wound and scar.

VI

Its Victories

Christ's Cross, restraining hell,
Has conquered Eden's curse,
Stormed Satan's citadel,
And won the universe.
Now to His faithful band
He gives that weapon bright
To arm both heart and hand
Against the evil sprite.

VII

In this auspicious Sign
Thou shalt be conqueror,
Said He to Constantine,
Who that proud Standard bore;
A glorious augury,
Of whose prodigious worth
The records all agree
In heaven and on earth!

VIII

Its Glory and Merit

Despite deceitful sense
And reason's fickle shift,
The Cross with confidence
We take as Truth's own gift.
A princess there we see
In whom, let faith confess,
We find all charity,
Grace, wisdom, holiness.

IX

God's love could not resist
Such beauty or its plea,
Which bade Him keep a tryst
With our humanity.
Coming to earth, He said:
This, Lord, and nothing more:
Thy saving Cross imbed
Here in My bosom's core.

X

He took it, found it fair,
An object not of shame
But honor, made it share
His love's most tender flame.
From childhood's morning hour
His longing kept in sight
As beauty would a flower
The Cross of His delight.

XI

At last in its caress
Long sought for eagerly,
He died of tenderness
And love's totality.

That dear supreme baptism
For which His heart had cried,
The Cross became His chrism,
Love's object undenied.

XII

Christ called the Fisherman
A Satan scandalous
When he but winced to scan
What Christ would bear for us.
Christ's Cross we may adore,
His Mother we may not.
O mystery and more!
O marvel beyond thought!

XIII

This Cross, now scattered wide
On earth, shall one day rise
Transported, glorified,
To the celestial skies.
Upon a cloudy height
The Cross, full-brillianted,
Shall, by its very sight,
Judge both the quick and dead.

XIV

Revenge, the Cross will cry
Against its sullen foes;
Pardon and joy on high
And blessedness for those
Of proved fidelity
In the immortal throng,
Singing its victory
With universal song.

XV

In life the saints aspired
To nothing but the Cross;
'Twas all that they desired,
Counting all else but loss.
Each one, in discontent
With such afflictions sore
As chastening heaven sent,
Condemned himself to more.

XVI

St. Peter, prison-chained,
Had greater glory there
Than when at Rome he gained
The first Christ-Vicar's chair.
Saint Andrew, faithful, cried:
O good Cross, let me yield
To thee and in thee hide,
Where death in Life is sealed.

XVII

See how the great St. Paul
Depicts with meagre gloss
His rapture mystical,
But glories in the Cross.
More admirable far,
More merit-rich is he
Behind his dungeon bar
Than in his ecstasy.

XVIII
Its Effects

Without a Cross, the soul
Is cowardly and tame;
Like fire to a coal
The Cross sets it aflame.
One who has suffered not,

In ignorance is bound;
Only in pain's hard lot
Is holy wisdom found.

XIX

A soul untried is poor
In value; new, untrained,
With destiny unsure
And little wisdom gained.
O sweetness sovereign
Which the afflicted feels
When pleased that to his pain
No human solace steals!

XX

'Tis by the Cross alone
God's blessing is conferred
And His forgiveness known
In the absolving word.
He wants all things to bear
The mark of that great seal;
Without it, nought is fair
To Him, no beauty real.

XXI

Wherever place is given
The Cross, things once profane
Become instinct with heaven
And shed away their stain.
On breast and brow, God's sign,
Worn proudly for His sake,
Will bless with Power divine
Each task we undertake.

XXII

It is our surety,

Our one protection,
Our hope's white purity,
Our soul's perfection.
So precious is its worth
That angels fain would bring
The blest soul back to earth
To share our suffering.

XXIII

This Sign has such a charm
That at the altar-stone
The priest can God disarm
And draw Him from His throne.
Over the sacred Host
This mighty Sign he plays,
Signals the Holy Ghost,
And the Divine obeys.

XXIV

With this adorable Sign
A fragrance is diffused
Most exquisite and fine,
A perfume rarely used.
The consecrated priest
Makes Him this offering
As incense from the East,
Meet crown for heaven's King.

XXV

Eternal Wisdom still
Sifts our poor human dross
For one whose heart and will
Is worthy of the Cross
Still seeks one spirit rare
Whose every pulse and breath
Is fortitude to bear
The Christ-Cross until death.

Ardent Apostrophe

XXVI

O Cross, let me be hushed;
In speech I thee abase.
Let my presumption, crushed,
Its insolence erase.
Since thee I have received
Imperfectly, in part,
Forgive me, friend aggrieved,
For my unwilling heart!

XXVII

Dear Cross, here in this hour,
I bow to thee in awe.
Abide with me in power
And teach me all thy law.
My princess, let me glow
With ardor in thine arms;
Grant me to chastely know
The secret of thy charms.

XXVIII

In seeing thee so fair,
I hunger to possess
Thy beauty, but I dare
Not in my faithlessness.
Come, mistress, by thy will
Arouse my feeble soul
And I will give thee still
A heart renewed and whole.

XXIX

For life I choose thee now
My pleasure, honor, friend,
Sole object of my vow,
Sole joy to which I tend.

For mercy's sake, print, trace
Yourself upon my heart,
My arm, my forehead, face;
And not one blush will start.

XXX

Above all I possess
I choose thy poverty;
And for my tenderness
Thy sweet austerity.
Now be thy folly wise
And all thy holy shame
As grandeur in my eyes,
My glory and my fame.

XXXI

When, by your majesty
And for your glory's sake,
You shall have vanquished me,
That conquest I shall take
As final victory,
Though worthy not to fall
Beneath thy blows, or be
A mockery to all.

— *English Rendition by Clifford J. Laube, Litt.D.*

Profile of Cardinal Arinze

Cardinal Francis Arinze is one of those rare persons who can communicate with others by simply looking at them. The first thing that impresses one about him is the smile in his eyes, a concrete sign of a life which is dedicated to sharing the love of Christ with people.

Such a gift for communication serves the cardinal well in his work as President of the Pontifical Council for Inter-Religious Dialogue, a post he has held since 1985 — the same year in which he was named cardinal by Pope John Paul II. He serves as a member of the Roman Curia, the Holy Father's direct staff.

Among other positions, His Eminence is also a member of the Executive Committees of the Congregation for the Doctrine of the Faith, the Congregation for the Evangelization of Peoples, and the Pontifical Council for the Laity, and he is one of the five cardinals on the presiding council of the Holy Father's central coordinating committee for the Jubilee Year 2000.

Cardinal Arinze was born in 1932 in Onitsha, Nigeria, from a family of African traditional religion. He was baptized Catholic at the age of 9.

"God's grace works in ways we do not understand,"

he says, recalling his childhood. "I was very impressed by that parish priest who baptized me, and after watching him for a long time, I felt the desire of becoming myself a priest." [The priest is now Blessed Cyprian Tansi.]

From that moment on, his path was the one indicated by Christ. He entered the seminary at the age of 13, was ordained a priest in 1958 and a bishop in 1965.

He was on the cutting edge of the evangelization movement in Nigeria. After Nigeria's civil war (1967-1970), Cardinal Arinze, while Archbishop of Onitsha and, later, President of the Nigerian Council of Bishops, was a major contributor to the mobilization of the native clergy, religious, and laity, and he helped in the evangelization which doubled the number of Catholics in the country in less than 14 years.

By the time Cardinal Arinze was called to Rome by the Holy Father in April 1984, 65.6% of the population of the Onitsha Archdiocese was Catholic, while the national average of Catholics was only 11.2% in a population of 89 million.

As an experienced leader in the Church and a man rooted in his Nigerian background, he understands the spiritual attack on the family, the importance of the parish, the potential of the laity, and the art of evangelization.

His Eminence is also a leading television personality in the United States and throughout the world. He is televised on the Apostolate for Family Consecration's Family Covenant, Spirit of John Paul II, and Be Not Afraid Family Hour series, which are shown throughout the world. Most importantly, Cardinal Arinze is a man of God, a man on fire for the Church and for the conversion of souls — a person for others!

Parts of this biography were taken from a cover story in Our Sunday Visitor.

68. Alone with God
*by Francis
Cardinal Arinze*

Apostolate for Family Consecration's
Peace of Heart Forum

Please obtain the video series #126-3365VK (set of 8 half-hour programs), which guides you through this section. We suggest that you gather a group of people to meet weekly to play the corresponding videotape and to discuss the material that you prayed and meditated on for the past week. You can use one of the following video/reading plans. See pages 588–613 for more details about the Peace of Heart Forums.

4-Week Video/Reading Plan

Session 1
Video 126-3351V *(show 126-3352 & 126-3353)*.
Read Introduction through Chapter 6 before the next session.

Session 2
Video 126-3354V *(show 126-3355 & 126-3356)*.
Read Chapters 7–11 before the next session.

Session 3
Video 126-3358V *(show 126-3359 & 126-3360)*.
Read Chapters 12–17 before the next session.

Session 4
Video 126-3361V *(show 126-3362 & 126-3363)*.

8-Week Video/Reading Plan

Session 1
Video 126-3351V *(show 126-3352)*.
Read Introduction through Chapter 3 before the next session.

Session 2
Video 126-3351V *(show 126-3353)*.
Read Chapters 4–6 before the next session.

Session 3
Video 126-3354V *(show 126-3355)*.
Read Chapters 7–8 before the next session.

Session 4
Video 126-3354V *(show 126-3356)*.
Read Chapters 9-11 before the next session.

Session 5
Video 126-3358V *(show 126-3359)*.
Read Chapters 12–13 before the next session.

Session 6
Video 126-3358V *(show 126-3360)*.
Read Chapters 14–15 before the next session.

Session 7
Video 126-3361V *(show 126-3362.*
Read Chapters 16-17 before the next session.

Session 8
Video 126-3361V *(show 126-3363.*

Complete video set 126-3365VK.

CONTENTS

Introduction

This little book is the fruit of retreat conferences which I gave to various groups of priests, brothers, sisters, and lay people between 1966 and 1984. In that period, several people encouraged me to put the conferences in writing. I finally took occasion of such a request from the Brothers of St. Stephen, in 1984, to prepare this book.

My hope is that the book will be found to be a useful companion to clerics, religious, and lay people who are doing long or short retreat periods, or who simply want suggestions for spiritual reading or meditation.

I express my gratitude to His Grace, Archbishop Stephen N. Ezeanya, Archbishop of Onitsha, for writing the Foreword to the book, and to Monsignor Hypolite Adigwe and his assistants for all the help and services needed to turn a hand-written document into a book.

Francis Card. Arinze
Vatican City
August 29, 1986

Foreword

In his Introduction to this book, His Eminence Francis Cardinal Arinze has defined a spiritual retreat as "a time set apart to listen to God, to be with Jesus, to give our souls time for spiritual rest, spiritual check up, or stock-taking or renewal." It is with a view to providing the priest, the religious and the laity with an aid towards making a successful retreat that the author has produced this work.

The topics are so well chosen and the book so carefully organized that the work covers the essential aspects of our Christian life on which one should reflect constantly. It recalls why man was created, the difficulties the soul encounters on its road to sanctity, the ways and means of overcoming them through the Sacraments and the sacramentals, and the practice of virtues.

Special emphasis is made on the religious vows of poverty, chastity, and obedience. Closely linked up with the vows are the practice of humility, constant prayer, the virtue of charity, and zeal in the apostolate. From the Introduction to the Conclusion, the author stresses the importance of devotion to the Blessed Virgin at every stage of the work.

With the publication of this book, His Eminence Cardinal Arinze has made yet another invaluable and timely contribution to the sanctification of souls. *Alone with God* is a book in which His Eminence has put together in a condensed form his years of experience gathered as a dedicated Shepherd and Pastor of souls during his ministry as a retreat preacher for all classes of people—priests, the religious, and the laity. It is also a fruit of years of scholarly work nourished and sustained by a life of close familiarity with our knowledge of the people and the nation.

Alone with God is a book for everyone—priests, the religious, and the laity. It is obvious that the author has this in view. Priests in particular, who are often charged with the mission of preaching retreats and giving spiritual direction to souls will find this book a very useful companion.

I therefore very warmly commend this book and recommend it to the entire people of God as a great help towards personal sanctification as we journey towards the Promised Land.

† Stephen N. Ezeanya
Archbishop of Onitsha
Feast of the Presentation
of the Blessed Virgin Mary
May 21, 1986

I. Are You Ready for a Spiritual Retreat?

A Time to Reflect

We know we have been working for God. We know that there is much work to be done in our parishes, schools, and church organizations. We know that there are many letters on our desks to be answered.

But we also know that the Lord wants us to listen to Him even more than He wants us to work for Him. We know that having too much to do and too little time to do it has its dangers—the danger to forget the God of works while concentrating on the works of God, the danger of apostolic noise-making and intense activity without much apostolic fruit or life.

A spiritual retreat is necessary as a time set apart to listen to God, to be with Jesus, to give our souls time for spiritual rest, spiritual check-up, or stock-taking or renewal.

Our daily work generally does not leave us enough time for a long conversation with God. The Christian life and the religious profession (and for priest the priestly vocation) are so precious and sacred that everything should be done to keep the flame of charity burning bright. Laxity can easily smuggle itself into our daily lives. Our resolutions can be forgotten. Our predominant fault can gradually reassert itself more and more. We can even go a little off our proper course. A retreat period is one of the best helps towards giving our spiritual life this needed attention.

Spiritual Rest

Jesus tells His disciples to come aside to a lonely place and rest awhile (cf. Mk. 6:31). A retreat is a time of rest, a type of spiritual sabbath rest or refreshment period. It should be marked by calm, joy, silence, and peace.

Your Cooperation is Required

Your retreat cannot succeed without you. You will be expected to listen to the talks, to take notes if you wish, and above all to reflect and to pray. It is you who are making the retreat. The retreat preacher is only trying to help you with suggestions.

The Gospels and the rest of Holy Scripture should be your companions. The documents of Vatican II, your Congregation's Constitutions and Rules for a religious, and, if there is still time, a suitable spiritual reading book are advisable.

Silence, interior and exterior, is a necessary condition for reflection and prayer. Special effort should be made at individual prayer, in addition to liturgical and other communal prayers.

A retreat should ordinarily end with some resolutions. These are useful as points of reference for the future. They can arise during the retreat, as you listen to the inspirations of the Holy Spirit.

We beg our Blessed Mother, Mary Immaculate, to obtain for us the grace to do this retreat with generosity and fidelity.

II. The End of Man

The Purpose is Most Important

The most important question we can ask about most things is to ask the purpose of their existence. Why do human beings exist? What is the end of man? What is man made for? What is it that, when we have got, we then relax, knowing that we have attained the purpose of our existence?

Unless a person has a clear idea of why he exists (and when I say he, I mean he or she), his journey through life is likely to remain aimless or wrongly aimed. Unless the five soccer forwards clearly see the goal posts of the opposing side, they are not likely to score a goal. The most important thing when a person is rushing to a place is that he should know to what place he is going and how he can reach there.

It is not enough to be in a hurry and to be going. It is also necessary, indeed vital, to know where one is going. Otherwise you may indeed run very well, but off the track. In the Olympic games you may indeed run very fast, but if you run outside the marked tracks and outside the given moment, you get no medal. If you were asked in an examination to write a composition on a railway engine and you wrote on the life story of a butterfly, how many marks do you suppose you would get? Nothing! Zero! You indeed wrote very well, but off the point!

We need to know why man exists in order to make sure that our lives are not wasted. Every creature has a purpose for its existence. Man surely does have.

Man is Made for Happiness

Man wants to be happy. Man is made for happiness. The monk and the nun enter the monastery because they want to be happy. Doctors are doctors because they want to be happy. So also teachers. So also Brothers of St. Stephen. The thief steals because he wants to be happy. For the same reason the thief kills a man and takes his 504 Peugeot car. The child who steals his mother's fish wants to be happy. The man who steals another man's wife wants to be happy. All these people want to be happy.

In What Does Happiness Consist?

But not all these people are happy. All the students who tackle a problem in arithmetic want to get the correct answer and are sincere. But not all of them get the correct answer. The correct answer is only one. The wrong answers are as many as there are ignorant students who do not know arithmetic!

All the mistakes which people have ever made, or will ever make, on the purpose of man's existence, are the wrong answers on where man's happiness lies. All these wrong answers are summarized under three headings by St. John when he warns us not to love the world nor the things that are in the world, for all that is in the world is the concupiscence of the flesh, the concupiscence of the eyes, and the pride of life (cf. 1 John 2:15-16). For the concupiscence of the flesh, substitute pleasure, whether of sex or of eating and drink. For the concupiscence of the eyes, substitute possessions. And for the pride of life, substitute power. There you have the three P's = P.P.P.: pleasure, possessions and power. These are the wrong reasons for man's existence. These are the three roads that do not lead to happiness for man. People have tried to get happiness out of one of them, or even of all three. Let us examine each more closely.

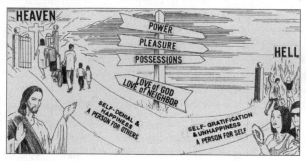

Solomon—A Good, Practical Example

Solomon had plenty of possessions, pleasure and power. Did he become happy? Let us see. When God told Solomon to request whatever he would, Solomon asked for wisdom so that he could govern the numerous people he inherited from his father David. God was pleased with Solomon's prayer because Solomon asked for wisdom and not for possessions, nor for military victory. So God promised to give him peace with all neighbors, abundance of wealth, and unheard-of wisdom. Solomon was so wise that when two women came to him for judgment, each of them claiming to be the mother of a live baby and holding that the other woman was the mother of the dead baby, Solomon solved the problem by wisely directing that each of the two babies be divided in two with a sword and each of the women receive a half. The real mother of the live baby emerged immediately. Was this Solomon happy? Let us see what happened to him.

Happiness is Not in Possessions

Can human happiness lie in the accumulation of possessions? Let us see. Solomon was fabulously rich. Read Ecclesiastes 2:1-11. "I did great things: built myself palaces, planted vineyards... I amassed silver and gold, the treasures of kings and provinces; acquired singing men and singing women and every human luxury, chest on chest of it. So I grew great, greater than anyone in Jerusalem before me; nor did my wisdom leave me. I denied my eyes nothing they desired... What vanity it all is, and chasing of the wind! There is nothing to be gained under the sun" (Eccles. 2:5-11). "Vanity of vanities. All is vanity! For all his toil, his toil under the sun, what does man gain by it?" (Eccles. 1:2-3).

Solomon had all those fantastic possessions. But they did not make him happy. Solomon was so rich that when the Son of God wanted to teach the apostles not to worry over material possessions, He gave the example of Solomon. He said that not even Solomon in all his regalia was robed or arrayed as the lilies of the field or the birds of the air (cf. Mt. 6: 25-34). Jesus is telling His Apostles to put their happiness, not in possessions, but in Divine providence.

Let us take an example more recent than that of Solomon. I shall withhold the names of the people involved. In 1923 a very important meeting was held at the X Hotel in Chicago. Attending this meeting were nine of the world's most successful financiers. Those present were: the President of the largest independent Steel Company, the President of the greatest Utility Company, the President of the largest Gas Company, the greatest Wheat Speculator, the President of the New York Stock Exchange, a member of the President's cabinet, the greatest "Bear" in Wall Street, the head of the world's Greatest Monopoly, and the President of the Bank of International Settlements.

Certainly we must admit that here were gathered a group of the world's most successful men, or at least men who had found the secret of "making money." Very well, 25 years later let us see where these men are.

The President of the largest independent Steel Company, Mr. B., went bankrupt and lived on borrowed money for five years before he died. The President of the greatest Utility Company, Mr. C., died a fugitive from justice and penniless in a foreign land. The President of the largest Gas Company, Mr. D., is now insane. The greatest Wheat Speculator, Mr. E., died abroad, insolvent. The President of the New York Stock Exchange, Mr. E., was recently released from Sing Sing Penitentiary. The member of the President's Cabinet, Mr. F., was pardoned from prison so he could die at home. The greatest "Bear" in Wall Street, Mr. G., committed suicide. The head of the Greatest Monopoly, Mr H., committed suicide. The President of the Bank of International Settlements, Mr. J., committed suicide.

All these men had learned well the art of making money, but not one of them seemed to be clear on the purpose of man's existence. Vanity of vanities. All is vanity...except...(complete it yourself!).

It is mistaken to think that the more money you have, the happier you will be. It does not follow. Of course if you have plenty of money there are many things you can do. You can have big houses in your village, at Onitsha, at Enugu, in Lagos, in London, in Los Angelus. Yes. You can have a private jet and fly from airport to airport. You can spend your holidays on the Alps, at the most expensive hotels. You can throw parties and squandermaniac feasts at the least provocation. But it is also my duty to tell you of some of your probable headaches: hypertension, obesity, more and more attention from the tax department of the government, nocturnal or even daylight visits by experienced thieves, envy and jealousy of many people, worry, accusations true and false, and probably finally prison or worse.

Just think back over the history of our country in the past 20 years. Where are now all those great ones who once were famous as rich people? Are you aware that as a poor Brother of St. Stephen you are most probably happier than most of them? Many rich people could smoke twenty-naira notes or hundred-dollar bills as cigarettes. Some husbands and wives are sitting on money. But happiness is far from them. Their home is like a hot oven. Their minds are not at rest. Their sleep is short and generally disturbed. They frequently consult the heart specialist .

Do not misunderstand me. Money is not bad in itself. And all rich people are not dishonest or irreligious. But one thing is certain: Money is not the road to happiness.

Happiness is Not in Pleasure

Other people have placed their happiness in pleasure. Although listening to good music is a pleasure, many people find that rather too sophisticated. They are more pedestrian in their tastes. They are looking for the pleasure of the taste or for pleasure of sex. Let us examine whether happiness has been found in either of these.

Those who place their happiness in pleasure of the taste concentrate on eating and drinking. And they do it to excess. The results are well known: tiredness, inability to study, drunkenness, car accident, useless or shameful words, disgrace. And no matter how much food or drink you may possess, you are not likely to be as rich as Solomon: "The daily provisions for Solomon were: thirty measures of fine flour and sixty measures of meal, ten fattened oxen, twenty free-grazing oxen, one hundred sheep, besides deer and gazelles, roebucks and fattened cuckoos" (1 Kings 5:2-3). Solomon had peace, security, abundance, and daily banqueting with his big household. Did he then become happy? Vanity of vanities.

Do you really believe that if you had all the types of food and wine you ever desired, you would then be happy? Even if you ate and drank with moderation, you would become hungry again the following day. And if you ate so much that you could not run if anyone chased you, and if you continued like that often, then not only will you not be happy, but some of the following things will begin to happen. You will have a headache. Your sleep at night will be poor. You will dream heavily. You will not be a good student or worker. You will get fat and the doctor will tell you things you would not like to hear. The doctor will tell you that your heart is overworked because of vast expanses of unmortified flesh. More seriously still, you will be spiritually weak because your spirit is not controlling your appetite for food and drink. Food is for man, not man for food.

Other people place their happiness in the pleasure of sex. Let us take the example of Solomon again. He looked for women. He loved them. He got them, not one or two, but a whole one thousand: 700 wives of royal rank in grade A, and 300 concubines in grade B. And what happened to Solomon. Read the Book of Kings. "King Solomon loved many foreign women: not only Pharaoh's daughter but Moabites, Edomites, Sidonians, and Hittites, from those peoples of whom Yahweh had said to the Israelites, 'You are not to go to them nor they to you, or they will surely sway your hearts to their own gods.' But Solomon was deeply attached to them. He had seven hundred wives of royal rank, and three hundred concubines. When Solomon grew old his wives swayed his heart to other gods; and his heart was not wholly with Yahweh his God as his father David's had been. Solomon became a follower of Astarte, the goddess of the Sidonians, and of Milcom, the Ammonite abomination. He did what was displeasing to Yahweh, and was not a wholehearted follower of Yahweh, as his father David had been. Then it was that Solomon built a high place for Chemosh the god of Moab on the mountain to the east of Jerusalem, and to Milcom the god of the Ammonites. He did the same for all his foreign wives, who offered incense and sacrifice to their gods" (2 Kings 11:1-8).

What happened to Solomon is very eloquent. He thought he would get happiness by having more women, more sex pleasure. He was grossly mistaken. The consequences were foolishness, idolatry, decline, and a shameful end. Solomon lost his great wisdom. He even began adoring idols.

None of you is likely to get one thousand women all for himself. To think therefore that if you get one you will become happy is to make a big mistake. And to imagine that if you in sacred vows sin with one woman you will become happy is to be a big fool. Look at the example of Solomon and draw the necessary conclusions. When you are tempted, and everyone will meet with temptation sometime in life, remember these considerations. The Book of Ecclesiasticus laments over Solomon's fall:

> "You amassed gold like so much tin, and
> made silver as common as lead. You aban-
> doned your body to women, you became the
> slave of your appetites. You stained your

honor, you profaned your stock, so bringing wrath on your children and grief on your posterity" (Ecclus. 47: 19-22).

Happiness is Not in Power

There are yet other people who place their happiness in power, in being on top, in reaching positions of authority, in being before the public eye, in occupying the first seat in the synagogue, in being popular. This is the mistake of aristocrats. For them, possessions and pleasure attract men of weaker material. But they regard themselves as men of sterner stuff.

This disease can affect religious brothers and sisters too. And this temptation to power can masquerade itself in such forms as "the good of the Church," "the right leadership for our Congregation," "reading the signs of the times in the world of today," "proper use of leadership qualities" and such-like catch phrases. Together with others, such people can say that uneasy lies the head that wears the crown. But they want to wear the crown. And they hope there will be no uneasiness. And even if there were, they still want to wear the crown.

A religious congregation, for example, is planning to elect a superior general. A member can think, or even say aloud to the others: "You know, brothers, that we need a strong and far-sighted leader. We need someone with a good education. I think I have a good plan for this congregation of ours. I am confident that our brothers will elect wisely. I know I am not worthy; but if you elect me you will see what I can do. Moreover, I hope you appreciate what I already accomplished. However, if you wish to elect another person, that is all right, go ahead, and I shall see how he will manage this difficult job!"

If a congregation elects such a person, he is likely to celebrate his "victory" for quite some time. He understands authority, not as a call to service (cf. Mt. 20:24-

28), but as an opportunity for enjoyment and domination, as a reward for past performance, as a pension post. If he is not elected, he is likely to become a problem child in the congregation.

Someone asked me in June 1984 whether the new assignment the Holy Father was giving me in the Vatican City was a promotion or a demotion, compared to my present post as Archbishop of Onitsha. I replied that I did not look at it in those terms but rather as assignments in the Church. The important thing is what God wants me to do. And He tells me through the Vicar of Christ.

The desire to have power, to be at the head, is in most human beings. But it has to be controlled and offered to the service of God and neighbor. There are some people who are so immoderate in their desire to be at the head, whether in Church, in state, in clubs, or in industries, that if they are put at the head, they dominate and oppress, and repress. And if they are not at the head, then they sabotage, they murmur, they originate and organize discontent and sell their unhappiness to unwary people who hitherto were at peace. They tell you that everybody in the group is discontented. But it is only themselves who are discontented!

Our conclusion is that happiness does not lie in power.

Happiness is Not in P.P.P.

Man's happiness, therefore does not lie in possessions, nor in pleasure, nor in power. These things are not bad in themselves. They should be given their proper value. They should not be overvalued. Possessions are useful, but we should not put our hearts on them. Pleasure has its proper place in moderate eating and drinking and in relations between husband and wife who are properly married, but pleasure is not to be made a motive for human action. Someone has to be in authority in every society, but the reason is service of others not the boosting of the ego.

Happiness Lies in God

Man is made for God. Only the possession of God can satisfy us. Our happiness lies in God alone. God has made us for Himself and our hearts are never at rest until they rest in Him, as St. Augustine discovered after making big mistakes in his youth (cf. St. Augustine, *Confessions* 1,1). The second question in the Penny Catechism goes to this most important point. Why did God make you? What is the purpose of human existence? In what does your real and lasting happiness lie? And the answer is unambiguous: God made me to know Him, to love Him and to serve Him in this world, and to be happy with Him forever in the next.

Whoever is looking for lasting happiness from creatures is making a mistake. Creatures are not able to give us that. Only God can. Through the prophet Jeremiah, God rebukes His unfaithful people: "My people have committed a double crime: they have abandoned me, the fountain of living water, only to dig cisterns for themselves, leaky cisterns that hold no water" (Jer. 2:13).

Our Earthly Life is a Journey

Our life on earth is really a journey. We are going, or are meant to be going, towards God in our heavenly home. We should never forget the purpose or target of our journey. And we should never turn away from it. A retreat helps us to stay on the correct tracks.

III. Sin

A Turning Away from God

Sin is a turning away from God who alone is the final end of man, who alone can make man permanently happy. "Consider carefully how evil and bitter it is for you to abandon Yahweh your God and not stand in awe of me" (Jer. 2:19).

Mortal sin is a total and complete turning away from God and a turning towards a creature. Venial sin is temporary interest in a creature without a total turning away from God.

Mortal Sin

Because mortal sin is a total turning away from God, it has awful consequences. It removes the state of grace, or the divine indwelling, from the soul. It causes a complete loss of all our merits (how much of these merits are regained when we repent, we do not know for certain). Mortal sin damages the spiritual machinery and also deals a psychological wound which is not easily totally healed even when the sinner repents.

Moreover, mortal sin can open the gateway to further mortal sins, not excluding the great sin of sacrilege. It promotes a deadening of conscience which should be delicate. Mortal sin disposes to cynicism, pessimism, and a spiritual philosophy of sadness or sourness, instead of Christian joy and optimism. Above all, mortal sin creates the danger of eternal damnation in hell, because whoever dies in a state of mortal sin will go to hell where he will suffer forever (cf. Mk. 9:42-47; Apoc. 20:15; Mt. 10:28, 7:13).

The Sense of Sin

The sense of sin is being made dull in the world of today. Some people speak and write as if it were impossible for most people to commit a mortal sin. This is false.

We should not lose sight of the greatness of God, of His surpassing holiness and His perfection. God dwells in light inaccessible. He is the source of life and goodness. We cannot think of Him as conniving at evil or ignoring it.

On the other hand, man is a creature. Man is not always ready to submit his will to God. He rebels. He has the effrontery to claim what he considers his right before God. Man is often lacking in courtesy, if not simple justice and truth, before his Creator. Man often behaves as if he were not the little creature that he is, or as if he were not a creature at all. At times, some people go even so far as to deny the existence of God and to insult Him with positive acts of defiance.

Let those who soft-pedal the idea of mortal sin tell us what to call oppression of the poor and the weak, the killing of thousands of unborn babies, the killing of old people who are sick, marriage infidelities, sexual relations between people who are not husband and wife, pornography, prostitution, child abuse, armed robbery, priests or religious betraying their ordination or profession vows, children of the Church sabotaging her from within, theologians deliberately teaching error against faith and morals and misleading many, national and international injustices, assassinations, terrorist attacks, and hijacking of airplanes leading to loss of life and property.

Who says that most people cannot commit mortal sin? Sin, unfortunately, does find its way into human behavior. No theologian should engage in such theological acrobatics or gymnastics as to talk of "fundamental option" in the sense that mortal sin is beyond the reach of most people. If a thief stole the car of such a theologian once, you would soon see the theologian going to the police to report a "serious matter." A sense of sin is a necessary consequence of our belief in God who is all holy, and our faith that we owe our love and loyalty to Him.

Venial Sin

The other type of sin is called venial sin. It is an offense against God, but not a total turning away from God. Consider the following actions: negligence in our duty in small matters; lies and exaggerations to get out of trouble, avoid blame, or to win praise; murmuring; complaining; gossiping; spreading discontent; stubbornness in little things; refusing to listen to the other person and annoying him; condemning people without hearing them, whether they are superiors, equals, or inferiors; anger; irritability; overweening ambition; careless friendships which can damage chastity; laziness; harshness; rudeness; envy; jealousy; and being thoughtless toward the needy. Circumstances can also make these actions mortal sins, just as an action which is objectively a mortal sin, could for an individual, be a venial sin because, for example, of lack of full knowledge or full consent.

Venial Sin should be Avoided

It is a wrong attitude to think that venial sin does not matter. It does matter. We can distinguish two types of venial sin.

There are errors of thoughtlessness and human weakness which we commit almost before we become aware of what is happening. They occur through lack of attention, and through rashness and habit, or character. We should strive to avoid them although it may not be easy to eliminate them altogether. Perhaps, "the virtuous man falls seven times, he stands up again" (Prov. 24:16), is said with reference to this type of fault.

There is deliberate venial sin, such as the acts listed in the section under the title "Venial Sin" above. These sins are deliberate, and therefore they are real obstacles to progress in the spiritual life. They are signs of ingratitude to God or of lack of fervor.

Venial sin does harm to the soul. It robs the soul of saving graces which would otherwise enrich it from God's hands. If a child despises the special gifts which his parents have gone to great trouble to buy, are the parents likely to give him more?

Venial sin beclouds our relations with God and makes us cold and weak in prayer and at Holy Communion. Deliberate venial sin casts doubt on a person's fervor in dedication to God. Venial sin weakens the ability of the soul to withstand the power of evil and to say a firm "No" to a temptation to mortal sin. The lax person commits many venial sins until it is difficult for the person to tell whether a certain action he committed is a venial sin or a mortal sin.

The saints advise us. St. John of the Cross says that if we neglect trifles, we are laying the foundation for great faults. St. Gregory the Great says that if we habitually commit little sins, we shall eventually not fear to fall into a mortal sin. And St. Theresa of Jesus says that the devil is happy when a person opens the door just a little, because the devil will make sure that the door will later stand entirely ajar.

How God has Punished Venial Sin

Those who imagine that venial sin does not matter much should reflect on the following ways in which God dealt with those we think committed what we call venial sins. Mary, the sister of Moses, complained and was struck with leprosy. Oza touched the Ark of the Covenant and was struck dead. The Bethsamites gazed at the Ark out of curiosity and many of them died. David, out of vanity, numbered his people and 70,000 people died in a plague. Moses and Aaron doubted for one moment, and both of them were excluded from entering the promised land. Ananias and Saphira told a lie about their own property, and both of them fell down and died. If all those who told lies today to priests or bishops fell down and died, there would be many corpses around our parish centers and even in corridors of some church offices. Who says that venial sin does not matter?

Turning Towards God

Sin should have no place in our lives. We should live for God. Our whole life should be a continuous movement towards God. And if anyone has had the misfortune to fall into sin, he should return to God. He should repent. He should do penance. That will be our next consideration: first, penance as a virtue, and then penance as a sacrament.

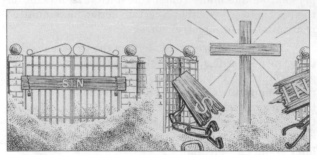

IV. Penance as a Virtue

What is Penance?

Penance as virtue is also called self-denial or mortification. It means denying ourselves something that is pleasant and allowed, or accepting or doing what is unpleasant, in order to make reparation for our faults or in order to arm ourselves better for spiritual combat.

We are children of a fallen race. Original sin has

made us weak. We are attracted by evil. And we are often lazy to do good. Baptism does not wipe away all the consequences of original sin. Moreover, we have committed personal sins which have further weakened us. And we need to do reparation for these offenses too. Without mortification the Christian will find it impossible to live the call of Christ with fidelity and generosity.

Jesus Tells Us to Do Penance

Our Lord and Savior is very clear on the necessity of penance. Indeed, He began His preaching with the message: "Repent, for the Kingdom of heaven is close at hand" (Mt. 4:17). "The Kingdom of heaven has been subjected to violence, and the violent are taking it by storm" (Mt. 11:12). "It is a narrow gate and a hard road that leads to life, and only a few find it" (Mt. 7:14).

The message is very clear. And if anyone still has any doubt, Jesus says further: "If anyone wants to be a follower of mine, let him renounce himself and take up his cross every day and follow me" (Lk. 9:23; cf. also Mt. 10:38). The entire sermon on the Mount is a call to penance.

St. Paul Taught the Same Doctrine

St. Paul is no less clear on the necessity for mortification. "Brethren, we are debtors, not to the flesh" (Rom. 8:12). "Those who belong to Christ have crucified that flesh with all its passions and desires" (Gal. 5:24). "I treat my body hard and make it obey me, for, having been an announcer myself, I should not want to be disqualified" (1 Cor. 9:27). "It makes me happy to suffer for you, as I am suffering now, and in my own body to do what I can to make up all that has still to be undergone by Christ for the sake of His body, the Church" (Col. 1:24). "As for me, the only thing I can boast about is the cross of our Lord Jesus Christ, through whom the world is crucified to me, and I to the world" (Gal. 6:14).

Other Scripture Models of Penance

The Holy Scripture shows us such models of mortified life as Abraham (who obeyed God to go out of his country and people and who was ready to sacrifice his only son Isaac), the prophets Isaiah, Jeremiah, Elisha, and Eliseus, to name a few, Tobias, the Macchabee brothers, and above all, St. John the Baptist. The book of Ecclesiasticus advises us to mortify our eyes, our tongue, and our appetite for food and drink and for sex.

Church History Models

The history of the Church is full of luminary examples of mortification. The early Christians lived a community life and shared their goods. Martyrs and virgins flourished out of the love of Christ. St. Anthony led a solitary life in the desert, and the religious life took root. Monks and nuns in cloisters lived lives of silence, fasting, prayer, and manual work. Christian kings and queens served lepers and shared their table with the poor. St. Thomas Aquinas and his fellow religious handed on to us monumental achievements in philosophy, theology, and asceticism because they had learned how to live mortified lives. St. Cecilia, St. Agnes, St. Maria Goretti, and the Martyrs of Uganda showed us how to live entirely for God with the basic instincts mortified with the help of God's grace.

Therefore, the Imitation of Christ says: "You cannot attain to perfect liberty unless you deny yourself in all things...The whole life of Christ was a cross and a martyrdom, and do you seek for yourself rest and joy...If indeed there had been anything better and more beneficial to man's salvation than suffering, Christ would certainly have shown it by word and example" (Imitation II, 12). There is no other way. It is Christ Himself who tells us: "Unless a wheat grain falls on the ground and dies, it remains only a single grain; but if it dies, it yields a rich harvest. Anyone who loves his life loses it; anyone who hates his life in this world will keep it for the eternal life" (John 12:24-25).

Common Sense Advises Mortification

Even natural reason, common sense, and the science of medicine advise self control. The person who does not control himself in matters of food and drink soon gets sick or is unable to do his work, or loses much money, or becomes an object of ridicule. An athlete has to control his eating habits and do many difficult exercises if he wants to win in the Olympic Games.

Consider the story of a secondary school soccer team which drove to another school for a soccer match. Their hosts delayed the lunch until 3:00 p.m. The visitors were very hungry. They were then led into the dining room. All kinds of attractive food and drink were there. The visiting boys helped themselves generously and forgot the match until they were called at 4:00 to the soccer field. They went. But they were too heavy with food. Some were slightly drunk. It was a disgraceful soccer match for their school. They were beaten 11-0. And all this because they had not learned to control their appetite for food and drink.

Apply this lesson to the spiritual life, where our battles are with the devil and his agents and with our human nature.

Mortifications Which Come Our Way

The safest kinds of mortification for us are not those which we go out to choose for ourselves, but rather those which come our way in life. It is harder to eat only one slice of bread at breakfast because you were given only one, although you wanted three, than to eat none at all because you decided to eat none.

Each of us, according to our state of life, has mortifying situations which come our way every day without our seeking them. Think of the sufferings involved in heat, cold, rain, sun, work assigned to us, the place to which you are posted, people's attitude to you which can be that of ingratitude, insult or even attack, false accusations, unpleasant decisions of superiors, defeat in an argument, community life (St. Theresa of Lisieux bore patiently the action of a sister near her in the chapel who always pronounced "s" as "sh"), food, house, means of transport which we do not like, not enough salt in food , expected letter from friend does not arrive, having to wear the same vest every day (this is a mortification particularly for religious men and women, especially women who by nature like to change dresses often), an unchanging daily time table, sickness, and old age.

If anyone bears these unpleasant situations with patience and love of God and with total self control and undisturbed joy, that person is on the road to sanctity.

Freely Chosen Acts of Mortification

There should also be room in our lives for freely chosen acts of mortification. For example, each of us needs deliberately to mortify the appetite for food and drink according to the person's condition and good advice from his spiritual director. Failure to do this makes the person weak and liable to faults and even falls in bigger matters.

Allied to the appetite for food and drink is the entire sense of feeling. The soft person seeks what is comfortable, sweet, easy, and nice-colored. He finds kneeling difficult. He does not stand erect. His movements are noisy. He sleeps longer than he should. His bed is too soft. His choice of clothes is too foppish. He is not mortified. He does not look like a disciple of Him who carried His cross up the rugged road to Mount Calvary, with a crown of thorns on His bleeding head. He wants to be a delicate member of a crucified Christ. St. Paul warns the Philippians: "I have told you often, and I repeat it today with tears, there are many who are behaving as enemies of the cross of Christ. They are destined to be lost. They make foods into their god...the things they think important are earthly things" (Phil. 3:18-19).

Because of the danger of exaggeration, pride, or illusion, it is advisable, at least for beginners, to obtain the guidance of their spiritual director in the choice of mortifications.

Penance Helps Our Movement Towards God

There is no doubt that penance helps our movement towards God in Whom alone is our total and permanent happiness. Penance also helps to make reparation for our sins and the sins of others and to keep our spiritual machinery in good combat form. There is no way of being a good follower of Christ if a person refuses to be mortified.

V. Penance as Sacrament

An Institution of Divine Mercy

It is the mercy of God which has given us the possibility of repentance and forgiveness, of pardon and peace, in the form of a sacrament. In this sacrament of reconciliation, God has made provisions for our repentance and spirit of penance, together with our open admission and confession of our guilt, to be met by His abundant mercy and elevated. When the sinner, with a desire for renewal and conversion, kneels before the priest and confesses his sins, the sinner, through the ministry of the priest and the Church, receives God's pardon. He is liberated from the chain of his sins. He is assured of pardon. The prodigal son is received back by the merciful Father.

Those who do not know the joy of this peace-giving sacrament have either not known the peace of being forgiven and being certain that one is forgiven, or they have tried to create substitutes for this sacrament. Some religions that are not Christian make rites that incorporate the idea of self accusation when seeking interior peace. Some people who think they are modern go to psychologists or psychoanalysts and pay big sums of money. Nobody can improve on what God has done.

Preparation for the Reception of this Sacrament

In preparing to go to the priest to receive pardon and peace, the penitent should pray for God's help. Then he should strive to recall his offenses against God or his neighbor. If the sinner has the terrible misfortune to have fallen into mortal sin, he should know that he is bound to confess it all. To conceal a mortal sin is to make a mockery of this sacrament of God's mercy.

The most important act of the penitent is true sorrow for his sins together with a resolution not to sin again. Without this firm determination and change of mind, there is no repentance, and therefore no absolution.

The danger in the confession of venial sins is that the penitent may be doing it out of routine and may not seriously repent and determine to take steps for a change of direction. It is very important that people who are striving for perfection, be they priests, laity, or religious, should bear this in mind. The sacrament of penance can be a great help to them on the road to union with God if they generously strive at each reception to change their lives and avoid faults confessed, together with battling against the underlying weaknesses which produce or worsen the faults.

Penance and Charity

The reception of the sacrament of reconciliation can help very much to promote the love of our neighbor. There is a danger that many penitents examine their consciences more often on matters touching prayer, chastity, and honesty in speech and action rather than on charity and duty to others. Both the first set and the second group of virtues and duties are necessary.

It is therefore not superfluous to suggest that penitents should examine their performance on such points as being a pleasant and considerate community member, anticipating the needs of those with whom we live and helping them, kindness in speech, patience with neighbors, kind thoughts for those who create problems for us, fidelity in the accomplishment of our duties, understanding authority as service and not as domination, help to the poor and the needy, and duties as a citizen.

Sometimes there is the possibility of a communal celebration of the rite of penance in the sense of celebration of the Word of God, and then everyone goes to confession and receives absolution one by one. This can help us to realize better that sin has consequences on the community of the Church.

Important Ministry for the Priest

The ministry of administering this sacrament of reconciliation is a very important one for the priest. It is the only spiritual direction which most Catholics actually receive in life, since there are so few priests. Considering also that every Catholic in mortal sin is bound to receive this sacrament before he receives Holy Communion (except in a few defined emergencies), and the Church instructs those particularly pursuing perfection to receive this sacrament frequently in order to develop ever more sensitive and delicate consciences (cf.

Canon 246, 4), this ministry of priests is also a difficult one. It is demanding. It can be tiresome. But the spiritual fruits are most abundant.

After Receiving the Sacrament

After receiving God's pardon and peace in this sacrament, the penitent should not forget to do the satisfaction or act of penance imposed on him by the priest, to thank God for His mercy, to beg the help of the Most Blessed Virgin Mary for fidelity to his resolutions, and then to strive to live a new life in the direction of his repentance and conversion.

VI. The Church

A reflection on the Church is important because it helps us to realize the greatness of the new family of God to which we have been called, and it aids us to appreciate the place of clerics, lay people,  and religious within the Church, together with their particular apostolates in the general apostolate of the Church. The best document is the Second Vatican Council Dogmatic Constitution on The Church. I shall merely touch here a few points from this rich book which will need constant study and prayer.

The Mystery of the Church

God created Man. Man rebelled against God. Original sin deprived man of grace and divine friendship. But "God loved the world so much that He gave His Son, so that everyone who believes in Him may not be lost but may have eternal life" (John 3:15-16).

God promised a Savior. Through the prophets, He taught us to hope for salvation. In the fullness of time, the Father sent His only begotten Son to become Man for our salvation. In the power of the Holy Spirit, Jesus preached and gathered the new family of God.

The Church is referred to as sheepfold, flock, field of God, building or house of God, the new Jerusalem. Founded on the apostles, given life by the Holy Spirit, fed by God's Word and sacraments, the Church, "like a pilgrim in a foreign land, presses forward amid the persecutions of the world and the consolations of God" (St. Augustine, *De Civ. Dei*, XVIII, 51, 2).

The People of God

In the Old Testament, God chose the people of Israel. In the New Testament, sealed in the Blood of Christ, God chose the Church as the new People of God. The head of this messianic people is Christ. Its heritage is the dignity and freedom of the sons of God in whose hearts the Holy Spirit dwells as in His temple. Its law is the new Commandment to love as Christ loved us. Its goal is the Kingdom of God (cf. Vatican II: The Church, n. 9).

All members of Christ share in His priestly, prophetic, and kingly powers in ways which have to be carefully explained. And this Church is the way to salvation. Although no one will be condemned to hell except through his own fault, it is only by being members of the Church that a person receives in abundance all the benefits of the redemption worked for us by Christ. Therefore the Church painstakingly fosters ecumenism and missionary work.

Clerics in the Church

It is the will of Christ that some men should be ordained ministerial priests in His Church, for the service of all the People of God who all share in the common priesthood by Baptism. The three orders of clerics, or the hierarchy, are made up of bishops, priests and deacons. The bishops, with the Pope, and under his authority, are the teachers of doctrine, high priests of sacred worship, and officers of good order. Priests are their co-operators in the same triple office. Deacons are ministers of the Word, of service, and of charity and helpers of the priests.

Since most Catholics are going to deal more with the priest in their Christian lives, a little more will now be said about the priest. The priest is ordained to sanctify, to preach, and to gather the People of God together. By the first assignment, he celebrates Holy Mass; he baptizes; he celebrates the other Sacraments; he blesses; and he prays in the name of the Church. By the second, he reads and explains Holy Scripture to the people; he teaches in the name of Christ and the Church; and he gives spiritual direction. As participator in the Kingly office of Christ, he is the leader of the Catholic community in the parish. Faith is needed to see in the priest an ambassador of Christ.

Lay People in the Church

Lay people are all Christians who by baptism are given a share in Christ and are called to live their lives of witness to Christ in the secular sphere. A secular quality is attached to the lay person. He is called to live his Christian life in the family, in marriage, in the arts and professions, in trade and commerce, in politics and government, in cultural settings and international relations. What makes him a lay person is that he is called to bring the spirit of Christ into these aspects of life in the earthly city from within, as an insider in the manner of leaven. This is what the lay apostolate is all about (cf. Vatican II: *The Church*, nn. 30-37; *The Church in the World of Today*, n. 43; *Laity* n. 7).

Religious in the Church

The radical or fundamental call for everyone is Baptism. At Baptism we are consecrated to God, and we make the most important and far-reaching vows in our lives of service of God.

From among all the baptized, Jesus chooses some to follow Him more closely in the life of the evangelical counsels. The religious life is proposed, not imposed. Those who answer this call renounce three of the more attractive things that we can have on earth: marriage, possessions, and doing our own will.

You will notice that the three religious vows of chastity, poverty, and obedience are an effort to dig out, at the roots, the three "concupiscences" which St. John warns us against, and which, as we saw above, when considering the final end of man, are the three possible wrong answers to where man's happiness can lie. They are the concupiscence of the flesh, the concupiscence of the eyes, and the pride of life (cf. 1 John, 2:15-16).

The religious is not saying that marriage, possessions, and doing our own will are bad. Indeed, if they were bad, they should not be offered to God, and it would be no virtue to do so. Rather the religious is saying that he wants to offer to God the three things on earth that most attract the human heart. And the religious is also saying that the seeking of these three goods, when it becomes immoderate, becomes an imperfection, or a sin, venial or mortal.

The religious state is a proof that the grace of Christ is stronger than the attractions of things of this world. In heaven there will be no marriage, no possessions, and no seeking our own will. There will be only seeing God as He is. The religious wants to anticipate that, as far as possible, on this earth. As the Council says: "The religious state reveals in a unique way that the kingdom of God and its over-mastering necessities are superior to all earthly considerations. Finally, to all men it shows wonderfully at work within the Church, the surpassing greatness of the force of Christ the King and the boundless power of the Holy Spirit" (Vatican II: *The Church*, n. 44).

It follows that religious brothers and sisters, monks and nuns, should live in such a way that this witness to Christ can really shine out in their lives. We shall consider this in greater detail in future pages, especially when we examine the three religious vows and the living of community life and a life of prayer and apostolate.

Everyone is Called to be Holy

Everyone is called to be holy. Holiness is not reserved to any particular group of people in the Church. It is a universal vocation for us all. Holiness is the perfection of charity according to each person's particular vocation. That person is holier who has more charity. "What God wants for you all is to be holy" (1 Thes. 4:3), St. Paul tells the Thessalonians.

The Church walks along this world as a pilgrim. We aspire after our home in heaven. The saints, who have already arrived there, are our models. They encourage us. We venerate them. They show the greatness of the redemption worked for us by Christ. The souls suffering in Purgatory can be helped by our sacrifices and prayers. We are all related in the communion of saints.

The greatest of the saints is the most Blessed Virgin Mary, Mother of God, Mother of the Church, symbol of the Church, and Mother of all Christians. A loving consideration of our Star of the Sea will be a fitting choice toward the end of this little book.

VII. The Sacred Liturgy

Exercise of the Priesthood of Christ

The Church of Christ prays. The work of redemption which Jesus Christ did for us goes on in the Church. In the Church, He continues to offer adoration, praise, thanksgiving, propitiation, and petition to His Heavenly Father.

Christ is always present in His Church, especially in her public acts of worship. He is present in the sacrifice of the Mass, not only in the ministering priest, but as God and Man under the forms of bread and wine. By His power He is present in the Sacraments so that He is the chief minister of each sacrament. He is present in His Word because it is He who speaks when Holy Scripture is read in the Church assembly. He is present in the public prayer of the Church, when the Church prays or sings, because He has promised that where two or three are gathered together in His Name, He is there in their midst (cf. Mt. 18:20).

The sacred liturgy is therefore the public worship of the Church, Head and members (cf. Vatican II: *Liturgy*, n. 7). It is an exercise of the priestly office of Jesus Christ. Therefore it is a sacred action of surpassing excellence.

Liturgical Renewal Introduced by Vatican II

The Second Vatican Council made a major effort to promote the renewal of the liturgy. It ordered (and in these twenty years the Church has almost completed) a revision of all the rites of public worship to make them more comprehensible to the people, to bring in better selected and more abundant texts of Holy Scripture, to encourage the vernacular, to emphasize the different ministries in the Church, to make the prayers for the hours of the day more meaningful, to render sacred music more conducive to prayer, to pay greater attention to the cultures of the various peoples in the world, and to help everyone to reap more abundant fruits from the celebration of the sacred mysteries.

In order that these aims may be achieved, it is clear that such cooperation as the following is required of us: study of the liturgy, more familiarity with Holy Scripture, silence and personal prayer, a well-prepared and prayerful carrying out of the liturgical rites, clean surroundings in Church, good sacred music, suitable items of sacred art and Church furnishings, and even good accommodation and acoustics.

Parts of the Sacred Liturgy

The sacred liturgy is made up of the sacraments, the sacramentals, and the liturgy of the hours.

The Sacraments

Baptism is the foundation of the other sacraments and the entire liturgy. It makes us Christians. It gives us power to offer Christian worship. We take a new name at Baptism, preferably the name of a saint in heaven, as an indication of our new life in Christ.

At Confirmation, we are strengthened by a special outpouring of the Holy Spirit so that we shall be strong and courageous enough to witness to Christ and to defend the Church.

Penance is already discussed. Holy Eucharist will be given separate treatment after this chapter.

The Anointing of the Sick puts the sick and suffering in union with Christ and gives them help. The revised rite has stressed that this is the sacrament of the sick, even if there is no danger of death. Prayer for recovery is one of the aspects of this sacrament.

Holy Orders gives ministers to the Church so that the People of God can be served and guided and so that sins can be forgiven and the Holy Eucharist celebrated.

Matrimony equips husbands and wives, whose mutual love is blessed and elevated in Christ, with graces for a basic apostolate in marriage and the family, which the Council calls the domestic church (cf. Vatican II: *The Church*, n. 11).

The Sacramentals

The sacramentals include such aspects of worship as the rites of religious profession, worship of the Holy Eucharist outside Mass, the dedication of churches and sacred objects, the blessing of people, things and places, and some prayers. In each of them, as in every act of the liturgy, the chief person at prayer is Christ. He associates the members of His Church with Him.

The Divine Office or Liturgy of the Hours

In order to "pray without ceasing" (1 Thes. 5:17), the Church as from ancient times had official public prayers to sanctify the different hours of the day and even the night. At present the Liturgy of the Hours includes the Office of Readings, Morning Prayer or Lauds, Offices of Terce, Sext and None, Vespers, and Compline.

Clerics and religious are bound to pray these hours each day for the Church and the world. It is better if the priests or religious who live together pray some of those Hours together. These beautiful combinations of psalms, sacred readings, chants, and prayers should be given great importance in our spiritual life. The different hours should be prayed as far as possible at their proper times in the day. Good knowledge of the psalms and Holy Scripture is a help. Silence and recollection are useful so that the individual can really make his own those beautiful prayers. If proper care is not taken, habit and familiarity can turn the Liturgy of the Hours into routine and oral recitations without much personal commitment.

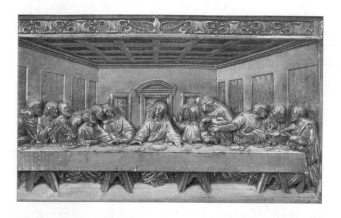

VIII. The Holy Eucharist

Institution

The night before He suffered, Jesus Our Savior gave us a special proof of His boundless love for us. He knew He would soon die for us on the cross, rise again, and ascend into heaven. He wanted to stay on with us even after His ascension. And He wanted to put into the hands of His Church His own sacrifice, which He was to offer the following day on Mount Calvary, so that the Church could offer it each day until the of the world in the forms of bread and wine.

He knew everything. He knew that everyone did not and would not believe in Him. He saw the children, the virgins, the good young people, the brave and loving mothers, the sick, the poor, and the dying. But He also saw the non-believers, the doubters, the scorners, and those who would commit sacrilege in His very sacrament of love.

And yet He did not hesitate to give the greatest sacrament of His Body and Blood: "He had always loved those who were His in the world, but now He showed how perfect His love was" (John 13:1). He took bread, said the blessing, broke it and gave it to His disciples saying: "Take...This is my Body which will be given up for you". He took the cup, blessed it and gave it to His disciples saying "Take...This is my Blood..." (Mt. 26:26-29).

The Second Vatican Council summarizes the doctrine on the institution of the Holy Eucharist: "At the Last Supper, on the night He was betrayed, our Savior instituted the Eucharistic sacrifice of His Body and Blood. This He did in order to perpetuate the sacrifice of the Cross throughout the ages until He should come again, and so to entrust to His beloved Spouse, the Church, a memorial of His death and resurrection: a sacrament of love, a sign of unity, a bond of charity, a paschal banquet in which Christ is consumed, the mind is filled with grace, and a pledge of future glory is given to us." (Vatican II, *Liturgy*, n. 47).

Relation with Calvary

This sacrifice of the Mass and the sacrifice of Calvary are one and the same because Christ is the chief priest and the victim in both. The only difference is in the manner of offering. On the Cross, Jesus offers Himself and sheds blood. At Mass, Jesus offers Himself through the ministry of the priest, in the form of a sacrament, in the form of bread and wine over which the words of consecration are said so that they became the Body and Blood of Christ. Also at Mass, Christians join with Christ and offer Him to God the Father with and through the ordained priest, who alone can consecrate bread and wine. And at Mass, the people also learn to offer themselves.

Graces of Holy Eucharist as Sacrifice

The Holy Eucharist as sacrifice, that is Holy Mass, is offered for the four major intentions which are also the summary of all the acts of religion.

Adoration of God is the primary aim. God is our

*Image of the vision that Sr. Lucia of Fatima had of the
Holy Sacrifice of the Mass in 1929.*

Creator. Holy Mass is our greatest act of public recognition of His greatness and of our condition as creatures.

Thanksgiving follows closely on adoration. We have received everything that we are or have from God: our being, health, gifts of nature and grace, Christian vocation, religious or priestly vocation, our achievements in life, indeed everything. It is right and just that we give Him thanks.

We are sinners. We need God's forgiveness. The Blood of Christ shed for our sins is adequate reparation because of Christ's infinite dignity. Holy Mass is a powerful way to request God to forgive us our sins.

We need many favors from God. We are not self sufficient. We need His grace in order to persevere in the Christian life. We stand in need of many gifts in this world. The Mass is an eloquent pleading before the throne of God for our many needs of nature and grace.

It means that we should request a priest to celebrate Mass for us, not only when we need something, but also to thank God and to praise Him.

Graces of Holy Eucharist as Sacrament

As sacrament the Holy Eucharist, or Holy Communion, makes us one with Christ, increases grace, decreases the attraction of sin, and is a pledge of life everlasting.

Holy Communion makes us one with Christ. We are united with Him in a sacred union with Him. We begin to share more and more of that mind which is in Christ Jesus. And this also includes union with my neighbor. If I receive Christ and my neighbor receives Christ, then I must love my neighbor. Otherwise my reception of Christ is not given its full meaning and power to change my life. You notice that before we receive Holy Communion, the Church wants us to exchange signs of peace or mutual love with our neighbor. This implies that anyone who does not love his neighbor should not approach the Eucharistic table. Love of one another is the new commandment of Christ. Holy Communion should be prepared for by greater efforts to love our neighbor.

The Holy Eucharist increases grace within us. Habitual grace is divine indwelling. God lives in us. This sacrament increases and intensifies this life of God in us.

Original sin makes us inclined to evil. This bad effect is not entirely removed by Baptism. Holy Communion increases love of God and therefore diminishes the attraction to sin. Sinners are really being enslaved by sin. Those who do God's will have the glorious liberty of the children of God. Fervent reception of Jesus in this sacrament of love increases our attachment to Him and our detachment from evil.

Jesus has promised that whoever eats His Body and drinks His Blood will have everlasting life. He has promised to raise that person up on the last day. He has warned that unless we receive Him in this sacrament, we shall not have life in us (cf. John 6). The Holy Eucharist, therefore, gives us a pledge of everlasting life.

The liturgical chant, "O Sacrum Convivium," has summarized these benefits of the reception of this Most Blessed Sacrament: "O sacred banquet in which Christ is received, the memorial of His passion is recalled, the mind is filled with grace and a pledge of future glory is given to us."

Devotion to Holy Mass

It is of central importance in our spiritual lives that we be intensely devoted to the Holy Eucharist. The celebration of this sacrifice and sacrament should be for us the center of our day. Everything connected with the material preparation for Holy Mass should be beautiful and clean: vestments, altar, sacred vessels, our own personal vest, Mass servers, and everything else.

A good preparation of all the texts for Mass helps to orient our souls and keep our attention. Punctuality is important. Hurry is harmful. Personal prayer before, during, and after Mass is necessary. It is a pity that many people limit themselves to prayers from a prayer-book. Another person's prayer can be of help to me. But I shall then move on to my own prayer. And my own prayer should be so personal to me that it could not be exactly like that of another person. Particularly after receiving Jesus in Holy Communion, I should speak to Him from my heart and also beg Him to help me listen to Him. He has things to tell me, if only I could sit at His feet and listen with love and desire!

Worship of the Holy Eucharist Outside of the Mass

The worship of the Holy Eucharist is not over when Mass is over. The Most Blessed Sacrament is reserved in the tabernacle so that we can visit Christ at different times during the day and night to adore Him, to tell Him that we love Him. Some visits can be brief, others long. We should form the habit of visiting Jesus in the chapel before we leave the house for work or for a journey, to tell Him where we are going and to request His help, guidance, and blessing. When we return, we should again visit Him to report on our journey, to thank Him, and perhaps to beg His forgiveness for what we did not do well. You notice that the Church wants the Blessed Sacrament to be reserved in a chapel in every religious house. Priests are expected to live near a parish church or other oratory. The Church wants to make sure that our lives are centered around the Holy Eucharist. If you forget to visit Jesus often during the day, how can you say that He is your great friend and that you love Him very much? Tell me the person you visit as often as possible and think about often, and I will tell you who is your dearest friend.

The Church wants a tabernacle lamp to be always burning before the Blessed Sacrament and also the tabernacle to be covered with a veil.

We also worship the Holy Eucharist outside Mass by Benediction of the Blessed Sacrament, by Eucharistic Processions, and by organized adoration for one hour, and in parishes occasionally a whole day or longer. Where our treasure is, there is our heart also. It is a praiseworthy habit to do a holy hour of adoration privately each day. In this period, one could also prayerfully read Holy Scripture and some spiritual book for part of the time. "I rejoiced when I heard them say: 'Let us go to God's house.'" So says Psalm 121 (122). Indeed, it is best to do most of our formal prayers in the chapel. Examples are the Liturgy of the Hours, Mental Prayer, the Rosary and the Way of the Cross.

Eucharistic Fervor Promotes the Entire Spiritual Life

A priest, religious, or lay person who centers his life on the Holy Eucharist, as suggested above, will find that Jesus will do great things for him.

Charity and unity will be promoted in the presbyterium of the diocese, in the parish, in the religious house, in the family, and in the place of work and recreation. Tensions in our relationships with our neighbor will be dissipated or at least systematically lowered. Coldness will be turned into warmth and Christian love.

Interior calm will grow in the individual. Irritability and restlessness and discontent will become less. Crosses will become less difficult to bear. The person will become more ready to acknowledge his faults and to ask for pardon. And he will be better prepared to forgive and forget.

Chastity will be better safeguarded. When a pot of meat is boiling hot, flies are not able to move in to eat of the meat. But if the fire is out, the water is cold, and the pot is open and unguarded, then flies will move in. If we are burning with the love and presence of Christ, the dirty flies of impurity will not be able to overcome us.

Eucharistic devotion helps a person to have a taste for spiritual things. It helps us to lift up our hearts. The Holy Eucharist is indeed the center of Christian worship and also the apex. In our individual lives, it is, or should be, the same.

IX. CHASTITY

Sexuality in God's Design

The book of Genesis tells us: "God created man in the image of Himself, in the image of God He created Him, male and female He created them" (Gen. 1:27). "God saw all He had made, and indeed it was very good"

(Gen. 1:31). Therefore to be a man or to be a woman comes from God. To be a man or to be a woman is to be created with inbuilt sexuality. Sexuality is a gift of God. It is good. It is acceptable to God. God blessed Adam and Eve saying to them: "Be fruitful, multiply, fill the earth and conquer it" (Gen. 1:28). God therefore also made marriage from the beginning as a very close form of community between a man and a woman.

Unfortunately, original sin upset the balance of man's friendship with God and life according to God's will. Terrible consequences followed, including consequences in matters touching sexuality. Man and woman began to find it difficult to act always according to right reason and God's law in matters touching their relationship as man and woman. Adam and Eve transmitted this difficulty to all their descendants except the Most Blessed Virgin Mary.

Chastity is the virtue which handles this difficulty. It is the virtue which moves man to act according to right reason and God's law in matters touching sexuality. By the grace of redemption, Christ redeemed marriage and made it a sacrament. And He also gave to some of His followers the still higher gift of virginity and of celibacy for the sake of the kingdom of heaven.

Sexual Relations are Correct Only Within Marriage

Between husband and wife, sexual relations or genital sexuality have their proper and only place. "The actions within marriage by which the couples are united intimately and chastely are noble and worthy ones. Expressed in a manner which is truly human, those actions signify and promote that mutual self-giving by which spouses enrich each other with a joyful and thankful will" (Vatican II; *The Church in the World of Today*, n. 49).

A reasonable person will easily see that a valid marriage, in which this intimate union has its only place, has four characteristics: permanence, fidelity, fertility, and moment of commitment. A marriage union is permanent until the death of one partner, in order to promote the procreation and education of children and the mutual love and growth of the spouses. It is marked by fidelity of the two spouses to each other, to the exclusion of every third party. Their sexual union is open to new life, and therefore they are happy, or should be, when a baby is arriving as a result of their union. And the marriage has a juridical moment of commitment or celebration and thus becomes valid also in the eyes of society. Sexual union which is lacking in any one of these four elements is wrong; it is a sin; it is not directed according to right reason and God's will; and the two people involved in it are bound to be wounded by the wrong act. Within a proper marriage, sexual relationship is directed towards growth, fulfillment, and happiness when it respects these four values.

Chastity is a Virtue for Everyone

It follows that chastity is a virtue for everyone: young person, single adult, husband and wife, priest and religious. Everyone is expected to practice this virtue according to his state of life. Only husband and wife can engage in genital sexuality. All others are excluded from it for the reasons given above, i.e. disorder, desecration and therefore, a sin.

Chastity is a virtue that protects marriage and the family. It is an attitude of reverence for the mystery of human life, for God's arrangement, and for the dignity of ourselves and our fellow human beings.

True, chastity is not the first of all the virtues. Charity is. But it remains true that after charity, it was chastity that greatly distinguished early Christians from pagans. Moreover, the unchaste person generally falls into many other sins against charity, justice, piety, truth, and honesty. And sins against chastity cause psychological disorders of more or less considerable proportions.

Chastity has been called the angelic virtue. In heaven we shall neither marry nor be married, but shall be as the angels of God (cf. Mt. 22:30).

Two Ways of Loving

Through human sexuality everyone is called somehow to fatherhood or motherhood. This is naturally carried out in marriage. It is spiritually carried out in consecrated celibacy by priests and religious who show loving concern for their neighbor. Marriage and consecrated celibacy are two ways of loving. The obligations of Christian chastity flow from these two vocations, each of which witnesses in its own unique way to the presence of the Kingdom of God. The sixth and ninth commandments are necessary in order to exclude contradictions and distortions of the profound meaning of sexuality and its expression in man's vocation. To abuse sex is to sin against God.

Chastity for Married People

Married people are to observe chastity according to their vocation. In all nobility and love, they are to be faithful to each other, to exclude all third persons, and to be ready to make the sacrifices which include abstaining from the marital act sometimes because of sickness, or absence of the marriage partner, or for other reasons. Moreover, they are to take care not to scandalize others and to train their children well. They should follow the theologically acceptable means of spacing children which are abstinence and natural family planning, and avoid the use of contraceptive drugs and means.

Chastity for Single Lay People

It is clear that lay people who are not married are bound to observe chastity and to refrain from all genital acts. This applies, for example, to young people, to the betrothed, to widows and widowers, and to single adults.

Chastity for Clerics

Deacons, priests, and bishops are required in the Latin Church, not only to be chaste but also to take the vow of celibacy for their whole lives. By this vow, they sacrifice the right to marry with all that this entails.

Although clerical celibacy is not of divine law, the Church has very good reasons for the discipline. Some reasons are Christological. The priest is another Christ. He should strive to imitate Christ. Christ lived a celibate life. As a spiritual father, the priest acts in the name of Christ towards the spouse of Christ, the Church. He handles the Body and Blood of Christ. It is fitting that he join Christ in the mystery of the Cross. The folly of the Cross consists in following a course which human wisdom judges foolish or useless. The priest is celibate "for the sake of the kingdom of God" (Lk. 18:29).

Another reason for clerical celibacy is ecclesiological. Priestly celibacy is a participation in the mystery of the Church. It is an expression of fidelity to the appeal and mission of Christ the Lord. It is a sign of complete consecration to Christ and the Church. For love of the Church and easier availability in the work of her apostolate, the priest is ready for sacrifices involved with celibacy, including a certain solitude or share in the abandonment of Golgotha.

A third reason for clerical celibacy is eschatological. Celibacy is a sign of a kingdom which is to come and which is not yet realized, except in part. The priest waits for the coming of the Lord in a very vigilant way and thus testifies to the community of the faithful that things of this world will pass away, including marriage.

Moreover, it is clear that not being weighed down by responsibility for a family, the priest has more liberty, affective and physical, to attend to things of the Church. Also not to be forgotten is the fact that to consecrate one's self to a cause which justifies the considerable sacrifice entailed by celibacy, is already to show great love of others, mastery of one's self, and uncommon maturity (cf. John Paul II: *Letter to all Priests on Holy Thursday*, 1979, n. 8).

Chastity for Religious and Members of Secular Institutes

In the Catholic Church it has been the tradition that all religious (brothers and sisters, monks and nuns) and members of secular institutes take the vow of perpetual chastity or celibacy. The person who so consecrates his chastity or virginity to God "for the sake of The Kingdom of heaven" (Mt. 19:12) sacrifices something that is good and dear to man. He more profoundly bears witness to the fact that human sexuality as exercised in marriage, although good in itself, is only one form of love. By their consecrated chastity, "religious give witness to all Christ's faithful of that wondrous marriage in which the Church has Christ as her only spouse, a marriage which has been established by God and which will be fully manifested in the world to come" (Vatican II: *Religious*, n. 12).

Not everybody is called to a life of consecrated celibacy. But those who are called by grace and who generously embrace this life out of love for Christ and in the desire to serve His Kingdom with greater freedom and single heartedness (cf. 1 Cor. 7: 32-35), will find in celibacy a means of profound self-fulfillment and growth in grace.

The Church has learned from experience and from the words of Christ that virginity for Christ is a vocation of "surpassing excellence". Consecrated virgins are rightly called brides of Christ, and religious profession is likened to a spiritual marriage. A breaking of a vow of celibacy by anyone would entail also the great sin of sacrilege.

Tensions in a Life of Celibacy

Some people have spoken of tensions in a life of celibacy. Let us examine three such tensions.

There is the fear of solitude, of psychological isolation, of the obligation to be alone all the time. The answer is that to a certain extent this tension exists. But it should not be exaggerated. If a consecrated celibate is generous and large hearted, and if genuine charity exists between him and those with whom he lives, his sense of solitude will not be very much more than that of a person who faces his individual responsibility with manly courage and sincerity. Moreover, other people have also a certain amount of solitude as single people in the world, as widows or widowers, as quarreling husbands and wives, and also as loving husbands and wives. Every person must at some stage be alone before God and answer for himself.

Others speak of the tension of the absence of fatherhood or motherhood. The answer is that the consecrated celibate has indeed no children according to the flesh, but many children according to the spirit, with effects carrying into eternity.

Some write about the difficulty of being always celibate. The answer is that in our fallen human condition, chastity will more or less remain a struggle for everyone: young or old, married or single, priest or religious. There is no need to exaggerate the problem for consecrated celibates.

Helps to Living Chastity

From the above considerations, it is possible to name some helps towards the cultivation and preservation of chastity according to each person's vocation in life. Let us list some.

A good family background is an excellent preparation. Wise and chaste parents who love their children and who conduct a home marked by joy, peace, calm, honesty, and nobility have already laid a good foundation. Growing children need parental understanding and guidance. A good school is a help.

Modesty and reserve are needed to protect the delicate virtue of chastity. In a way, chastity is as delicate as an egg. If you hold it too hard, it breaks up. If you hold it carelessly, it falls and breaks up. Modesty is the virtue which stands guard at the door to protect chastity. Modesty dictates and directs the becoming way to talk, walk, sit, dress, greet, write, and handle the usual situations involved in ordinary dealings between men and women.

Prayer, reflection, and silence are also needed. "As I know that I could not otherwise be continent except God gave it," says the Douay Version, "I went to the Lord and besought Him" (Wis. 8:21).

Humility, common sense, balance, and honesty are also needed. The chaste person is not proud. He does not rely on himself or his past records. He knows that we carry this treasure in earthen vessels. He knows that we must work out our salvation in fear and trembling. As long as we are on earth, a fall is possible. Therefore the chaste person relies on God. He does not take unnecessary risks. He does not engage in dangerous familiarities with the excuse of friendship. And he does not exploit his fellow human being.

Mortification is necessary. An athlete cannot hope to win a 100 meter race if he consumes two big plates of foufou and two big bottles of beer fifteen minutes before the race begins! "I chastise my body and bring it under subjection," St. Paul tells us (1 Cor. 9:27).

The sacraments help us to be chaste. The Sacrament of Penance gives us not only forgiveness but also strength to persevere. The Holy Eucharist is supremely powerful in giving us a taste for things of God and weaning us from the slavery to impurity. A fervent Eucharistic devotion will keep us near the Heart of Christ. Moreover, married people should live the community of life to which they are vowed. Priests should live the sacramental brotherhood in the unity of the presbyterium into which ordination introduces them. Religious profession is a sacramental not a sacrament. About religious and chastity, the Second Vatican Council says that "everyone should remember — superiors — especially that chastity has stronger safeguards in a community when true fraternal love thrives among its members" (Vatican II: *Religious*, n. 12).

Devotion to the Blessed Virgin Mary is a proven way of preserving chastity. She is "our tainted nature's solitary boast." She is mother of virgins. Those who fly to her refuge will not be disappointed.

Models of Chastity in the Bible

The Bible presents us with an impressive array of men and women who are models of chastity. In the Old Testament, Joseph, the son of Jacob, is outstanding. Servant of his master in Egypt, he refused to sin with his master's wife in spite of her insistent requests, and he suffered imprisonment in silence. God rewarded him abundantly.

John the Baptist was celibate. He gave his life for Christ. St. Joseph, husband of Mary Immaculate, is a model of humility, obedience, transparent chastity, and total fidelity. God trusted him with the care of Mary and Jesus, the two most precious human beings that ever walked this earth. Jesus, of course, was celibate. His Blessed Mother is Virgin before, during, and after the birth of her only Son. St. John the Evangelist, the beloved apostle to whom Christ entrusted His Mother, was a virgin. So was St. Paul.

Moreover, the Scripture calls Jerusalem a virgin (cf. Is. 23:12); Judith was praised for her chastity, and she won a big victory (cf. Jud. 15:10); St. Paul extols the dignity of celibacy (cf. 1 Cor. 7:9); and the Apocalypse says that only virgins can sing the song of the Lamb (cf. Apoc. 14:1).

Models of Chastity in Church History

Church history has presented us with an impressive array of men and women who lived chaste lives as consecrated virgins or religious or priests or as married people or widowers. It is enough to think of Saints Agnes, Thecla, Lucy, Cecilia, Gertrude, Margaret Mary Alacoque, Catherine, Clara, Scholastica, Theresa of Avila, Theresa of Lisieux, and Maria Goretti. Of the men saints, think of Saints Stephen, Ambrose, Thomas Aquinas, Peter Canisius, Ignatius of Loyola, Charles Borromeo, Aloysius Gonzaga, Francis de Sales, Francis Xavier, Francis of Assisi, Alphonsus Maria de Liguori, John Berchmans, John Mary Vianney, Martyrs of Uganda, and Maximilian Kolbe. These great specimens of redeemed humanity were not just holy people, but have also left a rich social, cultural, educational, medical, and social inheritance to all mankind

Chastity is a virtue which should distinguish all the followers of Christ. All of us should pray for the grace to love it and to live it with total fidelity.

X. POVERTY

The Purpose of Property

It is God's will that we human beings should make use of earthly goods during our pilgrimage on earth. We need a minimum of food, clothes, shelter, and other goods in order to live a dignified human existence.

By his labor and also by gifts and inheritance, man can acquire property. A person has a right to own the goods which he acquired in a just way. They help him to live a worthily human life and to discharge his duties to his family, his relatives, the Church, and society at large.

Property has a social dimension. Those who possess much of the goods of this world are bound to remember their neighbors who are in great need.

The goods of this world should be used by us to journey towards our heavenly home. They have no permanent value.

Detachment from Earthly Goods

Jesus teaches us detachment from earthly goods by word and example. "Blessed are the poor in spirit...the meek...those who cry...those who are persecuted for justice sake..." (Mt. 5:3-10). "You cannot be the slave both of God and of money" (Mt. 6:24). "That is why I am telling you not to worry about your life and what you are to eat, nor about your body and how you are to clothe it" (Mt. 6:25). He warns about the danger of riches: "It is easier for a camel to pass through the eye of a needle than for a rich man to enter the kingdom of heaven" (Mt. 19:24). He makes big promises to those who sacrifice earthly goods in order to follow Him: "Everyone who has left houses, brothers, sisters, father, mother, children, or land for the sake of my name will be repaid a hundred times over, and also inherit eternal life" (Mt. 19:29). He Himself was so poor that He had nowhere to lay His head. And when He died He was buried in a borrowed grave.

There is no doubt that the spirit of Christ is that of detachment from earthly goods. All Christians are bound to have this spirit and virtue of poverty. How a person practices it will depend on his vocation in life.

Poverty as Practiced by the Priest

Priests are spiritual leaders of both the laity and the religious. They should in their lives be models of the virtue of poverty so that the laity and the religious can be inspired to follow. Aware that the Lord is their portion and their inheritance (cf. Num. 18:20), they should take their hearts away from earthly things and attach them to Christ.

Therefore, a priest's housing facilities, means of transport, clothing, food, and general life style should be such as will not classify him with the well off and the powerful. The actual details can be discussed and can vary from culture to culture. But the general principle is there (cf. Vatican II: *Priests*, n. 17).

Priests should be good, honest, and careful administrators of Church property. Aware that the clergy and the poor should be maintained with these sacred funds, after divine worship is taken care of, priests should act in such a way as to generate confidence among the parishioners, their fellow priests, and the bishop, on their use of Church money. And they should be marked by generosity to the needy, the sick, and the old; to seminarians; and to aspirants to the religious life. Relatives of priests should not tempt the priest to nepotism because he did not become a priest in order to enrich them with Church property.

The Lord, through the prophets, was very severe on money-loving priests or pastors who were interested not so much in feeding the flock as in fleecing it. We can liken such to priests who call a parish good if there is much money in it (cf. Ezek. 33:1-9; 34:1-16; Mic. 3:58).

Poverty as Practiced by Religious

All religious in the Church take a vow of poverty. By this vow they sacrifice their right to own property. Therefore everything that comes to them as a result of their work or as gifts belongs to their religious congregation. In turn, the congregation looks after each member and helps the poor.

By this vow a religious shares in the poverty of Christ who became poor for our sake when before He had been rich, so that we might be enriched by His poverty (cf. 2 Cor. 8:9; Mt. 8:20). Religious are expected to be poor both in spirit and in fact, and to have their treasures in heaven (cf. Mt. 6:20).

Spirit of Poverty

The vow of poverty is not a vow of laziness. Religious are expected to be conscious that they are subject to the common law of work. Work is our way of showing love and solidarity with our community and the wider world.

It follows also that religious should have a high sense of responsibility and should use the goods made available to them with reasonable care. They should excel in their efforts to sacrifice the use of many creature comforts. They should be known to be hard-working and full of initiative. Church history is full of beautiful examples of religious in monasteries and in congregations who have accomplished much with little.

Religious should put aside all inordinate anxiety about earthly goods and trust in Divine Providence. Moreover, the suffering involved in going without necessary goods is part of the identification with the poor for which religious should be noted. It is a counter sign when religious, or their congregations, become known for opulence, a rich life style, and hardness of heart towards the poor.

Illusions about Poverty

There are some religious (brothers or sisters) who entertain false ideas about their poverty in the religious life. One illusion is that if they had not embraced the religious life, they would have been rich, they would not have been in need of so many things, and they would have been able to help their parents, brothers, sisters, cousins down to the seventh generation, and friends, with plenty of money. Perhaps this might have been so. But for most people it may not have been so because they would not have succeeded in becoming rich, and also because there are many rich people who do not give much to their relatives. Moreover, a religious brother or sister almost always has a reasonable availability of things necessary for a decent living and is looked after by his religious congregation when he is sick.

There are religious who go under the illusion that their present congregation is the cause of all their physical deprivations and that they know another congregation which looks after its members much better. Such religious are to be advised to make the full offering involved in their vowed life with all generosity and to stop deceiving themselves with daydreams!

Religious and Actual Poverty

Religious are expected to be poor, not only in spirit, but also in fact.

For example, their houses and furniture should be suitable, but not too rich. Their means of transport should be moderate and should not attract attention. Their vest should be of good but simple material. Here we see the centuries-old wisdom of the Church in having a religious habit for every order or congregation. The individual does not then waste money in making many other vests according to changing world fashions. And the mortification involved in wearing the same vest the whole year round is also part of the practice of poverty.

Religious houses and congregations are also expected to be poor. Of course they need some money in order to maintain their members, to train new ones, and to look after the sick and the old. But they should all the time remember that the accumulation of goods or funds is a continuing temptation both for individuals and for groups. Religious houses should also use their savings for the poor, for the seminaries, and for other needs of the Church. Their superiors should be in dialogue with the diocesan bishop on how the congregation can be involved in the programs of the diocese.

Desire for High Positions

It is human to desire to be placed in a high position in one's calling. Religious and priests are not spared this temptation. It is the temptation to high honor, to an appointment which gives a high sense of self-fulfillment, a sense of being somebody, a sense of having something to boast about or for which to be admired.

This temptation takes various forms according to people and places. For some it is the desire for top posts such as bishop, superior general, local superior, head of a school or college or hospital staff, etc. For others it is long university studies, high sounding academic degrees, and consequent professorship. For the same reason there is a temptation to look down on appointments such as the following: cooking, house-keeping, farming, breadmaking, and even teaching in kindergartens and primary schools and working as assistant priest in a poor parish.

The radical error in all this is a radical misunderstanding of the religious life or even the priesthood. They are not ladders for social promotion. The spirit of Christ is that of serving, not that of being served. Jesus did not approve of the maneuver of the two sons of Zebedee who tried to obtain top appointments at His right and His left in His kingdom. Nor did He approve of the anger and envy of the other ten apostles. He took the occasion to give them a lecture on His spirit of leadership, understood not as domination, but as service (cf. Mk. 10: 35-45). "Anyone who wants to become great among you must be your servant" (Mt. 10:43).

The spirit of poverty, therefore, also includes sacrifice of honors, power, and high position. A religious should in all simplicity accept whatever assignment is given him, without calculating whether these are high or low in the esteem of the world.

Poverty of the Religious Brother

In this respect, it is fitting to reflect on the poverty of the religious brother. This poverty, in a certain sense, consists in this, that many people do not place a religious brother high on the social ladder. It is because they have a false idea of what it means to be a brother. They think that a brother is a young man who did not succeed in becoming a priest, probably because he did not pass the examination. For the same reason, they think that a brother who has a university degree is a waste, and that if he is so intelligent he should have become a priest.

A person who thinks so should be plainly told that he is mistaken. The religious life is not a quest for prestige, high position, big name, or first seat in the synagogue. A religious is a Christian who is pursuing perfection in a state of consecration by the three vows recognized by the Church. Brothers are not struggling for high consideration, or for a seating position near the priests in the Church (because the priests are in the sanctuary since they have a Eucharistic ministry at the altar).

It is important that a religious brother should be very clear about his vocation to follow Christ who was so poor that He had nowhere to lay His head. It is bad enough if some lay people do not understand what a brother is. But if a brother also has doubt on his identity, if he has an identity crisis, then the situation is really grave. To be poor and to live poor is a powerful and convincing way to follow Christ in the world of today.

Witness of Poverty in the Nigeria of Today

In the Nigeria of today, there is an unbridled pursuit of riches. There is loud, high, and heavy spending at celebrations such as marriages, funerals, opening of new houses, and even receptions for newly ordained priests or professed religious. There is the phenomenon of the parade of wealth by the rich and of pretense at being rich by the poor. This disease has also invaded priests' rectories, brothers' fraternities, and convent corridors. The rich attract much attention, and if clerics and religious are not careful, they will be misled to paying more attention to the rich than to the poor.

All Christians should react against this situation in the spirit of Christ. And clerics and religious should lead this campaign which goes against the prevailing current in society. We cannot convert a materialistic society by ourselves joining its band-wagon.

Even the lyric poet Horace (65-3 B.C.) had the wisdom to write: "He who dreads poverty, lacks liberty ... and will remain forever a slave, because he has not learnt to be content with little" (Horace, *Epistles* I, 10). And the celebrated Greek philosopher Socrates (470-399 B.C.) says: "I think that to want as little as possible is to make the nearest approach to the gods, that the divine nature is perfection and that to be nearest to the divine nature is to be nearest to perfection" (*Socratic Discourses*: Plato and *Xenophon*, The Penguin Classics, p. 37; quoted by B. Fonlon. *An Open Letter to the Bishops of Buea and Bamenda*, 1973, pp. 14, 17).

Our Lord Himself summarizes it all: "How happy are the poor in spirit; theirs is the kingdom of heaven" (Mt. 5:3).

XI. OBEDIENCE

In the Steps of Our Master

Jesus obeyed. He obeyed His eternal Father. He obeyed Mary and Joseph. He obeyed even Pontius Pilate. "My food," He says, "is to do the will of the one who sent me, and to complete His work" (John 4:34; cf. also 5:30, 6:38). Jesus humbled Himself and became obedient unto death, even death on the cross (cf. Phil. 2:8).

Obedience in Holy Scripture

The Holy Scripture gives us many examples of people who submitted their wills to the will of God in acts of obedience nourished by faith, love, and trust. Abraham was commanded by God to leave his people and go out of his country to an unknown land which God promised him. He obeyed (cf. Gen. 11:1-4). Abraham was asked to sacrifice his son Isaac, and he was ready to do  it. Samuel was called by God. He obeyed (cf. 1 Sam. 3:5).

In the New Testament, St. Joseph was given various orders: to take into his home Mary, who was with child, to take the child and the mother and go into Egypt, to return from Egypt, and to leave Judea. He obeyed all these orders without a question (cf. Mt. 1:18-25; 2:19-23). Mary Immaculate obeyed her husband Joseph.

St. Paul obeyed the call of Christ and went on the difficult mission assigned to him (cf. Acts 9:6; 20:22-24). St. Stephen obeyed the guidance of the Holy Spirit (cf. Acts 6:8, 55).

The Bible extols obedience. Christ tells the Apostles that those who obey the Apostles are actually obeying Him (cf. Lk. 10:16). St. Paul advises obedience to earthly authorities because this authority comes from God (cf. Rom. 13:1-3, 5; Tit. 3:1). St. Peter does the same (cf. 1 Pet. 2:13-18).

On the other hand, Holy Scripture strongly disapproves of disobedience. Samuel blames Saul: "Is the pleasure of Yahweh in holocausts and sacrifices or in obedience to the voice of Yahweh? Yes, obedience is better than sacrifice, submissiveness better than the fat of rams. Rebellion is a sin of sorcery, presumption a crime of teraphim. Since you have rejected the word of Yahweh, He has rejected you as king" (1 Sam. 15:22-23). This is very clear. Adam and Eve disobeyed God and precipitated all of us into the state of a fallen race. Korah, Dathan and Abiram rebelled against Moses and Aaron, who were God's messengers, and the ground opened and swallowed them and all their families (cf. Num. 16 & 17). Miriam and Aaron complained against Moses, and Miriam was struck a leper (cf. Num. 12). The people disobeyed God at the waters of Meribah, and many were struck dead (cf. Num. 20).

Deuteronomy has summarized the spirit of obedience to God and trust in Him: "See, I set before you today a blessing and a curse: a blessing, if you obey the commandments of Yahweh our God that I enjoin on you today; a curse, if you disobey the commandments of Yahweh your God and leave that way I have marked out for you today" (Deut. 11:26-28).

Religious Obedience is Based on Faith

Obedience as a Christian virtue is based on faith. A superior is obeyed because the authority of God is recognized in the superior. For religious brothers and sisters there is the added motive of a vow. But every Christian has to practice this virtue according to the person's vocation. Children practice it by obeying their parents. Servants obey their masters. Teachers in a school obey their head teacher or principal. Priests obey their bishop and other diocesan officials appointed by him. Religious obey their superiors. Let us reflect more on this last point.

Obedience to Superiors by Religious

By the vow of obedience, religious brothers and sisters offer to God a total dedication of their own wills as a sacrifice. In this way, they unite themselves with greater steadiness and security to the saving will of

God. They follow the example of our Master, Jesus Christ, who came to do the will of the Father (cf. John 4:24; 5:30; Heb. 10:7; Ps. 39:9).

The Holy Spirit helps religious to see in their superiors the representatives of God. Through the sacrifice of their wills, they make themselves more totally at God's disposal and at the service of their brothers and sisters, at the service of the Church, and on the road to full growth in Christ (cf. Vatican II: *Religious*, n. 14).

The Duty of Superiors

It is not only those under authority who have a duty in this matter. Superiors have a duty also. They are to realize that to be put in a position of authority is to be called to serve others. It is not a position for rest, or enjoyment, and much less one of domination. A person is in authority, not to do what he likes, but to look for the will of God and to transmit it to the group which he is appointed to serve. The superior is the minister or mediator of God's will to the brothers or sisters. The superior must not mistake his whims and caprices, his likes and dislikes, and his funny ideas, for the will of God. Nor must he call for blind and foolish actions in the name of obedience. The superior is to be a model in seeking the will of God, in humbly bowing before it, and in simply transmitting it to the brothers and sisters.

The superior should, in faith, humility, and love, respect the persons of those whom he is appointed to serve. These persons have some God-given fundamental rights and dignity. Truth and justice are necessary virtues. Just as those who disobey are wrong, so those who give orders can be wrong too. Everyone will one day appear before the best Judge and be examined according to truth. God is no respecter of persons.

The Second Vatican Council wisely says to superiors: "As one who will render an account for the souls entrusted to him (cf. Heb. 13:17), each superior should himself be docile to God's will in the exercise of his office. Let him use his authority in a spirit of service for the brethren, and manifest thereby the charity with which God loves them. Governing his subjects as God's own sons, and with regard for their human personality, a superior will make it easier for them to obey gladly" (Vatican II: *Religious*, n. 14).

Dialogue

It follows that a spirit of dialogue should be normal in religious houses, and indeed in any other society, with the necessary adaptations. But dialogue is often misunderstood. It is not a session for the announcement of what is to be done, although announcements have sometimes to be made. It is not a meeting to allow the superior merely to hear the views of the others before deciding. It is not a gathering in which occasion is provided to attack the superior legitimately. It is not endless filibuster in which the tactic of the members is to talk, and talk and talk, and argue, and argue and argue, until the superior surrenders out of sheer tiredness.

Dialogue is a meeting of minds. It is a discussion in which people speak and also listen. It is a sincere exchange of views in which each person is willing to give and to receive. It is a common effort to identify a problem, to assess the difficulties, and to search together what would seem to be the best answer. The participants in a dialogue do not have the ready-made answer before they begin. They have their views. But they are prepared to change their ground in the light of better information. It is a fool or a stubborn person who refuses to change his views when the contrary arguments are clear and overwhelming.

Dialogue suggests that no one should be silenced. Even a person who is not very intelligent can sometimes propose a very wise solution. No one is wrong all the time. Even a clock that does not move is correct two times a day. No one has a monopoly on the guidance of the Holy Spirit. The wisdom, or even truth, of a proposition does not depend on the dignity of the person who propounded it.

Both the superior and all the other participants in a dialogue should be looking for the will of God. At the end of the dialogue session, the superior should be able to speak like the Apostles at the end of the Council of Jerusalem. "It has been decided by the Holy Spirit and by ourselves not to saddle you with any burden beyond these essentials" (Acts 15:28). The superior wants to transmit the will of God. Obviously, no matter how many hours the dialogue may have lasted, and even when there is no dialogue, the authority and responsibility of the superior to decide what is to be done and to give directives or orders, remains intact.

If a religious considers that what he is asked to do is really above his strength, or will do damage to him, to others or to the Church, it is his right, and sometimes even his duty, to explain his difficulties to the superior. He should be ready finally to abide by the decision of the superior.

Some Ways of Disobedience

Man, being a member of a fallen race, has throughout history found excuses for disobedience or invented ways of not obeying. Some religious or priests who are given appointments which they do not like, first try to find out how the superior or bishop arrived at that decision and who advised him. Others impute motives to the superior, generally without hearing him. There are others who resort to murmuring, which has been called the last refuge of a coward.

But some others who disobey are more active and militant. They demand dialogue in the sense of tiring the superior with endless arguments and threats until the superior surrenders in order to avoid a bigger evil. They lobby around among all those who they think can influence the superior to decide matters in the way it would suit them.

It is clear that priests can also disobey by setting aside the directives and liturgical rules of the Church for the celebration of the Holy Eucharist and other sacred rites and engaging in what some call "spontaneous or creative liturgy." Hypercriticism, by which some theologians disregard directives of the Church or make fun of the teaching authority of the Pope and the Bishops, is also a form of disobedience. So is the taking on of secular employment by priests or religious without, or worse still, against the approval of their bishops and superiors.

To obey is to make of our wills an offering to God. Obedience is better than sacrifice. The one who wants to follow Christ will have to learn to follow a Master who was obedient unto death, and death on a cross.

Xll. HUMILITY

Jesus was Humble

We learn humility in the school of Christ. He is our model. "Shoulder my yoke and learn from Me," He tells us, "for I am gentle and humble in heart, and you will find rest for your souls" (Mt. 11:29). He comes to do the Father's will. He comes, not to be served, but to serve (cf. Mt. 20:28). He took the nature of a slave (cf. Phil. 2:7). He teaches the Apostles that the greatest in the Kingdom of heaven is the one who humbles himself as a child (cf. Mt. 18:1-3). He rewards the humility of the Canaanite woman (cf. Mt. 15:28). He washes the feet of the Apostles (cf. John 13). Also by His poverty, labor, self-abnegation, patience, and especially perfect obedience, He taught us humility.

Humility is Based on Proper Esteem of Self

Humility is not pretense. It is based on truth. It is founded on proper esteem of self. We are God's creatures. We are redeemed by Christ. All the gifts of nature and grace which we have come from God's goodness. Humility demands that we honor and thank God for these gifts and refer the praise to Him and not to ourselves.

We also have faults. Everyone of us can, in quiet prayer, reflect on his defects. We should not dodge responsibility for these. We should accept that we are guilty of our lapses, instead of trying to blame people, the weather, the government, or our superiors.

The proud person has undue esteem of self. He exaggerates his good qualities. He does not refer his successes to God. And he finds it difficult to accept that he is wrong and to ask pardon.

Reasons for Humility

There are sound reasons why we should be humble. By ourselves we are nothing, we have nothing and can do nothing. All our greatness, including the very fact of our existence, comes from God. No one is good but God alone (cf. Lk. 18:18). "What do you have that has not been given to you? And if it was given, how can you boast as though it were not?" (1 Cor. 4:7). When we admire a picture, we give praise to the artist, not to the canvass. When a priest carries the Most Blessed Sacrament and goes to visit the sick, the people on the way genuflect to Christ in the Blessed Sacrament, not to the priest.

Another reason for humility is that in spite of all the endowments that God gave us, we have not profited sufficiently from His gifts as we should have. We have often opposed His plans and inspirations. We have inclinations to evil.

We must therefore admit that we are creatures entirely dependent on God's grace, deserving of no honor ourselves, but fully meriting contempt because of our opposition to God's will and our misuse of His gifts.

Signs of Humility

Humility is shy. It does not generally want to appear in public. The person who is humble generally does not know it as clearly as other people. Humility appears in the form of such virtues as obedience, patience, thanksgiving, praise, joy at other people's success, acceptance of other people's opinions, readiness for meaningful dialogue, charity, forgiveness, and self-control in community life.

The humble person is able to consider others better than himself. He does not condemn others. He finds it difficult to judge them. Indeed, Our Lord tells us not to judge others. We do not know the intentions of others. We can observe only their external actions. Appearances can be very deceptive. We generally cannot know all the circumstances necessary to judge a person properly. This shows how difficult the assignment of superiors is, and how necessary it is for others to sympathize with superiors, to help them, and to forgive them their mistakes of judgment of people or situations.

The humble person admits that he is wrong when he is wrong. He does not stubbornly stick to his opinion. Even when he is sure that he is right, he is moderate and calm in his statement of his position, and he has the patience and good sense to wait for a better day if his proposal is at present not accepted.

The humble person says his mind with all frankness during dialogue, but when the superior has finally decided what is to be done, the humble person, even if he had the contrary view, executes that command with calm, and also with all his gifts of nature and grace.

The humble person practices poverty in all its ramifications and does not get nervous over his nonattainment of high positions and big-sounding academic degrees.

The humble person does not seek popularity among human beings. Rather, he just wants to please God. He therefore does not fear to say or do a thing, or to take a decision which will make him unpopular, provided that prayer, reflection, and due consultation have clarified what God's will is.

The humble person is able to work as a good commission or committee member. He does not declare a state of emergency when his opinion is not accepted.

The humble person is patient under false accusation, persecution, ingratitude, and humiliations.

St. Benedict on Humility

St. Benedict gives the following twelve degrees of humility for a monk. Other people can adapt it to their own vocation:

1. To have the fear of God always before your eyes.
2. Not to love your own will nor take delight in satisfying your desires.

3. For love of God, to subject yourself to your superior.

4. Patience, calm, and perseverance in obeying difficult and unpleasant commands or suffering injuries.

5. Confessing and revealing thoughts and secret faults to the abbot.

6. Being content with anything, no matter how despicable, and regarding oneself as an unworthy servant.

7. Not just saying, but really believing oneself to be the worst of all.

8. Doing nothing outside the common rule of your monastery and the example of the elders.

9. Control of the tongue. Talking little.

10. Not too ready to laugh.

11. Gentle, calm, restrained and brief in speech.

12. Humility appearing in many ways of behavior.

(cf. St. Benedict's Rule for Monasteries, chapter 7).

In our following of Christ, humility occupies a quiet and most important place. The lack of this fundamental virtue is able to ruin any other virtue we may seem to have.

XIII. PRAYER

Necessity of Prayer

Prayer is an important exercise of the virtue of religion. It is a practical recognition of our dependence on God. It is an acknowledgement that our existence and ability to do good comes from God, and that cut off from God, we can achieve nothing (cf. John 15:5). Indeed, cut off from Him, we would lapse back into nothing.

Jesus, Our Model in Prayer

Our Lord Jesus Christ is our model of how to pray.

He taught us "about the need to pray continually and never lose heart" (Lk. 18:1). During His public life, on many occasions, He went off alone to pray, sometimes for the whole night (cf. Mk. 1:35; 6:46; Lk. 3:21; 5:16; 6:12; 9:18, 28). "He offered up prayer and entreaty, aloud and in silent tears" (Heb. 5:7).

He prayed so much that one of His disciples begged Him to teach them how to pray, and He taught them the magnificent and all-inclusive prayer, the Our Father (cf. Lk. 11:1f).

Jesus prayed for His Apostles especially at the last supper, the night before He suffered, after He gave them the wonderful sacrament of the Holy Eucharist and ordained them priests (cf. John 17). He prayed in a particular way for St. Peter, the head of the Apostles "that his faith might not fail" (Lk. 22:32).

Jesus prayed for Jerusalem, for all believers in Himself, and for those who crucified Him. He was in continuing prayer communion with His heavenly Father (Lk. 11:41).

Types of Prayer

Prayer is the raising up of our minds and hearts to God. It is spiritual communion with God. From the point of view of the contents of our prayer, we can distinguish four types of prayer according to the four major acts of religion: adoration, thanksgiving, asking pardon for sins, and petitions for things spiritual and temporal. All types are important. But the highest forms of prayers are those of adoration, of praise, of thanksgiving. Think of the first part of the angelic chant: Glory be to God in the Highest.

From the point of view of who is praying, we can

distinguish three types of prayer: liturgical prayer, communal prayer, and personal prayer. Liturgical prayer has already been examined. It is made up of sacraments, sacramentals and the Liturgy of the Hours. Communal prayers are prayers said together by a group of people. The words are generally written out beforehand. If the book containing them is meant for circulation, it should be approved by competent Church authority so that orthodoxy of doctrine can be safeguarded, because prayer influences faith and vice versa.

Personal or individual prayer needs special emphasis, because that is the type which most people find hardest. It demands more attention, or rather, the lack of attention is more easily noticed here than in the other two types. Personal prayer wells up from the depths of the heart of the individual. It is not copied from a book nor from another person. It is necessary in our spiritual lives, particularly during visits to the Most Blessed Sacrament, before and after receiving Holy Communion, at daily mental prayer, and at moments of joy, sorrow or danger. A person's level of spiritual growth can be gauged by his progress in personal prayer.

Qualities of Prayer

Prayer should be devout. To help us pray better, we should have an intention. Attention and recollection are necessary. A habitual practice of being in God's presence is a help. If set words are used, effort should be made to digest their meanings. Rushing is an enemy of good prayer. Prayer should be humble. God's majesty is supreme. We come before God as beggars. He knows everything. We are in no position to negotiate or bargain with Him. We should not try to issue Him an ultimatum.

When we pray, we should trust God. He wants to help us. He can help us. He loves us. He does help us. Therefore, in His hands we should relax (cf. James 1:5-

8; Mk. 11:24).

It follows that we should be resigned to God's will. Not our will but God's will is to be done (cf. Lk. 22:42). God does not need our advice on what is best for us.

Prayer should be persevering. We should knock and knock and continue to knock. That is what Our Lord taught us. And He granted the request of the Canaanite woman because she continued to pray (cf. Mt. 15:21-28; Lk. 18:1; Jdth. 4:11).

Difficulties in Prayer

Prayer is not without its difficulties. Some of them are due to our own fault and some are not. Distractions can be due to ill health, action of the non-guilty self, action of the guilty self, action of the devil, disturbance by other people, and other causes which Divine Providence knows. We should do our best to avoid distractions. But even when we have done all in our power some distractions are likely to remain sometime in our prayer as long as we are on pilgrimage on earth.

Sometimes we feel very dry at prayer. We do not feel inclined to pray. We should base ourselves on faith and not on feelings. We ought always to pray and not to lose heart (cf. Lk. 18:1). Aridity in prayer can also be the sign of the coming of a higher form of prayer. It is disastrous to give up prayer just because we feel dry.

Unsuitable surroundings can create problems. All things being equal, the chapel or church with the Most Blessed Sacrament is the ideal place for prayer. But of course, we should pray in our homes, places of work, at travel, at play, indeed everywhere.

Another difficulty at prayer is that many people are poor in personal prayer. They rely more on formal prayers said from prayerbooks. They have to learn that another person's private prayer can help us. But we should also develop our individual prayer. A child does not need a helping book in order to speak with his mother. A friend does not converse with his friend out of a speech writer's productions.

Advantages of Prayer

Prayer helps us to keep in union with God, without whom we are nothing and can do nothing.

Prayer helps us to reflect and to see ourselves as we are, i.e., as God sees us. Prayer is a spiritual mirror.

Prayer helps us to see when we are beginning to walk on the road to infidelity to God in matters of chastity, poverty, obedience, or other vows, and when we have begun to commit little robberies in a holocaust. Prayer helps us to look at ourselves in the mirror of Christ and to see our little acts in carelessness, not to talk of bigger ones, and our little concessions to human weakness.

Prayer and its concomitant reflection and silence help us to realize when we are getting difficult with people, irritable, intolerant, vain, or proud.

Prayer helps us to discover our selfishness and little acts of lack of charity towards our neighbor, together with our acts of anger (cf. John Paul II: *Letter to all Priests on Holy Thursday* 1979, n. 10).

Above all, prayer enables us to adore God, to recognize His greatness, and to be more and more completely at His disposal. It is therefore no surprise that St. Augustine says that he has learned to live well, who has learned to pray well. St. Alphonsus Maria de Liguori says that he who prays will be saved, and he who does not pray will be lost.

Prayer is the Soul of the Apostolate

Prayer gives life to our works of the apostolate. Without prayer our apostolic works will not bear spiritual fruit. We could be apostolic noise-makers. We could engage in hectic activities. The wheels of our car or motor cycle could rotate thousands of times each day.

But if we do not remain united with God in prayer, we would emerge as not much better than sounding drums or tinkling cymbals. Moreover, the active apostolic worker who does not pray is in danger of forgetting the God of works in order to concentrate on the works of God. He can even be in danger of sin.

The corridors of Church history are littered with the spiritual ruins of apostolic workers, including priests who neglected prayer. The fall of many priests begins on the day on which they began to be negligent with the Holy Eucharist, with the Liturgy of the Hours, with mental prayer, and with devotion to Our Blessed Lady. It is not a good argument to quote the saying, "to work is to pray." The saying would be correct if our apostolic works are indeed an outflow of our interior union with God, maintained and promoted through prayer. It would be false if work were not supported by prayer and if it were not given spiritual fertility by our dependence on God in prayer. Christ has warned us that cut off from Him we cannot achieve anything.

The busier we are, the more we should pray. St. Bernard warned Pope Eugenio IV (one of his monks who became Pope) that not only do the heavy engagements of the papal ministry not absolve him from much prayer, but rather that they oblige him to more prayer.

We should not forget what happened to St. Peter and the other two Apostles. Jesus told them to watch and pray. But they slept. And Judas did not sleep. When Judas led his gang to capture Jesus, Peter woke up from sleep and swung his sword. Jesus did not approve of this type of swordsmanship, this type of apostolic activism. And to prove the failure of the person who has not prayed, Peter and the other Apostles deserted their Master and fled. Peter rallied back, but he soon fell again. He denied his Master three times in front of a servant girl! Peter should have learned his lesson when he walked on the water to go to Jesus and then began to sink when he began looking at the fury of the waves instead of looking at Jesus and trusting in Him, and moving on in the strength of Jesus, without Whom we can do nothing. Apostolic workers, be they priests, lay people, or religious, should never forget this. Our help is in the name of the Lord who made heaven and earth.

XIV. CHARITY

Importance for Christian Perfection

Charity is love of God. It necessarily includes love of our neighbor. Indeed, love of our neighbor is generally a test of our love of God. St. John is very clear on this: "Anyone who says, 'I love God', and hates his brother, is a liar, since a man who does not love the brother that he can see cannot love God, whom he has never seen. So this is the commandment that He has given us, that anyone who loves God must also love his neighbor" (1 John 4:20-21; cf. also Mt. 7:12; 22:40).

Charity makes us like unto God: perfect (cf. Mt. 5:44; John 17:21-23). It makes us followers of Christ who gave love as His new commandment (cf. John 13:14; 15:12, 34). The last judgment will depend on our charity to our neighbor (cf. Mt. 25:15).

In this chapter we shall speak most of the time on

charity to our neighbor, as it is our simplest test of our love of God. But it must be borne in mind that charity is primarily the love of God. In this sense we say that charity is the queen and the form of all the virtues, because no other virtue is perfect and fully formed without charity. Also we say that holiness is the perfection of charity.

Motives for Love of Our Neighbor

We should love our neighbor because he is created by God, redeemed by Christ, called to be a member of the Church, and destined to see God in heaven. Christ, by becoming man, has in a way identified Himself with every man. What we do to others, He regards as done to Himself.

For some people, we have further reasons for charity because we share the same faith, or they are our priests or special consecrated people, or they are with us members of the same family, town, religious congregation, parish, diocese, etc. A close relationship is a motive for charity, although our charity must not stop there but should move onto other people.

Kind Thoughts About Others

Kind thoughts about other people do not cost us anything. And yet we, fallen children of Adam and Eve, often find them not easy, and we find the contrary happening often in our lives. But charity demands that we do not judge others, and if we have to, the judgment should be as favorable as possible. Jesus tells us: "Do not judge, and you will not be judged" (Mt. 7:1). "Always treat others as you would like them to treat you; that is the meaning of the Law and the Prophets" (Mt. 7:12; cf. also Lk. 6:31). "It is not for you," St. Paul tells us, "to condemn someone else's servant" (Rom. 14:4). "There must be no passing of premature judgment. Leave that until the Lord comes" (1 Cor. 4:5).

Unkind thoughts soon burst out into words and actions. They also nourish pride and self conceit.

Some Ways to Show Charity to Our Neighbor

Charity is not a matter of feeling. It is a decision. We may not feel like loving a certain person. But we can, for the very solid reasons examined above, decide to love him. Here are some helps.

We can and should pray for our neighbor, not only those of them who love us, but also, and particularly, for those who annoy or persecute us. And we should learn to thank God when other people do well.

There is an inclination in many of us to speak ill of others. This vice is all the more dangerous because it is not regarded as important by many people. And yet it is serious. And it often carries with it the violation of such commandments as the fourth, the fifth, and the eighth. It can wreck a community like a family, a presbyterium of priests, or a religious congregation. Uncontrolled dislike of other people causes the nastiest kind of slander.

Charitable speech to others also means avoidance of rough words, sarcasm, mocking and hurtful witticism, contempt of another's family, nationality or race, and refusal to listen to others.

Courtesy is a form of charity. Graciousness, gratitude, the answering of letters in time, the honoring of invitations, and punctuality are all different faces of the same virtue.

Brotherly correction done in the most considerate of ways is a form of charity (cf. Mt. 18:15-17).

Kind deeds are an expression of love. Our love should not be in words alone but also in deeds (cf. 1 John 3:18). Consideration for the needs of the members of our community to rest, to be left alone sometimes, to be helped, etc., is part of charity (cf. James 2:15-16). The spiritual and corporal works of mercy come under this category. It is, however, important to add that the one who gives to the needy must do it in such a way that the person who receives is not humiliated, but that his human dignity is fully respected. The one who gives should not blow a trumpet, and his right hand must not know what his left does. (cf. Mt. 6:1-4).

Hurts Against Charity

It follows that certain actions are hurts against charity. Let us name a few. Murmuring against the superior is destructive, not constructive. It is better to offer suggestions if one has any. Tale-bearing is the sister of murmuring.

To discuss the faults of others is generally not helpful. It can be charitable in some contexts when it is obviously full of love and a desire to help the other. It is not easy to do this with charity.

Ridicule of the opinions of other people is a hurt against love. Even when we have to disagree, we can do so with respect.

Envy and jealously are obviously opposed to love. We should rejoice when others do well. We all are companions in the journey of life, and more so in the Church.

Scandal is opposed to love. Our Lord has hard words on it: "Anyone who is an obstacle to bring down one of these little ones who have faith in me would be better drowned in the depths of the sea with a great millstone around his neck" (Mt. 18:6).

Control of the Tongue

The tongue deserves special consideration because of its role in promoting charity or the lack of it. We realize its importance when we reflect that out of the abundance of the heart, the mouth speaks.

St. James speaks eloquently of the power of the tongue to make or to mar, to praise God or to destroy our neighbor's reputation. He says that whoever controls his tongue completely is a perfect person. The passage is long, but I shall quote it all:

"After all, every one of us does something wrong,

over and over again; the only man who could reach perfection would be someone who never said anything
wrong – he would be able to control every part of himself. Once we put a bit into the horse's mouth to make it
do what we want, we have the whole animal under our
control. Or think of ships: no matter how big they are,
even if a gale is driving them, the man at the helm can
steer them anywhere he likes by controlling a tiny rud-
der. So is the tongue only a tiny part of the body, but it
can proudly claim that it does great things. Think how
small a flame can set fire to a huge forest; the tongue is
a flame like that. Among all the parts of the body, the
tongue is a whole wicked world in itself: it infects the
whole body; catching fire itself from hell, it sets fire to
the whole wheel of creation. Wild animals and birds,
reptiles and fish can all be tamed by man, and often are;
but nobody can tame the tongue – it is a pest that will
not keep still, full of deadly poison. We use it to bless the
Lord and Father, but we also use it to curse men who
are made in God's image: the blessing and the curse
come out of the same mouth. My brothers, this must be
wrong – does any water supply give a flow of fresh water
and salt water out of the same pipe? Can a fig tree give
you olives, my brothers, or a vine give figs? No more can
sea water give you fresh water." (James 3:2-12; cf. also
Ecclus. 19:4-12; 20:13-30; Prov. 10:19).

Anger and Prayer

Pity, compassion, tolerance, mercy, forgiveness or
forbearance (call it what you will, they are all different
names for charity) makes all the difference between success and failure in prayer.

Vision is impeded by dirt. If my soul is to see God in
prayer, every such impediment is to be removed. In particular, passionate thoughts are to be taken away. The
passion of anger is the most obvious. Another is concupiscence of the flesh.

Any yielding to anger, including rancor, peevishness and touchiness, is bound to be paid for at the time

of prayer. Prayer is the offshoot of gentleness, of the absence of anger, of charity. Macarius, the ancient spiritual master, said that if in correcting another, I allow myself to reach a point of anger, then I am only satisfying my own passion. I should not, in order to save another, lose my composure. St. Vincent de Paul said that at the age of nearly eighty years he reckoned that during his lifetime he used severe censure only three times, and exactly those three times he did not gain his objective, whereas he always succeeded with gentleness.

Anger, whatever form it may take, leaves in the soul a sediment of rancor. Since it offends against charity, it diminishes or destroys our chances of tasting and seeing how sweet the Lord is.

Mortification is necessary for the practice of charity because uncontrolled desire is the preparation for anger. When I blow up, it is generally because I desired something with natural desire and did not get it. Control desire, and you will control anger. What, in fact, would a person get angry about, if he cared nothing for food, wealth, or human glory, in short, if he cared nothing for pleasures, possessions, or power?

Charity in the Family

Charity begins at home. And we take "home" here at its most basic level of father, mother, and children. It is surprising how many occasions there are in the family to show genuine Christian love and self-control and, unfortunately, also the lack of it. Husbands and wives, parents and children, and brothers and sisters have to realize that their road to happiness and holiness goes through family joy, harmony, forgiveness, reconciliation – in one word, charity.

Charity in Religious Communities

Members of a religious congregation constitute a spiritual family. What has just been said about the natural family also applies to them. Religious should learn to share one another's joys and sorrows, hopes and plans, to show interest in the work of others, to encourage those who succeed, to celebrate their achievements with them, to have open hearts for each member, to share prayers, meals and games, to look after their sick and old members, to avoid factions, and, in short, to make every member feel at home.

Pastoral Charity by Priests

Particular ways in which priests can show charity are love of the Bishop and positive and friendly cooperation with him; community life among priests who are working in the same parish, seminary, or other such work; good advice to younger priests; help to priests in spiritual or material difficulty; promotion of a friendly and joyful spirit of working together among priests in the diocese; encouragement of religious and lay people; well-prepared spiritual conferences and homilies; patient hearing of Confessions; devout administration of the sacraments; patient bearing of injuries and false accusations; zeal to win for Christ those who do not yet know Him; and intense prayer permeated with the needs of the apostolate of the Church on the parish, diocesan, and world levels.

Model Prayer of St. Francis of Assisi

The famous prayer of St. Francis of Assisi is a model of charity in prayer:

> Lord, make me an instrument of your peace.
> Where there is hatred, let me sow love.
> Where there is injury, pardon.
> Where there is discord, unity.
> Where there is doubt, faith.
> Where there is error, truth.
> Where there is despair, hope.
> Where there is sadness, joy.
> Where there is darkness, light.
>
> Oh Divine Master, grant that I may not so much seek to be consoled as to understand, to be loved as to love. For it is in giving that

we receive. It is in pardoning that we are
pardoned. It is in dying that we are born to
eternal life.

XV. ZEAL IN THE APOSTOLATE

During a retreat we should reflect on how devoted
we are to spreading the Kingdom of Christ. In this chapter we shall consider zeal in itself and its major manifestations, a few areas of apostolate which need special
attention, and some of the qualities required in us.

Christ is the Center

Jesus Christ is the Gospel that we preach. He is the
Savior of the world (cf. John 4:42). Neither is there salvation in any other name. "For of all the names in the
world given to men, this is the only one by which we can
be saved" (Acts 4:12). Jesus is "the Way, the Truth and
the Life" (John 14:6). He is the soul of our message. He
is God's revelation to us. He is the central mystery of
our religion.

Desire to Share Christ with Others

Those who already have faith and love in Christ
cannot remain unconcerned when they see others who
do not yet know Christ. They must desire to share with
others this excelling knowledge of the Son of God made
man for us and our salvation. They want to bring Christ
to others so that others may have life and no longer go
hungry or thirsty (cf. John 6:35).

The Son of Man came to seek and to save that
which was lost (cf. Lk. 19:10). A person who loves Christ
intensely must be full of zeal, that all men may know
the one true God and Jesus Christ whom He has sent
(cf. John 17:3). St. Paul was full of this zeal. He tells the
Colossians: "I became the servant of the church when
God made me responsible for delivering God's message
to you, the message which was a mystery hidden for

generations and centuries and has now been revealed to his saints. It was God's purpose to reveal it to them and to show all the rich glory of this mystery to pagans. The mystery is Christ among you, your hope in glory: this is the Christ we proclaim, this is the wisdom in which we thoroughly train everyone and instruct everyone, to make all perfect in Christ. It is for this that I struggle wearily on, helped only by his power driving me irresistibly" (Col. 1:25-29).

Singlemindedness—Jesus Only

The person who engages in the apostolate should have his intentions clearly fixed on Jesus alone. This single minded intention needs purification and attention from time to time so that self and the world may not intrude to smuggle themselves in.

Jesus is our message. We should be on our guard to preach Jesus alone and not also to preach or project ourselves. Some of the Jews came "not only on account of Jesus but also to see Lazarus whom He had raised from the dead" (John 12:9). They did not have purity of intention. They were not seeking only Jesus. The apostle of Jesus should strive to work for Jesus and preach Him alone. Intrusions are a desire to attract public praise and fame, worry of what people think of us, immoderate desire for quick results, and desire for money or promotion through the apostolate.

Missionary Thrust

Missionary thrust is a normal part of zeal. A great desire to bring the message of Christ to peoples who do not yet know Christ should burn in all of us. Christians constitute only 33% of the total world population. Catholics are only 18%. Therefore we must painstakingly promote missionary work (cf. Vatican II: *The Church*, n. 16).

Missionary work is promoted by prayer and sacrifices, by material support for the apostolate in the missions, and by becoming a missionary priest, religious, or lay person. Moreover, even in areas that are regarded as Christian, there are many non-Christians and lapsed Christians. Individuals and groups have to contact them to bring them the message of Christ.

Catechesis or Religious Education

Catechesis or religious education in all its forms is one of the ways in which zeal for the Gospel shows itself. It is one of the chief duties of priests and bishops, but all other baptized also share in this apostolate, each person according to his vocation.

Religious education focuses on such areas as catechizing children, preparing people for the various sacraments, homilies at liturgical functions, spread of the Word of God by radio, press, and television, and teaching of religion in educational institutions. It also includes up-dating oneself on the best methods of catechesis, ongoing study, seminars for catechists, production of good catechetical books and aids, beautiful celebration of the liturgy with adequate participation by the congregation, and progress in love and knowledge of Holy Scripture.

The Poor, the Sick, and the Old

In the apostolate a special claim to attention belongs to the weaker people: the poor, the sick, and the old. They are very dear to God. Jesus paid much attention to them when He was on earth. Most of His miracles were worked in their favor.

There is no suggestion here that the rich people need no attention or that they should be neglected. Christ came for all. He also called Matthew. He had supper with Zacchaeus. The point being made here is that the weaker people should not be forgotten, because generally the rich and the strong attract much attention anyway.

Children and Youth

Children and young people were also very near to the heart of Jesus. He blessed little children and said that the Kingdom of heaven is for such (cf. Lk. 18:15-17).

Children and youth are the hope of the future. Foundations are laid early in life about what their character is likely to be and remain. Children can also be a door or a key to reaching parents who do not seem to care much about God and religion. Youth need to be trained in leadership skills so that they can help to win the world for Christ.

Girls and Women

Girls and women deserve special attention in the apostolate because they are the makers of the home, the heart of the family, the trainers of children, and the hope of introducing little ones to religion from childhood. They also have a big influence with men, especially within the family. If the mothers of families follow the example of the Immaculate Mother of God, we are more likely to have good marriages, to have a steady supply of well-trained young people who want to become priests or religious, and to have zealous lay apostles.

A negative proof of the importance of women in the apostolate is that the forces which fight against God and religion and which also sabotage or ruin the family (such as materialism, communism, freemasonry and hedonism), often find it easier to concentrate their attacks on women by confusing them about their role in the family and society, by ridiculing motherhood, by pornography, and by destroying women's desire to look up to Mary, Mother of God as their model.

Priestly and Religious Vocations

"The harvest is rich but the laborers are few, so ask the Lord of the harvest to send laborers to His harvest" (Lk. 10:2). The Church needs many young men for the priesthood. A good family, where there is prayer, joy, love, and forgiveness, and a parish that has a good training program of a team of altar servers and apostolic training of young men, are helps toward awakening priestly vocations. But direct appeals to young people individually or in groups, especially by priests, are also necessary.

Similar remarks can be made about vocations to the religious life. In some dioceses there has been established the organized preaching of religious vocations by teams of religious of many congregations who travel together to schools, colleges, and parish centers. We should not be shy in making appeals for Christ, nor should we allow children of this world to be wiser in their own generation than the children of light.

Study

Continuing study is needed for the promotion of the apostolate, especially by those who are leaders in the Church. Priests are in the first line in this matter. "The lips of the priest ought to safeguard knowledge; his mouth is where instruction should be sought, since he is the messenger of Yahweh Sabaoth" (Mal. 2:7). The Lord threatens priests who no longer study: "As you have rejected knowledge so do I reject you from my priest-hood; you have forgotten the teaching of your God" (Hosea 4:6).

But the need to study applies also to religious and leading laity and indeed to every Christian according to his vocation to the apostolate. Holy Scripture, the tradi-tional and living teaching of the Church, liturgy, cate-chetics, and the society, which has to be evangelized, together with its culture, are all areas of continued study and reflection.

Special mention should be made of the need to understand the people, customs, cultures, places, and times where the Gospel is to be spread. The situation of the family, the school arrangements, the condition of workers, urbanization, unemployment, and industrial-ization all fall under this title. The Gospel is being brought to a people who come from a definite context and not from a social void. The more we know about the social luggage which they have brought with them, the better we can bring Christ to them.

Organization of the Apostolate

Zeal in the spread of the Kingdom of God also includes good organization. For people in key positions such as bishops, priests, and leading religious and laity, this includes clear ideas based on sound doctrine and proven methods, a wise arrangement of work, prayer and rest, interview hours publicly announced and faith-fully honored, and ability to encourage others to bring out their best performance.

Organization of the apostolate calls for harmonious arrangements to channel the apostolates of clerics, laity, and religious into a beautiful orchestra which per-forms unto God's glory. This means foresight to remove, as far as possible, all possible causes of rivalry, clashes, jealousy, unnecessary duplication, frustration of some apostolic workers, discouragement of initiative, credibil-ity gap between those in authority and the people they are meant to lead, and absence of dynamic and convinced lay apostles in the political and cultural fields.

The charity of Christ urges us on. Jesus gave His life for us. We must be intensely desirous to spread His Good News.

XVI. HOLY MARY, OUR MOTHER

Close Associate of Christ in the Work of Our Salvation

Jesus Christ is our Saviour. He willed to associate His Blessed Mother with Himself in the work of our salvation. From the early days of original sin, God promised to give mankind a Redeemer. In the same prophecy, God spoke of the Woman, Mother of the Redeemer, who would crush the head of the devil (cf. Gen. 3:15). Through the prophets, God kept the hope of mankind alive in this promise (cf. Is. 7:14; Mic. 5:2-3).

In the fullness of time God sent His archangel Gabriel to a Virgin of Nazareth called Mary, whom He had already preserved from original sin and all personal sin, to announce to her that He wanted her to become the mother of the Son of God, who would take on human nature by the power of the Holy Spirit. Mary consented.

The Word became man. Mary became Virgin Mother of the Word made man.

Mary visited her cousin Elizabeth and thus brought Christ in her womb to sanctify John the Baptist not yet born. In Bethlehem, Mary brought Jesus into the world in a shepherd's manger. After forty days she presented Him in the temple. With St. Joseph she took the Child to Egypt to save Him from the swords of Herod's soldiers. These three exceptional figures lived many years thereafter in Nazareth.

Mary, with faith, love, and courage, gave her Son full freedom to carry out His public ministry. She maintained a prudent distance. But she came in at critical moments to help us to appreciate her power with her Son in getting the water changed into wine at Cana, in offering Jesus the occasion to emphasize that more important than being His Mother was her hearing the Word of God and keeping it, and especially in standing at the foot of the cross. Mary freely associated herself with her Son's passion and sacrifice on Mount Calvary. And she stayed on with the Apostles when the Holy Spirit descended on Pentecost Sunday. She was manifestly acting as the Mother of the Church, which is the Mystical Body of her Son. It is clear that Mary was closely associated with Christ in the work of our salvation.

Closely Related to the Church

It also follows that the Blessed Virgin Mary is closely related to the Church. She is Mother of Christ and therefore mother of the Mystical Body of Christ, the new People of God, the followers of Christ. She is the spiritual mother of every baptized person in a way analogous with the Church, which is our spiritual mother, especially by Baptism, the other sacraments, and the preaching of the Word of God.

Mary is also ever Virgin, before, during, and after the birth of Christ. The Church is mystically called virgin because she retains true faith in Christ and does not take away her belief and loyalty from Him.

Mary is a sign of what the Church is called upon to be: immaculate, faithful, humble, virgin, mother, loving, refuge of sinners, and the way to Christ.

Devotion to the Blessed Virgin Mary

Devotion to the Blessed Virgin Mary has therefore been traditional in the Church. She already prophesied that all generations would call her blessed (cf. Lk. 1:48). All generations have done precisely that. Devotion to Mary has been a normal mark of Christianity. Where it is lacking we suspect that something is wrong, that somebody has interfered with the divinely-established order somewhere, and that there is something missing. Saints have engaged in undeclared competitions in singing her praises. Cathedrals, churches, and other shrines have been named after her or one of her titles more than perhaps any other saint of the Christian faith. In Nigeria, for example, of 32 Cathedrals, 14 are named after her. Places of Marian pilgrimages, such as Lourdes and Fatima, are flooded by many pilgrims and are known for the sacraments of Penance and the Holy Eucharist.

Devotion to Mary leads to Jesus Christ. The Mother is the shortest road to her Son. She already had told the servants at Cana: "Do whatever He tells you" (John 2:5). She still says the same to us. True devotion to Mary leads to Jesus Christ the one Mediator between God and man. The doctrinal foundations of the greatness of the Blessed Virgin Mary and of her association with Christ in the work of our redemption explains such items of devotion to Mary as the Hail Mary, the Rosary, the dedication of Saturdays, May and October devotions, the taking of the name of Mary at Baptism, Confirmation and Religious Profession, and the building of historic and beautiful shrines, churches, and other places of pilgrimage.

Mary the Model of Every Christian

Mary is the model of every Christian in her faith, her obedience to God, her openness to the action of the Holy Spirit, her one hundred percent dedication to Jesus, her charity, and her self-offering.

For mothers of families and women in general, she is a sign of the true dignity of women as opposed to what so-called feminists say today. She is a model of chastity, virginity, motherhood, and a wife who loves and obeys her husband. For every Christian she is a sign of innocence, of the victory of grace over sin, of the power of the redemption worked by Christ. She is "our tainted nature's solitary boast."

Mary Model of the Religious

For all religious brothers and sisters, monks, and nuns, Mary is a model of total dedication and consecration to God. For her, God is everything. She always pleased God.

Religious will learn from Mary how to live lives of virginity or celibacy with fidelity and joy. Of course, she had no original sin. Religious, as all other people, do bear the consequences of original sin even after the guilt is removed by Baptism. Mary will teach them how to live the angelic virtues and produce much spiritual fruit in supernatural fatherhood or motherhood.

Mary was poor in things of this world. She put her heart in God, not on the passing things of this brief earthly existence. She had no high earthly position. She was among the poor in spirit. Religious aspire to be all that.

Mary obeyed. Handmaid of the Lord is what she

called herself. She obeyed God. She obeyed St. Joseph. She teaches religious how to offer the sacrifice of their wills, the sacrifice which is, in a sense, the most difficult of the three vows.

Beyond the three vows, Mary is a model for religious in community life, in self-sacrifice, in love of others, and in a life permeated by peace and joy.

Mary, Model of the Priest

Mary brought Jesus to the world, prepared the way for Him, lived for Him, projected Him and not herself, sacrificed Him, and stayed with His first followers. With Christ and from Christ, she learned to offer herself also.

In these ways she is the model of the priest who mediates divine life for souls, who is ordained entirely for Christ and the Church, who is to preach Christ not himself, who offers Christ at Mass every day, who handles Jesus in the Holy Eucharist with his anointed hands, who is the outstanding man of the Church in the parish, and who with Christ and through Christ learns daily to offer himself.

Mary shows the priest how to love Christ and the Church, how to serve them, how to be open to the action of the Holy Spirit, how to be humble, and how to bring Christ to others. Her faith, chastity, self-sacrifice, and silence in the face of great mysteries are examples for the priest.

Mary is Mother of Christ, the eternal High Priest. Therefore, every priest has special claims on Mary's motherhood and protection, since there is so much union between every ordained priest and Christ. St. John, the beloved Apostle, is the forerunner of every priest. Pope John Paul II dwells on this aspect of the priest's devotion to Mary in paragraph 10 of his 1979 Holy Thursday *Letter to all Priests*.

Mary, Our Hope at Our Last Hour

A Christian is encouraged to think that Mary will be with him at his last hour, that Mary will pray for him now and at the hour of his death. With the Church we can sing this concluding compline Hymn:

"Pray for us, O Patroness,
Be our consolation!
Lead us home to see your Son,
Jesus, our salvation!
Gracious are you, full of grace,
Loving as none other,
Joy of heaven and of earth,
Mary, God's own Mother."

XVII. GRACE AND GLORY

By Grace God Dwells in Us

Habitual grace means that God dwells in us, the Father, the Son and the Holy Spirit. "If anyone loves me he will keep my word, and my Father will love him, and we shall come to him and make our home with him" (John 14:23), Jesus assures us. "Make your home in me, as I make mine in you" (John 15:4).

Jesus is the natural Son of God. Grace makes us adopted sons of God. Grace makes us like Christ.

Grace is a Treasure

If a person had a check for one million dollars in his pocket, he would beware of thieves. A person who has the divine indwelling is expected to be much more careful. It is a pity if a Christian lived his life often forgetting the great Presence in him by grace. It is a disaster if a person in the state of grace betrayed the Divine Guest and handed himself over to mortal sin.

Grace is the Seed of Glory

Only death separates the person in the state of

grace from glory. Our prayer everyday should include a request for final perseverance, for fidelity to God in the state of grace until our death. The entire Christian life tends towards welcoming the Lord when He comes to each one of us at that supreme moment.

Death

We fear it. We have no personal experience of it. No one who has experienced it has returned to give us details. And yet we are sure that it will come. It comes to many people every day. One day it will be our turn. Our Lord tells us that the Son of Man will come at an hour we do not expect. Death is a certainty. Its hour is hidden from us.

It is in our own interest to think of our death, to prepare for it, to have our bags packed, to be ready to meet the Bridegroom at whatever hour He may call. It is better to do penance now, to take part at Holy Masses now, to receive Holy Communion with fervor now, to show charity to our neighbor now, and to spend ourselves in works of the apostolate now, than to hope that other people will do these works for us when we are dead.

In the context of a spiritual retreat, to prepare for our death also includes making reconciliation with those with whom we do not have good relations, making resolutions on how to combat our predominant fault, resolving to live with greater fidelity the duties of our state of life, and determining to pray more.

Hell

The doctrine on eternal damnation in hell-fire is one of the most austere tenets of our faith. It shows us the gravity of mortal sin. Some people have found this doctrine hard to accept. They have denied it outright and argued that a loving Father does not condemn his children to burn in the fire forever. Others try to soft-pedal the idea of hell, or they do not talk about it because they say that to preach it would cause morbid fears in people, or they so explain away mortal sin that hardly anyone can be regarded as capable of committing it.

But the fact is there. Our Lord tells us about those who have no charity, about those who refuse to believe and who will be lost, about those who sin against the Holy Spirit and who will not be forgiven in this world nor in the world to come, about the goats on his left who will go into everlasting fire, and about the outer darkness where there will be weeping and gnashing of teeth. "Go away from me," He will say to those without charity, "with your curse upon you, to the eternal fire prepared for the devil and his angels" (Mt. 25:41).

Hell exists. There is no need to try to ignore this harsh reality. We do not solve a difficult algebra homework assignment by denying the existence of algebra, nor by arguing that algebra is not important, nor by burning the algebra book. The way to avoid going to hell is to live lives of charity, as Jesus taught us.

Purgatory

People who die in the state of grace, but who still need to atone for temporal punishment due to venial sins go to Purgatory. They suffer intensely. We do not know for how long. But eventually they reach heaven. We on earth can help them with our prayers, sacrifices, good works, and especially the Holy Mass. And they will not forget us.

Heaven

God "will wipe away all tears from their eyes; there will be no more death, and no more mourning or sadness. The world of the past has gone" (Apoc. 21:4).

"How I love your palace
Yahweh Sabaoth!
How my soul yearns and pines
for Yahweh's courts!
My heart and my flesh sing for joy
to the living God ...
A single day in your courts
is worth more than a thousand elsewhere;
merely to stand on the steps of God's house
is better than living with the wicked"
(Ps. 83 (84):1, 2, 10).

Heaven is the terminus of our efforts, desires, aspirations and hopes. In heaven we see God face to face, as He is. This is the beatific vision, joy everlasting, happiness without end, the final end of man, the purpose of human existence, the only correct answer to the question "why does man exist?" He who does not reach heaven has failed. He who reaches heaven has succeeded. "How I rejoiced when they said to me, 'Let us go to the house of Yahweh'" (Ps. 121 (122):1).

Conclusion: Come Lord Jesus!

Let us go to Jesus so that we may have life and have it more abundantly. Let us live according to His life and teaching. Let us go to His Holy Mother, Mary Immaculate, and beg her to teach us how to be dedicated to Jesus, each of us according to his vocation in life.

With faith, love and hope, let us pray: Come, Lord Jesus.

69. The Mystery and Worship of the Eucharist

**Letter of the Supreme Pontiff
Pope John Paul II**

*To All the Bishops of the Church
February 24, 1980*

Part I

My venerable and dear brothers,

1. Again this year, for Holy Thursday, I am writing a letter to all of you. This letter has an immediate connection with the one which you received last year on the same occasion, together with the letter to the priests. I wish *in the first place to thank you cordially* for having accepted my previous letters with that spirit of unity which the Lord established between us, and also for having transmitted to your priests the thoughts that I desired to express at the beginning of my pontificate.

During the Eucharistic Liturgy of Holy Thursday, you renewed, together with your priests, the promises and commitments undertaken at the moment of ordination. Many of you, venerable and dear brothers, told me about it later, also adding words of personal thanks, and indeed often sending those expressed by your priests. Furthermore, many priests expressed their joy, both because of the profound and solemn character of Holy Thursday as the annual "feast of priests" and also because of the importance of the subjects dealt with in the letter addressed to them.

Those replies form a rich collection which once more indicates how dear to the vast majority of priests of the Catholic Church is the path of the priestly life, the path along which this Church has been journeying for centuries: how much they love and esteem it, and how much they desire to follow it for the future.

At this point I must add that *only a certain number of matters were dealt with in the letter to priests*, as was in fact emphasized at the beginning of the document.[1] Furthermore, the main stress was laid upon the pastoral character of the priestly ministry; but this certainly does not mean that those groups of priests who are not engaged in direct pastoral activity were not also taken into consideration. In this regard I would refer once more to the teaching of the Second Vatican

Council, and also to the declarations of the 1971 Synod of Bishops.

The pastoral character of the priestly ministry does not cease to mark the life of every priest, even if the daily tasks that he carries out are not explicitly directed to the pastoral administration of the sacraments. In this sense, the letter written to the priests on Holy Thursday was addressed to them all, without any exception, even though, as I said above, it did not deal with all the aspects of the life and activity of priests. I think this clarification is useful and opportune at the beginning of the present letter:

I. The Eucharistic Mystery in the Life of the Church and of the Priest

Eucharist and Priesthood

2. The present letter that I am addressing to you, my venerable and dear brothers in the episcopate—and which is, as I have said, in a certain way a continuation of the previous one—is also closely linked with the mystery of Holy Thursday, and is related to the priesthood. In fact I intend to devote it to the Eucharist, and in particular *to certain aspects of the Eucharistic Mystery and its impact on the lives of those who are the ministers of It:* and so those to whom this letter is directly addressed are you, the bishops of the Church; together with you, all the priests; and, in their own rank, the deacons too.

In reality, the ministerial and hierarchical priesthood, the priesthood of the bishops and the priests, and, at their side, the ministry of the deacons—ministries which normally begin with the proclamation of the Gospel—are in the closest relationship with the Eucharist. The Eucharist is the principal and central *raison d'être* of the sacrament of the priesthood, which effectively came into being at the moment of the institution of the Eucharist, and together with it.[2] Not without reason the words "Do this in memory of me" are said immediately after the words of eucharistic consecration, and we repeat them every time we celebrate the holy Sacrifice.[3]

Through our ordination—the celebration of which is linked to the holy Mass from the very first liturgical evidence[4]—we are united in a singular and exceptional way to the Eucharist. In a certain way we derive *from* it and exist *for* it. We are also, and in a special way, responsible for it—each priest in his own community and each bishop by virtue of the care of all the communities entrusted to him, on the basis of the *sollicitudo omnium ecclesiarum* that St. Paul speaks of.[5] Thus we bishops and priests are entrusted with the great "mystery of Faith," and while it is also given to the whole People of God, to all believers in Christ, yet to us has been entrusted the Eucharist also "for" others, who expect from us a particular witness of veneration and love towards this sacrament, so that they too may be able to be built up and vivified "to offer spiritual sacrifices."[6]

In this way our eucharistic worship, both in the celebration of Mass and in our devotion to the Blessed Sacrament, is like a life-giving current that links our ministerial or hierarchical priesthood to the common priesthood of the faithful, and presents it in its vertical dimension and with its central value. The priest fulfills his principal mission and is manifested in all his fullness when he celebrates the Eucharist,[7] and this manifestation is more complete when he himself allows the depth of that mystery to become visible, so that it alone shines forth in people's hearts and minds, through his ministry. This is the supreme exercise of the "kingly priesthood," "the source and summit of all Christian life."[8]

Worship of the Eucharistic Mystery

3. This worship is directed towards God the Father

through Jesus Christ in the Holy Spirit. In the first place towards the Father, who, as St. John's Gospel says, "loved the world so much that he gave his only Son, so that everyone who believes in him may not be lost but may have eternal life."[9]

It is also directed, in the Holy Spirit, to the incarnate Son, in the economy of salvation, especially at that moment of supreme dedication and total abandonment of Himself to which the words uttered in the Upper Room refer: "This is my body given up for you....This is the cup of my blood shed for you...."[10] The liturgical acclamation: "We proclaim your death, Lord Jesus" takes us back precisely to that moment; and with the proclamation of His resurrection we embrace in the same act of veneration Christ risen and glorified "at the right hand of the Father," as also the expectation of His "coming in glory." *Yet it is the voluntary emptying of Himself, accepted by the Father and glorified with the resurrection,* which, sacramentally celebrated together with the resurrection, brings us to adore the Redeemer who "became obedient unto death, even death on a cross."[11]

And this adoration of ours contains yet another special characteristic. It is compenetrated by the greatness of that human death, in which the world, that is to say each one of us, has been loved "to the end."[12] Thus it is also a response that tries to repay that love immolated even to the death on the cross: it is our "Eucharist," that is to say our giving Him thanks, our praise of Him for having redeemed us by His death and made us sharers in immortal life through His resurrection.

This worship, given therefore to the Trinity of the Father and of the Son and of the Holy Spirit, above all accompanies and permeates the celebration of the Eucharistic Liturgy. But it must fill our churches also outside the timetable of Masses. Indeed, since the Eucharistic Mystery was instituted out of love, and makes Christ sacramentally present, it is worthy of thanksgiving and worship. And this worship must be prominent in all our encounters with the Blessed Sacrament, both when we visit our churches and when the sacred species are taken to the sick and administered to them.

Adoration of Christ in this sacrament of love must also find expression *in various forms of eucharistic devotion*: personal prayer before the Blessed Sacrament, Hours of Adoration, periods of exposition—short, prolonged and annual (Forty Hours)—eucharistic benediction, eucharistic processions, eucharistic congresses.[13] A particular mention should be made at this point of the Solemnity of the Body and Blood of Christ as an act of

public worship rendered to Christ present in the Eucharist, a feast instituted by my predecessor Urban IV in memory of the institution of this great Mystery.[14] All this therefore corresponds to the general principles and particular norms already long in existence but newly formulated during or after the Second Vatican Council.[15]

The encouragement and the deepening of eucharistic worship are *proofs of that authentic renewal* which the council set itself as an aim and of which they are *the central point*. And this, venerable and dear brothers, deserves separate reflection. The Church and the world have a great need of eucharistic worship. Jesus waits for us in this sacrament of love. Let us be generous with our time in going to meet Him in adoration and in contemplation that is full of faith and ready to make reparation for the great faults and crimes of the world. May our adoration never cease.

Eucharist and Church

4. Thanks to the Council we have realized with renewed force the following truth: Just as the Church "makes the Eucharist" so "the Eucharist builds up" the Church[16]; and this truth is closely bound up with the mystery of Holy Thursday. The Church was founded, as the new community of the People of God, in the apostolic community of those Twelve who, at the Last Supper, became partakers of the body and blood of the Lord under the species of bread and wine. Christ had said to them: "Take and eat....Take and drink." And carrying out this command of His, they entered for the first time into sacramental communion with the Son of God, a communion that is a pledge of eternal life. From that moment until the end of time, *the Church is being built up through that same communion with the Son of God, a communion which is a pledge of the eternal Passover.*

Dear and venerable brothers in the episcopate, as teachers and custodians of the salvific truth of the Eucharist, we must always and everywhere preserve this meaning and this dimension of the sacramental encounter and intimacy with Christ. It is precisely these elements which constitute the very substance of eucharistic worship. The meaning of the truth expounded above in no way diminishes—in fact, it facilitates—the eucharistic character of spiritual drawing together and union between the people who share in the sacrifice, which then in Communion becomes for them the banquet. This drawing together and this union, the prototype of which is the union of the Apostles about Christ at the Last Supper, express the Church and bring her into being.

But the Church is not brought into being only through the union of people, through the experience of brotherhood to which the Eucharistic Banquet gives rise. The Church is brought into being when, in that fraternal union and communion, we celebrate the sacrifice of the cross of Christ, when we proclaim "the Lord's death until he comes,"[17] and later, when, being deeply compenetrated with the mystery of our salvation, we approach as a community the table of the Lord, in order to be nourished there, in a sacramental manner, by the fruits of the holy Sacrifice of propitiation. Therefore in eucharistic Communion we receive Christ, Christ Himself; and our union with Him, which is a gift and grace for each individual, brings it about that in Him we are also associated in the unity of His body which is the Church.

Only in this way, through that faith and that disposition of mind, is there brought about that building up of the Church, which in the Eucharist truly finds its "source and summit," according to the well-known expression of the Second Vatican Council.[18] This truth, which as a result of the same Council has received a new and vigorous emphasis,[19] must be a frequent theme of our reflection and teaching. Let all pastoral activity be nourished by it, and may it also be food for ourselves and for all the priests who collaborate with us, and likewise for the whole of the communities entrusted to us. In this practice there should thus be revealed, almost at every step, *that close relationship between the Church's spiritual and apostolic vitality* and *the Eucharist, understood in its profound significance* and from all points of view.[20]

Eucharist and Charity

5. Before proceeding to more detailed observations on the subject of the celebration of the holy Sacrifice, I wish briefly to reaffirm the fact that eucharistic worship constitutes the soul of all Christian life. In fact, Christian life is expressed in the fulfilling of the greatest commandment, that is to say, in the love of God and neighbor, and this love finds its source in the Blessed Sacrament, which is commonly called the sacrament of love.

The Eucharist signifies this charity, and therefore

recalls it, makes it present *and at the same time brings it about.* Every time that we consciously share in it, there opens in our souls a real dimension of that unfathomable love that includes everything that God has done and continues to do for us human beings, as Christ says: "My Father goes on working, and so do I."[21] Together with this unfathomable and free gift, which is *charity* revealed in its fullest degree in the saving sacrifice of the Son of God, the sacrifice of which the Eucharist is the indelible sign, there also springs up within us a lively response of love. We not only know love; we ourselves *begin to love.* We enter, so to speak, upon the path of love and along this path make progress. Thanks to the Eucharist, the love that springs up within us from the Eucharist develops in us, becomes deeper and grows stronger.

Eucharistic worship is therefore precisely the expression of that love which is the authentic and deepest characteristic of the Christian vocation. This worship springs from the love and serves the love to which we are all called in Jesus Christ.[22] A living fruit of this worship is the perfecting of the image of God that we bear within us, an image that corresponds to the one that Christ has revealed in us. As we thus become adorers of the Father "in spirit and truth,"[23] we mature in an ever fuller union with Christ, we are ever more united to Him, and—if one may use the expression—we are ever more in harmony with Him.

The doctrine of the Eucharist, sign of unity and bond of charity, taught by St. Paul,[24] has been in subsequent times deepened by the writings of very many saints who are living examples for us of Eucharistic worship. We must always have this reality before our eyes, and at the same time we must continually try to bring it about that our own generation too may add new examples to those marvelous examples of the past, new examples no less living and eloquent, that will reflect the age to which we belong.

Eucharist and Neighbor

6. *The authentic sense of the Eucharist becomes of itself the school of active love for neighbor.* We know that this is the true and full order of love that the Lord has taught us: "By this love you have for one another, everyone will know that you are my disciples."[25] The Eucharist educates us to this love in a deeper way; it shows us, in fact, what value each person, our brother or sister, has in God's eyes, if Christ offers Himself equally to each one, under the species of bread and wine. If our Eucharistic worship is authentic, it must make us grow in awareness of the dignity of each person. The awareness of that dignity becomes the *deepest motive of our relationship with our neighbor.*

We must also become particularly sensitive to all human suffering and misery, to all injustice and wrong, and seek the way to redress them effectively. Let us learn to discover with respect the truth about the inner self that becomes the dwelling place of God present in the Eucharist. Christ comes into the hearts of our brothers and sisters and visits their consciences. How the image of each and every one changes, when we become aware of this reality, when we make it the subject of our reflections! The sense of the Eucharistic Mystery leads us to a love for our neighbor, to a love for every human being.[26]

Eucharist and Life

7. Since therefore the Eucharist is the source of charity, it has always been at the center of the life of Christ's disciples. It has the appearance of bread and wine, that is to say of food and drink; it is therefore as familiar to people, as closely linked to their life, as food and drink. The veneration of God, who is love, springs, in eucharistic worship, from that kind of intimacy in which *He Himself, by analogy with food and drink, fills our spiritual being,* ensuring its life, as food and drink do. This "eucharistic" veneration of God therefore strictly corresponds to His saving plan. He Himself, the Father, wants the "true worshippers"[27] to worship Him precisely in this way, and it is Christ who expresses this desire, both with His words and likewise with this sacrament in which He makes possible worship of the Father in the way most in conformity with the Father's will.

From this concept of eucharistic worship there then stems the whole *sacramental style of the Christian's life.* In fact, leading a life based on the sacraments and animated by the common priesthood means in the first place that Christians desire God to act in them in order to enable them to attain, in the Spirit, "the fullness of Christ himself."[28] God, on His part, does not touch them only through events and by this inner grace; He also acts in them with greater certainty and power through the sacraments. The sacraments give the lives of Christians a sacramental style.

Now, of all the sacraments it is the Holy Eucharist that brings to fullness their initiation as Christians and confers upon the exercise of the common priesthood that sacramental and ecclesial form that links it—as we mentioned before[29]—to the exercise of the ministerial priesthood. In this way eucharistic worship is the *center and goal of all sacramental life.*[30] In the depths of eucharistic worship we find a continual echo of the sacraments of Christian initiation: Baptism and Confirmation. Where better is there expressed the truth that we are not only "called God's children" but "that is what we are"[31] by virtue of the sacrament of Baptism, if not precisely in the fact that in the Eucharist we become partakers of the body and blood of God's only Son? And what predisposes us more to be "true witnesses of Christ"[32] before the world—as we are enabled to be by the sacrament of Confirmation— than Eucharistic Communion, in which Christ bears witness to us, and we to Him?

It is impossible to analyze here in greater detail the links between the Eucharist and the other sacraments, in particular with the sacrament of family life and the sacrament of the sick. In the encyclical *Redemptor hominis*[33] I have already drawn attention to the close link between the sacrament of Penance and the sacrament of the Eucharist. *It is not only that Penance leads to the Eucharist, but that the Eucharist also leads to Penance.* For when we realize who it is that we receive in Eucharistic Communion, there springs up in us almost spontaneously a sense of unworthiness, together with sorrow for our sins and an interior need for purification.

But we must always take care that this great meeting with Christ in the Eucharist does not become a mere habit, and that we do not receive Him unworthily, that is to say, in a state of mortal sin. The practice of the virtue of penance and the sacrament of Penance are essential for sustaining in us and continually deepening that spirit of veneration which man owes to God Himself and to His love so marvelously revealed. The purpose of these words is to put forward some general reflections on worship of the Eucharistic Mystery, and they could be developed at greater length and more fully. In particular, it would be possible to link what has been said about the effects of the Eucharist on love for others with what we have just noted about commitments undertaken towards humanity and the Church in Eucharistic Communion, and then outline the picture of that "new earth"[34] that springs from the Eucharist through every "new self."[35] *In this sacrament* of bread and wine, of food and drink, *everything that is human really undergoes a singular transformation and elevation.* Eucharistic worship is not so much worship of the inaccessible transcendence as worship of the divine condescension, and it is also the merciful and redeeming transformation of the world in the human heart.

Recalling all this only very briefly, I wish, notwithstanding this brevity, to create a wider context for the questions that I shall subsequently have to deal with: These questions are closely linked with the celebration of the holy Sacrifice. In fact, in that celebration there is expressed in a more direct way the worship of the Eucharist. This worship comes from the heart, as a most precious homage inspired by the faith, hope and charity which were infused into us at Baptism. And it is precisely about this that I wish to write to you in this letter, venerable and dear brothers in the episcopate, and with you to the priests and deacons. It will be followed by detailed indications from the Sacred Congregation for the Sacraments and Divine Worship.

II. The Sacred Character of the Eucharist and Sacrifice

Sacred Character

8. Beginning with the Upper Room and Holy Thursday, the celebration of the Eucharist has a long history, a history as long as that of the Church. In the course of this history the secondary elements have undergone certain changes, *but there has been no*

change in the essence of the "Mysterium" instituted by the Redeemer of the world at the Last Supper. The Second Vatican Council too brought alterations, as a result of which the present liturgy of the Mass is different in some ways from the one known before the Council. We do not intend to speak of these differences: It is better that we should now concentrate on what is essential and immutable in the Eucharistic Liturgy.

There is a close link between this element of the Eucharist and its sacredness, that is to say, its being a holy and sacred action. Holy and sacred, because in it are the continual presence and action of Christ, "the Holy One" of God,[36] "anointed with the Holy Spirit,"[37] "consecrated by the Father"[38] to lay down His life of His own accord and to take it up again,[39] and the High Priest of the New Covenant.[40] For it is He who, represented by the celebrant, makes His entrance into the sanctuary and proclaims His Gospel. It is He who is "the offerer and the offered, the consecrator and the consecrated."[41] The Eucharist is a holy and sacred action, because it constitutes the sacred species, the *Sancta sanctis*, that is to say, the "holy things (Christ, the Holy One) given to the Holy," as all the Eastern liturgies sing at the moment when the eucharistic Bread is raised in order to invite the faithful to the Lord's Supper.

The sacredness of the Mass, therefore, is not a "sacralization," that is to say, something that man adds to Christ's action in the Upper Room, for the Holy Thursday supper was a sacred rite, a primary and constitutive liturgy, through which Christ, by pledging to give His life for us, Himself celebrated sacramentally the mystery of His passion and resurrection, the heart of every Mass. Our Masses, being derived from this liturgy, possess of themselves a complete liturgical form, which, in spite of its variations in line with the families of rites, remains substantially the same. The sacred character of the Mass is a sacredness instituted by Christ. The words and actions of every priest, answered by the conscious active participation of the whole eucharistic assembly, echo the words and actions of Holy Thursday.

The priest offers the holy Sacrifice *in persona Christi*; this means more than offering "in the name of" or "in place of" Christ. *In persona* means in specific sacramental identification with "the eternal High Priest"[42] who is the author and principal subject of this sacrifice of His, a sacrifice in which, in truth, nobody can take His place. Only He—only Christ—was able and is always able to be the true and effective "expiation for our sins and...for the sins of the whole world."[43] Only His sacrifice—and no one else's—was able and is able to have a "propitiatory power" before God, the Trinity, and the transcendent holiness. Awareness of this reality throws a certain light on the character and significance of the priest celebrant who, *by confecting the holy Sacrifice and acting "in persona Christi,"* is sacramentally (and ineffably) brought into that most profound *sacredness*, and made part of it, spiritually linking with it in turn all those participating in the eucharistic assembly.

This sacred rite, which is actuated in different liturgical forms, may lack some secondary elements, but it can in no way lack its essential sacred character and sacramentality, since these are willed by Christ and transmitted and regulated by the Church. Neither can this sacred rite be utilized for other ends. If separated from its distinctive sacrificial and sacramental nature, the Eucharistic Mystery simply ceases to be. It admits of no "profane" imitation, an imitation that would very easily (indeed regularly) become a profanation. This must always be remembered, perhaps above all in our time, when we see a tendency to do away with the distinction between the "sacred" and "profane," given the widespread tendency, at least in some places, to desacralize everything.

In view of this fact, *the Church has a special duty to*

safeguard and strengthen the sacredness of the Eucharist. In our pluralistic and often deliberately secularized society, *the living faith* of the Christian community—a faith always aware of its rights vis-à-vis those who do not share that faith—ensures respect for this sacredness. The duty to respect each person's faith is the complement of the natural and civil right to freedom of conscience and of religion.

The sacred character of the Eucharist has found and continues to find expression in the terminology of theology and the liturgy.[44] This sense of the objective sacred character of the Eucharistic Mystery is so much part of the faith of the People of God that their faith is enriched and strengthened by it.[45] Therefore the ministers of the Eucharist must, especially today, be illumined by the fullness of this living faith, and in its light they must understand and perform all that is part, by Christ's will and the will of His Church, of their priestly ministry.

Sacrifice

9. The Eucharist is above all else a sacrifice. It is the sacrifice of the Redemption and also the sacrifice of the

New Covenant,[46] as we believe and as the Eastern
Churches clearly profess: "Today's sacrifice," the Greek
Church stated centuries ago, "is like that offered once by
the Only-begotten Incarnate Word; it is offered by Him
(now as then), since it is one and the same sacrifice."[47]Accordingly, precisely by making this single sacrifice of our salvation present, man and the world are
restored to God through the paschal newness of
Redemption. This restoration cannot cease to be: it is
the foundation of the "new and eternal covenant" of God
with man and of man with God. If it were missing, one
would have to question both the excellence of the sacrifice of the Redemption, which in fact was perfect and
definitive, and also the sacrificial value of the Mass. In
fact, the Eucharist, being a true sacrifice, brings about
this restoration to God.

Consequently, the celebrant, as minister of this sacrifice, is the authentic *priest*, performing—in virtue of
the specific power of sacred ordination—a true sacrificial act that brings creation back to God. Although all
those who participate in the Eucharist do not confect
the sacrifice as He does, they offer with Him, by virtue
of the common priesthood, their own *spiritual sacrifices*
represented by the bread and wine from the moment of
their presentation at the altar. For this liturgical action,
which takes a solemn form in almost all liturgies, has a
"spiritual value and meaning."[48] The bread and wine
become in a sense a symbol of all that the eucharistic
assembly brings, on its own part, as an offering to God
and offers spiritually.

It is important that this first moment of the Liturgy
of the Eucharist in the strict sense should find expression in the attitude of the participants. There is a link
between this and the offertory "procession" provided for
in the recent liturgical reform[49] and accompanied, in
keeping with ancient tradition, by a psalm or song. A
certain length of time must be allowed, so that all can
become aware of this act, which is given expression at

the same time by the words of the celebrant.

Awareness of the act of presenting the offerings should be maintained throughout the Mass. Indeed, it should be brought to fullness at the moment of the consecration and of the anamnesis offering, as is demanded by the fundamental value of the moment of the sacrifice. This is shown by the words of the Eucharistic Prayer said aloud by the priest. It seems worthwhile repeating here some expressions in the third Eucharistic Prayer that show in particular the sacrificial character of the Eucharist and link the offering of our persons with Christ's offering: "Look with favor on your Church's offering, and see the Victim whose death has reconciled us to yourself. Grant that we, who are nourished by his body and blood, may be filled with his Holy Spirit, and become one body, one spirit in Christ. May he make us an everlasting gift to you."

This sacrificial value is expressed earlier in every celebration by the words with which the priest concludes the presentation of the gifts, asking the faithful to pray "that my sacrifice and yours may be acceptable to God, the almighty Father." These words are binding, since they express the character of the entire Eucharistic Liturgy and the fullness of its divine and ecclesial content.

All who participate with faith in the Eucharist become aware that it is a "sacrifice," that is to say, a "consecrated Offering." For the bread and wine presented at the altar and accompanied by the devotion and the spiritual sacrifices of the participants are finally consecrated, so as to become *truly, really and substantially* Christ's own body that is given up and His blood that is shed. Thus, by virtue of the consecration, the species of bread and wine re-present[50] in a sacramental, unbloody manner the bloody propitiatory sacrifice offered by Him on the cross to His Father for the salvation of the world. Indeed, He alone, giving Himself as a propitiatory Victim in an act of supreme surrender and immolation, has reconciled humanity with the Father, solely through His sacrifice, "having canceled the bond which stood against us."[51]

To this sacrifice, which is renewed in a sacramental form on the altar, the offerings of bread and wine, united with the devotion of the faithful, nevertheless bring their unique contribution, since by means of the consecration by the priest they become sacred species. This is made clear by the way in which the priest acts during the Eucharistic Prayer, especially at the consecration, and when the celebration of the holy Sacrifice and participation in it are accompanied by awareness that "the Teacher is here and is calling for you."[52] This call of the Lord to us through His Sacrifice opens our hearts, so that, purified in the mystery of our Redemption, they may be united to Him in Eucharistic Communion, which confers upon participation at Mass a value that is mature, complete and binding on human life: "The Church's intention is that the faithful not only offer the spotless victim but also learn to offer themselves and daily to be drawn into ever more perfect union, through Christ the Mediator, with the Father and with each other, so that at last God may be all in all."[53]

It is therefore very opportune and necessary to continue to actuate a new and intense education, in order to discover all the richness contained in the new liturgy. Indeed, the liturgical renewal that has taken place since the Second Vatican Council has given, so to speak, greater visibility to *the Eucharistic Sacrifice*. One factor contributing to this is that the words of the Eucharistic Prayer are said aloud by the celebrant, particularly the words of consecration, with the acclamation by the assembly immediately after the elevation.

All this should fill us with joy, but we should also remember that *these changes demand new spiritual awareness and maturity*, both on the part of the celebrant—especially now that he celebrates "facing the people"—and by the faithful. Eucharistic worship matures and grows when the words of the Eucharistic Prayer, especially the words of consecration, are spoken with great humility and simplicity, in a worthy and fitting way, which is understandable and in keeping with their holiness; when this essential act of the Eucharistic Liturgy is performed unhurriedly; and when it brings about in us such recollection and devotion that the participants become aware of the greatness of the mystery being accomplished and show it by their attitude.

III. The Two Tables of the Lord and the Common Possession of the Church

The Table of the Word of God

10. We are well aware that from the earliest times the celebration of the Eucharist has been linked not only with prayer but also with the reading of Sacred Scripture and with singing by the whole assembly. As a result, it has long been possible to apply to the Mass the comparison, made by the Fathers, with the two tables, at which the Church prepares for her children the word of God and the Eucharist, that is, the bread of the Lord. We must therefore go back to the first part of the sacred mystery, the part that at present is most often called the *Liturgy of the Word*, and devote some attention to it.

The reading of the passages of Sacred Scripture chosen for each day *has been subjected by the Council* to new criteria and requirements.[54] As a result of these norms of the Council a new collection of readings has been made, in which there has been applied to some extent the principle of continuity of texts and the principle of making all the sacred books accessible. The insertion of the Psalms with responses into the liturgy makes the participants familiar with the great wealth of Old Testament prayer and poetry. The fact that these texts are read and sung in the vernacular enables everyone to participate with fuller understanding.

Nevertheless, there are also those people who, having been educated on the basis of the old liturgy in Latin, experience the lack of this "one language," which in all the world was an expression of the unity of the Church and through its dignified character elicited a profound sense of the Eucharistic Mystery. It is therefore necessary to show not only understanding but also full respect towards these sentiments and desires. As far as possible these sentiments and desires are to be accommodated, as is moreover provided for in the new dispositions.[55] The Roman Church has special obligations towards Latin, the splendid language of ancient Rome, and she must manifest them whenever the occasion presents itself.

The possibilities that the post-conciliar renewal has introduced in this respect are indeed often utilized so as to make us *witnesses of and sharers in the authentic celebration of the Word of God.* There is also an increase in the number of people taking an active part in this celebration. Groups of readers and cantors, and still more often choirs of men or women, are being set up and are devoting themselves with great enthusiasm to this aspect. The Word of God, Sacred Scripture, is beginning to take on new life in many Christian communities. The faithful gathered for the liturgy prepare with song for listening to the Gospel, which is proclaimed with the devotion and love due to it.

All this is noted with great esteem and gratitude, but it must not be forgotten that complete renewal makes yet other demands. These demands consist in *a new sense of responsibility towards the Word of God* transmitted through the liturgy in various languages, something that is certainly in keeping with the universality of the Gospel and its purposes. The same sense of responsibility also involves the performance of the corresponding liturgical actions (reading or singing), which must accord with the principles of art. To preserve these actions from all artificiality, they should express such capacity, simplicity and dignity as to highlight the special character of the sacred text, even by the very manner of reading or singing.

Accordingly, these demands, which spring from a new responsibility for the Word of God in the liturgy,[56] go yet deeper and *concern the inner attitude* with which the ministers of the Word perform their function in the liturgical assembly.[57] This responsibility also concerns *the choice of texts. The choice has already been made by the competent ecclesiastical authority, which has also made provision for the cases in which readings more suited to a particular situation may be chosen.*[58] Furthermore, it must always be remembered that only the Word of God can be used for Mass readings. The reading of Scripture cannot be replaced by the reading of other texts, however much they may be endowed with undoubted religious and moral values. On the other hand such texts can be used very profitably in the homily. Indeed the homily is supremely suitable for the use of such texts, provided that their content corresponds to the required conditions, since it is one of the tasks that belong to the nature of the homily to show the points of convergence between revealed divine wisdom and noble human thought seeking the truth by various paths.

The Table of the Bread of the Lord

11. The other table of the Eucharistic Mystery, that of the Bread of the Lord, also requires reflection from the viewpoint of the present-day liturgical renewal. This is a question of the greatest importance, since it concerns a special act of living faith, and indeed, as has been attested since the earliest centuries,[59] it is a manifestation of *worship of Christ, who in Eucharistic Communion entrusts Himself to each one of us*, to our hearts, our consciences, our lips and our mouths, in the form of food. Therefore there is special need, with regard to this question, for the watchfulness spoken of by the Gospel, on the part of the pastors who have charge of eucharistic worship and on the part of the People of God, whose "sense of the faith"[60] must be very alert and acute particularly in this area.

I therefore wish to entrust this question to the heart of each one of you, venerable and dear brothers in the episcopate. You must above all make it part of your care for all the churches entrusted to you. I ask this of you in the name of the unity that we have received from the Apostles as our heritage, collegial unity. This unity came to birth, in a sense, at the table of the Bread of the Lord on Holy Thursday. With the help of your brothers in the priesthood, do all you can to *safeguard the sacred dignity of the eucharistic ministry and that deep spirit of Eucharistic Communion* which belongs in a special way to the Church as the People of God, and which is also a particular heritage transmitted to us from the Apostles, by various liturgical traditions, and by unnumbered generations of the faithful, who were often heroic witnesses to Christ, educated in "the school of the cross" (Redemption) and of the Eucharist.

It must be remembered that the Eucharist as the table of the Bread of the Lord is a continuous invitation. This is *shown in the liturgy when the celebrant says: "This is the Lamb of God. Happy are those who are called to his supper"*[61]; it is also shown by the familiar Gospel parable about the guests invited to the marriage banquet.[62] Let us remember that in this parable there are many who excuse themselves from accepting the invitation for various reasons.

Moreover our Catholic communities certainly do not lack people who *could participate* in Eucharistic Communion *and do not*, even though they have no serious sin on their conscience as an obstacle. To tell the truth, this attitude, which in some people is linked with an exaggerated severity, has changed in the present century, though it is still to be found here and there. In fact what one finds most often is not so much a feeling of unworthiness as a certain lack of interior willingness, if one may use this expression, a lack of Eucharistic "hunger" and "thirst," which is also a sign of lack of adequate sensitivity towards the great sacrament of love and a lack of understanding of its nature.

However, we also find in recent years another phenomenon. Sometimes, indeed quite frequently, everybody participating in the eucharistic assembly goes to Communion; and on some such occasions, as experienced pastors confirm, there has not been due care to approach the sacrament of Penance so as to purify one's conscience. This can of course mean that those approaching the Lord's table find nothing on their conscience, according to the objective law of God, to keep them from this sublime and joyful act of being sacramentally united with Christ. But there can also be, at least at times, another idea behind this: the idea of the Mass as *only* a banquet[63] in which one shares by *receiving the body of Christ in order to manifest, above all else, fraternal communion.* It is not hard to add to these reasons a certain human respect and mere "conformity."

This phenomenon demands from us watchful attention and a theological and pastoral analysis guided by a sense of great responsibility. We cannot allow the life of our communities to lose the good quality of sensitiveness of Christian conscience, guided solely by respect for Christ, who, when He is received in the Eucharist, should find in the heart of each of us a worthy abode. This question is closely linked not only with the practice of the sacrament of Penance but also with a correct sense of responsibility for the whole deposit of moral teaching and for the precise distinction between good and evil, a distinction which then becomes for each person sharing in the Eucharist the basis for a correct judgment of self to be made in the depths of the personal conscience. St. Paul's words, "Let a man examine himself,"[64] are well known; this judgment is an indispensable condition for a personal decision whether to approach Eucharistic Communion or to abstain.

Celebration of the Eucharist places before us many other requirements regarding the ministry of the eucharistic table. Some of these requirements concern only priests and deacons, others concern all who participate in the Eucharistic Liturgy. Priests and deacons must remember that the service of the table of the Bread of the Lord imposes on them special obligations which refer in the first place to Christ Himself *present in the Eucharist* and secondly to all who actually participate in the Eucharist or who might do so. With regard to the first, perhaps it will not be superfluous to recall

the words of the *Pontificale* which on the day of ordination the bishop addresses to the new priest as he hands
to him on the paten and in the chalice the bread and
wine offered by the faithful and prepared by the deacon:
*"Accipe oblationem plebis sanctae Deo offerendam.
Agnosce quod agis, imitare quod tractabis, et vitam
tuam mysterio dominicae crucis conforma."*[65] This last
admonition made to him by the bishop should remain as
one of the most precious norms of his eucharistic ministry.

It is from this admonition that the priest's attitude
in handling the bread and wine which have become the
body and blood of the Redeemer should draw its inspiration. Thus it is necessary for all of us who are ministers of the Eucharist to examine carefully our actions at
the altar, in particular the way in which we handle that
food and drink which are the body and blood of the Lord
our God in our hands: the way in which we distribute
Holy Communion; the way in which we perform the
purification.

All these actions have a meaning of their own.
Naturally, scrupulosity must be avoided, but God preserve us from behaving in a way that lacks respect, from
undue hurry, from an impatience that causes scandal.
Over and above our commitment to the evangelical mission, our greatest commitment consists in exercising
this mysterious power over the body of the Redeemer,
and all that is within us should be decisively ordered to
this. We should also always remember that to this ministerial power we have been sacramentally consecrated,
that we have been chosen from among men "for the good
of men."[66] We especially, the priests of the Latin
Church, whose ordination rite added in the course of the
centuries the custom of anointing the priest's hands,
should think about this.

In some countries *the practice of receiving
Communion in the hand* has been introduced. This practice has been requested by individual episcopal confer-

ences and has received approval from the Apostolic See. However, cases of a deplorable lack of respect towards the eucharistic species have been reported, cases which are imputable not only to the individuals guilty of such behavior but also to the pastors of the church who have not been vigilant enough regarding the attitude of the faithful towards the Eucharist. It also happens, on occasion, that the free choice of those who prefer to continue the practice of receiving the Eucharist on the tongue is not taken into account in those places where the distribution of Communion in the hand has been authorized. It is therefore difficult in the context of this present letter not to mention the sad phenomena previously referred to. This is in no way meant to refer to those who, receiving the Lord Jesus in the hand, do so with profound reverence and devotion, in those countries where this practice has been authorized.

But one must not forget the primary office of priests, who have been consecrated by their ordination to represent Christ the Priest: for this reason their hands, like their words and their will, have become the direct instruments of Christ. Through this fact, that is, as ministers of the Holy Eucharist, they have a primary responsibility for the sacred species, because it is a total responsibility: they offer the bread and wine, they consecrate it, and then distribute the sacred species to the participants in the assembly who wish to receive them. Deacons can only bring to the altar the offerings of the faithful and, once they have been consecrated by the priest, distribute them. How eloquent therefore, even if not of ancient custom, is the rite of the anointing of the hands in our Latin ordination, as though precisely for these hands a special grace and power of the Holy Spirit is necessary!

To touch the sacred species and *to distribute them with their own hands* is a privilege of the ordained, one which indicates an active participation *in the ministry of the Eucharist.* It is obvious that the Church can grant this faculty to those who are neither priests nor deacons, as is the case with acolytes in the exercise of their ministry, especially if they are destined for future ordination, or with other lay people who are chosen for this to meet a just need, but always after an adequate preparation.

A Common Possession of the Church

12. We cannot, even for a moment, forget that the Eucharist is a special possession belonging to the whole Church. It is the *greatest gift* in the order of grace and of sacrament that the divine Spouse has offered and unceasingly offers to His spouse. And precisely because it is such a gift, all of us should in a spirit of profound faith let ourselves be guided by a sense of truly Christian responsibility. A gift obliges us ever more profoundly because it speaks to us not so much with the force of a strict right as with the force of personal confidence, and thus—without legal obligations—it calls for *trust and gratitude.* The Eucharist is just such a gift and such a possession. We should remain faithful in every detail to what it expresses in itself and to what it asks of us, namely, thanksgiving.

The Eucharist is a common possession of the whole Church as the sacrament of her unity. And thus the Church has the strict duty to specify everything which concerns participation in it and its celebration. We should therefore act according to the principles laid down by the last Council, which, in the Constitution on the Sacred Liturgy, defined the authorizations and obligations of individual bishops in their dioceses and of the episcopal conferences, given the fact that both act in collegial unity with the Apostolic See.

Furthermore we should follow the directives issued by the various departments of the Holy See in this field: be it in liturgical matters, in the rules established by the liturgical books in what concerns the Eucharistic Mystery,[67] and in the Instructions devoted to this mystery, be it with regard to *communicatio in sacris*, in the norms of the *Directorium de re oecumenica*[68] and in the *Instructio de peculiaribus casibus admittendi alios christianos ad communionem eucharisticam in Ecclesia catholica*.[69] And although at this stage of renewal the possibility of a certain "creative" freedom has been permitted, nevertheless this freedom must strictly respect the requirements of substantial unity. We can follow the path of this pluralism (which arises in part from the introduction itself of the various languages into the liturgy) only as long as the essential characteristics of the celebration of the Eucharist are preserved, and the norms prescribed by the recent liturgical reform are respected.

Indispensable effort is required everywhere to ensure that within the pluralism of eucharistic worship envisioned by the Second Vatican Council the unity of which the Eucharist is the sign and cause is clearly manifested.

This task, over which in the nature of things the Apostolic See must keep careful watch, should be assumed not only by each *episcopal conference* but by every minister of the Eucharist, without exception. Each one should also remember that he is responsible for the common good of the whole Church. The *priest as minister*, as celebrant, as the one who presides over the eucharistic assembly of the faithful, should have a special *sense of the common good of the Church*, which he represents through his ministry, but to which he must also be subordinate, according to a correct discipline of faith. He cannot consider himself a "proprietor" who can make free use of the liturgical text and of the sacred rite as if it were his own property, in such a way as to stamp it with his own arbitrary personal style. At times this latter might seem more effective, and it may better correspond to subjective piety; nevertheless, objectively it is always a betrayal of that union which should find its proper expression in the sacrament of unity.

Every priest who offers the holy Sacrifice should recall that during this Sacrifice it is not *only* he with his community that is praying but the whole Church, which is thus expressing in this sacrament her spiritual unity, among other ways by the use of the approved liturgical text. To call this position "mere insistence on uniformity" would only show ignorance of the objective requirements of authentic unity, and would be a symptom of harmful individualism.

This subordination of the minister, of the celebrant, to the *Mysterium* which has been entrusted to him by the Church for the good of the whole People of God, should also find expression in the observance of the liturgical requirements concerning the celebration of the holy Sacrifice. These refer, for example, to dress, and in particular to the vestments worn by the celebrant. Circumstances have of course existed and continue to exist in which the prescriptions do not oblige. We have been greatly moved when reading books written by priests who had been prisoners in extermination camps, with descriptions of Eucharistic Celebrations without the above-mentioned rules, that is to say, without an altar and without vestments. But although in those conditions this was a proof of heroism and deserved profound admiration, nevertheless in *normal conditions* to ignore the liturgical directives can be interpreted as a lack of respect towards the Eucharist, dictated perhaps by individualism or by an absence of a critical sense concerning current opinions, or by a certain *lack of a spirit of faith.*

Upon all of us who, through the *grace* of God, are ministers of the Eucharist, there weighs a particular responsibility for the ideas and attitudes of our brothers and sisters who have been entrusted to our pastoral care. It is our vocation to nurture, above all by personal example, every healthy manifestation of worship towards Christ present and operative in that sacrament of love. May God preserve us from acting otherwise and weakening that worship by "becoming unaccustomed" to various manifestations and forms of eucharistic worship which express a perhaps "traditional" but healthy piety, and which express above all that "sense of the faith" possessed by the whole People of God, as the Second Vatican Council recalled.[70]

As I bring these considerations to an end, I would like to ask forgiveness—in my own name and in the name of all of you, venerable and dear brothers in the episcopate—for everything which, for whatever reason, through whatever human weakness, impatience or negligence, and also through the at times partial, one-sided and erroneous application of the directives of the Second Vatican Council, may have caused scandal and disturbance concerning the interpretation of the doctrine and the veneration due to this great sacrament. And I pray the Lord Jesus that in the future we may avoid in our manner of dealing with this sacred mystery anything which could weaken or disorient in any way the sense of reverence and love that exists in our faithful people.

May Christ Himself help us to follow the path of true renewal towards that fullness of life and of eucharistic worship whereby the Church is built up in that unity that she already possesses, and which she desires to bring to ever greater perfection for the glory of the living God and for the salvation of all humanity.

Conclusion

13. Permit me, venerable and dear brothers, to end these reflections of mine, which have been restricted to a detailed examination of only a few questions. In undertaking these reflections, I have had before my eyes all the work carried out by the Second Vatican Council, and have kept in mind Paul VI's Encyclical *Mysterium Fidei*, promulgated during that Council, and all the documents issued after the same Council for the purpose of implementing the post-conciliar liturgical renewal. A very close and organic *bond exists between the renewal of the liturgy and the renewal of the whole life of the Church.*

The Church not only acts but also expresses herself in the liturgy, lives by the liturgy and draws from the liturgy the strength for her life. For this reason liturgical renewal carried out correctly in the spirit of the Second Vatican Council is, in a certain sense, the measure and the condition for putting into effect the teaching of that Council which we wish to accept with profound faith, convinced as we are that by means of this Council the Holy Spirit "has spoken to the Church" the truths and given the indications for carrying out her mission among the people of today and tomorrow.

We shall continue in the future to take special care to promote and follow the renewal of the Church according to the teaching of the Second Vatican Council, *in the spirit of an ever living Tradition.* In fact, to the substance of Tradition properly understood belongs also a correct re-reading of the "signs of the times," which require us to draw from the rich treasure of Revelation "things both new and old."[71] Acting in this spirit, in accordance with this counsel of the Gospel, the Second Vatican Council carried out a providential effort to renew the face of the Church in the sacred liturgy, most often having recourse to what is "ancient," what comes from the heritage of the Fathers and is the expression of the faith and doctrine of a Church which has remained united for so many centuries.

In order to be able to continue in the future to put into practice the directives of the Council in the field of liturgy, and in particular in the field of eucharistic worship, *close collaboration is necessary* between the competent department of the Holy See and each episcopal conference, a collaboration which must be *at the same time vigilant and creative.* We must keep our sights fixed on the greatness of the most holy Mystery and at the same time on spiritual movements and social changes, which are so significant for our times, since they not only sometimes create difficulties but also prepare us for a new way of participating in that great Mystery of Faith.

Above all I wish to emphasize that the problems of the liturgy, and in particular of the Eucharistic Liturgy, must not be *an occasion for dividing Catholics and for threatening the unity of the Church.* This is demanded by an elementary understanding of that sacrament which Christ has left us as the source of spiritual unity. And how could the Eucharist, which in the Church is the *sacramentum pietatis, signum unitatis, vinculum caritatis,*[72] form between us at this time a point of division and a source of distortion of thought and of behavior, instead of being the focal point and constitutive center, which it truly is in its essence, of the unity of the Church herself?

We are all equally indebted to our Redeemer. We should all listen together to that spirit of truth and of love whom He has promised to the Church and who is operative in her. In the name of this truth and of this love, in the name of the crucified Christ and of His

Mother, I ask you, and beg you: Let us abandon all opposition and division, and let us all unite in this great mission of salvation which is the price and at the same time the fruit of our redemption. The Apostolic See will continue to do all that is possible to provide the means of ensuring that unity of which we speak. Let everyone avoid anything in his own way of acting which could "grieve the Holy Spirit."[73]

In order that this unity and the constant and systematic collaboration which leads to it may be perseveringly continued, I beg on my knees that, through the intercession of Mary, holy spouse of the Holy Spirit and Mother of the Church, we may all receive the light of the Holy Spirit. And blessing everyone, with all my heart I once more address myself to you, my venerable and dear brothers in the episcopate, with a fraternal greeting and with full trust. In this collegial unity in which we share, let us do all we can to ensure that the Eucharist may become an ever greater source of life and light for the consciences of all our brothers and sisters of all the communities in the universal unity of Christ's Church on earth.

In a spirit of fraternal charity, to you and to all our confreres in the priesthood I cordially impart the apostolic blessing.

From the Vatican, February 24, First Sunday of Lent, in the year 1980, the second of the Pontificate.

Joannes Paulus PP. II

FOOTNOTES

1. Cf. Chapter 2: AAS 71 (1979), pp. 395f.

2. Cf. Ecumenical Council of Trent, Session XXII, Can. 2: *Conciliorum Oecumenicorum Decreta,* ed. 3, Bologna 1973, p. 735.

3. Because of this precept of the Lord, an Ethiopian Eucharistic Liturgy recalls that the Apostles "established for us patriarchs, archbishops, priests and deacons to celebrate the ritual of your holy Church": *Anaphora Sancti Athanasii: Prex Eucharistica,* Haenggi-Pahl, Fribourg (Switzerland) 1968, p. 183.

4. Cf. *La Tradition apostolique de saint Hippolyte,* nos. 2-4, ed. Botte, Münster-Westfalen 1963, pp. 5-17.

5. 2 Cor. 11:28.

6. 1 Pt. 2:5.

7. Cf. Second Vatican Council, Dogmatic Constitution on the Church *Lumen gentium,* 28; AAS 57 (1965), pp. 33f.; Decree on the Ministry and Life of Priests *Presbyterorum Ordinis,* 2, 5: AAS 58 (1966), pp. 993, 998; Decree on the Missionary Activity of the Church Ad gentes, 39: AAS 58 (1966), p. 986.

8. Second Vatican Ecumenical Council, Dogmatic Constitution on the Church *Lumen gentium,* 11: AAS 57 (1965), p. 15.

9. Jn. 3:16. It is interesting to note how these words are taken up by the liturgy of St. John Chrysostom immediately before the words of consecration and introduce the latter: cf. *La divina Liturgia del nostro Padre Giovanni Crisostomo, Roma-Grottaferrata* 1967, pp. 104f.

10. Cf. Mt. 26:26-28; Mk. 14:22-25; Lk. 22:18-20; 1 Cor. 11:23-25; cf. also the Eucharistic Prayers.

11. Phil. 2:8.

12. Jn. 13:1.

13. Cf. John Paul II, Homily in Phoenix Park, Dublin, 7: AAS 71 (1979), pp. 1074ff.; Sacred Congregation of Rites, instruction *Eucharisticum mysterium*: AAS 59 (1967), pp. 539-573; *Rituale Romanum, De sacra communione et de cultu Mysterii eucharistici extra Missam, ed. typica*, 1973. It should be noted that the value of the worship and the sanctifying power of these forms of devotion to the Eucharist depend not so much upon the forms themselves as upon interior attitudes.

14. Cf. *Bull Trasiturus de hoc mundo* (Aug. 11, 1264): *Aemilii Friedberg, Corpus Iuris Canonici*, Pars II. *Decretalium Collectiones*, Leipzig 1881, pp. 1174-1177; *Studi eucharistici*, VII Centenario della Bolla 'Transiturus,' 1264-1964, Orvieto 1966, pp. 302-317.

15. Cf. Paul VI, encyclical letter *Mysterium Fidei:* AAS 57 (1965), pp. 753-774; Sacred Congregation of Rites, Instruction *Eucharisticum Mysterium*: AAS 59 (1967), pp. 539-573; *Rituale Romanum, De sacra communione et de cultu Mysterii eucharistici extra Missam, ed. typica*, 1973.

16. John Paul II, encyclical letter *Redemptor Hominis*, 20: AAS 71 (1979), p. 311; cf. Second Vatican Ecumenical Council, Dogmatic Constitution on the Church, *Lumen gentium*, 11: AAS 57 (1965), pp. 15f; also, note 57 to Schema II of the same dogmatic constitution, in *Acta Synodalia Sacrosancti Concilii Oecumenici Vaticani II*, vol. II, periodus 2a, pars I, public session II, pp. 251f.; Paul VI, address at the general audience of September 15, 1965: *Insegnamenti di Paolo VI*, III (1965), p. 103; H. de Lubac, *Méditation sur l'Eglise*, 2 ed., Paris 1963, pp. 129-137.

17. 1 Cor. 11:26.

18. Cf. Second Vatican Ecumenical Council, Dogmatic Constitution on the Church *Lumen gentium*, 11: AAS 57 (1965) pp. 15f; Constitution on the Sacred Liturgy *Sacrosanctum Concilium*, 10: AAS 56 (1964), p.

102; Decree on the Ministry and Life of Priests, *Presbyterorum Ordinis*, 5: AAS 58 (1966), pp. 997f.; Decree on the Bishops' Pastoral Office in the Church *Christus Dominus*, 30: AAS 58 (1966), pp. 688f.; Decree on the Church's Missionary Activity, *Ad gentes*, 9: AAS 58 (1966), pp. 957f.

19. Cf. Second Vatican Ecumenical Council, Dogmatic Constitution on the Church *Lumen gentium*, 26: AAS 57 (1965), pp. 31f.; Decree on Ecumenism *Unitatis Redintegratio,* 15: AAS 57 (1965), pp. 101f.

20. This is what the Opening Prayer of Holy Thursday asks for: "We pray that in this Eucharist we may find the fullness of love and life": *Missale Romanum, ed. typica altera* 1975, p. 244; also the communion epiclesis of the Roman Missal: "May all of us who share in the body and blood of Christ be brought together in unity by the Holy Spirit. Lord, remember your Church throughout the world; make us grow in love": Eucharistic Prayer II: *ibid.*, pp. 458f.; Eucharistic Prayer III, p. 463.

21. Jn. 5:17.

22. Cf. Prayer after communion of the Mass for the Twenty-second Sunday in Ordinary Time: "Lord, you renew us at your table with the bread of life. May this food strengthen us in love and help us to serve you in each other": *Missale Romanum, ed. cit.*, p. 361.

23. Jn. 4:23.

24. Cf. 1 Cor. 10:17; commented upon by St. Augustine: *In Evangelium Ioannis* tract. 31, 13; PL 35, 1613; also commented upon by the Ecumenical Council of Trent, Session XIII, can. 8; *Conciliorum Oecumenicorum Decreta*, ed. 3, Bologna 1973, p. 697, 7; cf. Second Vatican Ecumenical Council, Dogmatic Constitution on the Church, *Lumen gentium*, 7: AAS 57 (1965), p. 9.

25. Jn. 13:35.

26. This is expressed by many prayers of the *Roman Missal*: the Prayer over the Gifts from the Common, "For those who work for the underprivileged"; "May we who celebrate the love of your Son also follow the example of your saints and grow in love for you and for one another": *Missale Romanum, ed. cit.*, p. 721; also the Prayer after Communion of the Mass "For Teachers": "May this holy meal help us to follow the example of your saints by showing in our lives the light of truth and love for our brothers": *ibid.*, p. 723; cf. also the Prayer after Communion of the Mass for the Twenty-second Sunday in Ordinary Time, quoted in note 22.

27. Jn. 4:23.

28. Eph. 4:13.

29. Cf. above, no. 2.

30. Cf. Second Vatican Ecumenical Council, Decree on the Missionary Activity of the Church Ad *gentes*, 9, 12: AAS 58 (1966), pp. 958-961f.; Decree on the Ministry and Life of Priests *Presbyterorum Ordinis*, 5: AAS 58 (1966), p. 997.

31. 1 Jn. 3:1.

32. Second Vatican Ecumenical Council, Dogmatic Constitution on the Church *Lumen gentium*, 11: AAS 57 (1965), p. 15.

33. Cf. no. 20: AAS 71 (1979), pp. 313f.

34. 2 Pt. 3:13.

35. Col. 3:10.

36. Lk. 1:34; Jn. 6:69; Acts 3:14; Rev. 3:7.

37. Acts 10:38; Lk. 4:18.

38. Jn. 10:36.

39. Cf. Jn. 10:17.

40. Heb. 3:1; 4:15, etc.

41. As was stated in the ninth-century Byzantine liturgy, according to the most ancient codex, known for-

merly as B*arberino di San Marco* (Florence), and, now
that it is kept in the Vatican Apostolic Library, as
Barberini Greco 366 f. 8 verso, lines 17-20. This part has
been published by F.E. Brightman, *Liturgies Eastern
and Western*, I. *Eastern Liturgies*, Oxford 1896, p. 318,
34-35.

42. Opening Prayer of the Second Votive Mass of the
Holy Eucharist: *Missale Romanum, ed. cit.*, p. 858.

43. 1 Jn. 2:2; cf. *ibid.*, 4:10.

44. We speak of the *divinum Mysterium*, the
Sanctissimum, the *Sacrosanctum*, meaning what is
sacred and *holy* par excellence. For their part, the
Eastern churches call the Mass *raza* or *mysterion,
hagiasmos, quddasa, qedasse*, that is to say "consecration" par excellence. Furthermore there are the liturgical rites, which, in order to inspire a sense of the sacred,
prescribe silence, and standing or kneeling, and likewise professions of faith, and the incensation of the
Gospel book, the altar, the celebrant and the sacred
species. They even recall the assistance of the angelic
beings created to serve the Holy God, i.e., with the
Sanctus of our Latin churches and the *Trisagion* and
Sancta Sanctis of the Eastern liturgies.

45. For instance, in the invitation to receive communion, this faith has been so formed as to reveal comple-
mentary aspects of the presence of Christ the Holy One:
the epiphanic aspect noted by the Byzantines ("Blessed
is he who comes in the name of the Lord: The Lord is
God and *has appeared to us*" *La divina Liturgia del
santo nostro Padre Giovanni Crisostomo*, Roma-
Grottaferrata 1967, pp. 136f.); the aspect of relation and
union sung of by the Armenians (Liturgy of St. Ignatius
of Antioch: "*Unus Pater sanctus nobiscum, unus Filius
sanctus nobiscum, unus Spiritus sanctus nobiscum*":
*Die Anaphora des heiligen Ignatius von Antiochien,
übersetzt von A. Rücker, Oriens Christianus*, 3ª ser., 5
[1930], p. 76); and the hidden heavenly aspect celebrated by the Chaldeans and Malabars (cf. the antiphonal

hymn sung by the priest and the assembly after Communion: F.E. Brightman, *op. cit.*, p. 299).

46. Cf. Second Vatican Ecumenical Council, Constitution on the Sacred Liturgy *Sacrosanctum Concilium*, 2, 47: AAS 56 (1964), pp. 83f.; 113; Dogmatic Constitution on the Church *Lumen gentium*, 3 and 28: AAS 57 (1965), pp. 6, 33f.; Decree on Ecumenism *Unitatis Redintegratio,* 2: AAS 57 (1965), p. 91; Decree on the Ministry and Life of Priests *Presbyterorum Ordinis,* 13: AAS 58 (1966), pp. 1011f., Ecumenical Council of Trent, Session XXII, chap. I and II: *Conciliorum Oecumenicorum Decreta*, ed. 3, Bologna 1973, pp. 732f. especially: *una eademque est hostia, idem nunc offerens sacerdotum ministerio, qui se ipsum tunc in cruce obtulit, sola offerendi ratione diversa (ibid.,* p. 733).

47. *Synodus Constantinopolita adversus Sotericum* (January 1156 and May 1157): Angelo Mai, *Spicilegium romanum,* t. X, Rome 1844, p. 77; PG 140, 190; cf. Martin Jugie, Dict. Theol. Cath., t. X, 1338; T*heologia dogmatica christianorum orientalium,* Paris, 1930, pp. 317-320.

48. *Instituto Generalis Missalis Romani,* 49c: *Missale Romanum, ed. cit.,* p. 39; cf. Second Vatican Ecumenical Council, Decree on the Ministry and Life of Priests *Presbyterorum Ordinis,* 5: AAS 58 (1966), pp. 997f.

49. *Ordo Missae cum populo,* 18: *Missale Romanum, ed. cit.,* p. 390.

50. Cf. Ecumenical Council of Trent, Session 22, chap I, *Conciliorum Oecumenicorum Decreta*, ed. 3, Bologna 1973, pp. 732f.

51. Col. 2:14.

52. Jn. 11:28.

53. *Instituto Generalis Missalis Romani,* 55f.: *Missale Romanum, ed. cit.,* p. 40.

54. Cf. Constitution on the Sacred Liturgy *Sacrosanctum Concilium*, 35, 51: AAS 56 (1964), pp. 109, 114.

55. Cf. Sacred Congregation of Rites, Instruction *In edicendis normis*, VI, 17-18; VII, 19-20: AAS 57 (1965), pp. 1012f.; Instruction *Musicam Sacram*, IV, 48: AAS 59 (1967), p. 314; Decree *De Titulo Basilicae Minoris,* II, 8: AAS 60 (1968), p. 538; Sacred Congregation for Divine Worship, Notif. *De Missali Romano, Liturgia Horarum et Calendario*, I, 4: AAS 63 (1971), p. 714.

56. Cf. Paul VI, Apostolic Constitution *Missale Romanum*: "We are fully confident that both priests and faithful will prepare their minds and hearts more devoutly for the Lord's Supper, meditating on the scriptures, nourished day by day with the words of the Lord": AAS 61 (1969), pp. 220f.; *Missale Romanum, ed. cit.*, p. 15.

57. Cf. *Pontificale Romanum. De Institutione Lectorum et Acolythorum*, 4, *ed. typica,* 1972, pp. 19f.

58. Cf. *Instituto Generalis Missalis Romani*, 319-320: *Missale Romanum*, ed. cit., p. 87.

59. Cf. Fr. J. Dölger, *Das Segnen der Sinne mit der Eucharistie. Eine altchristliche Kommunionsitte: Antike und Christentum, t.* 3 (1932), pp. 231-244; *Das Kultvergehen der Donatistin Lucilla von Karthago. Reliquienkuss vor dem Kuss der Eucharistie, ibid.*, pp. 245-252.

60. Cf. Second Vatican Ecumenical Council, Dogmatic Constitution on the Church *Lumen gentium*, 12, 35; AAS 57 (1965), pp. 16, 40.

61. Cf. Jn. 1:29; Rv. 19:9.

62. Cf. Lk. 14:16ff.

63. Cf. *Instituto Generalis Missalis Romani*, 7-8: *Missale Romanum, ed. cit.*, p. 29.

64. 1 Cor. 11:28.

65. *Pontificale Romanum. De Ordinatione Diaconi, Presbyteri et Episcopi, ed. typica*, 1968, p. 93.

66. Heb. 5:1.

67. Sacred Congregation of Rites, Instruction *Eucharisticum Mysterium:* AAS 59 (1967), pp. 539-573; *Rituale Romanum. De sacra communione et de cultu Mysterii eucharistici extra Missam, ed. typica*, 1973; Sacred Congregation for Divine Worship, *Litterae circulares ad Conferentiarum Episcopalium Praesides de precibus eucharisticis:* AAS 65 (1973), pp. 340-347.

68. Nos. 38-63: AAS 59 (1967), pp. 586-592.

69. AAS 64 (1972), pp. 518-525. Cf. also the *Communicatio* published the following year for the correct application of the above-mentioned Instruction: AAS 65 (1973), pp. 616-619.

70. Cf. Second Vatican Ecumenical Council, Dogmatic Constitution on the Church *Lumen gentium,* 12: AAS 57 (1965), pp. 16f.

71. Mt. 13:52.

72. Cf. St. Augustine, *In Evangelium Ioannis tract.* 26, 13: PL 35, 1612f.

73. Eph. 4:30.

70. The Credo of the People of God
Proclaimed by His Holiness Pope Paul VI
on June 30, 1968

Reflection for Sundays

With this solemn liturgy we end the celebration of the nineteenth centenary of the martyrdom of the holy apostles Peter and Paul, and thus close the Year of Faith. We dedicated it to the commemoration of the holy apostles in order that we might give witness to our steadfast will to be faithful to the deposit of the faith[1] which they transmitted to us, and that we might strengthen our desire to live by it in the historical circumstances in which the Church finds herself in her pilgrimage in the midst of the world.

We feel it our duty to give public thanks to all who responded to our invitation by bestowing on the Year of Faith a splendid completeness through the deepening of their personal adhesion to the word of God, through the renewal in various communities of the profession of faith, and through the testimony of a Christian life. To our brothers in the episcopate especially, and to all the faithful of the holy Catholic Church, we express our appreciation and we grant our blessing.

A Mandate

Likewise, we deem that we must fulfill the mandate entrusted by Christ to Peter, whose successor we are, the last in merit; namely, to confirm our brothers in the faith.[2] With the awareness, certainly, of our human weakness, yet with all the strength impressed on our spirit by such a command, we shall accordingly make a profession of faith, pronounce a creed which, without being strictly speaking a dogmatic definition, repeats in substance, with some developments called for by the spiritual condition of our time, the creed of Nicea, the creed of the immortal tradition of the holy Church of God.

In making this profession, we are aware of the disquiet which agitates certain modern quarters with regard to the faith. They do not escape the influence of a world being profoundly changed, in which so many certainties are being disputed or discussed. We see even Catholics allowing themselves to be seized by a kind of passion for change and novelty. The Church, most assuredly, has always the duty to carry on the effort to study more deeply and to present, in a manner ever better adapted to successive generations, the unfathomable mysteries of God, rich for all in fruits of salvation. But at the same time the greatest care must be taken, while fulfilling the indispensable duty of research, to do no injury to the teachings of Christian doctrine. For that would be to give rise, as is unfortunately seen in these days, to disturbance and perplexity in many faithful souls.

Await Word

It is important in this respect to recall that, beyond scientifically verified phenomena, the intellect which God has given us reaches *that which is*, and not merely the subjective expression of the structures and development of consciousness; and, on the other hand, that the task of interpretation—of hermeneutics—is to try to understand and extricate, while respecting the word expressed, the sense conveyed by a text, and not to recreate, in some fashion, this sense in accordance with arbitrary hypotheses.

But above all, we place our unshakable confidence in the Holy Spirit, the soul of the Church, and in theological faith upon which rests the life of the Mystical Body. We know that souls await the word of the Vicar of Christ, and we respond to that expectation with the instructions which we regularly give. But today we are given an opportunity to make a more solemn utterance.

On this day which is chosen to close the Year of Faith, on this feast of the blessed apostles Peter and

Paul, we have wished to offer to the living God the homage of a profession of faith. And as once at Caesarea Philippi the apostle Peter spoke on behalf of the twelve to make a true confession, beyond human opinions, of Christ as Son of the living God, so today his humble successor, pastor of the Universal Church, raises his voice to give, on behalf of all the People of God, a firm witness to the divine Truth entrusted to the Church to be announced to all nations.

We have wished our profession of faith to be to a high degree complete and explicit, in order that it may respond in a fitting way to the need of light felt by so many faithful souls, and by all those in the world, to whatever spiritual family they belong, who are in search of the Truth.

To the glory of God most holy and of our Lord Jesus Christ, trusting in the aid of the Blessed Virgin Mary and of the holy apostles Peter and Paul, for the profit and edification of the Church, in the name of all the pastors and all the faithful, we now pronounce this profession of faith, in full spiritual communion with you all, beloved brothers and sons.

Profession of Faith

We believe in one only God, Father, Son and Holy Spirit, creator of things visible such as this world in which our transient life passes, of things invisible such as the pure spirits which are also called angels,[3] and creator in each man of his spiritual and immortal soul.

We believe that this only God is absolutely one in His infinitely holy essence as also in all His perfections, in His omnipotence, His infinite knowledge, His providence, His will and His love. He is *He who is*, as He revealed to Moses;[4] and He is *love*, as the apostle John teaches us:[5] so that these two names, being and love, express ineffably the same divine reality of Him who has wished to make Himself known to us, and who,

"dwelling in light inaccessible,"[6] is in Himself above every name, above every thing and above every created intellect. God alone can give us right and full knowledge of this reality by revealing Himself as Father, Son and Holy Spirit, in whose eternal life we are by grace called to share, here below in the obscurity of faith and after death in eternal light. The mutual bonds which eternally constitute the Three Persons, who are each one and the same divine being, are the blessed inmost life of God thrice holy, infinitely beyond all that we can conceive in human measure.[7] We give thanks, however, to the divine goodness that very many believers can testify with us before men to the unity of God, even though they know not the mystery of the most holy Trinity.

The Father

We believe then in the Father who eternally begets the Son; in the Son, the Word of God, who is eternally begotten; in the Holy Spirit, the uncreated Person who proceeds from the Father and the Son as their eternal love. Thus in the Three Divine Persons, *coaeternae sibi et coaequales*,[8] the life and beatitude of God perfectly one superabound and are consummated in the supreme excellence and glory proper to uncreated being, and always "there should be venerated unity in the Trinity and Trinity in the unity."[9]

The Son

We believe in our Lord Jesus Christ, who is the Son of God. He is the Eternal Word, born of the Father before time began, and one in substance with the Father, homoousios to Patri,[10] and through Him all things were made. He was incarnate of the Virgin Mary by the power of the Holy Spirit, and was made man: equal therefore to the Father according to His divinity, and inferior to the Father according to His humanity;[11] and Himself one, not by some impossible confusion of His natures, but by the unity of His person.[12]

He dwelt among us, full of grace and truth. He proclaimed and established the Kingdom of God and made us know in Himself the Father. He gave us His new commandment to love one another as He loved us. He taught us the way of the beatitudes of the Gospel: poverty in spirit, meekness, suffering borne with patience, thirst after justice, mercy, purity of heart, will for peace, persecution suffered for justice sake. Under Pontius Pilate He suffered—the Lamb of God bearing on Himself the sins of the world, and He died for us on the cross, saving us by His redeeming blood. He was buried, and, of His own power, rose on the third day, raising us by His resurrection to that sharing in the divine life which is the life of grace. He ascended to heaven, and He will come again, this time in glory, to judge the living and the dead: each according to his merits—those who have responded to the love and piety of God going to eternal life, those who have refused them to the end going to the fire that is not extinguished.

And His Kingdom will have no end.

The Holy Spirit

We believe in the Holy Spirit, who is Lord, and Giver of life, who is adored and glorified together with the

Father and the Son. He spoke to us by the prophets; He was sent by Christ after His resurrection and His ascension to the Father; He illuminates, vivifies, protects and guides the Church; He purifies the Church's members if they do not shun His grace. His action, which penetrates to the inmost of the soul, enables man to respond to the call of Jesus: Be perfect as your Heavenly Father is perfect (Mt. 5:48).

We believe that Mary is the Mother, who remained ever a Virgin, of the Incarnate Word, our God and Savior Jesus Christ,[13] and that by reason of this singular election, she was, in consideration of the merits of her Son, redeemed in a more eminent manner,[14] preserved from all stain of original sin[15] and filled with the gift of grace more than all other creatures.[16]

Joined by a close and indissoluble bond to the Mysteries of the Incarnation and Redemption,[17] the Blessed Virgin, the Immaculate, was at the end of her earthly life raised body and soul to heavenly glory[18] and likened to her risen Son in anticipation of the future lot of all the just; and we believe that the Blessed Mother of God, the New Eve, Mother of the Church,[19] continues in heaven her maternal role with regard to Christ's members, cooperating with the birth and growth of divine life in the souls of the redeemed.[20]

Original Offense

We believe that in Adam all have sinned, which means that the original offense committed by him caused human nature, common to all men, to fall to a state in which it bears the consequences of that offense, and which is not the state in which it was at first in our first parents—established as they were in holiness and justice, and in which man knew neither evil nor death. It is human nature so fallen, stripped of the grace that clothed it, injured in its own natural powers and subjected to the dominion of death, that is transmitted to all men, and it is in this sense that every man is born in sin. We therefore hold, with the Council of Trent, that original sin, is transmitted with human nature, "not by imitation, but by propagation" and that it is thus "proper to everyone."[21]

Reborn of the Holy Spirit

We believe that Our Lord Jesus Christ, by the sacrifice of the cross redeemed us from original sin and all the personal sins committed by each one of us, so that, in accordance with the word of the apostle, "where sin abounded, grace did more abound."[22]

We believe in one Baptism instituted by our Lord Jesus Christ for the remission of sins. Baptism should be administered even to little children who have not yet been able to be guilty of any personal sin, in order that, though born deprived of supernatural grace, they may be reborn "of water and the Holy Spirit" to the divine life in Christ Jesus.[23]

Baptism

We believe in one, holy, catholic, and apostolic Church built by Jesus Christ on that rock which is Peter. She is the Mystical Body of Christ; at the same time a visible society instituted with hierarchical organs, and a spiritual community; the Church on earth, the pilgrim People of God here below, and the Church filled with heavenly blessings; the germ and the first fruits of the Kingdom of God, through which the work and the sufferings of Redemption are continued throughout human history, and which looks for its perfect accomplishment beyond time in glory.[24] In the course of time, the Lord Jesus forms His Church by means of the sacraments emanating from His plenitude.[25] By these she makes her members participants in the Mystery of the Death and Resurrection of Christ, in the grace of the Holy Spirit who gives her life and movement.[26] She is therefore holy, though she has sinners in her bosom, because she herself has no other life but that of grace: it is by living by her life that her members are sanctified; it is by removing themselves from her life that they fall into sins and disorders that prevent the radiation of her sanctity. This is why she suffers and does penance for these offenses, of which she has the power to heal her children through the blood of Christ and the gift of the Holy Spirit.

The Word

Heiress of the divine promises and daughter of Abraham according to the Spirit, through that Israel whose scriptures she lovingly guards, and whose patriarchs and prophets she venerates; founded upon the apostles and handing on from century to century their ever-living word and their powers as pastors in the successor of Peter and the bishops in communion with him; perpetually assisted by the Holy Spirit, she has the charge of guarding, teaching, explaining and spreading the Truth which God revealed in a then veiled manner by the prophets, and fully by the Lord Jesus. We believe all that is contained in the word of God written or handed down, and that the Church proposes for belief as divinely revealed, whether by a solemn judgment or by the ordinary and universal magisterium.[27] We believe in the infallibility enjoyed by the successor of Peter when he teaches ex cathedra as pastor and teacher of all the faithful,[28] and which is assured also to the episcopal body when it exercises with him the supreme magisterium.[29]

We believe that the Church founded by Jesus Christ and for which He prayed is indefectibly one in faith, worship and the bond of hierarchical communion. In the bosom of this Church, the rich variety of liturgical rites and the legitimate diversity of theological and spiritual heritages and special disciplines, far from injuring her unity, make it more manifest.[30]

One Shepherd

Recognizing also the existence, outside the organism of the Church of Christ, of numerous elements of truth and sanctification which belong to her as her own and tend to Catholic unity,[31] and believing in the action of the Holy Spirit who stirs up in the heart of the disciples of Christ love of this unity,[32] we entertain the hope that the Christians who are not yet in the full communion of the one only Church will one day be reunited in one flock with one only shepherd.

We believe that the Church is necessary for salvation, because Christ, who is the sole mediator and way of salvation, renders Himself present for us in His body which is the Church.[33] But the divine design of salvation embraces all men; and those who without fault on their part do not know the Gospel of Christ and His Church, but seek God sincerely, and under the influence of grace endeavor to do His will as recognized through the promptings of their conscience, they, in a number known only to God, can obtain salvation.[34]

Sacrifice of Calvary

We believe that the Mass, celebrated by the priest representing the person of Christ by virtue of the power received through the Sacrament of Orders, and offered by him in the name of Christ and the members of His Mystical Body, is the sacrifice of Calvary rendered sacramentally present on our altars. We believe that as the bread and wine consecrated by the Lord at the Last Supper were changed into His body and His blood which were to be offered for us on the cross, likewise the bread and wine consecrated by the priest are changed into the body and blood of Christ enthroned gloriously in heaven, and we believe that the mysterious presence of the Lord, under what continues to appear to our senses as before, is a true, real and substantial presence.[35]

Transubstantiation

Christ cannot be thus present in this sacrament except by the change into His body of the reality itself of the bread and the change into His blood of the reality itself of the wine, leaving unchanged only the properties of the bread and wine which our senses perceive. This mysterious change is very appropriately called by the Church *transubstantiation*. Every theological explanation which seeks some understanding of this mystery must, in order to be in accord with Catholic faith, maintain that in the reality itself, independently of our mind, the bread and wine have ceased to exist after the Consecration, so that it is the adorable body and blood of the Lord Jesus that from then on are really before us under the sacramental species of bread and wine,[36] as the Lord willed it, in order to give Himself to us as food and to associate us with the unity of His Mystical Body.[37]

The unique and indivisible existence of the Lord glorious in heaven is not multiplied, but is rendered present by the sacrament in the many places on earth where Mass is celebrated. And this existence remains present, after the sacrifice, in the Blessed Sacrament which is, in the tabernacle, the living heart of each of our churches. And it is our very sweet duty to honor and adore in the blessed Host which our eyes see, the Incarnate Word whom they cannot see, and who, without leaving heaven, is made present before us.

Temporal Concern

We confess that the Kingdom of God begun here below in the Church of Christ is not of this world whose form is passing, and that its proper growth cannot be confounded with the progress of civilization, of science or of human technology, but that it consists in an ever more profound knowledge of the unfathomable riches of Christ, an ever stronger hope in eternal blessings, an ever more ardent response to the love of God, and an ever more generous bestowal of grace and holiness among men. But it is this same love which induces the Church to concern herself constantly about the true temporal welfare of men. Without ceasing to recall to her children that they have not here a lasting dwelling, she also urges them to contribute, each according to his vocation and his means, to the welfare of their earthly city, to promote justice, peace and brotherhood among men, to give their aid freely to their brothers, especially to the poorest and most unfortunate. The deep solicitude of the Church, the Spouse of Christ, for the needs of men, for their joys and hopes, their griefs and efforts, is therefore nothing other than her great desire to be present to them, in order to illuminate them with the light of Christ and to gather them all in Him, their only Savior. This solicitude can never mean that the Church conform herself to the things of this world, or that she lessen the ardor of her expectation of her Lord and of the eternal Kingdom.

We believe in the life eternal. We believe that the souls of all those who die in the grace of Christ— whether they must still be purified in purgatory, or whether from the moment they leave their bodies Jesus takes them to paradise as He did for the Good Thief— are the People of God in the eternity beyond death, which will be finally conquered on the day of the Resurrection when these souls will be reunited with their bodies.

Prospect of Resurrection

We believe that the multitude of those gathered around Jesus and Mary in paradise forms the Church of Heaven, where in eternal beatitude they see God as He is,[38] and where they also, in different degrees, are associated with the holy angels in the divine rule exercised by Christ in glory, interceding for us and helping our weakness by their brotherly care.[39]

We believe in the communion of all the faithful of

Christ, those who are pilgrims on earth, the dead who are attaining their purification, and the blessed in heaven, all together forming one Church; and we believe that in this communion the merciful love of God and His saints is ever listening to our prayers, as Jesus told us: Ask and you will receive.[40] Thus it is with faith and in hope that we look forward to the resurrection of the dead, and the life of the world to come.

Blessed be God Thrice Holy. Amen.

FOOTNOTES

1. Cf. 1 Tim. 6:20.
2. Cf. Lk. 22:32.
3. Cf. Dz.-Sch. 3002.
4. Cf. Ex. 3:14.
5. Cf. 1 Jn. 4:8.
6. Cf. 1 Tim. 6:16.
7. Cf. Dz.-Sch. 804.
8. Cf. Dz.-Sch. 75.
9. Cf. *ibid.*
10. Cf. Dz.-Sch. 150.
11. Cf. Dz.-Sch.76.
12. Cf. *ibid.*
13. Cf. Dz.-Sch. 251-252.
14. Cf. *Lumen Gentium*, 53.
15. Cf. Dz.-Sch. 2803.
16. Cf. *Lumen Gentium*, 53.
17. Cf. *Lumen Gentium*, 53, 58, 61.
18. Cf. Dz.-Sch. 3903.
19. Cf. *Lumen Gentium*, 53, 58, 61, 63; Cf. Paul Vl,

Alloc. for the Closing of the Third Session of the Second Vatican Council: AAS LVI [1964] 1016; Cf. Exhort. Apost. Signum Magnum, Introd.

20. Cf. *Lumen Gentium*, 62; cf. Paul Vl, Exhort. Apost. Signum Magnum, p. 1, n. 1.

21. Cf. Dz.-Sch. 1513.

22. Cf. Rom. 5:20.

23. Cf. Dz.-Sch. 1514.

24. Cf.. *Lumen Gentium*, 8, 5.

25. Cf. *Lumen Gentium*, 7, 11.

26. Cf. Sacrosanctum Concilium, 5, 6; cf. *Lumen Gentium*, 7, 12, 50.

27. Cf. Dz.-Sch. 3011.

28 Cf. Dz.-Sch. 3074.

29. Cf. *Lumen Gentium*, 25.

30. Cf. *Lumen Gentium*, 23; cf. Orientalium Ecclesiarum 2, 3, 5, 6.

31. Cf. *Lumen Gentium*, 8.

32. Cf. *Lumen Gentium*, 15.

33. Cf. *Lumen Gentium,* 14.

34. Cf. *Lumen Gentium,* 16.

35. Cf. Dz.-Sch. 1651.

36. Cf. Dz.-Sch. 1642,1651-1654; Paul Vl, Enc. Mysterium Fidei.

37. Cf. S. Th., 111, 73, 3.

38. Cf. 1 Jn. 3:2; Dz.-Sch. 1000.

39. Cf. *Lumen Gentium*, 49.

40. Cf. Lk. 10:9-10; Jn. 16:24.

73. Light, Salt, and Leaven
Lay People's Role in the Church's Mission
by Bishop Alvaro del Portillo of Opus Dei

"Mission Impossible." No other expression can summarize the command given to a small group of people on the Mount of Olives, early one spring morning at the dawn of the Christian era: You will receive power when the Holy Spirit comes upon you, and then you will be my witnesses not only in Jerusalem but throughout Judea and Samaria, and indeed to the ends of the earth (Acts 1:8). Christ's last words had all the appearance of insanity. Neither rich nor learned nor influential, how were those simple people from this lost corner of the Roman empire, supposed to carry to the whole world the message of a recently executed man?

Within the span of three hundred years, a large part of the Roman world had converted to the Christian way of life. The doctrine of the Crucified had conquered the persecutions of the powerful, the contempt of the learned, and the hedonist's resistance to moral demands. Christianity is today the world's greatest spiritual force. Only God's grace can explain it. But his grace has worked through men and women who lived up to the mission they received.

Christ did not speak of this mission as a mere possibility. He gave his disciples an imperative command. Thus we read in St. Mark: Go out to the whole world; proclaim the Good News to all creation. He who believes and is baptized will be saved; he who does not believe will be condemned (Mk 16:15-16). And similarly in St. Matthew: Go, therefore, make disciples of all nations; baptize them in the name of the Father and of the Son and of the Holy Spirit, and teach them to observe all the commands I gave you. And know that I am with you always; yes to the end of time (Mt 28:19-20). Such words bring to mind Christ's prayer to the Father during the Last Supper: As you sent me into the world, I have sent them into the world (Jn 17:18). The Second Vatican Council, in commenting on these words, stated: "The Church has received this solemn mandate of Christ to proclaim the saving truth from the apostles and must carry it out to the very ends of the earth." (1)

Everyone's Task

Whenever there is talk of the Church's mission, people often mistakenly assume that this responsibility lies with the clergy. But the mission that Christ entrusts to his disciples must be carried out by all the members of the Church. Everyone, each according to his or her own condition, has to join in this common endeavor. (2) The Council reminded us that "the Christian vocation by its very nature is also a vocation to the apostolate...In the Church there is a diversity of ministry but a oneness of mission. Christ conferred on the Apostles and their successors the duty of teaching, sanctifying, and ruling in his name and power. But the laity likewise share in the priestly, prophetic and royal office of Christ and therefore have their own share in the mission of the whole people of God in the Church and in the world." (3) All Christians are made one body with Christ through baptism and participate in his redemptive mission. Each and every one therefore must actively work to pass on to all men and women the gospel Jesus preached.

Although the apostolic dimension of the Christian vocation has always been present in the Church, it seemed for a long time that the saving mission had been entrusted to only a few. The rest of the faithful, the vast majority, had but a passive role to play. The Second Vatican Council has returned to the beginnings, emphasizing that the universal call to apostolate is not just a possibility but a real duty: "On all Christians therefore is laid the pre-eminent responsibility of working to make the divine message of salvation known and accepted by all people throughout the world." (4)

Where Only Lay People Can Reach

Do lay people as such have a specific role within the Church's mission? The Second Vatican Council has already given exact guidelines. Ordinary faithful, says the Constitution *Lumen Gentium*, "are called there by God that by exercising their proper function and led by the spirit of the Gospel they may work the sanctification of the world from within as a leaven. In this way they may make Christ known to others, especially by the testimony of a life resplendent in faith, hope and charity." (5) And further on: "the laity are called in a special way to make the Church present and operative in those places and circumstances where only through them can it become the salt of the earth." (6) For example, the Church is present in a hospital not only in the chaplain; she is there too in the Christian faithful who, as doctors and nurses, work to give the patients good professional services and personal attention. In a neighborhood, the church building will always be an indispensable point of reference; but the only way to reach those who do not attend its services is through Christian families.

The Apostolic Exhortation *Christifideles Laici*, taking into account work done in the 1987 Synod of Bishops, explores this doctrine more deeply. Referring to the laity's mission, the Pope warned of two dangers: "the temptation of being so strongly interested in Church services and tasks that some fail to become actively engaged in their responsibilities in the professional, social, cultural, and political world; and the temptation of legitimizing the unwarranted separation of faith from life, that is, a separation of the Gospel's acceptance from the actual living of the Gospel in various situations in the world." (7) Against these two extremes, the Pope remarked that what distinguishes lay men and women is their "secular character" since

God calls them to "sanctify themselves in marriage or the celibate life, in a family, in a profession, and in the various activities of society." (8)

The Synod tried in this way to avoid the double risk pointed out by the Pope. By encouraging the mission of lay people in temporal affairs, it sidesteps the temptation to retreat into the Church so as to escape from a hostile or indifferent society. By calling for a strong unity of faith and life, the bishops seek to avoid the loss of Christian identity. To be salt for the earth, one must be in the world. But this salt must never become insipid.

The specific mission of lay people is thus clear: to bring Christ's message to all earthly concerns: one's family, professional occupation, social activities...And, with the help of grace, to transform them into an encounter with God.

The First Christians

However, all this is not something new that took shape only after Vatican II. The Christians of the first hour, those who knew Christ and the Apostles personally or who belonged to immediately-following generations, were strongly conscious of their mission in the world. Tertullian, for instance, writes: "We live as other men and women. We share your Forum, meat market, baths, shops, factories, inns, market days, and the rest of your business enterprises. We are sailors like yourselves, we serve in the army, we engage in farming and trading; in addition, we place the products of our labor at your service." (9)

And we can still read in a venerable document from Christian antiquity: "Christians are not distinguished from the rest of mankind by either country, speech, or customs; the fact is they nowhere settle in cities of their own; they use no peculiar language; they cultivate no eccentric mode of life... While they dwell in both Greek and non-Greek cities, as each one's lot was cast, and conform to the customs of the country in dress, food and mode of life in general, the whole tenor of their way of living stamps it as worthy of admiration and admittedly extraordinary." (10) While remaining where they were, the first Christians had notably changed their behavior as the same document says further on: "They marry like others and beget children; but they do not expose their offspring...They find themselves in the flesh, but do not live according to the flesh. They spend their days on earth, but hold citizenship in heaven. They obey the established laws, but in their private lives rise above the laws... In a word, what the soul is in the body, that the Christians are in the world." (11)

This attitude and their fervent apostolic activity resulted in the Christian faith spreading astoundingly in a brief space of time. Doubtless, those brothers and sisters of ours had God's grace. But, in addition, we know that their response was always heroic: not only when facing torture but also in every moment of their lives. It is not a surprise that Tertullian could write: "We were born yesterday and already fill the earth: cities, islands, towns, villages, the army, the imperial palace, the senate, the Forum. Only your temples we have left for you." (12)

Opus Dei's Spirit

Allow me to change tactics slightly. The universal call to sanctity and apostolate, so clear in the first Christians and recalled by the latest Council (13), is one of the basic principles informing the spirit of the Prelature of Opus Dei. Since 1928, its founder, the Servant of God Josemaria Escriva, never ceased saying that sanctity and apostolate were a right and duty for each baptized person. For instance he wrote in 1934: "Your duty is to sanctify yourself. Yes, even you. Who thinks that this task is only for priests and religious? To everyone, without exception, our Lord said: 'Be perfect, as my heavenly Father is perfect.' " (14) And again on our apostolic mission: "Through the world still echoes that divine cry: 'I have come to cast fire upon the earth, and what will I but that it be kindled?' And you see: it has nearly all died out...Don't you want to spread the blaze?" (15)

Monsignor Escriva can well be considered a pioneer of the Second Vatican Council. Cardinal Poletti clearly asserted it when introducing the beatification process of Opus Dei's founder: "For having proclaimed the universal call to holiness, since 1928 when he founded Opus Dei, Msgr. Josemaria Escriva has been recognized by all as a forerunner of the Council in what was precisely the marrow of its teaching." (16)

Word and Example

In an increasingly materialistic society, the Christian's task is similar to that of Christ's first disciples: to pass on the Good News by example and word.

In this life we never know the effects of our behavior on those around us, the good example or scandal we have given. The first and essential obligation for any Christian is to act in harmony with the faith, consistent with professed beliefs. "You are the light of the world. A city built on a hill cannot be hidden. Nor do men light a lamp and put it under a bushel, but on a stand, and it gives light to all in the house. Let your light so shine before men, that they may see your good works and give glory to your Father who is in heaven."(Mt 5:14-16)

However, example is not enough. "An apostolate of

this kind does not consist only in the witness of one's way of life; a true apostle looks for opportunities to announce Christ by words addressed either to non-believers with a view to leading them to faith, or to the faithful with a view to instructing, strengthening and encouraging them to a more fervent life." (17)

This charge is not addressed to "specialist" apostles. The Council reminded everyone of the obligation that each lay person has to do apostolate on his or her own initiative. "The individual apostolate, flowing generously from its source in a truly Christian life, is the origin and condition of the whole lay apostolate, even of the organized type, and it admits of no substitute. Regardless of status, all lay persons (including those who have no opportunity or possibility for collaboration in associations) are called to this type of apostolate and obliged to engage in it. This type of apostolate is useful at all times and places, but in certain circumstances it is the only one appropriate and feasible." (18)

The occasions for apostolate are countless. One's entire life should be constantly apostolic. Nevertheless, I would like to consider two areas that are the axes of most people's life: work and family.

Through Professional Work

Professional work is one of the places where friendships are born and develop. Possibilities for apostolate here might seem to be restricted to a few persons, but we should not forget that deep, trusting relationships spring up with those who work at our side, enabling us frequently to help them in decisive and lasting ways.

Some jobs (I am thinking, for example, of teaching or working in the mass media) offer an opportunity to reach hundreds and even thousands of persons. However, it would be a mistake to think that only these professions can be occasions for apostolate. On the contrary, all Christians in whatever job or circumstance should help those around them find the Christian mean-

ing of life. Ordinarily, there will be no need for great eloquence and sermons. It will be enough to practice what
Opus Dei's founder called "the apostolate of friendship
and confidence," which he described in this manner:
"Those words whispered at the proper time into the ear
of your wavering friend; that helpful conversation you
manage to start at the right moment; the ready advice
that improves his studies; and the discreet indiscretion
by which you open for him unsuspected horizons for his
zeal — all that is the 'apostolate of friendship.' " (19)

Apostolic zeal is shown in real concern for others,
which normally finds an outlet in personal conversation
between two friends. "A Christian's apostolate — and
I'm talking about an ordinary Christian living as just
one more man or woman among equals — is a great
work of teaching. Through real, personal, loyal friendship, you create in others a hunger for God and you help
them to discover new horizons. Naturally, simply: with
the example of your faith lived to the full, with a loving
word full of the force of divine truth." (20)

This apostolic effort is not limited to individuals.
With a spirit of freedom and responsibility, Christians
ought to see to it that the whole spectrum of social structures and institutions help all men and women draw
closer to God. The Council saw this infusion of a
Christian spirit into the temporal order as the characteristic mission of the lay faithful. In his apostolic
exhortation *Christifideles Laici*, the Pope calls on
Christians who work in the fields of science, technology,
medicine, politics, economics and culture, (21) asking
them not to shrink from their responsibility to build a
more humane, and therefore a more Christian, world.

The inspiration and principles needed for such an
endeavor are to be found in the Church's social doctrine.
But this doctrine will take on life only when men and
women — whether on Wall Street or in a humble corner
shop — see their work as something more than a mere
source of income or a rung upon the social ladder. Men

and women are needed — whether in City Hall or in neighborhood associations — who will work to foster a more humane society; educators are required — whether university professors or grade school teachers — who will help create a Christian culture.

Importance of the Family

Along with all this apostolic endeavor centered around work, the apostolate done in and through the family will always have a fundamental importance. For parents, their first and most important apostolate, entrusted to them directly by God, is the education of their children.

The family is "the first and vital cell of society." (22) On its health depends the entire society's health or sickness. Society will be more fraternal if all family members learn how to sacrifice for each other. Tolerance and respect in human relationships depends on the mutual understanding between parents and children. Loyalty will have a resurgence in society at large if marital fidelity is properly valued. And materialistic consumerism will decline if the happiness of home is not calculated only in material possessions.

The role of example is crucial in the education of children. John Paul II has commented about his own father: "My father was admirable, and almost all the memories of my childhood and adolescence are connect-

ed with him...The mere fact of seeing him on his knees
had a decisive influence on my early years. He was so
hard on himself that he had no need to be hard on his
son; his example alone was sufficient to inculcate discipline and a sense of duty." (23) And Cardinal Luciani —
later John Paul I — wrote: "In reality, the first book of
religion that children read is the parents themselves. It
is a good thing if the father says to the boy: 'There is a
monk confessor at church, don't you think you could
take advantage of the opportunity?' Better still if he
says: 'I'm going to church, to Confession; do you want to
come along?' " (24) Example given in all circumstances
— loyalty to friends, work habits, sobriety and temperance, joy in adversity, concern for others, generosity —
are engraved forever in the children's hearts.

Then, parents must give generous attention to their
children's education. The founder of Opus Dei used to
tell business people: "The most important business you
have is raising your children well." This will come about
if parents become friends with their children; if children
always can open their hearts trustingly to their parents
when troubles of any kind crop up. St. Thomas More
wrote: "When I have returned home, I must talk with
my wife, chat with my children, and confer with my servants. All this activity I count as business when it must
be done — and it must be unless you want to be a
stranger in your own home. Besides, one must take care
to be as agreeable as possible to those whom nature has
supplied, or chance has made, or you yourself have chosen, to be the companions of your life." (25)

True, the frantic pace of modern times does not
seem to foster this calm dedication to children. We have
more and more of everything, except time for others.
There is a risk that parents may be devoured by work,
even though it is done for the sake of their children's
future. But their future well-being depends a lot more
on the time parents have generously given rather than
on the material comfort provided. Children do not com-

plain so much of not having been given this or that by their parents, as of parents who have not given themselves to the family.

Families Open to All

But a Christian aware of his or her mission as leaven for the world cannot be satisfied with home duties and obligations. In a highly competitive world, it is normal to seek at home, in one's own family, the much-needed affection and security so often lacking in the world at large. It is also understandable that many parents strive to protect their own family's welfare. At the same time, the Christian family is always an "open" family.

"The family, like the Church, ought to be a place where the Gospel is transmitted and from which the Gospel radiates...Such a family becomes the evangelizer of many other families, and of the neighborhood of which it forms part." (26) A Christian family striving to live up to its ideals, despite its limitations and difficulties, is always attractive, even from a human perspective. More so if such a family is truly open to others, fostering an apostolic spirit with relatives, colleagues, neighbors, friends of the children. Thus will be realized the ideal held up by John Paul II when he wrote: "the Church of the home is also called to be a luminous sign of Christ's presence and of his love for those who are far away, for families who do not yet believe, and for those Christian families who no longer live in accordance with the faith that they once received." (27)

At the same time, all families are subjected to exterior influences coming from legislation, school and public opinion. To protect one's own family as well as to help others, a Christian should work towards the creation of a favorable social climate for the family.

As we read in the Apostolic Exhortation *Familiaris Consortio*, "Families should be the first to take steps to see that the laws and institutions of the State not only do not offend but support and positively defend the rights and duties of the family. Along these lines, families should grow in awareness of being 'protagonists' of what is known as 'family politics' and assume responsibility for transforming society." (28)

A New Evangelization

The first Christians transformed society as they strove to fulfill Christ's command: "They, going out, preached everywhere, the Lord working with them and confirming the word by the signs that accompanied it." (Mk 16:20)

At the threshold of the third millennium, in the midst of a society that seems to be frantically fleeing God, Christians are called to carry out a new evangelization "in and from the ordinary, material and secular activities of human life. He (Christ) waits for us everyday, in the laboratory, in the operating room, in the army barracks, in the university chair, in the factory, in the workshops, in the fields, in the home and in all the immense panorama of work. Understand this well: there is something holy, something divine hidden in the most ordinary situations, and it is up to each one of you to discover it." (29)

As John Paul II has written, "This will be possible if the lay faithful will know how to overcome in themselves the separation of the Gospel from life, to again take up in their daily activities in family, work, and society, an integrated approach to life that is fully brought about by the inspiration and strength of the Gospel." (30) The world hungers for coherent Christians: people who stumble and fall, but who are determined to get up and go forward, under the protection of holy Mary, along the way leading to the Father through Jesus Christ, the Way, the Truth and the Life.

FOOTNOTES

1 Dogmatic Constitution on the Church *Lumen Gentium*, 17 (N.C.W.C. translation has been used for all quotes from Vatican II).

2 Cf. Ibid., 30.

3 Decree on the Apostolate of Lay People *Apostolicam Actuositatem*, 2.

4 Ibid., 3.

5 Dogmatic Constitution on the Church *Lumen Gentium*, 31.

6 Ibid., 33.

7 Apostolic Exhortation *Christifideles Laici*, 2.

8 Ibid., 15.

9 Tertullian, *Apology of Christians*, 42.

10 Epistle to Diognetus, 5.

11 Ibid., 5 and 6.

12 Tertullian, *Apology of Christians*, 1.

13 John Paul II has written: "It is possible to say that this call to holiness is precisely the basic charge entrusted to all the sons and daughters of the Church by a Council which intended to bring a renewal of Christian life based on the Gospel. This charge is not a simple moral exhortation but an undeniable requirement arising from the mystery of the Church." (Apostolic Exhortation *Christifideles Laici*, 16)

14 Josemaria Escriva, *The Way*, 291.

15 Ibid., 801.

16 Decreto di Introduzione della Causa di Beatificazione del Servo di Dio Josemaria Escriva de Balaguer y Albas.

17 *Apostolicam Actuositatem*, 6.

18 Ibid., 16.

19 Josemaria Escriva, The Way, 973.

20 Josemaria Escriva, Christ Passing By, 149.

21 Cf. nn. 38, 42-44.

22 *Apostolicam Actuositatem*, 11.

23 Andre Frossard, Be Not Afraid, p. 14.

24 Illustrissimi: Letters from Pope John Paul I, p. 223.

25 St. Thomas More, Utopia.

26 Apostolic Exhortation *Evangelii Nuntiandi*, 71. Quoted in John Paul II, Apostolic Exhortation on The Role of the Christian Family in the Modern World *Familiaris Consortio* 52.

27 *Familiaris Consortio*, 54.

28 Ibid., 44.

29 Conversations with Monsignor Josemaria Escriva, 114.

30 *Christifideles Laici,* 34.

74. Seven Prayers in the Lord's Prayer for Nurturing New Covenant Life
by Fr. Bernard Geiger, O.F.M., Conv.

Begin each prayer with: Our Father, who art in Heaven, that is, in every heart that loves You, because that is where You dwell.

1. **Hallowed be thy name**: Yes, Father; therefore, enlarge the twin mystical sapphires of our **Gifts of Knowledge** and **Infused Faith** (also see 53L). For these are permanent capacities You have given us to receive and use the light of knowledge and the power of faith which Your Holy Spirit wants to bring us from Jesus' fullness of grace and truth in Mary. Only with these can we make acts and develop habits of supernatural knowledge and faith. Only with these can we dispel our ignorance of You and every tendency or vice of mind-darkening covetousness. And only with these can we know and appreciate the Kingdom of Love which You have established for Your glory and our salvation, and thus hold Your Name sacred.

Father, let Your Holy Spirit constantly irradiate us with the light of Mary's knowledge and the power of her faith. May she help us use these to learn all that You want us to know, and believe all that You want us to believe. For Mary is the Immaculata, Your daughter, the Woman Full of Grace, whom You have sent to help Jesus, Your Son and hers, replace the Ancient Serpent's evil empire with Your Kingdom of Love. With these actual graces may we share her knowledge of You as Infinite Goodness-in-Person; her knowledge of Your Call, Plan and New Covenant; her knowledge of who Jesus and she are, of who each one of us is in Your Plan; her knowledge of how much You love us; of how much we need Your merciful love; how much You need and want our love, and of how You have created in each of us a need for each other's love. Only with our love can

Your love form Your Kingdom of Love, and bring about the fulfillment of Your Plan and our Covenant. With this knowledge and our infused Faith, we do believe, we do adore You; we accept again and keep in mind Your Call and Plan, and Your New Covenant with us. We celebrate Your goodness and all that You are doing through them.

2. **Thy kingdom come:** Father, enlarge the twin mystical topazes of our **Gifts of Understanding** and **Infused Hope**. These are the permanent capacities You have given us to receive and use the light of understanding and the power of hope which Your Holy Spirit wants to bring us from Jesus through Mary. These powers alone enable us to make acts and develop habits of supernatural understanding and hope. With them we bind ourselves ever more securely to Jesus our King and Head, and so expand and strengthen Your Kingdom. With them we dispel our incomprehension of You and Your wonderful Plan, and every tendency to mind-numbing gluttony. Only with them can we understand our relationships in the Holy Spirit with You, with Jesus, Mary, Joseph and everyone else, and totally commit our lives to You in them.

Father, send Your Holy Spirit to fill us with the light of Mary's understanding and power of hope. May she help us use these to understand and commit ourselves to all that You want us to understand and be committed to. May she share with us her understanding of Jesus, Your Son and hers, Your Eternal Word-Made-Man, Your Infinite Truth-in-Person in Whom, through Whom, and for Whom You created us; the One Whom You have sent to live in us so that we might live in Him, and form His Mystical Body. With these graces, we commit ourselves again to the New Covenant that You have made with us in Jesus. May our humility, gratitude and commitment grow constantly stronger.

3. **Thy will be done on earth as it is in heaven:** And so, Father, may Your Holy Spirit, the Eternal Immaculate Conception of Your Son's and Your eternal mutual love, Your Infinite Unity-in-Person, enlarge the twin mystical rubies of our **Gifts of Piety** and **Infused Charity-Love**. These are the permanent capacities You have given us in Baptism to receive and use the light of piety and the power of charity-love which He brings us from Jesus through Mary. These actual graces enable us to make acts and develop habits of supernatural piety and charity. Only with them can we dispel every sense of alienation, isolation and hostility, and every tendency or vice of that false love which is lust. With these graces, You and Jesus actually begin to live in us, and we to live in You and in one another in Jesus. With the gift of piety and the virtue of charity-love, Your reign of love actually begins to govern our minds and hearts.

Father, may Your Holy Spirit constantly immerse us in Mary's light of piety and power of charity-love. May she help us to use this light to see and acknowledge the identity that You give us with yourself, with Jesus, with the Holy Spirit, with Mary herself, with one another, and with every other person and group. May she help us to use the power of her charity to become, like her, the person You call each of us to be in Your Church and Kingdom of Love. With this power and her help, we do love you. We give ourselves to You and to each other to obey Your Call, Plan and New Covenant, as Mary does. We say "Yes" to all Your love, and all that You wish to give us, and "Yes" to all that You ask of us. In this way, may we constantly grow in our love for You. May we grow in obedience and self-giving, and thus permit Your love to work in us without hindrance.

4. **Give us this day our daily bread**: That is, Father, may Your Holy Spirit enlarge in us the mystical pearls of our **Gifts of Wisdom**, and our mystical diamonds of **Infused Prudence**. These are the permanent capacities You gave us in Baptism to receive and use the light of wisdom and power of prudence which He brings us from Jesus' fullness of grace and truth in Mary. These energies enable us to make acts and develop habits of supernatural wisdom and prudence. Only with these graces, can we dispel our false self-images and every tendency or vice of pride. Through them, You nurture and energize Your reign of love in us, and build up Your Kingdom.

Father, may Your Holy Spirit constantly inundate us with Mary's light of wisdom and power of prudence.

May she help us to use her light of wisdom to see the whole sweep of Your vision for Jesus, herself and us. Especially may she help us always take into account the potential You have given us in Jesus for fulfilling Your Call, Plan and New Covenant, the means that You give us for this purpose, especially through the Eucharist, and the opportunities we have for doing so. May she help us to use her power of prudence to set goals for Jesus that will actualize this potential, and to prioritize them as long-range, middle-range and short-range. May she help us to plan projects that effectively utilize the means You give, and to carry out the programs to develop the talents, resources, arts, skills, associations, structures, quality controls, and so on, that we'll need in order to accomplish them. We choose now to do these things so that our prudence may grow in penetration, universality and practicality.

5. **Forgive us our trespasses as we forgive those who trespass against us:** Yes, Father, let Your Holy Spirit enlarge in us the twin mystical jacinths of our **Gifts of Counsel** and **Infused Justice**. These are the permanent capacities You have given us in Baptism to receive and use the light of counsel and power of justice which Your Holy Spirit brings to us from Jesus through Mary. Only with these can we make acts and develop habits of supernatural counsel and justice. With them we dispel our evil cunning, and every tendency or vice of envy. By them we are reconciled with You. With them we rightly implement Your reign of love in ourselves and others.

Father, let Your Holy Spirit constantly transfuse us with the light of Mary's counsel and power of her justice. May she help us to use these to totally forgive ourselves and others as You have forgiven us. And may she help us to unite ourselves with Jesus as He offers His Body, Blood, Soul and Divinity to You in reparation for all our sins and failings. May she help us to use them to establish daily agendas, and discern the practical things we must do at each moment in every situation to achieve the goals that she has helped us to set. In particular, may she help us to plan the strategies and tactics, the day-to-day policies and procedures, the checks and balances, the schedules, timing and routines necessary to carry out our projects. With these actual graces and with the power of Jesus' justice, help us to always order ourselves to do what most pleases Him. May we thus develop fidelity, exactitude and promptness in our justice.

6. **Lead us not into temptation:** Rather, Father, let Your Holy Spirit enlarge in us the twin mystical emeralds of our **Gifts of Fear of the Lord** and **Infused Temperance**. For these are the permanent capacities You gave us in Baptism to receive the light of reverence and power of temperance which Your Spirit brings to us from Jesus through Mary. Only with these can we make acts and develop habits of supernatural reverence and temperance. With them alone can we really dispel our insensitivity to You and others, and every tendency or vice of sloth. With them, we develop and use our impelling and repelling emotions to serve Your reign of love.

Father, let Your Holy Spirit constantly permeate us with the light of Mary's reverence for You and the power of her temperance. May she help us to use the light of her reverence to contemplate frequently the delight, desire and joy that she, Jesus and the saints have in each and all of us, Your creatures, and in our commitments to Your Call, Plan and New Covenant; and the horror, disgust, aversion and sorrow that they feel for sin, and thus stir up and develop these same explosive emotions in ourselves to shape them into these same fundamental attitudes. May she help us to use her power of temperance to harness our explosive, animating emotions and attitudes in order to seal our commitments to Jesus. We choose to do this now so as to toughen and seal these in peace, quiet meekness, and strength, and thus overcome all temptations to neglect or abandon them.

7. **But deliver us from evil:** And so, Father, let Your Holy Spirit enlarge the twin mystical amethysts of our **Gifts of Fortitude** and our **Infused Fortitude**. These are the permanent capacities that You give us in Baptism to receive and use the light of mental fortitude and the power of "intestinal" fortitude which Your Spirit brings us from Jesus through Mary. These enable us to make acts and develop habits of supernatural fortitude of both mind and heart. With them, we dispel false consciences in ourselves and every tendency or vice of cruel, vicious or uncontrolled anger. With them, we develop and use our productive and defensive emotions, too, to serve Your reign of love.

Father, may Your Holy Spirit constantly immerse us in the energies of Mary's fortitude of mind and heart. May she help us to use the light of her mental fortitude to contemplate frequently the courage, confident commitment and enthusiasm which she, Jesus, and the saints had for carrying out Your Call, Plan and New Covenant; and the fear, despair and anger which they had, respectively, for whatever would either threaten this effort, or divert them from it, or obstinately and persistently oppose it. May she thus help us stir up and develop these same driving-emotions and attitudes in ourselves. May she then help us to use the power of her fortitude of heart to always focus these emotions and attitudes on the commands we give ourselves, either to expedite our work for Jesus, or to overcome all threats, diversions and obstacles to it. We choose now to do this and thus achieve constantly greater perseverance, patient endurance, and invincibility in our efforts to fulfill Your will and Plan. Amen.

Seven separate prayers: Choose only one of the seven petitions. Begin with the words, "Our Father, etc.," then pray one or both paragraphs of the petition chosen. Pray a different petition each day of the week. Or, continue to peacefully pray just one petition daily for three weeks or so.

77. The Five Dimensions of the Responsibility of the Present Moment

by Jerome F. Coniker

1. One of the most basic responsibilities of our baptismal consecration is to live for God alone and to draw our family and others to Him.

As Catholic families, we are called to be instruments of the Holy Family to bring other families to God. If enough of us allow ourselves to be used by God, we will see the greatest period of peace and evangelization that the world has ever known. **The Third Millennium can be a time when our children and grandchildren can grow up in a society of light and Truth.**

At this point, you are probably thinking, "How can he talk this way when the evil we see today is so pervasive?"

I believe many people are coming to the realization that unless we turn back to God in prayer, and then vigorously evangelize and catechize, we are going to slip into a totally dark age that will only be reversed after a long period of persecution and purification. This purification could last far beyond our lifetime.

In both the Old and New Testaments, we found 177 warnings from God to His people to stop sinning. Seventy times they responded with repentance and were blessed, rather than chastised. This should give us hope. But 107 times they didn't repent, and they were chastised. This should warn us.

A People of Hope

2. **The stakes are high, but we are a people of hope. We have been given a great gift for our troubled times—Pope John Paul II. If we follow his teachings, we can cross the threshold of hope into the Third Millennium, which he has said can be**

the greatest period of peace and religion that the world has ever known.

Let us respond to the Holy Father's challenge, especially to the **"sleeping giant of the laity,"** at this time in history.

Responsibility of the Present Moment

3.   Those of you who have come to Catholic Familyland hear us talking about the **responsibility of the present moment**. In our particular charism, we believe that the responsibility of the present moment is the essence of holiness because it helps to bring us into union with God's will for us every moment of the day. Until enough people live this way, we will never see peace in our families and society.

How can we, as laymen, be deeply united with God? Hasn't it been the tradition of Catholics to think that only those who are priests and religious sisters and brothers are called to really be one with God? Sometimes we think that lay men or women, who live in the world, can also be part of the world, and not really be committed to transforming it into God's Kingdom on Earth.

Consecration means to be set apart for the exclusive use of God. The whole world should be set apart for God. In his letter to the first Christians, St. Peter wrote, "You are a chosen race, a royal priesthood, a consecrated nation, a people set apart" (1 Peter 2:9).

Pope John Paul II referred to the three vocations of the priesthood, religious and laity when he taught:

The role of the ministerial priest is to be the bridge between heaven and earth. In the Holy Sacrifice of the Mass only the ministerial priest brings down the Body, Blood, Soul and Divinity of Our Lord — the very center of our Faith. Only the ministerial priest can forgive sins in the Name of Jesus Christ Our Lord.

The role of the religious (who are also members of the Priesthood of the Faithful) is to be outside of the world, but to serve the world.

The role of the laity (who are also members of the Priesthood of the Faithful) is to remain in the world, **not to be of the world, but to transform the world into God's kingdom upon earth.**

Public Reign of Christ

4.   Let's take a deeper look at the laity. Many lay people don't even realize that we as lay members of the Church are not called to be of the world, but rather to transform it. We can help to bring about the public reign of Christ so the Faith will reign in our daily lives within our communities.

What does this mean—the public reign of Christ? I believe it means that most every parish will have Perpetual Adoration, where entire families come at specified times to adore and be with Our Lord. Churches will be left open for people to stop in and visit Our Lord 24 hours a day. Catholics will imitate some of their Protestant brethren in bringing their entire family to church for an evening of family worship during the week, to participate in what we call our *Be Not Afraid Family Hours.* And our traditional devotions will be practiced by the majority of families.

It means that employers will be fair with their employees, and that employees will do the very best at their jobs because they know they are doing it for the Lord.

Clothing styles will be modest, and the media will be moral. And most of all, God's laws will prevail in all dimensions of our society and the Ten Commandments will be the standard by which decisions are made in our courts and legislatures.

What's so wrong with that?! Why can't we live and work for this goal? This is what we're called to do—to transform our world into God's kingdom on earth!

We pray for the public reign of Christ everyday in the Our Father: "Thy kingdom come, Thy will be done on earth as it is in heaven." This means we hope and pray for the reign of God's peace, the civilization of love of which the Holy Father has often spoken and has asked us to work for. This can become a reality when we really do God's will, as it is done in heaven.

Is it Impossible?

5.   You say that's impossible? It isn't. It isn't if we really work for it and make heroic sacrifices. Anything is possible with God's grace (cf. Mark 10:27).

In many of our encounters with Mother Teresa, she told us that holiness is not a luxury for the few, but an obligation for all of us. It is our will, combined with God's grace, that will transform us into His image.

But we have to make an act of the will and will to be holy with all of our hearts. We have to ask for it in prayer, and we have to prove that we have this desire by doing God's will. This is done by fulfilling the responsibility of the present moment. **When we are receptive to these graces and act upon them, God will make us holy. Holiness is union with God.**

Today our society is anything but holy. Due to the lack of adequate formation, there were many misrepresentations of the Second Vatican Council and its directives. As a result of this and other factors, much confusion was wrought in the Church. **However, we know that Vatican II was truly led by the Holy Spirit and has made a special call to the laity to become holy.**

This is why it is so important for Catholic laymen of today to study the *Catechism of the Catholic Church*, the documents of the Second Vatican Council, and papal documents. These teachings are so rich and put forth such clarity on the laity's call to sanctify their daily activities and to fulfill their obligation to evangelize.

The Truth Makes Us Free

6.   Our families have a responsibility to know the Truth. In many ways we become slaves to our own ignorance. We need to spend less time watching TV and more time studying Church teachings. We have to study our Faith and share it. We have to find out what the Holy Father is telling the people of today.

Fatima—A Beginning, Not an End

7.   After living near Fatima in Portugal for two years, Gwen and I were privileged to have an audience with the Bishop of Leiria, where Fatima is located. The Bishop told us to go back to America and use the Fatima message to get people's attention, so they could begin to live a spiritual life.

The Bishop told us that the purpose of Our Lady's apparitions was to bring us to Jesus Christ and into the heart the Church. He went on to say

that the heart of the Church is where the Pope is.

Mary Draws Us to Jesus

8.   The Hearts of Jesus and Mary are never to be separated. She is God's Mother and He has placed her in the dignified position as Mother of the Church.

Mary always draws us into the heart of the Church. We, as laymen, can reach the deepest degree of union with God by consecrating ourselves to Jesus through His mother, according to the formula of St. Louis de Montfort, by developing a deep prayer life, by studying the truths of our Faith, and by accepting the responsibilities of our state in life as lay men and women. Pope John Paul II has given us so many rich teachings about Mary and St. Joseph, who are perfect models, and about the Sacrament of Matrimony and family life.

St. Therese the Little Flower, Patroness of Missionaries

9.   St. Therese has now been elevated to a Doctor of the Church. One of the books she read over and over during her short life was the classic by Fr. Pierre de Caussade, S.J., entitled, *Abandonment to Divine Providence*.

In the Apostolate for Family Consecration **we have coined the phrase "responsibility of the present moment" from the term used in this book, "grace of the present moment".**

By fulfilling the responsibility of every moment which means doing what we should be doing at the time that we should be doing it and in the way that we know we are supposed to do it, we can live a life of deep interior union with God.

Attitude Makes the Difference

10. Our attitude makes all the difference in the world. When fulfilling our responsibilities, we can literally transform every act of our day into a meritorious act by uniting ourselves with Christ. This means that a mother at home, cleaning the house or changing the diapers of her child, can transform these everyday tasks into great spiritual acts of mercy.

We can transform the work that we do into a sacrificial offering to God, whether it be putting a wheel on a car in the factory or writing a legal brief in the office. We can convert every act of our day into a meritorious act of love, if we do it for the Lord — if we have that commitment!

God's Will

11. What does it mean to do **God's Will? How does this impact on the Mystical Body of Christ?** We know that if we are in the state of grace, and are doing God's Will through virtuous acts, prayers, or the reception of the sacraments, we grow in sanctifying grace. That is, we share in God's own life and **God's presence grows within us. At the same time, we can also atone or repair for the sins of the world.**

When someone sins, he gives the devil more power to tempt everyone. This brings about more selfishness and evil in the world and more persecution of the innocent and the poor.

However, we also have to understand that we gain no merit in the Mystical Body of Christ if we are not in the state of sanctifying grace, and therefore, cannot repair for the effects of sin in the world. **That is why frequent reception of the Sacrament of Penance is so essential.** This sacrament helps keep our consciences from becoming so eroded that we can no longer discern good from evil in each present moment.

Most people might ask, "How can a layman live the responsibility of the present moment in a practical way?" Our lives are so erratic and we don't have the order of living, for instance, as that which is found in a monastery, where the monks and nuns live in a strict routine. **Laymen, on the contrary, should expect to experience a healthy tension in managing all the dimensions of their lives in order to do God's Will in each present moment.**

Five Dimensions

12. There are five dimensions to the concept of "responsibility of the present moment." This is depicted in the diagram of the "Supernatural House" illustrated on the next page.

We need to maintain a balance of all five responsibilities, or dimensions. Otherwise, our "supernatural house" will collapse, and we will have no protection from the onslaughts of the world, the flesh, and the devil.

These five dimensions, these five basic responsibilities that we must make time for each day are:

1. our sacramental life
2. our prayer and formation life
3. our family and community life
4. our work in the home, factory, office, or field
5. our apostolic life — our evangelization responsibilities to share our Faith with our families, neighbors, and the world.

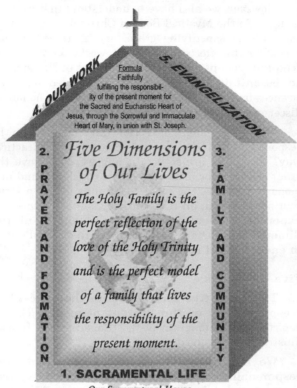

Our Supernatural House

The house diagram contains the following text:

4. OUR WORK

5. EVANGELIZATION

Formula
Faithfully fulfilling the responsibility of the present moment for the Sacred and Eucharistic Heart of Jesus, through the Sorrowful and Immaculate Heart of Mary, in union with St. Joseph.

2. PRAYER AND FORMATION

3. FAMILY AND COMMUNITY

Five Dimensions of Our Lives

The Holy Family is the perfect reflection of the love of the Holy Trinity and is the perfect model of a family that lives the responsibility of the present moment.

1. SACRAMENTAL LIFE

The First Dimension: Sacraments

13. The very foundation of our supernatural life is the Sacraments. In Section 950, under "Communion of the Sacraments", the *Catechism of the Catholic Church* states:

"The fruit of all the sacraments belongs to all the faithful. All the sacraments are sacred links uniting the faithful with one another and binding them to Jesus Christ, and above all Baptism, the gate by which we enter into the Church. The communion of saints must be understood as the communion of the sacraments. The name 'communion' can be applied to all of them, for they unite us to God. But this name is better suited to the Eucharist than to any other, because it is primarily the Eucharist that brings this communion about."

Without frequent confession (at least monthly), we are building on sand. In Section 1457, the *Catechism of the Catholic Church* goes on to teach:

"Anyone who is aware of having committed a mortal sin must not receive Holy Communion, even if he experiences deep contrition, without having first received sacramental absolution, unless he has a grave reason for receiving Communion and there is no possibility of going to confession. Children must go to the sacrament of Penance before receiving Holy Communion for the first time."

In Section 1458 the Catechism continues to teach:

"Without being strictly necessary, confession of everyday faults (venial sins) is nevertheless strongly recommended by the Church. Indeed the regular confession of our venial sins helps us form our conscience, fight against evil tendencies, let ourselves be healed by Christ and progress in the life of the Spirit. By receiving more frequently through this sacrament the gift of the Father's mercy, we are spurred to be merciful as he is merciful."

The *Be Not Afraid Family Hours* truly do form consciences and dispose families to go to Confession, which further disposes them to fervently adore and receive our Eucharistic Lord.

Second Dimension: Our Prayer & Formation Life

14. One of the supporting walls of our "supernatural house" is our prayer and formation life, meaning that we must pray everyday and learn our Faith. The Church teaches us how to pray. She teaches about the great treasures of the Church found in Sacred

Scripture, the *Catechism of the Catholic Church*, and the Vatican Council documents, as well as the writings of the saints, the popes, and the doctors of the Church— all presented in such a cohesive way in our Family Catechism and our Family Wisdom Curriculum.

The Third Dimension: Our Family & Community

15. At the Second World Meeting of Families, the Holy Father said, **"Today the basic struggle for human dignity is centered on the family and life." His theme for this world gathering was "The Family: Gift and Commitment, Hope for Humanity".**

The destiny of the world depends on the family. If we do not have a good family life, we will be unstable in everything we do.

One of the reasons why there is so much confusion in our society today is because a stable family life is literally non-existent. The family stabilizes society. When the family is not formed in the Truth, it loses its very moorings. If we neglect the family, everything will crumble.

Fourth Dimension: Our Work

16. Very few of us consider work to be meritorious. Great leaders in the Church, like Blessed Monsignor Escrivá, have said that work is at the very heart of our holiness, because it is fulfilling one of our major responsibilities in our life.

In fact, Pope John Paul II has written an encyclical on the dignity of work. By reading this encyclical, you can penetrate the tremendous gift that God has given us to bring order into our world.

Therefore, a mom at home taking care of the family (the home manager), and a dad in the factory, office, or the field can grow in merit just by offering their work to the Lord.

We can grow in merit by doing our work as perfectly as we can and by doing it for the Lord. In this way we can transform our work into a living sacrifice, a prayer, which enables us to grow in sanctifying grace, God's presence within us, and to grow in our capacity to know, love and serve God throughout all eternity.

St. Paul said in Colossians 3:23: "Whatever your work is, put your heart into it, as if it were for the Lord, and not for men, knowing that the Lord will repay you by making you His heirs."

Fifth Dimension: Evangelization

17. When looking at the diagram of the five dimensions of our lives, we see evangelization as being half of the roof—meaning it is as important as our work.

What does a roof do? It protects the structure from the rain and snow that can erode the foundation and the walls. Also, the roof literally holds the sides together. If you have ever seen the construction of a house, workers rapidly try to get the roof frame built in order to hold the walls together so it doesn't collapse.

Evangelization is a basic responsibility. We must teach the Faith and share it with our families, neighbors, and the entire world. **This is the area where most of us fall flat on our faces.**

Our culture does not look at the apostolic life as an essential responsibility that must be carried out by the laity. In many instances, people feel that catechesis and evangelization is the obligation of the priest and religious and that lay people can do it when they have time.

The Holy Father and the teachings of the Second Vatican Council make it very clear that **we have no alternative**—we must evangelize and catechize!

Now, it is true that at times we may have to modify the time we spend for evangelization because of involvement in extraordinary family or workplace circumstances, but we must never abandon it — we must see to it that this responsibility is carried out.

We should look at our obligation to do apostolate — which is to evangelize and catechize — just as we look at our work and our careers. If we were in charge of a major task at work and a problem came up in our home life, we are still responsible enough to call our place of work and make sure that someone took care of that particular task.

We should place the same emphasis on evangelization as we do on our work and careers. If we don't, we will not be fulfilling our missionary mandate to evangelize and spread the Gospel. We may try to find some excuse to walk away from the obligation to save souls. "Woe to me if I do not preach the Gospel," said St. Paul. (1 Cor. 9:16))

A "Blueprint" for the Laity

18.   Pope John Paul II has written so much for the laity. In his apostolic letter, *Christifideles Laici* (Lay Members of Christ's Faithful People), His Holiness gave us a complete blueprint on what we, as lay members, should do and how we should do it.

This document is not only a synthesis of the Synod of Bishops teachings about the laity, but also of the Fathers of the Church, Scripture, and the rich teachings of the Second Vatican Council. It clearly shows us that we have a responsibility to evangelize. We recommend this as regular spiritual reading for our members and friends. It is available through the Family Apostolate and other Catholic bookstores.

Our Lord teaches us in Matthew 7:21 and 10:28:

"It is not those who say Lord, Lord, who will enter the Kingdom of Heaven, but those who do the will of my Father."

"Do not fear those who can kill the body, but those

who can kill both the body and the soul."

Our Lord also said in Luke 9:23 :

"If anyone wishes to be a follower of mine, let him renounce himself, take up his cross everyday and follow me."

Our Lord is saying that we must "take up our crosses" everyday—**accept our responsibilities and follow Him.**

Evangelization is not easy, particularly for those busy parents who home-school their children. However, it can be done! It is a matter of prioritizing and setting time aside. My daughter and son-in-law, Maureen and Matt, home-school six of their eight children, and they still make time to evangelize others by helping conduct our *Be Not Afraid Family Hours* at their local parish in Kenosha, Wisconsin.

Mother Teresa's Idea

19. The *Be Not Afraid Family Hours* are a powerful means to share the Faith and to fulfill our obligation to evangelize our families and communities.

These Family Hours are one-hour videotape programs which Mother Teresa recommended that we use weekly, in churches, with our families in order to stop abortion and to save family life.

We currently have 72 Family Hour videos available and more are in production. They are produced in series of nine video novenas, focused on a particular devotion or theme. The first few minutes cover the particular theme of the Family Hour such as St. Joseph, the Immaculate Conception, the Living Eucharist, the Holy Rosary, Healing Through Consecration, Divine Mercy, Purgatory, and Mary, Life, & the Sacraments. Other features are:

— the dramatized Rosary with different mysteries acted out each week. The children love this.

— a brief review of the Family Catechism with Roman Curia Cardinal Arinze, to motivate people to use the Vatican-approved Family Catechism that is cross-referenced with the *Catechism of the Catholic Church, Veritatis Splendor* and other vital documents. Families must be grounded in order to defend their Faith in these spiritually perilous times.

— a song with very moving pictures that clearly depict spiritual realities, such as the Real Presence of Jesus in the Eucharist.

— a closing message from both Pope John Paul II and Mother Teresa of Calcutta (who originated this idea).

Our Bad Reputation

20. Laymen have a bad reputation for dropping the ball when it comes to this fifth dimension—evangelization. That is why when people go to talk to their parish priests and ask them if they can run our Family Hours on video in the parish church, in many cases the first thing the priest wonders is if he will be the one left "holding the ball" as soon as some trouble at home occurs. Keep in mind that in some parishes where there were once five priests, there is now only one or two. The laity must now do their part.

For the most part, we have found that priests are willing to cooperate. Sadly enough, experience proves that so often when the laity start something in the parish, they don't finish it. **We must change that reputation—we must become more responsible evangelizers and do our part.**

Most people are afraid of the word "evangelization" because they don't know how to evangelize. The *Be Not Afraid Family Hours* on video in homes or churches every week **are a perfect and natural means to**

evangelize our neighbors.

The Family Hours on video are an ideal way to teach the Faith to our media culture. We simply have to call and invite people each week to this event.

Become First-Class Evangelizers

21. Since its founding in 1975, the Apostolate for Family Consecration has developed tri-media evangelization and catechetical programs which the laity can confidently use, as first-class evangelizers and catechists, without having to obtain a doctorate degree in theology.

We can use our talents to bring people to these Family Hours on video in homes and in churches, and then let the greatest teachers of the world, such as Pope John Paul II, Mother Teresa, and Cardinal Arinze, teach the Faith through the vibrant means of video, **while Confessions are being heard.**

By drawing families into deeper union with Our Eucharistic Lord, they can grow in sanctifying grace. This can be a spiritual power that can change the course of history and play a major role in bringing about the civilization of love by unleashing the power of the Church that is in the Holy Eucharist and the Sacrament of Penance.

Think of the tug on Jesus' heart when children are in the churches with their parents, praying the Rosary and petitioning Our Lady to talk to Her Son about their problems and the needs of the poor all over the world.

In summary, families should come together every week in the Eucharistic Presence of Our Lord in the churches to see the *Be Not Afraid Family Hour* videotapes, to learn about their Faith, to examine their consciences, and **to go to Confession. This helps them to live a moral lifestyle that will sustain them**

through the unbelievable temptations coming at them everyday from TV, the press, music, and the education system.

A Complete Reversal

22. All of the harm that has been sown so deeply in family life over the past thirty years can be reversed through the powerful means of the *Be Not Afraid Family Hours* and the Vatican-approved *Apostolate's Family Catechism.* The Family Catechism systematically draws the entire family into the *Catechism of the Catholic Church* and *Veritatis Splendor.*

The Holy Father and his Roman Curia have blessed this method. They have encouraged us year after year, both in writing and in person. We are praying that you truly live the responsibility of the present moment and carry this great gift out to our time. Simply acquire our Save the Family Program and get started.

The family has to be restored through a very aggressive evangelization and catechetical program that reflects the teachings of the Pope and the Magisterium of the Church. Our Family Hours on video and tri-media catechetical programs truly do that.

Moving with God

23. The five dimensions of living the responsibility of the present moment bring us into a life of union with God.

Mother Teresa said that everything must begin with prayer (dimensions 1 & 2) and the fruit of prayer is a deepening of faith (dimension 2) and the fruit of faith is love (dimensions 1, 2, & 3) and the fruit of love is service (dimensions 3, 4, & 5) and the fruit of service is peace (union with God).

When we are determined to do God's Will at every moment of the day and ask for the grace to do it as perfectly as we can, we will become more aware of His presence. This enables us to pray constantly (cf. 1 Thess 5:17) **because we will be communing with God in a very natural way throughout our day. That's what prayer is—talking to God, and knowing that we are in His Presence, as Cardinal Arinze says, "Just loving Him!"**

Sometimes we don't have to talk when we are with our loved ones. We are just there in their presence. When we experience this with God, it can evolve into the **highest form of prayer,** which the Church calls contemplation.

A Formula for Life

24. **The five dimensions of living the responsibili-**

**ty of the present moment give you a formula for
life. They will frequently create a healthy tension
that will keep your life in balance.** We know that
we're not in heaven yet! We're part of the Church militant on earth. We're going through military maneuvers
all the time in order to do battle with the world, the
flesh and the devil—with our own weaknesses and the
weaknesses of others.

Spiritual Time Management

25. Keeping a balance among these five dimensions
basically amounts to spiritual time management (prudence). We have to ask God for the grace each day to
plan our time wisely in order to give adequate attention
to these five dimensions.

Throughout the day we must challenge ourselves
and qualify what we are doing. We must not go to
extremes and focus too much on just one or two of the
dimensions. We need to seek God's Will. We will be
more responsive to His inspirations when we have an
adequate prayer and formation life.

God will start to clearly show us what we should do.
As married couples, we must take the time to dialogue
with our spouses, to pray together, and to call on the
graces of the Sacrament of Matrimony. As we do this,
God will give us and our families the grace to do His
Will.

Keep in mind what John said in 4:34:

26. "My food is to do the will of the One who sent Me
and complete His work."

**That is our task—to do the Will of God by
completing the work that He has given us to do.**
Pope John Paul II said that each of us is a unique gift of
God **with an unrepeatable mission**. Each of us has a
unique role to fulfill in the Church. This role cannot be
carried out by anyone else. If we don't step up to the

challenge and fulfill this responsibility, souls will not be touched and will not reach their full potential in God. Some may even be lost because we did our own will instead of God's.

Our Lord said in John 17:15-17: "Father, do not remove them from the world, but protect them from the evil one...Consecrate them in truth."

The Apostolate's catechetical and evangelization programs will protect your family and neighbors from the evil one through the dual dimensions of Pope John Paul II's consecration: Totus Tuus and Consecrate them in Truth.

Take up the challenge and start or join an Apostolate Lay Ecclesial Team or start a committee to run the Family Hours in your church and help consecrate your family and neighbors in the Truth through the Family Hours and the Vatican-approved Apostolate's Family Catechism.

[In the USA call 1-800-For-Mary. In the Philippines call (632) 800-4440]

102. Rich in Mercy
Dives in Misericordia
by Pope John Paul II

Retranslation and Outline
by Fr. George Kosicki, C.S.B.

Apostolate for Family Consecration's
Peace of Heart Forum

Please obtain the video series #126-3853VK (set of 8 half-hour programs), which guides you through this section. We suggest that you gather a group of people to meet weekly to play the corresponding videotape and to discuss the material that you prayed and meditated on for the past week. You can use one of the following video/reading plans. See pages 588–613 for more details about the Peace of Heart Forums.

4-Week Video/Reading Plan

Session 1
Video 126-3847V *(show 126-3847.1 & 126-3847.2)*.
Read Introduction through Chapter III before the next session.

Session 2
Video 126-3848V *(show 126-3848.1 & 126-3848.2)*.
Read Chapters IV–V before the next session.

Session 3
Video 126-3850V *(show 126-3850.1 & 126-3850.2)*.
Read Chapters VI–VIII before the next session.

Session 4
Video 126-3851V *(show 126-3851.1 & 126-3851.2)*.
Complete video set: Resource #126-3853VK

8-Week Video/Reading Plan

Session 1
Video 126-3847V *(show 126-3847.1)*.
Read Intro–Chapter I before the next session.

Session 2
Video 126-3847V *(show 126-3847.2)*.
Read Chapters II–III before the next session.

Session 3
Video 126-3848V *(show 126-3848.1)*.
Read Chapter IV before the next session.

Session 4
Video 126-3848V *(show 126-3848.2)*.
Read Chapter V before the next session.

Session 5
Video 126-3850V *(show 126-3850.1)*.
Read Chapter VI before the next session.

Session 6
Video 126-3850V *(show 126-3850.2)*.
Read Chapter VII before the next session.

Session 7
Video 126-3851V *(show 126-3851.1)*.
Read Chapter VIII before the next session.

Session 8
Video 126-3851V *(show 126-3851.2)*.

*Complete video set:
Resource #126-3853VK*

Acknowledgment

My special thanks go to Father Francis Jaworski, M.I.C. (Provincial Superior of the Marians of the Immaculate Conception, Association of Marian Helpers, Stockbridge, MA), for his patient and careful checking of the original Polish text as the English translation was read aloud. We were both enriched in hearing the message of mercy once again.

Introduction

Why a fresh translation of the encyclical "Rich in Mercy"?

The message of the encyclical on Divine Mercy needs to be made clear and strong. It needs to continue to reach those it should. The message is so important and the needs of the times are so urgent that the message must be broadcast again and again in the fullness of its power.

The original Polish text, written in longhand by Pope John Paul II in his native tongue, flows ever so smoothly, using words that are delicately and specifically chosen. The Latin and English translations, which had to be done quickly and immediately for the Vatican Polygot Press, do not convey the full strength and beauty of the original text.

The intention of this translation, using the original Polish as well as the English and Latin Vatican Polygot Press translations as a basis, is to convey the spiritual power of the message. There are a number of factors that would need to be combined to do this with the greatest force: a knowledge of Polish, an ease with the existential philosophical mode of thinking of John Paul II, a thorough grasp of his message of mercy and the origins of his concern about mercy, and a knowledge of the English language. The author cannot claim expertise in all of the above needed factors, but is very much aware of the urgency of the message of mercy and the origins of the concern of Pope John Paul. May his inadequacy in Polish and English, and his weakness in existential philosophy, be overcome by his burning desire to convey the Holy Father's message of mercy.

The origins of the knowledge and concern of Pope John Paul II for the message of Divine Mercy come from his personal involvement with the messages of Divine Mercy revealed to the Servant of God, Sister Faustina

Kowalska (1905-1938) in his home archdiocese of Cracow, Poland. During the 1930's Sister Faustina received revelations from Our Lord telling her of His infinite mercy for mankind. He asked that His mercy be made known to everyone now, "while it still is the time for mercy." As Archbishop of Cracow, the then Karol Wojtyla introduced Sister Faustina's cause for canonization. He was instrumental in conscripting the leading Polish theologian, the Reverend Professor Ignacy Rozycki, to prepare a definitive study of her writings and the heroicity of her life. After ten years of exhaustive study, Professor Rozycki submitted a highly favorable document of support for the cause of her canonization.

Now is the time to proclaim God's great mercy, while it is still the time of His mercy. Today is the day of His mercy, before the day of His judgment. In regard to the translation itself, the author tried to bring out the force of the Pope's message by using the English phrases and words that seemed to be as strong as his words. The changes made most often were an addition of the phrase or word referred to in a reflexive pronoun. Often, the sentences or paragraphs were so long that the "it" became ambiguous and the sentence lost its force. This repeating of the subject makes the sentences clear and strong. In some chapters, sentences were divided in order to convey the full impact of the message.

Three kinds of summaries of the encyclical are presented as aids to understanding the message:

- An **Abstract** which gives the sequence of the topics and the flow of the main concepts;

- A **Schematic Summary** which gathers the key points in sweeping statements that can be used to teach, preach, and help to remember this message of mercy; and

- A **Sense-line Summary** which stresses the main points of each section in short phrases, conveying the strength of the message.

A Trilogy of Encyclicals

The three encyclicals of Pope John Paul II form a trilogy, as he himself expressed in the third letter. The first letter, *Redeemer of Man*, points out Jesus Christ as "the center of history and the universe" who reveals to each and every person their identity and dignity. He further points out that the Church is the link and the way to Christ for every person, no matter what the problems. The second letter of the trilogy is this one, *Rich in Mercy*, in which John Paul II points out the Father as rich in mercy. The Father's mercy is shown to be revealed in Christ Jesus, mercy incarnate, as the answer to the lack of peace in the world. In the third letter of the trilogy, *Lord and Giver of Life*, John Paul II shows that the Holy Spirit is the one who convicts us of our greatest sin, namely, the practical atheism of the world. At the same time, he shows that the Holy Spirit brings our sins to the cross to be washed in the blood of Jesus, so that we might receive His saving love and mercy for eternal life.

This trilogy is a clear response to the greatest problems of our day. Sin is the issue of our day, and mercy is the answer.

—*Rev. George Kosicki, C.S.B.*

Abstract

The theme of the encyclical letter *Dives in Misericordia* is Divine Mercy. Pope John Paul II develops the thesis that to practice, proclaim, and pray for mercy is the mission of the Church and the whole world. The letter is divided into eight chapters with fifteen subtopics.

The Pope expands the biblical text Jn. 14:9, "He who sees Me sees the Father," by discussing the revelation of mercy and the incarnation of mercy. He encourages us all to open our minds and hearts more widely to Christ.

"The Messianic Message" of Chapter Two describes "When Christ began to do and to Teach." The Messiah is a clear sign of God who is love. Through His lifestyle and through His actions, Jesus revealed that love is present in the world.

Reconciliation & Penance—the Sacrament of Mercy

"The Old Testament" is the topic of Chapter Three. The concept of mercy and its history are developed. Mercy is contrasted with God's justice.

"The Parable of the Prodigal Son" is the topic of Chapter Four. It brings focus to the relationship between justice and love that is manifested as mercy. In this parable, love is transformed into mercy. A particular focus on human dignity is presented, as well as the faithfulness of a Father's love.

In "The Paschal Mystery," Chapter Five, mercy is revealed in the Cross and Resurrection. It emphasizes that love is present in the world and that this love is more powerful than any kind of evil. Believing in this love means believing in mercy. "Love More Powerful Than Death, More Powerful Than Sin" is expanded. A discussion of Mary, the Blessed Mother of Jesus and the "Mother of Mercy", concludes, the chapter.

Chapter Six proclaims "Mercy...from Generation to Generation" and discusses the need for mercy for our generation. There are sources of uneasiness and a lack of peace attributed to our times. The question, "Is Justice Enough?" is raised. The Pope calls for a deeper power of love, for justice is not enough.

"The Mercy of God in the Mission of the Church" stresses the Church's role to profess and proclaim the mercy of God, the most stupendous attribute of the Creator and Redeemer. "The Church Seeks to Put Mercy into Practice" for "Blessed are the Merciful, for they shall obtain mercy." True mercy is, so to speak, the most profound source of justice. Mercy is also the most perfect incarnation of "equality" between people. All people are invited to proclaim and introduce into life the mystery of mercy supremely revealed in Jesus Christ. "It is precisely in the name of this mystery that Christ teaches us to forgive always." "... He who forgives and he who is forgiven encounter one another at an essential point, namely, the dignity or essential value of the person..."

The encyclical letter ends with "The Prayer of the Church in Our Times." Prayer is needed to overcome modern man's lack of courage to utter the word "mercy." The Pope exhorts us to call upon the God who loves all people and desires every true good for each individual. He prays that the Love which is in the Father may once again be revealed at this stage of history. He concludes by pointing out that the very reason for the Church's existence is to reveal God, who is Love and Mercy Itself.

Schematic Summary of Rich in Mercy

The Papal Letter *Rich in Mercy* proclaims mercy as:

- The prophetic word of our time: the now word is MERCY!

- The content, power, and mission of Christ and His Church.

- The summary of the Gospel: "Blessed are the merciful for they shall obtain mercy."

- The parable of mercy: the Prodigal Son - the essence of mercy in the restored value of man.

- The answer to the question of "a lack of peace."

- The summons to the Church and by the Church to practice, preach, and plead for mercy.

- The revelation of Jesus, mercy incarnate, centered in the crucified risen Jesus, continued in the Heart of Mary.

- The prayer for the presence of love, which is greater than evil, sin and death.

- The plea for us and the whole world.

A Sense-Line Summary of Rich in Mercy

I. He Who Sees Me Sees the Father

Jesus
has revealed God
who is rich in mercy
as the Father.

Christ crucified
is the center of all;
He reveals to us
the mercy
of the Father. (1)

God is visible
in and through Christ,
visible in His mercy.
Christ is mercy,
incarnate and personified.
Is mercy a threat?
No.
God is the Father of mercies

especially to the suffering.
This letter is a summons
To the Church and
By the Church
for mercy. (2)

II. The Messianic Message

When Christ began
to do and teach,
He proclaimed
liberty to the oppressed.
The words and actions of Jesus
make the Father present,
the Father who is love and mercy.
Jesus demanded of the people
the same love and mercy
as a condition of mercy:
"the merciful shall obtain mercy." (3)

III. The Old Testament

The Hebrew Bible
is a history of special experiences
of the mercy of the Lord.
Mercy is a special power of love
which prevails over sin
and infidelity of the Chosen People.
Mercy is the content of intimacy
with their Lord.
Mercy is Hesed:
goodness, grace, love fidelity.

Mercy is Rahamim:
love of a mother, tender, the heart's womb.
The Old Testament
encourages the suffering to appeal
to mercy.
Mercy is more powerful
and more profound than justice.

Mercy is love vis-a-vis justice.
Mercy is involved in mystery of creation
and in the mystery of election. (4)

IV. The Parable of the Prodigal Son

Mary's canticle brings Old Testament mercy
to the New Testament:
"Mercy from generation to generation."
Zachariah's canticle remembers
God's covenant of mercy,
both "hesed" and "rahamim".
The parable of the Prodigal Son
expresses the essence of Divine Mercy.
Each of us
in each age
is the prodigal.
The dignity of the son
in the father's house
is greater than his possessions
or their lack.
The son's turning point
is the awareness
of the loss of his dignity
as His father's son.
Love is transformed into mercy
as it goes beyond
the precise norm of justice. (5)

The father is faithful
to his fatherhood.
The son's humanity is saved.
Mercy has the interior form
of agape-love.
The son is restored
to value
and not humiliated.

Conversion
is the most concrete working of mercy

in the human world.
Mercy restores value,
promotes good,
draws good from evil,
causes rejoicing.
Mercy is the fundamental
content and power
of Christ's mission. (6)

V. The Paschal Mystery

The Father in Christ's paschal mystery
reveals the depth of love
and the greatness of man.
The paschal mystery
is a superabundance
of justice
that bears upon sin
and restores love.
It reveals mercy in its fullness.
The Cross is the final word
of Christ's messianic mission,
speaking unceasingly of God
the Father as merciful.
Believing in the crucified Son
is believing in love
present in the world.
Believing in the crucified Son
is believing in mercy.

The Cross is witness
to the strength of evil
in the world.
In Christ on the Cross
Justice is done
to sin and death
at the price
of sacrifice and death.
The Cross is
the radical revelation

of mercy.
The Resurrection perfects
the revelation of mercy and
foretells a new heaven.
In this our time,
love is revealed as mercy.
In the end,
mercy will be revealed as love.

The Church's program,
like Christ's mission,
is mercy.
With the Cross at the center,
Christ crucified is the Word
that does not pass away.
He is the one who stands at the door
and knocks. (7)

Our love of God
is an act of mercy
to the Son of the Father.
"Blessed are the merciful,
for they shall obtain mercy"
is a synthesis
of the whole Good News.
By the Resurrection
Jesus experienced mercy —
the very love of the Father —
more powerful than death!
In the Paschal Mystery
Christ reveals himself
as the inexhaustible source
of mercy —
He is the definitive incarnation
of mercy;
its living sign. (8)

In this age, too,
"His mercy is from
generation to generation..."

Mary, who obtained mercy
like no other,
shares in revealing
God's mercy
by the sacrifice of her heart.
Mary experienced
the mystery of Mercy
and also has the deepest knowledge
of mercy.
She knows its price.
She received into her heart
the mystery of mercy.
Mary is the Mother of mercy.
What Jesus came to reveal,
her heart continues to reveal
as the merciful love
of a mother. (9)

VI. Mercy...from Generation to Generation

Our generation, too,
is included
in His mercy.
This age has tremendous potential
but
there is a lack of peace and
a sense of powerlessness
in regard to the situation
in the world. (10)

There is increasing fear
of destruction
because of atomic stockpiles,
fear of oppression
because of materialism
and abuse of power.
There is a gigantic remorse
over inequity
between rich and poor nations.
This is why

the moral lack of peace
is destined to become
even more acute.
This lack of peace
reaches out for solutions.
This lack of peace
is stronger
than all emergency measures. (11)

Justice alone is not enough!
The Church shares with the people
the desire for a just life.
Often programs that start
with the idea of justice
suffer in practice
from distortions.
The Church shares
in the lack of peace
caused by the decline
of fundamental values,
the crisis in truth,
desacralization of relationships
and the common good. (12)

VII. The Mercy of God in the Mission of the Church

In face of the lack of peace,
the Church must witness
to mercy
by professing
and proclaiming it.

Mercy is
the great attribute of God
towards His people.
The Heart of Christ
is the center of the revelation
of the merciful love
of the Father.

The Church lives authentic life
when she draws near
to the source, Christ's Heart,
and dispenses
and professes mercy.
Mercy is
the most stupendous attribute
of the Creator and Redeemer.
The source
of the Savior's mercy is:
the Word of God;
Eucharist — love more powerful than death
Reconciliation — love greater than sin.
God, who is love,
cannot reveal Himself
other than as mercy.
Mercy, like God,
is infinite —
infinite in readiness
and power to forgive.
Conversion —
consists in the discovery
of mercy and
a rediscovery of the Father. (13)

"Blessed are the merciful,
for they shall obtain mercy."
Man attains God's mercy
as he is merciful.
Mercy is
reciprocal and bilateral —
the one who gives
is also the beneficiary.
As man respects
the dignity of man,
Christ receives mercy
as done unto Himself.
Mercy is the most profound source of justice
and the most perfect incarnation

of the "equality" of justice.
Mercy makes
the world more human
because it introduces
forgiveness.
The Church must proclaim
and introduce mercy —
the source of forgiveness
from our wellspring, the Savior.

Forgiveness is for everyone —
for all time —
not a cancellation
of the requirement of justice,
not an indulgence
toward evil
but the love necessary so that
man may affirm himself
as man —
as the father affirmed
the dignity
of his Prodigal Son. (14)

VIII. The Prayer of the Church in Our Times

The Church must proclaim
and practice mercy.
Yet,
in these critical times
she cannot forget
the right and duty
to appeal for mercy
especially when the world
moves away from mercy.
"Loud cries" for mercy
ought to be the cry
of the Church of our times.
Modern man is anxious
about the solution
to the terrible tensions
of our times, and lack of courage

to cry for mercy.
So all the more
the Church must cry:
"MERCY!"
Everything said in this encyclical
must be continually transformed
into an ardent prayer for mercy
and for all of mankind,
even if the world deserves
another "flood."

Let us appeal to God
Through Christ,
mindful of the words of
Mary's magnificat
which proclaims:
"Mercy from age to age,"
let us cry out
to the God of Mercy Himself
for this present generation!
Let us offer our cry
with Christ on the Cross:
"Father, forgive them."
Let us offer our cry
for the love of God
and for the love of man.

May the love of the Father
be revealed again
by the work of the Son
and the Holy Spirit.
May that love be shown
to be present
in the modern world
and to be more powerful
than evil, sin and death.
We pray through the intercession of
Mary
Who does not cease to proclaim:
"Mercy...from generation to generation." (15)

*His Holiness considers this to be
his most important encyclical.*

The Encyclical *Rich in Mercy*
by Pope John Paul II

Venerable Brothers and dear sons and daughters, greetings and apostolic blessings!

I. He Who Sees Me Sees the Father (cf. Jn. 14:9)

1. The Revelation of Mercy

"God who is rich in mercy" (Eph. 2:4) is the one whom Jesus Christ revealed to us as *Father*. It is his very own Son who revealed Him and made Him visible in Himself. How memorable that moment when Philip, one of the twelve Apostles, turning to Christ said: "Lord, show us the Father and we shall be satisfied";

and Jesus gave the following reply, "Have I been with you so long and yet you do not know me...? He who has seen me has seen the Father" (Jn. 14:8-9). These words were spoken during the farewell discourse, toward the end of the paschal supper, which started the events of those holy days, which were to prove once and for all, that "God, who is rich in mercy, out of the great love with which He loved us, even when we were dead through our trespasses made us alive together with Christ" (Eph. 4:2-5a).

Following the teachings of the Second Vatican Council and responding to the special needs of the times in which we live, I have devoted the Encyclical *Redemptor Hominis* to the truth about man, a truth which is revealed in its fullness and in its perfection in Christ. A no less important need in these critical and difficult times impels me to draw attention once again in Christ to the countenance of the "Father of mercies and God of all comfort" (2 Cor.1:3). We read in the Constitution *Gaudium et Spes* (22), "Christ the new Adam ... fully reveals man to himself and brings to light his most high calling," and does it "in the very revelation of the mystery of the Father and His love." The above words I have quoted are clear testimony to the fact that man cannot bring about the full dignity of his humanity without reference to God, not only in a theoretical way but in the full reality of his existence. Man and his higher calling are revealed in Christ *through the revelation of the mystery of the Father and His love.*

And so it is fitting that we now turn to the mystery of love. The multiple experience of the Church and modern man call for this reflection on love. It is also demanded by the pleas of so many human hearts, their sufferings and hopes, by their doubts and expectations. While it is true that every human being is the pathway for the Church, as I expressed in my Encyclical *Redemptor Hominis*, at the same time the Gospel and the whole Tradition unchangingly shows us that we must follow this way with every human being just as Christ has opened up His way by revealing in Himself the Father and His love (*Ibid.*). In Christ Jesus every path to man, as it has been assigned once and for all to the Church in the changing context of our times, is simultaneously an approach to the Father and His love. The Second Vatican Council has confirmed this truth for needs of our times.

The more the Church's Mission is centered on man, the more it is "man-centered," the more it must be confirmed and made really "God-centered;" that is to say, directed in Jesus Christ to the Father. While the various currents of thought both in the past and at the present have tended and still tend to separate man-centeredness and God-centeredness, and even to set them in opposition to each other. The Church, following Christ, seeks to join the two together in human history in a deep and living way. This principle of joining together man-centeredness and God-centeredness in Christ is also one of the basic principles, perhaps the most important one, of the teaching of the last Council. Since in the present phase of the Church's history we have put before ourselves as our primary task the *implementation of the teachings of the great Council*, we must act upon this with faith, and with an open mind and with all our hearts. In the Encyclical *Redemptor Hominis* I tried to show that the deepening and the many-faceted enrichment of the Church's consciousness, which came thanks to the Council, must open our minds and our hearts more widely to Christ. In this present Encyclical I want to say that openness to Christ, who as the Redeemer of the world fully "reveals man to himself," can only be achieved through an ever more mature relationship to the Father and His love.

2. The Incarnation of Mercy

Although God "dwells in unapproachable light" (1 Tm. 6:16), at the same time He speaks to man in the language of the entire universe: "ever since the creation of the world his invisible nature, namely, his eternal power and deity, has been clearly perceived in the things that have been made" (Rom. 1:20). This indirect and imperfect knowledge, achieved by the intellect seeking God by means of creatures of the visible world, falls short of "The vision of the Father." "No one has ever seen God," writes St. John in order to stress more fully the truth that "the only Son, who is in the bosom of the Father, he has made him known (Jn. 1:18). This "making known" reveals God in the most profound mystery of His being, one and three, surrounded by "unapproachable light" (1 Tm. 6:16). Yet through this "making known" by Christ we know God above all in His relationship of love for man: in His philanthropy (Titus 3:4). Precisely here "His invisible nature becomes "visible" in a special way, incomparably more visible than through all the other "things that have been made." The invisible *God becomes visible in Christ and through Christ,* through His actions and His words, and finally through His death on the cross and His Resurrection.

In this way, in and through Christ, God becomes remarkably visible in His mercy. This attribute of divinity is emphasized which the Old Testament defined as "mercy," using various concepts and terms. Christ gives the whole Old Testament tradition of mercy its ultimate meaning. Not only does He speak of mercy and explain it by the use of comparisons and parables, but above all *He Himself incarnates mercy and personifies it. In a sense, Christ Himself is mercy.* To the one who sees mercy in Him, who finds mercy in Him, to that one God becomes "visible" in a remarkable way as the Father "who is rich in mercy" (Eph. 2:4).

The present day mentality, more perhaps than that of people in the past, seems opposed to a God of mercy, and in fact tends to exclude from life and to remove from the human heart the very idea of mercy. The word and concept of "mercy" seem to disturb man who, thanks to the enormous development of science and technology, never before known in history, has become the master of the earth and has subdued it and dominated it (cf. Gen 1:28). This "domination over the earth" sometimes understood in a one-sided and superficial way, seems to leave no room for mercy. In this regard we can profitably refer to the picture of "man's situation in the world today" as described at the beginning of the Constitution *Gaudium et Spes*. Here we read the following sentences: "In the light of the foregoing factors there appears the dichotomy of a world that is at once powerful and weak, capable of doing what is noble and what is base, disposed to freedom and slavery, progress and decline, brotherhood and hatred. Man is growing conscious that the forces he has unleashed are in his own hands and that it is up to him to control them or be enslaved by them" (*Gaudium et Spes*, No. 9: AAS 58 1966, p. 1032).

The situation of the contemporary world not only displays transformations that give grounds for hope in a *better future for man on earth*, but also reveals threats of many kinds far surpassing those known up until now. Without ceasing to point out these threats on various occasions (such as in addresses to the UNO, to the UNESCO, to the FAO and elsewhere), the Church must at the same time examine them in the light of the truth received from God.

The truth revealed in Christ, about God who is the "Father of mercies" (2 Cor. 1:3), enables us to "see" Him as remarkably close to man, especially when man is suffering, when he is under threat at the very heart of his existence and human dignity. And for this reason many people and groups guided by a lively faith are turning almost spontaneously to the mercy of God in today's situation in the Church and world. They are certainly being urged by Christ Himself, who through his Spirit works in the mystery of human hearts. This mystery of God revealed by Christ as "Father of Mercies," in the midst of the threats to man in our age, becomes like a remarkable summons directed to the Church.

In the present Encyclical I want to follow this summons. I want to draw from the eternal and incomparable language of revelation and faith, with all its simplicity and depth, words to express in this same language once more, before God and humanity, the great anxieties of our time.

Revelation and faith teach us not only to meditate in the abstract upon the mysteries of God as "Father of Mercies," but also to make recourse to that mercy in the name of Christ and in union with Him. Did not Christ say that our Father who "sees in secret" (Mt. 6:4, 6, 18) is as if He were always waiting for us to call upon Him in every need, and at the same time come to know ever deeper His mystery: the mystery of the Father and His love (cf. Eph. 3:18; also Lk. 11:5-13).

Therefore I want these considerations to bring this mystery closer to everyone. At the same time I want them to be a heartfelt appeal of the Church for mercy which humanity and the world need so much. And they need mercy even though they do not realize it.

II. The Messianic Proclamation

3. When Christ Began to Do and Teach

In the presence of His own townspeople, living in Nazareth, Christ recalls the words of the prophet Isaiah: "The Spirit of the Lord is upon Me, because He has anointed Me to preach the good news to the poor. He has sent me to proclaim release to captives and recovery of sight to the blind, to set at liberty those who are oppressed, to proclaim the acceptable year of the Lord" (Lk. 4:18-19). These sentences, recorded by St. Luke, are *his first messianic declaration*. They are followed by actions and words known through the Gospel. Through these actions and words Christ makes the Father present among men. Significantly, the people involved are, above all, the poor, those without means of livelihood, those deprived of their freedom, the blind who cannot see the beauty of creation, those living with anguished hearts or suffering from social injustice, and finally sinners. For these especially the Messiah becomes a remarkably clear sign of God who is love, He becomes a sign of the Father. In this visible sign the people of our time can "see" the Father just like those people of times past.

It is significant that, when the messengers sent by John the Baptist came to Jesus to ask Him: "Are you He who is to come, or shall we look for another?" (Lk.7:19). Jesus answered them by referring to the same testimony with which He has begun his teaching at Nazareth: "Go and tell John what it is that you have seen and heard: the blind receive their sight, the lame walk, lepers are cleansed, and the deaf hear, the dead are raised up, the poor have the good news preached to them." Then He concluded: "And blessed is he who takes no offense at Me!" (Lk. 7:22-23).

Especially by His life-style and His actions, Jesus showed that *love is present in the world* in which we live. This love is an effective love, a love that turns to man and embraces everything that makes up his humanity. This love is especially recognized in contact with suffering, injustice and poverty encompassing the whole historical "human condition," which in various ways shows man's limitation and frailty, both physical and moral. It is exactly in this way and with this scope that love is revealed and called "mercy" in the language of the bible.

Christ then reveals God, who is Father, who is "love," as St. John will express in his letter (1 Jn. 4:16); Christ reveals God as "rich in mercy," as we read in St. Paul (Eph. 2:4). This truth is not just the subject of a teaching, but is a reality made present to us by Christ. *Making the Father present as love and mercy* is, in Christ's own consciousness, the fundamental proof of His mission as the Messiah. He points this out by the words He uttered first in the synagogue in Nazareth and later in the presence of His disciples and the messengers of John the Baptist.

On the basis of this way of making present God who is Father of love and mercy, Jesus makes mercy one of the principal *topics of His preaching.* As usual, He primarily teaches "in parables," because they best explain the essence of things. It is enough to recall the parable of the Prodigal Son (Lk. 15:11-32) or the parable of the Good Samaritan (Lk. 10:30-37), but also by way of contrast, consider the parable of the merciless servant (Mt. 18:23-25). However, there are many passages in the teaching of Christ that show love — mercy under some ever new aspect. We need only consider the Good Shepherd, who goes in search of the lost sheep (Mt. 18:12-14; Lk. 15:8-10). St. Luke is the evangelist who distinguishes himself in the number of times he treats mercy in the teaching of Christ and so his Gospel has earned forever the title: "The Gospel of Mercy."

When one speaks of teaching, one encounters a major problem of meaning of terms and content of concepts, especially the content of the *concept of "mercy"* (in relationship to the concept of "love"). A grasp of the content of these concepts is key to understanding the very reality of mercy and this is what is most important for us. But before devoting a further section of our consideration to establishing the meaning of the terms and clarifying the content of the concept of "mercy," we must note that Christ, in revealing the love — mercy of God, at the same time *demanded from the people* that they also be guided in their lives by love and mercy. This demand forms the very essence of the messianic proclamation, and the very essence of the Gospel's distinguishing character (*ethos*). The teacher expresses that both, in the form of the commandment which He calls "the greatest" (Mt. 22:38), and also in the form of a blessing when in the Sermon on the Mount He proclaims: "Blessed are the merciful, for they shall obtain mercy" (Mt. 5:7).

In this way the messianic proclamation about mercy keeps the characteristic divine-human dimension. Christ the very fulfillment of the messianic prophecy — by becoming the incarnation of love, which is seen with special force in the face of the suffering, the unfortunate and sinners, makes present and so more fully reveals the Father, who is God "rich in mercy." At the same time, by becoming for people a model of merciful love for others, Christ proclaims by His actions, even more than by His words, the call to mercy which is one of the essential elements of the Gospel's distinguishing character (**ethos**). Here, it is not just a case of fulfilling a command or an obligation of an ethical nature; it is also a case of satisfying a very major condition so that God could reveal Himself to man: "The merciful…shall obtain mercy."

III. The Old Testament

4. The concept of "mercy" in the Old Testament has a long and rich history. We have to refer back to it in order that the mercy revealed by Christ may shine forth more clearly. By revealing mercy both through his actions and His teaching, Christ addressed Himself to people who, not only knew the concept of mercy, but who also, as the *people of God of the Old Covenant,* had

drawn from their age-long history a *special experience of the mercy of God*. This experience was social and communal, as well as individual and interior.

Israel was, in fact, the people of the covenant with God, a covenant that it broke many times. Whenever it became aware of its infidelity — and in the history of Israel there was no lack of prophets and others, who awakened this awareness — it appealed to mercy. In this regard, the books of the Old Testament give us very many examples.

Among the events and texts of greater importance, one may recall: the beginning of the history of the judges (cf. Judges 3:7-9); the prayer of Solomon at the inauguration of the temple (cf. 1 Kings 8:22-53); the request of the prophet Micah for forgiveness (cf. Micah 7:18-20); the consoling messages of Isaiah (cf. Is. 1:18; 51:4-16); the cry of the Jews in exile (cf. Bar. 2:11-3:8); and the renewal of the covenant after the return from exile (cf. Neh. 9).

It is significant that the prophetic teachings on mercy link the sin of the people with the distinct image of love on God's part. God loves Israel with the love of a special choosing, much like the love of a spouse (cf. Hosea 2:21-25; Is. 54:6-8) and for this reason pardons its faults and even its infidelities and betrayals. When He finds repentance and true conversion, He brings His people back to grace (cf. Jer. 31:20; Ez. 39:25-29). In the preaching of the prophets, *mercy signifies a special*

power of love, which *prevails over the sin and infidelity* of the chosen people.

In this broad "social" context, mercy appears to correlate with the interior experience of individuals languishing in a state of guilt or enduring every kind of suffering and misfortune. *Both physical and moral evil*, namely sin, cause each of the sons and daughters of Israel to turn to the Lord and beseech His mercy. In this way David turns to Him, conscious of the seriousness of his guilt (cf. 2 Sam .11; 12; 24:10); Job too, after his rebellion, turns to him in his tremendous misfortune (Job, *passim*); so also does Esther, knowing the mortal threat to her own people (Esther 4:17 ff.); and we find still other examples in the books of the Old Testament (cf. e.g., Neh. 9:30-32; Tob. 3:2-3; 11-12; 8:16-17; 1 Mac. 4:24).

At the root of this many-sided conviction, which is both communal and personal and which is proven by the whole of the Old Testament down through the centuries, is the basic experience of the chosen people at the Exodus. The Lord saw the affliction of His people reduced to slavery, heard their cry, knew their oppression, and decided to deliver them (cf. Ex. 3:7f.). In this act of salvation by the Lord, the prophet perceived His love and compassion (cf. Is. 63:9). This is precisely the ground upon which the people and each of its members based their certainty of the mercy of God, which can be invoked in all tragic circumstances.

Added to this is the fact that sin too constitutes man's misery. The people of the Old Covenant experienced this misery from the time of the Exodus, when they set up the golden calf. The Lord Himself triumphed over this act of breaking the covenant when He solemnly revealed to Moses that He was a "God merciful and gracious, slow to anger and abounding in steadfast love and faithfulness" (Ex. 34:6). It is in this central revelation that the whole of the chosen people and each of its members will find, every time that they have sinned, the strength and the motive for turning to the Lord to remind Him of what He had revealed about Himself (cf. Num. 14:18; 2 Chr. 30:9; Neh. 9:17; Ps. 86; Wis. 15:1; Sir. 2:11; Joel 2:13) and to beseech His forgiveness.

Thus, in deeds and in words, the Lord revealed His mercy from the very beginnings of the people which He chose for Himself. In the course of its history, this people continually entrusted themselves to the God of Mercies, both when stricken with misfortune and when they became aware of their sin. All the subtleties of love become manifest in the Lord's mercy toward those who are His own; He is their Father (cf. Is. 63:16), for Israel is His firstborn son (cf. Ex. 4:22). The Lord is also the bridegroom of her whose name the prophet proclaims: *Ruhamah,* "Beloved" or "she has obtained pity" (cf. Hos. 2:3).

Even when the Lord is exasperated by the infidelity of His people and thinks of finishing with them, it is still His tenderness and generous love for those who are His own which overcome His anger (cf. Hos. 11:7-9; Jer. 31:20; Is. 54:7f.). Thus it is easy to understand why the psalmists, when they desire to sing the highest praises of the Lord, break forth into hymns to the God of love, tenderness, mercy, and fidelity (cf. Ps. 103 and 145).

From all this it follows that mercy does not pertain only to the notion of God, but it is something that characterizes the life of the whole people of Israel and each of its sons and daughters. *Mercy is the content of intimacy with their Lord*, the content of their dialogue with Him. Precisely under this aspect, mercy is presented in the individual books of the Old Testament with a great richness of expression. It may be difficult to find in these books a purely theoretical answer to the question of what mercy is in itself. Nevertheless, the terminology that is used is in itself able to tell us much about this subject. (For footnote see Appendix A)

The Old Testament proclaims the mercy of the Lord by the use of many terms with related meanings; they are differentiated by their particular content, but *it could be said that they all converge from different directions on one single fundamental concept* to express its surpassing richness and at the same time bring it close to man under its different aspects. The Old Testament encourages people suffering from misfortune, especially those weighed down by sin, as well as the whole of Israel, who had entered into the covenant with God *to appeal for mercy*, and enables them to count upon it. It reminds them of His mercy in times of failure and loss of trust. So, in turn, the Old Testament *gives thanks and glory* for mercy every time that mercy is made manifest in the life of the people or in the lives of individuals.

In this way, mercy is in a certain sense contrasted with God's justice, and in many cases is shown to be not only more powerful than that of justice but also more profound. Already the Old Testament teaches that, although justice is an authentic virtue in man, and in God signifies transcendent perfection, nevertheless love is "greater" than justice: greater in the sense that it is primary and fundamental. Love, so to speak, conditions justice and, in the final analysis, justice serves love. The primacy and superiority of love in the face of justice — and this is a mark of the whole of revelation — *are revealed precisely through mercy*. This seemed so obvious to the psalmists and prophets that the very term justice ended up meaning the salvation accomplished by the Lord and His Mercy (Ps. 40:11; 98:2f; Is. 45:21; 51:5; 56:1). *Mercy differs from justice, but it is not in opposition to it*, if we admit in the history of man, as the Old Testament precisely does, the presence of God, who as Creator has already linked Himself to His creature with a particular love. Love, by its very nature, excludes hatred and ill will toward the one to whom He once gave the gift of himself: *Nihil odisti eorum quae fecisti* "you hold nothing of what you have made in abhorrence" (Wis. 11:24). These words indicate the profound basis of the relationship between justice and mercy in God, in His relations with man and the world. They tell us that we must seek the life-giving roots and intimate reasons for this relationship by going back to "the beginning," *in the very mystery of creation*. They foreshadow in the context of the Old Covenant the full revelation of God, who is "love" (1 Jn. 14:16).

Connected with the mystery of creation is the *mystery of election*, which in a special way shaped the history of the people whose spiritual father is Abraham by virtue of his faith. Nevertheless, through this people which journeys forward through the history of both, the Old Covenant and the New, that mystery of the election refers to every human being, to the whole great human family. "I have loved you with an everlasting love, therefore I have continued my faithfulness to you" (Jer. 31:3). "For the mountains may depart...my steadfast love shall not depart from you, and my covenant of peace shall not be removed" (Is. 54:10). This truth, once proclaimed to Israel, involves a perspective of the whole history of man, a perspective both temporal and ultimate (eschatological) (Jon. 4:2-11; Ps. 145:9; Sir. 18:8-14; Wis. 11:23-12:1). Christ reveals the Father within the framework of the same perspective and on ground already prepared, as many pages of the Old Testament writings demonstrate. At the end of this revelation, on the night before He dies, he says to the Apostle Philip these memorable words: "Have I been with you so long, and yet you do not know me...? He who has seen me has seen the Father" (Jn. 14:9).

IV. The Parable of the Prodigal Son

5. An Analogy

At the threshold of the New Testament, two voices resound in St. Luke's Gospel in unique harmony about the mercy of God, a harmony which forcefully echoes the whole Old Testament tradition. They express the semantic elements linked to the differentiated terminology of the Ancient Books. *Mary*, entering the house of Zechariah, *magnifies* the Lord with all her soul for "His *mercy*," which "from generation to generation" is bestowed on those who fear Him. A little later, as she recalls the election of Israel, she proclaims the mercy which He who has chosen

Israel holds "in remembrance" for all time (cf. Lk. 1:49-54).

In both places it is a case of *hesed*, i.e., the fidelity that God manifests to His own love for the people, fidelity to the promises that will find their definitive fulfillment precisely in the motherhood of the Mother of God (cf. Lk. 1:49-54).

Afterwards, in the same house, when John the Baptist is born, his father *Zechariah* blesses the God of Israel and glorifies the mercy God promised to our fathers and for "remembering" His holy covenant (cf. Lk. 1:72). Here too it is a case of mercy in meaning of *hesed*, insofar as in the following sentences, in which Zechariah speaks of the "tender mercy of our God," there is clearly expressed the second meaning, namely, *rahamim* (Latin translation: *viscera misericordiae*), which rather identifies God's mercy with a mother's love.

In His teaching, Christ Himself draws on this

inheritance of mercy from the Old Testament, simplifies
it and deepens it. This is most clearly seen in the parable of the Prodigal Son (Lk 15:14-32). Even though the
word "mercy" is not used in the parable, the deepest
meaning of divine mercy is described. The words of the
Old Testament for mercy are not used, but the drama
played out between the loving father and his two sons —
a drama of love and prodigality — helps us to understand the "mystery of mercy."

The younger son asks and receives from his father
the portion of the inheritance that is due to him and
leaves home for a faraway country and spends it all in a
prodigal way, "in loose living." This is a picture of every
man in every age, beginning with Adam who was the
first to lose the inheritance of grace and original justice.
The analogy at this point is very wide-ranging. The
parable indirectly touches upon every break of the
covenant of love, every loss of grace, every sin. In this
analogy there is less emphasis than in the prophetic tradition on the unfaithfulness of the whole people of
Israel, although *the analogy of the Prodigal Son* may
extend to this also. "When he had spent everything," the
son "began to be in need," especially as "a great famine
arose in that country" to which he had gone, after leaving his father's house. And in this situation "he would
gladly have fed on" anything, even "the pods that swine
ate," the swine that he herded for "one of the citizens of
that country." But even this was refused him.

The parable then turns to the inner man. The
inheritance that the son had received and wasted was
merely a quantity of material goods, but more important than these goods was his dignity as a son in his
father's house. The situation in which he found himself
when he lost the material goods should have made him
aware of the love of that dignity. He had not thought of
it earlier, when he had asked his father to give him the
part of the inheritance, that was due to him, in order to
go away. He seems not to be conscious of it even now,

when he says to himself: "How many of my father's hired servants have bread enough to spare, but I perish here with hunger." He measures himself by the measuring stick of the goods that he has lost and "has not," against the goods that the hired hands "have" in his father's house. These words express, above all, his attitude toward material goods; yet, under their surface is hidden the tragedy of lost dignity, the consciousness of squandered sonship.

Then comes his decision: "I will arise and go to my father and I will say to him, `Father, I have sinned against heaven and before you; I am no longer worthy to be called your son. Treat me as one of your hired servants'" (Lk 15:18-19). These are words that reveal more deeply the real problem. The sense of a wasted dignity grew as a result of the whole situation over the material goods in which the Prodigal Son found himself because of his folly and his sin. When he decides to return to his father's house, he asks his father to receive him no longer as a son but as an employee.

At first sight he seems to be acting because of hunger and poverty, yet his motive is permeated by a consciousness of a deeper loss: to be a hired hand in his father's house. This certainly is a great humiliation and shame. Nevertheless, the Prodigal Son is ready to undergo that humiliation and shame. He realizes that he no longer has any right except to be an employee in his father's house. His decision is taken in full awareness of what he has already deserved and of what he can still have by right in accordance with the norms of justice. Exactly this reasoning shows that at the center of the Prodigal Son's consciousness is found a sense of a lost dignity, a sense of that worth which comes from being a son of a father. And so, with his decision made, he sets out on his way.

In the parable of the Prodigal Son, the word "justice" is not used even once, just as the word "mercy" is not used. But justice is related to love, and is seen as mercy, and described with great precision in the Gospel parable. It becomes evident that love becomes mercy when it is necessary to cross the precise bounds of justice — precise and often too narrow. The Prodigal Son, having wasted everything he had received from his father, felt he deserved, after his return to work in his father's house as a servant, to be earning a living and gradually building up a certain provision of material goods, but never in the amount he had before he departed. This would be demanded by the order of justice, especially since as son he not only squandered his portion of inheritance, which he received from the father, but he also touched his father and offended him by his whole conduct. Because this conduct had in his own eyes deprived him of dignity as a son, it could not be a matter of indifference to the father. It had to hurt him. It had to involve him in some way. It was, after all, his own son, and that relationship could never be changed or destroyed by any kind of behavior. The Prodigal Son is aware of this; and this awareness makes him see clearly his lost dignity, and evaluate honestly his position, which he might still earn in his father's house.

6. Special Focus on Human Dignity

This precise picture of the state of the soul of the Prodigal Son allows us to understand with similar precision what the mercy of God really is. There is no doubt that this simple yet penetrating parable reveals to us God who is Father. The conduct of the father in the parable, his whole way of acting, shows his inner attitude and the individual threads of mercy from the Old Testament in a new synthesis full of simplicity and depth. The father of the Prodigal Son is *faithful to his own fatherhood, and faithful to his love* which he had lavished on his son as son. This fidelity of the father shows itself first in his immediate readiness to welcome his son home when he returns with his inheritance squandered. Then this fidelity is even more fully shown in his joy, so generously lavished on the returned

Prodigal Son that it stirs up the protests and jealousy of the elder brother, who never left the father and never abandoned his house.

This fidelity of the father to himself — known as *hesed* in the Old Testament — is at the same time charged with affection. We read that as soon as the father saw his Prodigal Son returning home "he had compassion, ran to meet him, then threw his arms around his neck and kissed him (Lk . 15:20). He certainly acted with a flood of deep affection and this explains his generosity toward his son, which so angered the elder brother. Yet, the fundamental reason for this emotion must be sought at a deeper level. Note that the father is aware that a fundamental good has been saved: the good of his son's humanity. Although he squandered the inheritance, *his humanity is saved*. Even more, it has been, in a way, *found again*. The words of the father to the elder son show this: "It was fitting to make merry and be glad, for this your brother was dead and is alive; he was lost and is found." In the same chapter of the Gospel according to St. Luke, we read the parable of the sheep that was found (Lk. 15:3-6), and the parable of the coin that was found (Lk. 15:8-9). Each time there is an emphasis on the same joy as in the case of the Prodigal Son. So the fatherly fidelity is totally concentrated on the humanity of the lost son and his dignity. This explains above all his joyous emotion at the moment of the son's return home.

Going on, one can therefore say that love for the son, the love that springs from the very essence of fatherhood, in a way obliges the father to be concerned about his son's dignity. This concern is the measure of his love, the love of which Saint Paul was to write: "Love is patient and kind...love does not insist on its own way; it is not irritable or resentful... but rejoices in the right... hopes all things, endures all things...and never ends" (1 Cor. 13:4-8). Mercy — as Christ presented it in the parable of the Prodigal Son has the *inner form of love*, called agape in the New Testament. This love is able to reach down to every prodigal son, to every human misery, and above all to every form of moral misery, sin. When this happens, the person who is the receiver of the mercy doesn't feel put down, but rather is lifted up and "restored to value." The father first and foremost expresses his joy to him that he has been "found again" and that he has "returned to life." This joy shows that a good has remained intact: even if he is a Prodigal Son he does not cease to be a real son of his father. Thus joy also shows that a good has been found again, namely, the return of the prodigal to the truth about himself.

What took place between the father and the son in Christ's parable cannot be evaluated "from the outside." Our prejudices against mercy are mostly the result of evaluating only from the outside. At times, by following this "outside" method of evaluation, we see in mercy above all an *inequality* between the one offering it and the one receiving it. As a result, we are ready to conclude that mercy hurt the receiver because it hurts the dignity of man. The parable of the Prodigal Son shows us that the reality *is in fact otherwise*: the interplay of mercy is based on the common experience of that good which is man, on the common experience of the dignity that is his by right. This common experience makes the Prodigal Son begin to see himself and his behavior in their full truth (such a vision of truth is real humility). On the other hand, by this same common experience, the son becomes a very special good to the father. The father sees so clearly the good, so perfectly accomplished by a radiation of truth and love, that he seems to forget all the evil which the son had committed.

The parable of the Prodigal Son expresses in a simple but profound way *the reality of conversion*. Conversion is the most concrete expression of the work of love and presence of mercy in this human world. The true and full meaning of mercy is not just looking penetratingly and even compassionately at moral, physical or material evil. Mercy is true and full when it restores to value, lifts up higher, draws good from all the forms of evil in the world and in man. Understood in this way, mercy is the fundamental content of the messianic proclamation of Christ and the real power of His mission. This is the way His disciples and followers understood and practiced mercy. Mercy never ceased to reveal itself in their hearts and in their actions, especially in the creative proof of love which does not allow itself to be "conquered by evil but overcomes evil with good" (Rom. 12:21). The genuine face of mercy has to be constantly revealed anew. In spite of many prejudices mercy seems to be especially needed in our times.

V. The Pascal Mystery

7. Mercy Revealed in the Cross and Resurrection

The messianic message of Christ and His entire activity among people end with the Cross and the Resurrection. We have to penetrate deeply into this final event which especially in the language of the Council is defined as the *Pascal mystery* if we wish to express in depth the truth about mercy as it has been revealed to the utmost in the history of our salvation. At this point of our considerations we shall have to draw closer still to the content of the Encyclical *Redemptor Hominis*. In fact, the reality of the redemption, in its human dimension, reveals the unheard of greatness of man, "which gained for us so great a Redeemer" (*Exultet*, Easter Vigil liturgy). At the same time the *divine dimension* of the Redemption enables us, I would say, in the most experimental and "historical" way, to uncover the depth of that love which does not recoil before the extraordinary sacrifice of the Son. This sacrifice in its human dimension is offered to express the fidelity of the Creator and Father toward human beings, created in His image and chosen from "the beginning," in this Son for grace and glory.

The events of Good Friday and, even before that, in the prayer in Gethsemane, introduce a fundamental change into the whole course of the revelation of love and mercy in the messianic mission of Christ. The one who "went about doing good and healing" (Acts 10:38) and "curing every sickness and disease" (Mt. 9:35) now Himself seems to deserve the greatest mercy and to appeal for mercy when He is arrested, abused, condemned, scourged, crowned with thorns, nailed to the cross and amid agonizing torments hands over His spirit (Mk. 15:37; Jn. 19:30). It is then that He especially deserves mercy from the people to whom He had extended only good, yet He does not receive it in return. Even those who are closest to Him cannot protect Him and snatch Him from the hands of the oppressors. At this final stage of His messianic activity the words which the prophets, especially Isaiah, uttered concerning the servant of Yahweh are fulfilled in Christ: "Through His stripes we are healed" (Is. 53:5).

Christ, as the man who suffers really and in a terrible way in the Garden of Olives and on Calvary, addresses Himself to the Father, that Father whose love He had preached to the people, to whose mercy He had borne witness through all of His activity. But He is not spared — not even He — the terrible suffering: *"God did not spare his own Son,"* but "For our sake God made him to be sin who knew no sin" (2 Cor. 5:21). St. Paul sums up in a few words the whole depth of the Cross and at the same time the divine dimension of the reality of the Redemption. Indeed this Redemption is the ultimate and definitive revelation of the holiness of God, who is the absolute fullness of perfection: fullness of justice and of love, since justice is based on love, flows from it and tends toward it. In the passion and death of Christ, in the fact that the Father did not spare His own Son, but "for our sake made him sin" (2 Cor. 5:21), absolute justice is expressed, for Christ undergoes the passion and cross because of the sins of humanity. This constitutes even a "superabundance" of justice, for the sins of man are "compensated for" by the sacrifice of the Man-God. Nevertheless, this justice, which is true justice "in good measure," is born completely from love: from the love of the Father and of the Son, and completely bears fruit in love. Precisely for this reason the divine Justice revealed in the Cross of Christ is "in God's measure," because it it born from love and is accomplished in love, bearing the fruits of salvation. The divine dimension of redemption is put into effect not only by meting out justice against sin, but also by restoring to love that creative power in man, thanks to which he once more has access to the fullness of life and holiness that came from God. In this way redemption involves the revelation of mercy in its fullness.

The Paschal mystery is the culmination of this revealing and effecting mercy, which is able to justify man, to restore justice in the sense of that salvific order which God willed from the beginning in man and, through man, in the world. The suffering Christ speaks in a special way to man, and not just to the believer! The non-believer also will be able to discover in Him the eloquence of solidarity with the human lot, as also the harmonious fullness of selfless dedication to the cause of man, to truth and to love. And yet the divine dimension of the Paschal mystery goes still deeper. The Cross on Calvary, the Cross upon which Christ conducts His final dialogue with the Father, emerges from the very depth of love that man, created in the image and likeness of God, has been given as a gift, according to God's eternal plan. God, as Christ revealed Him, does not merely remain closely linked with the world as the Creator and the ultimate source of existence. He is also Father: He is linked to man, whom He called into existence in the visible world, by a bond still more intimate that that of creation. It is a love which not only creates the good but also grants participation in the very life of God: Father, Son and Holy Spirit. For He who loves desires to give Himself.

The Cross of Christ on Calvary stands on the road of that *admirable commercium*, of the *wonderful self-communication of God to man*. This includes the *call* to man to share in the divine life by giving himself, and with him the whole world, to God, and like an adopted son to become a sharer in the truth and love which is in God and proceeds from God. It is precisely on the road of man's eternal election to the dignity of being an adopted child of God that there stands in history the Cross of Christ, the only-begotten Son, who, as "light from light, true God from true God" (Nicene Creed), came to give the final witness to the wonderful *covenant of God with humanity, of God with every human being*. This covenant, as old as man, goes back to the very mystery of creation. Afterwards many times renewed with one single chosen people, it is equally the new and final covenant. It was established there on Calvary, and is not limited to a single people, to Israel, but is open to each and every one.

What else, then, does the Cross of Christ say to us, the Cross that in a sense is the final word of His messianic proclamation and mission? And yet this is still not the last word of the God of the Covenant: the last word will be declared at dawn when first the women and then the Apostles came to the tomb of the crucified Christ, see the tomb empty and for the first time hear the words: "He is risen from the dead." They will repeat this message to others and will be witnesses to the Risen Christ. Yet, even in the glorification of the Son of God, the Cross remains; that Cross, which through all the messianic testimony of the Son of Man, who suffered death upon it, speaks and never ceases to speak of God the Father, who is absolutely faithful to His eternal love for man. "God so loved the world that He gave His only Son, that whoever believes in Him should not perish but have eternal life" (cf. Jn. 3:16). It means believing that love is present in the world and that this love is more powerful than any kind of evil in which individuals, humanity, or the world are entangled. Believing in this love means believing in mercy. For mercy is an indispensable dimension of love; it is as it were love's second name. At the same time, mercy is the specific manner in which love is revealed and realized in the face of the reality of evil that is in the world, evil which touches and entraps man, penetrates even into his heart and can cause him to "perish in Gehenna" (Mt. 10:28).

8. Love More Powerful than Death, More Powerful than Sin

The Cross of Christ on Calvary is also a witness to the strength of evil against the very Son of God. The Son of God who alone among all the Sons of men was by His nature absolutely innocent and free from sin, and whose coming into the world was untainted by the disobedience of Adam and the inheritance of original sin. And here, precisely in Him, in Christ, justice is done to sin at the price of His sacrifice, of His obedience "even to death" (Phil. 2:8). Him who was without sin "God made sin for our sake" (2 Cor. 5:21). Justice is also brought to bear upon death, which from the beginning of man's history has been allied to sin. Death has justice done to it at the price of the death of the one who was without sin and who alone was able by means of His own death to inflict death upon death (cf. 1 Cor. 15:54-55). In this way *the Cross of Christ*, on which the Son, consubstantial with the Father, renders *full justice to God*, is also a *radical revelation of mercy*; in other words, of love that goes against what constitutes the very root of evil in the history of man: against sin and death.

The Cross is the deepest condescension of God toward man and to what man, especially in difficult and painful moments, looks as his unhappy lot. The Cross is like a touch of eternal love upon the painful wounds of man's earthly existence; it is the total fulfillment of the messianic program that Christ once formulated in the synagogue at Nazareth (cf. Lk. 4:18-21) and then repeated to the messengers sent by John the Baptist (cf. Lk. 7:20-23). According to the words once written in the prophecy of Isaiah (cf. Is. 35:5; 61:1-3), this program consisted in the revelations of merciful love for the poor, the suffering and prisoners, for the blind, the oppressed and sinners. In the Paschal mystery the limits of the many-sided evil in which man becomes a sharer during his earthly existence are surpassed: the Cross of Christ, in fact, makes us understand the deepest roots of evil, which are fixed in sin and death; thus the Cross becomes a final (eschatological) sign. Only in the final (eschatological) fulfillment and the final renewal of the world *will love conquer, in all the elect, the deepest sources of evil*, bringing as its fully mature fruit the kingdom of life and holiness and glorious immortality. The foundation of this final fulfillment is already contained in the Cross of Christ and in His death. The fact that Christ "was raised the third day" (1 Cor. 15:4) constitutes the final sign of the messianic mission, a sign that perfects the entire revelation of merciful love in a world that is subject to evil. At the same time it constitutes the sign that foretells "a new heaven and a new earth" (Rev. 21:1), when God "will wipe away every tear from their eyes, there will be no more death or mourning, no crying, no pain, for the former things have passed away" (Rev. 21:4).

In the final (eschatological) fulfillment, mercy will be revealed as love; while in the temporal phase, in human history, which is at the same time the history of sin and death, love must be revealed as mercy and must also be fulfilled as mercy. Christ's messianic program, the program of mercy, becomes the program of His people, the program of the Church. At the very center there is always the Cross, for it is the Cross that the revelation of merciful love attains its peak. Until "the former things pass away" (cf. Rev. 3:20), the Cross will remain the "place" about which still other words of the book of Revelation can be applied: "Behold, I stand at the door and knock; if anyone hears my voice and opens the door, I will come in and eat with him and he with Me" (Rev. 3:20). In a remarkable way God also reveals His mercy *when He prompts man to have "mercy" toward His own Son, toward the Crucified One.*

Christ, precisely as the Crucified One, is the Word that does not pass away (cf. Mt. 24:35), and He is the one who stands at the door and knocks at the heart of every man (cf. Rev. 3:20), without restricting his freedom, but instead, seeking to draw from this very freedom love, which is not only an act of solidarity with the suffering Son of Man, but also a kind of "mercy" shown by each one of us to the Son of the eternal Father. In the whole of the revelation of mercy through the Cross, could man's dignity be more highly respected and ennobled, for, in obtaining mercy, he is in a sense the one who at the same time "shows mercy"? In a word, is not this the position of Christ with regard to man when He says: "As you did it to one of the least of these...you did it to me"? (Mt. 25:40)

Do not the words of the Sermon on the Mount: "Blessed are the merciful for they shall obtain mercy" (Mt. 5:7), constitute in a certain sense, a synthesis of the whole of the Good News, of the whole of the "wonderful exchange" *(admirable commercium)* contained therein? This exchange is a law of *the very plan of salvation*, a law which is simple, strong and at the same time "easy." Demonstrating from the very start what the "human heart" is capable of ("to be merciful"), do not these words from the Sermon on the Mount reveal in the same perspective the deepest mystery of God: that inscrutable unity of Father, Son and Holy Spirit, in which love, containing justice, sets in motion mercy, which in turn reveals the perfection of justice?

The Paschal Mystery is Christ at the summit of the revelation of the inscrutable mystery of God. It is precisely then that the words pronounced in the Upper Room are completely fulfilled: "He who has seen me has seen the Father" (Jn. 14:9). In fact, Christ, whom the Father "did not spare" (Rom. 8:32) for the sake of man and who in His passion and in the torment of the Cross did not obtain human mercy, has revealed in His Resurrection the fullness of the love that the Father has for Him and, in Him for all people. "He is not God of the dead, but of the living" (Mk. 12:27). In His Resurrection, Christ has revealed the God of merciful love, precisely because *He accepted the Cross as the road to the Resurrection*. And it is for this reason that when we recall the Cross of Christ, His passion and death, our faith and hope are centered on the Risen One: on that Christ who "on the evening of that day, the first of the week,...breathed on them, and said to them: 'Receive the Holy Spirit. If you forgive the sins of any, they are forgiven; if you retain the sins of any, they are retained'" (Jn. 20:19-23).

Here is the Son of God who in His Resurrection experienced in a radical way mercy shown to Himself, that is to say, the love of the Father which is *more powerful than death*. And it is also the same Christ the Son of God, who at the end of His messianic mission and in a certain sense, even beyond the end, reveals Himself as the inexhaustible source of mercy (like a well that cannot be emptied), of the same love that, in a subsequent perspective of the history of salvation in the Church, is to be everlastingly confirmed as *more powerful than sin.* The Paschal Christ is the definitive incarnation of mercy. The living sign of the Paschal Christ is salvific in history and in the final times (in eschatology). In the same spirit, the liturgy of Eastertide places on our lips the words of the Psalm: "I will sing of the mercies of the Lord forever" (Ps. 88:2).

9. Mother of Mercy

These words of the Church at Easter: "I will sing of the mercies of the Lord forever," re-echo the full prophetic content of the words Mary uttered during her visit to Elizabeth, the wife of Zechariah: "His mercy is from generation to generation." At the very moment of the Incarnation, these words open up a new perspective of salvation history. After the Resurrection of Christ, this perspective is new on both the historical and final (eschatological) level. From that time onwards, there is a succession of new generations of individuals in the immense human family, in ever-increasing size; there is also a succession of new generations of the People of God, marked with the sign of the Cross and of the Resurrection and "sealed" (cf. 2 Cor. 1:21-22) with the sign of the Paschal Mystery of Christ, the radical revelation of the mercy that Mary proclaimed on the threshold of her kinswoman's house: "His mercy is from generation to generation" (Lk. 1:50).

Mary is also the one who experienced mercy in a remarkable and exceptional way, as no other person has. At the same time, still in an exceptional way, she paid for her share in revealing God's mercy by the sacrifice of her heart. This sacrifice is intimately linked with the Cross of her Son at the foot of which she was to stand on Calvary. Her sacrifice is a unique sharing in the revelation of mercy, that is, a sharing in the absolute fidelity of God to His own love, to the covenant that He willed from eternity and that He entered into in time with man, with the people, with humanity; it is a sharing in that revelation that was decisively fulfilled through the Cross. *No one has experienced to the same degree as the Mother of the Crucified One* the mystery of the Cross, the overwhelming encounter of divine transcendent justice with love: that "kiss" given by mercy to justice" (cf. Ps. 85:11). No one as much as Mary has accepted into their heart that mystery, that truly divine dimension of the Redemption accomplished on Calvary by means of the death of her Son, together with the sacrifice of her maternal heart and with her final "fiat."

Mary, then, is also the one who knows to the fullest the mystery of God's mercy. She knows its price, she knows how great it is. In this sense we call her the *Mother of mercy*, God's Mother (*Theotokos*) of Mercy or the Mother of the God of Mercy. Each one of these titles contains its own deep theological meaning. Each of them expresses the special preparation of her soul, of her whole personality, so that she was able to see through the complex events, first of Israel, then of every individual and the whole of humanity, that mercy "from generation to generation" (Lk. 1:50) which people share in, according to the eternal design of the most Holy Trinity.

The above titles which we attribute to the God-bearer speak of her above all, however, as the Mother of the Crucified and Risen One; *as the one* who experienced mercy in an exceptional way, and *in an equally exceptional way* "merits" that mercy throughout her earthly life and particularly at the foot of the Cross of her Son. Finally, these titles speak of her as one who, through her hidden and at the same time incomparable sharing in the messianic mission of her Son, was called in a special way to bring close to people that love which He had come to reveal. That love finds its most concrete expression in all of the suffering, the poor, those deprived of their own freedom, the blind, the oppressed and sinners; just as Christ spoke of Isaiah, first in the synagogue at Nazareth (cf. Lk. 4:18) and then in response to the question of the messengers of John the Baptist (cf. Lk. 7:22).

Mary shared precisely in this "Merciful" love, which proves itself above all in contact with moral and physical evil. She shared singularly and exceptionally by her heart as the Mother of the Crucified and Risen One. This "merciful" love does not cease to be revealed in her and through her in the history of the Church and all mankind. This revelation is especially fruitful, because it is based on the remarkable docility of the maternal heart of the God-bearer, on her unique sensitivity and fitness to reach all who accept this merciful love most easily from a mother's side. This is one of the great life-giving mysteries of Christianity, a mystery intimately connected with the mystery of the Incarnation.

"The motherhood of Mary in the order of grace," as the Second Vatican Council explains, "lasts without interruption from the consent she faithfully gave at the Annunciation and which she sustained without hesitation under the Cross, until the eternal fulfillment of all the elect. In fact, being assumed into heaven she has not laid aside this office of salvation but by her manifold intercession she continues to obtain for us graces of eternal salvation. By her maternal charity, she takes care of the brethren of her Son who still journey on earth surrounded by dangers and difficulties, until they are led into their blessed home" (*Lumen Gentium*, 62).

VI. "Mercy from Generation to Generation"

10. An Image of Our Generation

We have every right to believe that our generation too is included in the words of the God-bearer when Mary glorified that mercy shared in "from generation to generation" by those who are guided by the fear of the Lord. The words of *Mary's Magnificat* carry a prophetic content that concerns not only the past of Israel but also the whole future of the People of God on earth. In fact, all of us now living on earth are *the generation* that is aware of the approach of the third millennium and that profoundly feel the turning point that is occurring in history.

The present generation considers itself in a privileged position: progress provided it with countless possibilities that only a few decades ago were undreamed of. Men's creative activity, his intelligence and his work, have brought about profound changes both in the field of science and technology and in that of social and cultural life. Man has extended his power over nature and has acquired deeper knowledge of the laws of social behavior. He has seen the obstacles and distances between individuals and nations dissolve or shrink through an increased sense of what is universal. There is a clearer awareness of the unity of the human race, an acceptance of mutual dependence in authentic solidarity, and a desire and possibility of making contact with one's brothers and sisters beyond artificial and geographic divisions and racial limits. Today's young people, especially are conscious that the progress of science and technology can produce not only new material goods but also a wider sharing in their mutual understanding. The extraordinary progress made in the field of information and data processing, for instance, will increase man's creative capacity and provide access to the intellectual and cultural notes of other peoples. New communication techniques will encourage greater participation in events and a wider exchange of ideas. The achievements of biological, psychological and social science help man to penetrate deeper the riches of his own being. It is true that too often this progress is still the privilege of the industrialized countries, but it cannot be denied that the prospect of enabling every people and every country to benefit from it has long ceased to be pure utopia when there is a real political desire for it.

But side by side with all this, or rather as part of it, there are also the difficulties that appear whenever there is growth. There stands out a lack of peace (anxiety) and a powerlessness regarding the profound response that man knows that he must give. The picture of the world today presents deeper recurring shadows and imbalances. The pastoral constitution of the Second Vatican Council, *Gaudium et Spes*, is certainly not the only document that deals with the life of this generation, but it is a document of special importance. "The dichotomy affecting the modern world," we read in it, "is, in fact, a symptom of a *deeper dichotomy* that is *in man himself.* He is the meeting point of many conflicting forces. In his condition as a created being he is subject to a thousand shortcomings, but feeling untrammeled in his inclination and destined for a higher form of life. Torn by a welter of anxieties he is compelled to choose between them and repudiate some among them. Worse still, feeble and sinful as he is, he often does the very thing he hates and does not do what he wants. And so he feels himself divided, and the result is a host of discords in social life" (*Gaudium et Spes*, 10).

Towards the end of the introductory exposition we read: "...in the face of modern developments there is a growing body of men who are asking the most fundamental of all questions or are glimpsing them with a keener insight: What is man? *What is the meaning of suffering, evil, death, which have not been eliminated by all this progress? What is the purpose of these achievements, purchased at so high a price?"* (Ibid.)

In the span of fifteen years since the end of the Second Vatican Council, has this picture of tensions and threats that mark our epoch become less disquieting? It seems not. On the contrary, the tension and threats, that in the Council document seem only to be outlined, not showing their real degree of danger hidden within them, have revealed themselves more clearly these years; they have in a different way confirmed that danger, and do not permit us to cherish the illusions of the past.

11. Sources of the Lack of Peace

[Note: In this section (#11) and in other places, Pope John Paul II uses the word "Niepokoj" in the Polish text, literally meaning "non-peace" or better "non-shalom." It is a rich word carrying the meaning of a lack of shalom, the lack of right order with God and man and the good associated with such a life. The dictionary translates "niepokoj" as: trouble, disquiet, anxiety, unrest, uneasiness, restlessness, concern, worry, agitation. The word carries with it the sense of evil and anxiety referred to in the prayer that follows the Lord's Prayer in the Eucharist: "Deliver us, Lord, from every evil, and grant us peace in our day. In your mercy keep us free from sin and protect us from all anxiety as we wait in joyful hope for the coming of our Savior, Jesus Christ." The Latin translation uses a series of words to translate this word "niepokoj," used repeatedly in this section, the English equivalent being: solicitude, trepidation, anxiety, anguish, inquietude, conturbation. The Vatican Polygot Press translation uses the word "uneasiness." In this present translation, "lack of peace" is used.

The lack of peace in men's hearts and in the world is the central issue of the encyclical and the answer to this

lack of peace is mercy. The use of "lack of peace" is impor-
tant in order to relate the message of this encyclical to
the Gospel message of peace (Jn 20:20-21), to the
embolism after the Lord's Prayer in the Roman liturgy,
and to the message of Our Lady's apparitions at Fatima
and other places. The problem in the modern world is
lack of peace; the answer is mercy.]

As a result of the situation, the feeling of being
under threat is growing in the world. There is a growing
fear grounded in experience that is connected with the
prospect of a conflict that in view of today's atomic
stockpiles could mean the partial self-destruction of
humanity, as said in the Encyclical *Redemptor Hominis*.
But the threat does not merely concern what human
beings can do to human beings through the means provided by military technology. The threat also concerns
many other dangers produced by a materialistic society
which in spite of "humanistic" declarations accepts the
primacy of things over persons. Modern man rightly
fears that by the use of the means invented by this type
of society, individuals and the environment, communities, societies and nations can fall victim to the abuse of
power by other individuals, environments and societies.
The history of our century offers many examples of this.
In spite of all the declarations on the rights of man in all
his dimensions, that is to say, in his bodily and spiritual existence, we cannot say that these examples belong

only to the past.

Man rightly fears falling victim to an oppression that will deprive him of his interior freedom, of the possibility of expressing the truth of which he is convinced, of the faith that he professes and of the ability to obey the voice of conscience that tells him the right path to follow. The technical means at the disposal of modern society conceal within themselves, not only the possibility of self-destruction through military conflict, *but also the possibility of a* "peaceful" *subjection of individuals of environment*, of entire societies and nations that for one reason or another might prove inconvenient for those who possess the necessary means and are ready to use them without scruple. Let us not forget the continued existence of torture practiced with impunity, systematically used by authority as a means of domination and political oppression.

Then, alongside the awareness of biological threat, there is a growing awareness of yet another threat, even more destructive of what is essentially human, what is intimately bound up with the dignity of the person and their right to truth and freedom.

All this is happening against the background of the *gigantic remorse* caused by the fact that side by side with wealthy and surfeited people and societies, living in plenty and ruled by consumerism and pleasure, the same human family contains individuals and groups *that are suffering from hunger*. There is no scarcity of little children dying of hunger under their mothers' eyes. There is no scarcity of entire areas of poverty, shortages and underdevelopment in various parts of the world, and in various socio-economic systems. This fact is universally known. *The state of inequality* between individuals and between nations not only exists; it is increasing. It still happens that, side by side with those who are wealthy and living in plenty, there exist those who are living in want, suffering misery, and often actually dying of hunger; and their number reaches millions, even hundreds of millions. This is why a moral lack of peace is destined to become even more acute. It is obvious that a fundamental defect, or rather a series of defects, indeed a defective machinery is at the root of contemporary economics and materialistic civilization, which does not allow the human family to break free from such radically unjust situations.

This picture of today's world is filled with much evil, both physical and moral, so as to make it a world entangled in contradictions and tensions, and at the same time full of threats to human freedom, conscience and religion. *This picture explains the lack of peace* felt by contemporary man. This lack of peace is experienced not only by those who are disadvantaged or oppressed, but also by those who possess the privileges of wealth, progress and power. Although there is no scarcity of people trying to understand the sources of the lack of peace, or trying to react against it with emergency measures offered by technology, wealth or power, still in the depth of the human spirit this *lack of peace is stronger than all emergency measures*. This lack of peace concerns the fundamental problems of all human existence as the analysis of the Second Vatican Council rightly pointed out. This lack of peace is tied to the very meaning of man's existence in the world and is a lack of peace about the future of man and all mankind. This lack of peace reaches out for decisive solutions, which now seem to be confronting the human race.

12. Is Justice Enough?

It is not difficult to see that in the modern world the *sense of justice* has been re-awakening on a vast scale. Without doubt, this sense of justice emphasizes that which goes against justice in relationship between individuals, social groups and "classes," between individual peoples and states, and finally between whole political systems; indeed, between what are called "worlds." This deep and multiple trend, at the basis of which the contemporary conscience has placed justice, gives proof of the ethical character of the tensions and struggles pervading the world.

The Church shares with the people of our time this profound and ardent desire for a life which is just in every aspect. She does not fail to examine the various aspects of the sort of justice that life of people and society demands. This is confirmed by the field of Catholic social doctrine, greatly developed in the course of the last century. In line with this teaching proceed the education and formation of human consciences in the spirit of justice, and also individual undertakings especially in the sphere of the apostolate of the laity, which are developing in precisely this spirit.

And yet, it would be difficult not to notice that very often *programs which start from the idea of justice* and which ought to assist its fulfillment among individuals, groups and human societies, in practice *suffer from distortions*. Although they continue to appeal to the idea of justice, nevertheless, experience shows that other negative forces have gained the upper hand over justice, such as spite, hatred and even cruelty. In such cases, the desire to annihilate the enemy, limit his freedom or even force him into total dependence, becomes the fundamental motive for action. This contrasts with the essence of justice which by its nature tends to establish equality and harmony between the parties in conflict. This kind of abuse of the idea of justice and the practical distortion of it show how far human action can *deviate from justice itself*, even when it is being undertaken in the name of justice.

Christ did not challenge His listeners in vain, faithful to the doctrine of the Old Testament, for their attitude which was manifested in the words: "An eye for an eye and a tooth for a tooth" (Mt 38). This was the form of distortion of justice at that time. Today's forms continue to be modeled on it. It is obvious, in fact, that in the name of alleged justice (for example, historical justice or class justice) the neighbor is sometimes destroyed, killed, deprived of liberty or stripped of fundamental human rights. The experience of the past and of our own time demonstrates that *justice alone is not enough,* that it can even lead to the negation and destruction of itself, if *that deeper power, which is love,* is not allowed to shape human life in its various dimensions. It has been precisely historical experience that, among other things, has led to the formulation of the saying: *summum ius, summa iniuria* (the highest justice is the highest offense). This statement does not detract from the value of justice and does not minimize the significance of the order that is based upon it; it only indicates, under another aspect, the need to draw from the powers of the Spirit which condition the very order of justice, powers which are still more profound.

The *Church,* having before her eyes the picture of the generation to which we belong, shares the lack of peace of so many of the people of our time. Moreover, the Church is troubled by *the decline of many fundamental values,* which constitute unquestionable good not only for Christian morality but simply *for human morality, for moral culture*: these values include respect for human life from the moment of conception, respect for marriage in its indissoluble unity, and respect for the stability of the family. Moral permissiveness strikes especially at this most sensitive sphere of life and society. Hand in hand with this go the crisis of truth in human relationships, lack of responsibility for what one says, the purely utilitarian relationship between individual and individual, the loss of a sense of the authentic common good and the ease with which it is alienated. Finally, there is the "desacralization" that often turns into "dehumanization"; the individual and the society for whom nothing is "sacred" suffer moral decay in spite of appearances.

VII. The Mercy of God in the Mission of the Church

In connection with this picture of our generation, a picture which must awake a deep lack of peace, there come to mind once more those words which, by reason of the Incarnation of the Son of God, resounded in Mary's *Magnificat,* and which sing of "mercy from generation to generation." The Church of our time, taking these inspired words deeply to heart and applying them to her own experience and to the suffering of the human family, must become especially and profoundly conscious of the need to *bear witness in her whole mission to God's mercy*, following in the footsteps of the tradition of the Old and the New Testament, and above all of Jesus Christ Himself and His Apostles. The Church must bear witness to the mercy of God revealed in Christ, in the whole of His mission as Messiah, *professing it*, in the first place as a salvific truth of faith and as necessary for life in harmony with faith, and then seeking to *introduce* it and to *incarnate* it in the lives of both her faithful and as far as possible in the lives of all people of good will. Finally, the Church professing mercy and not stepping back from it in life has the right and duty to call upon the mercy of God, *imploring mercy* in the face of all the manifestations of physical and moral evil, before all the threats that cloud the whole horizon of the life of humanity today.

13. The Church Professes the Mercy of God and Proclaims It

The Church must *profess and proclaim God's mercy in all its truth*, as it has been handed down to us by revelation. We have sought, in the foregoing pages of the present document, to sketch at least an outline of this truth, which finds such rich expression in the whole of Sacred Scripture and in Sacred Tradition. In the daily life of the Church, the truth about the mercy of God, expressed in the Bible, resounds like a continuous echo through the many readings of the Sacred Liturgy. The authentic sense of the faith of the People of God witnesses to this truth as is shown by various expressions of personal and community piety. It would be difficult to make a list or summary of them all, because most of them are vividly written in the depths of people's hearts and consciences. If some theologians claim that mercy is greatest of the attributes and perfections of God, then to this the Bible, Tradition and the whole faith life of the People of God provide unique proof. It is not here a question of the perfection of the inscrutable essence of God in the mystery of divinity itself, but the perfection and attribute whereby man, in the inner truth of his existence, meets the living God ever so closely and ever so often. According to the words of Christ to Philip (cf. Jn. 14:9-10), "seeing the Father," the "seeing" of God through faith, finds in this very meeting with His mercy a unique moment of inner simplicity and truth. It is a meeting with mercy similar to the simplicity and truth that we find in parable of the Prodigal Son.

"He who has seen me has seen the Father" (Jn. 14:9). The Church professes the mercy of God Himself, the Church lives by it in her wide experience of faith. She also lives by it in her teaching, constantly contemplating Christ, concentrating on Him, on His life and on His Gospel, on His Cross and Resurrection, on His whole mystery. Everything that contributes to "seeing" Christ in the Church's living faith and teaching brings us nearer to "seeing the Father" in the holiness of His mercy. The Church seems to profess and venerate the mercy of God in an extraordinary way when she turns to Heart of Jesus. In fact, it is precisely this drawing close to Christ in the mystery of His Heart which allows us to stop and dwell on this central point. The Heart of Christ is the point at which it is the easiest for mankind to preach the revelation of the Father's merciful love, a revelation which makes up the central content of the messianic mission of the Son of God.

The *Church* lives an authentic life when she *professes* and *proclaims* the most stupendous attribute of the Creator and Redeemer and when she brings people close to the sources of the Savior's *mercy*, of which she is the trustee and dispenser. Of great significance in this matter is the constant pondering on the Word of God, and above all a conscious and mature participation *in the Eucharist* and *in the sacrament of Penance or Reconciliation.* The Eucharist brings us ever nearer to that love which is more powerful than death: "For as often as we eat this bread and drink this cup," we proclaim not only the death of the Redeemer but also His Resurrection, "until He comes in glory" (cf. 1 Cor. 11:26, an acclamation of the Roman Missal). The same Eucharistic rite celebrated in memory of Christ who in His messianic mission revealed His Father to us by means of His Word and Cross, witnesses to the inexhaustible *love,* in whose strength He unceasingly wants to unite Himself with us and make us one, going out to meet every human heart. The road for this meeting is cleared for everyone, by the sacrament of Penance or Reconciliation, even those weighed down with great faults. In this sacrament every person can experience in an extraordinary way, mercy, that is, that love which is more powerful than sin. This has already been spoken of in the Encyclical *Redemptor Hominis;* but it will be fitting to return once more to this fundamental theme.

It is precisely because sin exists in the world, which "God so loved that He gave His only Son" (Jn. 3:16), that God who "is love" (Jn. 4:8), cannot reveal Himself otherwise than as mercy. This mercy declares not only the deepest truth about love, the love which is God and is God's, but this mercy also declares the inner truth of man and the world, which is man's temporary homeland.

Mercy in itself, as a perfection of the infinite God, is also infinite. So too then is the Father's readiness infinite and inexhaustible to receive the prodigal children, who return to His home. *Infinite are the readiness and power of forgiveness* which flow continually from the inexpressible value of the sacrifice of the Son. No human sin can prevail over this power or even limit it! On the part of man only a lack of goodwill can limit it, a lack of readiness to be converted and to repent, in other words, persistence in obstinacy, oppressing grace and truth, especially in the face of the witness of the Cross and Resurrection of Christ.

For this reason, the Church professes and proclaims conversion. Conversion to God always depends upon *discovering His mercy*, that is, in discovering that love which is patient and kind (cf. 1 Cor. 13:4) as only the Creator and Father can be. This love of the "God and Father of our Lord Jesus Christ" (2 Cor. 1:3) is faithful down to the uttermost consequences in the history of His covenant with man: even to the Cross, the death and Resurrection of the Son. Conversion to God is always the fruit of the "rediscovery" of this Father, who is rich in mercy.

Genuine knowledge of the God of mercy, the God of tender love, is a constant and inexhaustible source of conversion, not only a single inner act but also a permanent capability, as a state of the soul. Those who come to know God in this way, who "see" Him in this way, can live only in a state of being continually converted to Him. They live, then, *in statu conversionis* (in a state of conversion) which marks out the deepest element of the pilgrimage of every man and woman on earth *in statu viatoris* (in the state of a pilgrim). It is obvious that the Church professes the mercy of God, revealed in the crucified and risen Christ, not only by the word of her teaching but above all through the deepest pulsation of the life of the whole People of God. By means of this testimony of life, the Church fulfills the mission proper to the People of God, the mission which is a sharing and, in a sense, a continuation of the messianic mission of Christ Himself.

The contemporary Church is profoundly conscious that only relying on the mercy of God will she be able to carry out the tasks that arise from the teaching of the Second Vatican Council, above all the ecumenical task which aims at uniting all who confess Christ. As she makes many efforts in this direction, the Church confesses with humility that only that love which is more powerful than the weakness of human divisions *can ultimately bring about that unity* which Christ implored from the Father and which the Spirit never ceases to beseech for us "with sighs too deep for words" (Rom. 8:26).

14. The Church Seeks to Put Mercy into Practice

Jesus Christ taught that mankind not only receives and experiences the mercy of God, but that it is also called "to practice mercy" toward others: "Blessed are the merciful, for they shall obtain mercy" (Mt. 5:7). The Church sees in these words a call to action, and she tries to practice mercy. If all the Beatitudes of the Sermon on the Mount indicate the way of conversion and of reform of life, then the one referring to those who are merciful is particularly eloquent in this regard. Mankind attains to the merciful love of God, His mercy to the extent that he himself is interiorly transformed in the Spirit of that love toward his neighbor.

This most essential evangelical process is not just a single breakthrough of heart but a whole style of life, an essential attribute of the Christian vocation. It consists in the constant discovery and persevering practice of *love as a unifying and elevating power* despite all difficulties of psychological or social nature. It is a question, in fact, of a *merciful love* which, by its essence, is creative love. In mutual relations between persons, merciful love is never a one-sided act or process. Even in the case in which everything would seem to indicate that only one party is giving and offering, and the other only receiving and taking, (for example, in the case of a doctor giving treatment, a teacher teaching, parents supporting and bringing up their children, a benefactor helping the needy), in reality the one who gives is always also a beneficiary. In any case, he too can easily find himself in the position of the one who receives, who obtains a benefit, who experiences merciful love; he too obtains mercy.

In this sense, Christ crucified is for us the loftiest model, inspiration and encouragement. When we base our life on *this impressive model,* we are able with all humility to show mercy to others, knowing that Christ accepts it as if it were shown to Himself (cf. Mt. 25:34-40). On the basis of this model, we must also continually purify all our actions and intentions in which mercy is understood and practiced in only one direction, that is, as a good done to others. An act of merciful love is only really such when we are deeply convinced at the moment of performing it that we are at the same time receiving mercy from the people who are accepting it from us. If this two-directional and mutual quality is absent, our actions are not yet true acts of mercy, nor has there yet been fully completed in us that conversion to which Christ has shown us the way by His words and example, even to the Cross. We are not yet sharing fully in the *magnificent source of merciful love* that has been revealed to us by Him.

Thus, the way which Christ showed to us in the Sermon on the Mount about the blessing of the merciful is much richer than what we sometimes find in ordinary human opinion. These opinions see mercy as a one-sided act or process, presupposing and maintaining a certain distance between the one practicing mercy and the one benefitting from it, between the one who does good and the one who receives it. Hence this approach attempts to free interpersonal and social relationships from mercy and to base them solely on justice. Such opinions about mercy, however, fail to see the fundamental link between mercy and justice spoken of by the whole biblical tradition, and above all by the messianic mission of Jesus Christ. *True mercy is the deepest source of justice.* If justice is in itself suitable for judging between nations and distributing among them objective goods in an equitable manner, then love and only love (including that kindly love we call "mercy") is capable of restoring man to himself.

Equalizing mercy that is truly Christian is also in a certain sense the *most perfect incarnation of "equalizing"* between people, and therefore, also the most perfect incarnation of justice as well, insofar as justice aims at the same result in its own sphere. However, the "equalization" brought about by justice is limited to the realm of objective and extrinsic goods, while love and mercy bring about that people meet one another in that value which is man himself, with the dignity that is proper to him. At the same time, this "equalizing" of people through "patient and kind" love (cf. 1 Cor. 13:4) does not take away differences. The person who gives becomes more generous when he or she feels at the same time benefited by the person accepting his or her gift. Also the person who accepts the gift with the awareness that, in accepting it, he or she too is doing good, is in his or her own way serving the greater cause of the dignity of the person. This most profoundly contributes to uniting people among themselves.

Thus, mercy becomes an indispensable element for shaping mutual relationships between people, in a spirit of deeper respect for what is human, and in a spirit of mutual brotherhood. It is impossible to establish this bond between people, if they wish to regulate their mutual relationships only according to the measure of justice. In every sphere of interpersonal relationship, justice must experience a profound "correction" by that love which as St. Paul proclaims "is patient and kind" or, in other words, possesses the characteristics of the *merciful love* which is so much of the essence of the Gospel and Christianity. Let us remember, furthermore, that *merciful tenderness and sensitivity* so eloquently spoken of in the parables of the Prodigal Son (cf. Lk. 15:11-32), the parable of the lost sheep and in the lost coin (cf. Lk. 15:1-10). Consequently, merciful love is especially indispensable between those who are closest to one another; between husbands and wives, between parents and children, between friends; and it is indispensable in education and in pastoral work.

Its sphere of action is not limited to this. Paul VI more than once indicated the "civilization of love" (cf. close of the Holy Year, December 25, 1975) as the goal toward which all efforts in the cultural and social fields as well as in the economic and political fields should tend. It must be added that this good will never be reached if in our thinking and acting concerning the vast and complex spheres of human society we stop at the criterion of "an eye for an eye, a tooth for a tooth" (Mt. 5:38) and do not try to transform it in its essence, by complementing it with another spirit. Certainly, the Second Vatican Council also leads us in this direction, when it speaks repeatedly of the need to make the world ever more human (*Gaudium et Spes*, 40; AAS 58, 1966 Paul VI; *Paterna cum benevolentia,* 1-6 SSD 61, 1977 pp. 7-9, 17-23), and says that the realization of this task is precisely the mission of the Church in the modern world. Society can become ever more human only if we introduce into the many-sided setting of interpersonal relationships, not merely justice, but also that "merciful love" which constitutes the messianic message of the Gospel.

This human world can become "even more human" only when we introduce into all the mutual relationships which form its moral aspect, the moment of forgiveness, which is so much of the essence of the Gospel. Forgiveness demonstrates the presence in the world of *the love which is more powerful than sin*. Forgiveness is also the fundamental condition for reconciliation, not only in the relationship of God with man, but also in relationships between people. If we eliminate forgiveness from this world, then it would be nothing but a world of cold and unfeeling justice, in the name of which each person would claim his or her own rights *vis-a-vis* others; the various kinds of selfishness latent in man would transform life and human society into a system of oppression of the weak by the strong, or into an arena of permanent strife between one group and another.

For this reason the Church must acknowledge as her chief duty the *proclamation and introduction into life*, the mystery of mercy, so perfectly revealed in Jesus Christ at every stage of history, especially in our modern age. Not only for the Church herself as the community of believers but also in a certain sense for all humanity. This mystery is the source of a life different from the life which can be built by human beings who are exposed to the oppressive forces of the threefold concupiscence active within them (cf. 1 Jn. 2:16). It is precisely in the name of this mystery of mercy that Christ teaches us to forgive always. How often we repeat the words of the prayer which He Himself taught us, asking *"forgive us* our trespasses *as we forgive* those who trespass against us," which means those who have committed an offense against us (Mt. 6:12). It is difficult, frankly, to express the deep value of the attitude which these words describe and form. How much these words say to everyone about others and at the same time about themselves! The consciousness of usually being debtors to each other goes hand in hand with the call to fraternal solidarity, which St. Paul expressed in his concise exhortation to "forbear one another in love" (Eph. 2; cf. Gal. 6:2). What a lesson of humility is to be found here for man, for both one's neighbors and oneself! What a school of good will for each day in various situations of our life. If we were to ignore this lesson of forgiveness, what would remain of any truly "humanist" program of life and education?

Christ emphasizes so insistently the need to forgive others that when Peter asked Him how many times he should forgive his neighbor, He answered with the symbolic number of "seventy times seven" (Mt. 18:22), meaning that he must be able to forgive everyone every time. It is obvious that such a generous requirement of *forgiveness does not cancel out the objective requirements*

of justice. Properly understood, justice is, so to speak, the goal of forgiveness. In no passage of the Gospel message does forgiveness, or mercy as its source, mean tolerance toward evil, toward scandals, toward injury or insult. In every case reparation for evil and scandal, compensation for injury, and satisfaction for insult are conditions of forgiveness.

Thus the fundamental structure of justice always enters into the sphere of mercy. Mercy, however, has the power to confer on justice a new content, which is expressed most simply and fully in forgiveness. Forgiveness, in fact, shows that over and above the process of "equalizing" and "truce" which is specific to justice, love is necessary, so that persons may affirm themselves as human. Fulfillment of the conditions of justice is especially indispensable in order that love may reveal its own image. In analyzing the parable of the Prodigal Son, we have already called attention to the fact that he who forgives and he who is forgiven meet one another at a vital point, namely, the dignity or essential value of the person, a point which cannot be lost. The confirming of this point of dignity of the person or finding it anew is a source of the greatest joy.

The Church rightly considers it her duty and the duty of her mission to *guard the authenticity of forgiveness,* both in life, behavior and in educational and pastoral work. She protects it simply by guarding its source, which is the mystery of the mercy of God Himself as revealed in Jesus Christ.

The basis of the Church's mission, in all the spheres spoken of in the numerous pronouncements of the most recent Council and in the centuries old experience of the apostolate, is none other than "drawing from the wells of the Savior" (cf. Is. 12:3); this is what provides many guidelines for the mission of the Church in the lives of individual Christians, of individual communities, and also of the whole People of God. This "drawing from the wells of the Savior" can be done only in the spirit of poverty to which we are called by the words and example of the Lord: "You received without pay," (Mt. 10:8). Thus, in all the ways of the Church's life and ministry, through the evangelical poverty of her ministers and stewards and of her whole People which bears witness to "the mighty works" of its Lord — the Lord has all the more revealed Himself as the God who is "rich in mercy."

VIII. The Prayer of the Church in Our Times

15. The Church Appeals to the Mercy of God

The Church proclaims the truth about God's mercy which is made known in the crucified and risen Christ and she makes it known in various ways. The Church also tries to be merciful to people through people because she considers this to be an indispensable condition for a better, "more human" world, today and tomorrow.

And yet at no time and in no period of history — especially at a turning point like ours – can the Church forget about *prayer, which is a cry for the mercy of God* in the midst of the many forms of evil that weigh upon mankind and threaten it. This imploring of mercy is precisely the fundamental right and at the same time the duty of the Church in Christ Jesus. It is the right and duty of the Church toward God and at the same time toward humanity.

The more the human conscience succumbs to secularization and loses its sense of the very meaning of the word "mercy," the more it moves away from God and the mystery of mercy. Therefore *the Church has all the more the right and the duty* to appeal to God's mercy with "loud cries" (Heb. 5:7). Such "loud cries" ought to be the cry of the Church of our times to God for mercy as she announces and proclaims the certainty of that mercy in the crucified and risen Christ, that is, the Paschal Mystery. This mystery carries within itself the fullest revelation of mercy, namely, that love is more powerful than death, more powerful than sin and every evil, that love lifts man from his deepest falls and frees him from his greatest threats.

Modern man feels these threats. What has been said on this point is only a beginning. Modern man often asks about the solutions of these terrible tensions which have built up in the world between peoples. And if at times he *lacks the courage to utter this word "mercy,"* or if his conscience is empty of religious content and he does not find the equivalent, so much greater is the *necessity for the Church to utter this word*, not only in her own name but also in the name of all people of our time.

It is necessary that everything that I have said in this present letter on mercy be *continuously changed and transformed into an ardent prayer*, into a cry for mercy on the people of the modern world with all their needs and threats. *May this cry be filled with that truth about mercy* which has found such rich expression in the Sacred Scriptures, in Tradition, and in the authentic life of faith of countless generations of the People of God. Like the sacred writers, let us cry out to God who cannot despise anything that He has made, (Gen. 1:31; Ps. 145:9; Wis. 11:24), Him who is faithful to Himself, His fatherhood and His love. And like the prophets, let us appeal to that love which has maternal characteristics — and, like a mother, goes after each of her children, after each lost sheep, even if the lost are in the millions, even if the evil in the world outweighs honesty, even if mankind deserves, because of its sins, a kind of modern "flood," as did the generation of Noah.

Let us then appeal also to that kind of fatherly love revealed to us by Christ in His messianic mission, which reached its ultimate expression in His cross, in His death and in His resurrection! Let us appeal to God through Christ, mindful of the words of Mary's *Magnificat* which proclaims "mercy from age to age." Let us cry out for God's own mercy for this present generation! May the Church, which like Mary continues to be the spiritual mother of humankind, express in this prayer her total maternal concern, as well as that trusting love from which is born the most burning need for prayer.

Let us cry out, guided by that faith, hope and love that Christ grafted in our hearts. This cry for mercy is at the same time an expression of our love of God, from whom modern man has distanced himself and made of Him a stranger, proclaiming in various ways that he doesn't "need" God. This then is mercy, the *love of God* whose insult — rejection by modern man — we feel deeply and are ready to cry out with Christ on the cross, "Father, forgive them, for they do not know what they do" (Lk. 23:34 RSV).

This cry for mercy is at the same time *love for all of mankind*. Mercy is love for all peoples without exception or division: without difference of race, culture, language, or world-view, without distinction between friends and enemies. This cry for mercy is love for all people. Mercy desires every true good for each individual and for every human community, for every family, for every nation, for every social group, for youth, adults, parents, and for the elderly and the sick. It is love for everyone, without exception or division. This cry for mercy is love for all people, the care which ensures for everyone all true good, and removes and drives away every sort of evil.

And if any of our contemporaries do not share the faith and hope which bid me, as a servant of the mysteries of God (cf. 1 Cor. 1:1), to implore the mercy of God Himself for mankind in this hour of history, *then may they understand the reason for my concern. It is dictated by love* for mankind, for all that is human and which, according to the intuitions of many of our contemporaries, is threatened by an immense danger.

The same mystery of Christ, which reveals to us the great vocations of mankind, which obliged me to proclaim in the Encyclical *Redemptor Hominis* mankind's incomparable dignity, also obliges me to announce mercy as God's merciful love revealed in that same mystery of Christ. This mystery of Christ also obliges me to appeal to this mercy and implore this mercy on our difficult and critical times of the Church and of the world as we approach the end of the second millennium.

In the name of Jesus Christ crucified and risen from the dead, in the spirit of His messianic mission, which endures in the works of mankind, *we lift up our voice and plead*: that the love which is in the Father, may once again be revealed at this stage of history; and that, through the work of the Son and the Holy Spirit, this love which is in the Father, may be once again shown to be present in our modern world as more powerful than evil and more powerful than sin and death. We plead this through the intercession of Mary, who does not cease to proclaim "mercy from generation to generation," and also through the intercession of the saints in whom have been completely fulfilled the words of the Sermon on the Mount: "Blessed are the merciful, for they shall obtain mercy" (Mt. 5:7).

It is not permissible for the Church, for any reason, to withdraw into herself as she continues the great task of implementing the Second Vatican Council. In this implementing we can rightly see a new phase of the self-realization of the Church — in keeping with the age in which it has been our destiny to live. The reason for her existence is, in fact, to reveal God, that Father who allows us to "see" Himself in Christ (cf. Jn. 14:9). No matter how strong the resistance of human history may be, no matter how estranged the civilization of the world, no matter how great the denial of God in the human world, so much the greater must be our closeness to that mystery which, hidden for centuries in God, was then truly shared with man, in time, through Jesus Christ.

With my Apostolic Blessing.

Given in Rome, at St. Peter's, on the thirtieth day of November, the First Sunday of Advent, in the year 1980, the Third of my Pontificate.

Joannes Paulus PP.

Appendix A: Footnote for Section III "The Old Testament"

In describing mercy, the books of the Old Testament use two expressions in particular, each having a different semantic nuance. First there is the term *hesed*, which indicates a profound attitude of "goodness." When this is established between two individuals, they do not just wish each other well; they are also faithful to each other by virtue of an interior commitment, and therefore also *by virtue of a faithfulness to themselves*. Since *hesed* also means "grace" or "love," this occurs precisely on the basis of this fidelity. The fact that the commitment in question has not only a moral character but almost a juridical one makes no difference. When in the Old Testament the word *hesed* is used of the Lord, this always occurs in connection with the covenant that God established with Israel. This covenant was, on God's part, a gift and a grace for Israel. Nevertheless, since, in harmony with the covenant entered into, God has made a commitment to respect it, *hesed* also required in a certain sense a legal content. The juridical commitment on God's part ceased to oblige whenever Israel broke the covenant and did not respect its conditions. But precisely at this point, *hesed*, in ceasing to be a *juridical obligation*, revealed its deeper aspect: it showed itself as what it was at the beginning, that is, as love that gives, love more powerful than betrayal, grace stronger than sin.

This fidelity *vis-a-vis* the unfaithful "daughter of my people" (cf. Lam 4:3, 6) is, in brief, on God's part, *fidelity to Himself*. This becomes obvious in the frequent recurrence together of the two terms *hesed we' met* (= grace and fidelity), which could be considered a case of *hendiadys* (cf. e.g. Ex. 34:6; 2 Sm. 2:6; 15:20; Ps. 25 [24]:10; 40 [39]:11-12; 85 [84]:11; 138 [137]:2; Mi. 7:20). "It is not for your sake, O house of Israel, that I am about to act, but for the sake of my holy name" (Ez. 36:22). Therefore Israel, although burdened with guilt for having broken the covenant, cannot lay claim to God's *hesed* on the the basis of (legal) justice; yet it can and must go on hoping and trusting to obtain it, since the God of the Covenant is really "responsible for his love." The fruits of this love are forgiveness and restoration to grace, and the re-establishment of the interior covenant.

The *second word* which in the terminology of the Old Testament serves to define mercy is *rahamim*. This has a different nuance from that of *hesed*. While *hesed* highlights the marks of fidelity to self and of "responsibility for one's own love" (which are in a certain sense masculine characteristics), *rahamim, in its very root, denotes the love of a mother (rehem* = mother's womb). From the deep and original bond — indeed the unity — that links a mother to her child there springs a particular relationship to the child, a particular love. Of this love one can say that it is completely gratuitous, not merited, and that in this aspect it constitutes an interior necessity: an exigency of the heart. It is, as it were, a "feminine" variation of the masculine fidelity to self, expressed by *hesed*. Against this psychological background, *rahamim* generates a whole range of feelings, including goodness and tenderness, patience and understanding, that is, readiness to forgive.

The Old Testament attributes to the Lord precisely these characteristics, when it uses the term *rahamim* in speaking of Him. We read in Isaiah: "Can a woman forget her suckling child, that she should have no compassion on the son of her womb? *Even these may forget, yet I will not forget you*" (Is. 49:15). This love, faithful and invincible, thanks to the mysterious power of motherhood, is expressed in the Old Testament texts in various ways: as salvation from dangers, especially from enemies; also as forgiveness of sins — of individuals and also of the whole of Israel; and finally in readiness to fulfill the (eschatological) promise and hope, in spite of human infidelity, as we read in Hosea: "I will heal their faithlessness, I will love them freely" (Hos. 14:5).

In the terminology of the Old Testament we also find other expressions, referring in different ways to the same basic content. But the two terms mentioned above deserve special attention. They clearly show their *original anthropomorphic aspect*: in describing God's mercy, the biblical authors use terms that correspond to the consciousness and experience of their contemporaries. The Greek terminology in the Septuagint translation does not show as great a wealth as the Hebrew: therefore it does not offer all the semantic nuances proper to the original text. At any rate, the New Testament builds upon the wealth and depth that already marked the Old.

In this way, we have inherited from the Old Testament — as it were in a special synthesis — not only the wealth of expressions used by those books in order to define God's mercy, but also a specific and obviously anthropomorphic "psychology" of God: *the image of His anxious love*, which in contact with evil, and in particular with the sin of the individual and of the people, *is manifested as mercy*. This image is made up not only of the rather general content of the verb *hanan* but also of the content of *hesed* and *rahamim*. The term *hanan* expresses a wider concept: it means in fact the manifestation of grace, which involves, so to speak, a constant predisposition to be generous, benevolent and merciful.

In addition to these basic semantic elements, the Old Testament concept of mercy is also made up of what is included in the verb *hamal*, which literally means "to spare" (a defeated enemy) but also "to show mercy and compassion," and in consequence forgiveness and remission of guilt. There is also the term *hus*, which expresses pity and compassion, but especially in the affective sense. These terms appear more rarely in the biblical texts to denote mercy. In addition, one must note the word *'emet*, already mentioned: it means primarily "solidity, security" (in the Greek of the Septuagint: "truth") and then "fidelity," and in this way it seems to link up with the semantic content proper to the term *hesed*.

800. Summary of Recommended Spiritual Practices

For Second Degree and above members of the AFC

The habit of developing a prayer life takes time. Once committed to memory, most of the recommended prayers and practices can be worked into our daily, weekly, and monthly routines. The reflective recitation of written prayers (which takes about 7 minutes a day), however, should be just a part of our prayer life. You may want to use our audiotape on prayer (160-760A). It features our daily prayers and practical insights on prayer by Francis Cardinal Arinze, Bishop Fremiot Torres Oliver, and Sr. John Vianney. Ask about our prayer and meditation audio album on the daily themes stated in section 805 (160-761AK).

The Rosary can be a great opportunity for meditation. It should be used primarily as a means of meditating upon its Mysteries, Sacred Scripture, the virtues and gifts of the Holy Spirit, the words of the Our Father and Hail Mary prayers, or other dimensions of our Faith.

For rapid spiritual growth, make an appointment with God each day by setting aside one-half to one hour for quiet, reflective reading and mental prayer. Sometimes this quiet time can be spent by just remaining in God's presence while you thank Him for His Passion, goodness, and mercy.

To maintain a balanced perspective about the Church's gifts, try to include the daily themes specified in Section 805 during your mental prayer time with the Lord, His Mother, and His Heavenly Court.

Please don't "speed read" your spiritual books and prayers—just slowly read until the Holy Spirit moves you to pause and reflect on a certain Truth. Don't worry about completing your readings, but let them serve as a springboard into meditation.

In order to better understand The Apostolate's spirituality, frequently read sections 42a and 77 (FCPB-DM).

A Note of Caution

Once we have developed the habit of working prayer and quiet reflective reading time into our daily lives (adjusting our schedules to accommodate it), we should not become anxious when duties of state may prohibit completing some of our spiritual practices. We try to integrate these practices into our lives in a fluid, non-coercive way. When changes in our day-to-day activities occur, we should avoid losing our peace if we are unable to complete all of our spiritual exercises. God is our All. It is never His Will that we strain ourselves to the point of losing interior peace in order to follow our schedule of spiritual practices. We should, however, still make an appointment with God for our daily prayer time and strive to keep that appointment even more than we would do with other very important people.

Key Scriptures for Reflection on a Consecrated Way of Life

Consecration: Jn. 1:12, 8:35 [Our Lord describes consecration in Jn. 17]; 2 Cor. 4:7-10; Gal. 4:1-7; 2 Tim. 2:21.

Christ's definition of consecration and formula for protecting our families: John 17:3, 4, 6, 15, 17, & 22: *"And eternal life is this: to know You...I have glorified You on earth and finished the work that You gave Me to do...I have made Your name known...I am not asking You to remove them from the world, but to protect them from the evil one...Consecrate them in the truth ...that they may be one as We are one."*

What we should do: 1 Timothy 4:13, 16: *"Make use of the time until I arrive by reading to the people, preaching and teaching...Take great care about what you do and what you teach...in this way you will save both yourself and those who listen to you."*

Work: Eph. 6:7: *"Work hard and willingly, but do it for the sake of the Lord and not for the sake of men."* Also see 1 Cor. 15:58, 16:15; 2 Tim. 4:5.

Gratitude: Deut. 8:10; Ps. 100:4, 107:22; Col. 1:12, 3:15-16; 1 Thes. 5:18.

Suffering: Rm. 5:3-5; 1 Cor. 1:18-19, 10:13; 2 Cor. 4:7-10, 17-18, 6:4-10; Heb. 12:6-7, 5:10-111; 1 Peter 5:10-11; and 1 Pet. 4:1-2: *"Think of what Christ suffered in this life, and then arm yourselves with the same resolution that He had: anyone who in this life has bodily suffering has broken with sin, because for the rest of his life on earth he is not ruled by human passions but only by the will of God."*

Prayer: Ps. 65:2; Prov. 15:29; 1 Chron. 16:11; Mt. 7:7, 21:22, 26:41; Mk. 9:29; Lk. 6:12, 18:1; Jn. 15:7, 16:24, 17:15; Acts 6:4; Rm. 12:12; Eph. 6:18; Col. 4:2; 1 Thes. 5:17; Jas. 5:13, 1 Pet. 3:12.

Joy: Mt. 2:10-11; Lk. 15:5; Jn. 15:11, 17:13; Acts 5:41; Phil. 4:4-9; 1 Thes. 5:16; 1 Pet. 1:8.

Unity: Lk. 11:17, 22:26; Jn. 17:21-22; Rm. 12:5; 1 Cor. 1:10, 10:17; 2 Cor. 13:11; Eph. 4:3; Phil. 1:27; 1 Thes. 5:12-18; Heb. 13:17; 1 Pet.3:8, 5:3-5.

Confidence in God's Grace: When you feel helpless in your trials, reflect on St. Paul's Second Letter to the Corinthians, 12:9-10: *"But He has said, 'My grace is enough for you: My power is at its best in weakness.' So I shall be very happy to make my weaknesses my special boast so that the power of Christ may stay over me, and that is why I am quite content with my weaknesses, and with insults, hardships, persecutions, and the agonies I go through for Christ's sake. For it is when I am weak that I am strong."*

805. Recommended Daily Practices

Daily attendance at Mass (FCPB #29b) is suggested (if the responsibilities of your state in life permit, see section #77), followed by prayer #4 (FCPB). Try to pray the following daily prayers: #'s 2a, 2b, 2d, 2e, 2f, 2g, & 2h (FCPB); and to recite the [family] Rosary (FCPB #6a-9), part of #10 (FCPB), and the "Chaplet of Divine Mercy" (FCPB #20f) when possible. Try to pray the "Angelus" (FCPB #2c) three times a day (possibly at meals along with prayers 34a and 34b). Try to read or listen to tapes on Sacred Scripture each day, preferably while praying the Rosary; and read or listen to tapes on consecration, preferably from the works of St. Louis de Montfort, St. Maximilian Kolbe, or Pope John Paul II. Draw closer to Jesus through frequent Acts of Spiritual Communion (FCPB #11a).

Try to listen to spiritual audiotapes in the morning and during other times, such as when traveling or cleaning. As you go about your activities, dialogue with members of the Holy Family and your Guardian Angel often; for that is what prayer really is—a dialogue with God and His heavenly court.

Write out a "key card" containing the virtue and Scripture verse which will help you overcome your primary fault. Examine your conscience at least once a day using your "key card" and try to reflect on part of First Corinthians 13 (FCPB #2i). During your morning and evening prayer time and other times of the day, visualize yourself practicing the virtues that are the exact opposite of your faults. (See sections 53b and 53L.)

FCPB = All Family Consecration Prayer & Meditation Books
FCPB-DM = Divine Mercy Edition
FCPB-MC = Marian Consecration Edition
FCPB-JS = St. Joseph & the Communion of Saints Edition
FCCI = Family Consecration Classics I Edition

A spiritual guide who understands the teachings of Vatican II and Pope John Paul II on the role of the laity and who understands the AFC's spirituality should assist you in selecting your daily meditative spiritual reading, which normally includes the Peace of Heart Forum book used in your Lay Ecclesial Team formation sessions. Choose from the following recommendations:

- daily Mass reading reflections from the *In Conversation with God* series

- the Apostolate's *Family Consecration Prayer & Meditation Books*

- AFC Covenants

- *Abandonment to Divine Providence*, by Fr. Jean-Pierre de Caussade

- spiritual works by Blessed Josemarie Escriva, Pope John Paul II, or AFC founder, Jerome Coniker

- choose spiritual works and prayers from the following daily themes to help you focus your prayers and thoughts, but don't try to read everything at once. Always leave time for quiet mental prayer.

Sundays: Pray for the Holy Father, the Pope; bishops; priests; and all consecrated celibates. Thank the Holy Trinity for blessings received, and ask for the grace to do God's Will. Reflect on the meaning of the Resurrection of Jesus from the dead. Try to read part of Pope Paul VI's proclamation on the Apostles' Creed (FCPB-DM #70) or pray part of #34 (FCPB) or #21 (FCPB) or read from the Pope's newspaper *L'Osservatore Romano*.

Mondays: Pray to the Holy Spirit for the gifts of charity, apostolic zeal, and wisdom. Particularly pray for the Poor Souls in Purgatory and invoke them to intercede for the work of the Apostolate for Family Consecration. Reflect on eternity: Heaven, hell and Purgatory. Try to read part of Pope John Paul II's encyclical on the Holy Spirit (FCCI #101), part of #45 (FCPB-JS) or 45a (FCPB), or part of #46 (FCPB). Apostolate chaplains are asked to offer the votive Mass of the Holy Spirit or one for deceased relatives, friends, and benefactors of The Apostolate, if the liturgical calendar permits.

Tuesdays: Pray to and invoke the angels and saints to intercede for all families and members of The Apostolate and for their work. If possible, read from Pope John Paul II's teaching on the angels (FCPB-JS #36) or recite #40 (FCPB). Apostolate chaplains are asked to offer the votive Mass of the Angels or Saints or for vocations in the AFC, if the liturgical calendar permits.

Wednesdays: Honor St. Joseph. Ask St. Joseph to protect The Apostolate, to help you keep your commitments, and to protect and inspire couples to draw on the graces of the Sacrament of Matrimony. We ask members to read part of Pope John Paul II's Apostolic Letter on St. Joseph (FCPB-JS #66) or *Familiaris Consortio* (FCCI #109) or pray #14 (FCPB), and to replace the Rosary with the "Seven Sorrows and Joys of St. Joseph Chaplet" (FCPB #14a). Apostolate chaplains are asked to offer the votive Mass in honor of St. Joseph, if the liturgical calendar permits.

Thursdays: Pray for an increased devotion to the Holy Eucharist, and call down the Precious Blood of Jesus upon the work, families, and members of The Apostolate and upon the deceased members of your family. We recommend that you try to read part of Pope John Paul II's letter on the Eucharist (FCPB-DM #69) and pray #11a (FCPB). Apostolate chaplains are asked to offer the votive Mass of the Holy Eucharist; the Precious Blood; or Jesus Christ, Eternal High Priest, if the liturgical calendar permits.

Fridays: Make reparation to the Sacred Heart of Jesus, and pray for the intentions at the foot of the altars in the AFC centers and for increased First Friday devotions. We encourage people to pray the "Mercy of God, Way of the Cross" (FCPB #59) on First Fridays and all Fridays of Lent. Try to pray #22 (FCPB) or part of Pope John Paul II's encyclical on Divine Mercy (FCPB-DM #102). Apostolate chaplains are asked to offer the votive Mass of the Sacred Heart or of the Divine Mercy, if the liturgical calendar permits.

Saturdays: Honor Our Lady, and pray for increased devotion to her Immaculate Heart and the spreading of the daily family Rosary, consecration, and First Saturday Communion of Reparation devotions. Try to read something about Our Lady, particularly from Pope John Paul II's encyclical *Mother of the Redeemer* (FCPB–MC #104), one of St. Louis de Montfort's works (FCPB #49; FCPB-MC #48, 50, or 67), the prayer by St. Maximilian Kolbe (FCPB #50b), or prayer #2 (FCPB). Apostolate chaplains are asked to offer a votive Mass in honor of one of Mary's titles if the liturgical calendar permits. Note: See First Saturday Reparation Promise (FCPB-MC #33).

Occasionally reflect on part of Pope Paul VI's January 1, 1967, statement on reparation (FCPB #42) and FCPB-DM #42a, and the 17th chapter of St. John's Gospel (FCPB-DM #50f). Daily live the norms for indulgences; ask Our Lady to apply your indulgences to the Poor Souls of your loved ones and others in Purgatory (FCPB-DM #45a).

806. Weekly Practices
*For Second & Third Degree and Life Members
of Lay Ecclesial Teams*

– weekly attendance at Lay Ecclesial Team meetings, with formation, spiritual insight sharing, evangelization strategy, and reports

– weekly attendance at a *Be Not Afraid Family Hour*® or other Apostolate Ecclesial Team outreaches

– weekly Ecclesial Team evangelization work assignment of at least two hours

807. Recommended Monthly Practices

For Second & Third Degree and Life Members

– confession twice a month when possible

– meditate on and live the virtue and Scripture of the month.

St. Alphonsus suggests to focus on the following virtues for each month, which the AFC has adopted:

Jan:	Mortification	July:	Love of God
Feb:	Recollection	Aug:	Love of Neighbor
Mar:	Deepening Prayer Life	Sept:	Poverty
Apr:	Self-Denial	Oct:	Chastity
May:	Faith	Nov:	Obedience
June:	Hope	Dec.	Humility

– First Fridays: Mass and Stations of the Cross (FCPB #59) if possible

– First Saturdays: Mass, *First Saturday Cenacles* on video (see pages 582 and 583), and, if possible, a morning of recollection on Divine Mercy, Mary, St. Joseph, or Pope John Paul II's teachings. Try to renew your consecration with prayer #49.

808. Yearly Practices/Events/Retreats

For Second & Third Degree and Life Members

– renewal of St. Louis de Montfort's Marian consecration, February 20–March 25 (FCPB-MC #51)

AFC members strive to attend two or three of the following events each year:

– weekend silent retreats for all Second Degree and above Disciple and Apostle members (required) and seven-day retreat for all Catholic Corps, Mystical Rose, and Tower of David members

– Evangelization & Catechetical Training Retreats and

Marriage Get-away Weekends

– Holy Family Fests

– Totus Tuus "Consecrate Them in Truth" Family Conferences

850. Degrees of AFC Membership

First Degree members are fully practicing Catholics who commit at least 5 hours each week to apostolic formation and service in a Lay Ecclesial Team or at an AFC center. First Degree members follow the policies and procedures regarding the use of AFC outreach programs. They may, however, be living a spirituality/commitment to other Church-approved associations distinct from the AFC and are not required to fulfill the AFC's daily prayers and spiritual practices.

Second Degree members are fully practicing Catholics who embrace the AFC spirituality and commit to all of its spiritual practices. Apostolic formation and service in a Lay Ecclesial Team or at an AFC center becomes their primary endeavor outside of family and career responsibilities. Second Degree members follow the AFC's policies and procedures and their respective membership covenant and renew their commitment every six months for a minimum of three years.

Third Degree members have fulfilled all of the requirements of Second Degree membership for at least three years and renew their commitments every year for a minimum of five years before the AFC considers confirming their commitment as **Life members**.

851. Types of AFC Membership

Sacri-State members: Anyone can become a Sacri-State member by offering his/her prayers (Oblate Sacri-State) and/or physical suffering (Suffering Sacri-State) for a particular active member or couple, or for the general work and mission of the AFC. Priests can be Oblate Sacri-state members by offering their available Masses for the AFC's work and mission.

Sacri-State members strive to daily pray the Family Apostolate's Morning Offering (#2a).

Disciple members: Those of any degree who have made a commitment to assist the Lay Ecclesial Teams or AFC centers on a voluntary basis for a minimum of four hours per week and who attend a weekly *Be Not Afraid Family Hour* or other Lay Ecclesial Team or AFC center outreach program.

Apostle members: Those of any degree who are married or are open to marriage and who devote themselves to full-time work in the AFC.

Catholic Corps members: Second & Third Degree and Life members who make apostolic celibate commitments and devote themselves to full-time work in the AFC. Some Catholic Corps men have been ordained priests and assigned by their Bishop for life-time service as chaplains for the AFC.

Mystical Rose members: Second & Third Degree and Life members who are widows and are self-supporting and who make a celibate commitment while devoting themselves to full-time work in the AFC.

Tower of David members: Second & Third Degree and Life members who are widowers and are self-supporting and who make a celibate commitment while devoting themselves to full-time work in the AFC.

Cooperator members are those of any faith who watch or listen to the AFC's television or radio programs, benefit from the various multi-media AFC resources, or have attended AFC functions. Cooperators may also occasionally volunteer their apostolic services or financially support the work of the AFC.

534

*Please be loyal to the following benefactors of the
Apostolate for Family Consecration.*

535

SHARP & FELLOWS, INC.
SINCE 1877

**POPULAR CHILDREN'S TRAIN RIDE IDEAL FOR MALLS,
SPECIAL EVENTS, AMUSEMENT FLEA MARKETS, AND
MORE!! IT'S A ONE PERSON BUSINESS.**

DESCRIPTION:

COMPLETE TRAINS AVAILABLE!
ELECTRIC 24 VOLT
TRAIN LOCOMOTIVE PLUS CAR BODIES
CAR BODIES ARE PLASTIC
CAR BODIES COLORS ARE RED, YELLOW, AND GREEN
TRACK AVAILABLE IN A VARIETY OF LENGTHS
MAXIMUM WEIGHT PER CAR IS 400 LB (6 CHILDREN)
MAXIMUM SAFE OPERATING SPEED IS 4 MPH
EASY MAINTENANCE
EASY ASSEMBLY
EASY TO OPERATE
COMPLETE WITH OPERATING MANUAL

INFORMATION:

SOME TRAINS ARE STILL ON LOCATION AND OPERATING
LENDER'S LIQUIDATION SALE
UNITS FOR SALE OR LEASE — FINANCING AVAILABLE
FOR MORE INFORMATION,
PLEASE CALL 1-800-486-2500 AND ASK FOR MIKE

**P.O. Box 603660, Cleveland, OH 44103
PHONE: (216) 870-2700 • FAX: (216) 881-0999**

*The eyes of the Lord are upon those who love Him, a mighty protection
and strong support...He lifts up the soul and gives light to the eyes; He
grants healing, life, and blessing. (Sir. 34:16-17)*

538

Wisdom will praise herself, and will glory in the midst of her people (Sir. 24:1). So now sing praise with all your heart and voice, and bless the name of the Lord (Sir. 39:35).

The Apostolate for Family Consecration
Families Building the Civilization of Love

in the Spirit of Pope John Paul II

The Apostolate for Family Consecration (AFC) was founded by Jerry and Gwen Coniker, parents of 13 and grandparents of 35. An international association of Christ's faithful, The Family Apostolate was officially approved by the Church in the Holy Year of 1975. Its John Paul II Holy Family Center, known as Catholic Familyland, is located on 950 acres in rural Bloomingdale, Ohio, an hour's ride from Pittsburgh. The AFC also has a major center in Manila, Philippines.

The Family Apostolate is called to an extraordinary mission — to help families get to Heaven, and to show them how to bring as many souls as possible with them! Its motto is, "All for the Sacred and Eucharistic Heart of Jesus, all through the Sorrowful & Immaculate Heart of Mary, all in union with St. Joseph."

In our day, the "culture of death" seeks to dismantle Christian family life through sin and deception — contraception, abortion, euthanasia, violence, sexual immorality, infidelity, divorce, substance abuse, faithlessness, despair, suicide, and so many other evils. The AFC is an **"apostolate of hope,"** responding to the challenge of helping families to build the "civilization of love and life" envisioned by Pope John Paul II, consecrating them to Jesus, through Mary, in TRUTH and grace.

The AFC seeks to help transform families, neighborhoods, schools, and parishes into evangelizing communities, consecrating them in the truths of the Catholic faith, and nourishing them with the timeless, Eucharistic, Marian, and family-centered spirituality of Pope John Paul II.

To accomplish this end, the AFC creatively uses tri-media communication resources (videos, audios, books), which feature many of the most outstanding teachers of the Faith today. Complete evangelization and catechetical systems are produced which are designed for effective use in homes, schools, parishes, or by any spiritual organization.

The AFC does not treat symptoms of family breakdown but applies lasting **remedies** to the underlying spiritual causes—sin and ignorance of God's loving designs. The remedies are the grace of Jesus and consecration to His Truth (cf. Jn. 17), by way of His Mother's Immaculate Heart, as she requested at Fatima. Mary most perfectly leads us to Jesus, and St. Joseph protects us along the way.

The AFC offers concrete apostolic techniques, tactics, and training for cooperative efforts in evangelization and catechesis, plus an array of support ministries. These include radio & television programs, weekend conferences, assorted retreats, and an evangelization and catechetical training institute, all aimed at producing the following spiritual fruits (T-R-U-T-H):

Tapping more fully the treasure of grace made available in the Sacraments, particularly the Eucharist, Penance, Matrimony, and Baptism — teaching St. Louis de Montfort's formula for faithfully living out our baptismal consecration to Jesus, through Mary;

Repairing more heroically for sin and the widespread ignorance of God by responsibly and fervently fulfilling the Church's **mandate** to know our Faith (catechesis) and to share it with others (evangelization);

Uniting the family with God and one another, the family with the parish, parents with teachers, and families with neighbors — building the "civilization of love;"

Teaching the Faith in a systematic, "fail-safe" way by means of continuous, in-depth, easy-to-use, modern communication resources. This relieves much of the burden for the average lay person, catechist, or busy pastor to present with theological precision the fullness of Catholic truth, through audio and video;

Helping to reinforce families and awaken the sleeping giant of the Catholic laity by strengthening families and fostering neighborhood support groups (called Lay Ecclesial Teams, see pages 634–635) focused on the Truth and centered on the Eucharist, Mary, and the Papacy.

Through its tri-media evangelization resources and systems, the AFC seeks to build the "civilization of love" as envisioned by Pope John Paul II. (p. 555)

Overview of the Family Apostolate's Ministries

Tri-Media Communication Resources:
Catechetical & Evangelization Systems
to Consecrate Families and Parishes in the Truth

Founded in 1975

Activities at Catholic Familyland®

Totus Tuus Family Conferences™

The Totus Tuus "Consecrate Them in Truth" Family
Fest Conferences will enable families and individuals to continually experience the rich teachings of
Cardinals, Bishops, Roman Curia members, and
other great leaders in the Church. These all present
the vibrant spirituality and priorities of Pope John
Paul II, as we enter the Third Millennium. These conferences educate, motivate, and inspire families to be
families for others. During these conferences, workshops are held which teach how to use The
Apostolate's Vatican-approved tri-media resources.
Dioceses and spiritual associations are encouraged
to send their leaders to attend the conferences and
workshops.

Holy Family Fests

The seven-day Holy Family Fests enable families to
experience Catholic community life at "Catholic
Familyland." Families pray, work, and play together
in an atmosphere which promotes healthy family

values. The Family Fests help to unite families with God and one another and inspire families to go back and evangelize and catechize their parishes and neighborhoods.

Marriage Get-Away Weekends

Marriage Get-Away weekends are centered around the Sacraments of Reconciliation and the Holy Eucharist—a special time to learn the Church's teachings on the powerful Sacrament of Matrimony, and a time to enrich and renew one's marriage.

Lay Ecclesial Team Evangelization System™

The *Lay Ecclesial Team Evangelization System* offers the laity a practical structure to nourish family life through the Catholic faith. It enables parents and youth within the parish and neighborhood community (and in many cases, other spiritual associations), to take part in a coordinated evangelization and catechetical program which uses fail-safe, approved tri-media resources on a continuing basis. This system simultaneously renews family, neighborhood, and parish life. (See pages 634–635.)

Evangelization & Catechetical Training Institute

The Evangelization and Catechetical Training Institute is another outreach of the Apostolate for Family Consecration. It teaches the *Family Wisdom Curriculum* system to parents, teachers, and administrators, and also teaches The Apostolate's *Lay Ecclesial Team Evangelization System* to qualified couples and associations. (See pages 555 and 632–635.)

Communication Resources/Systems

The Apostolate's video library of exclusive productions contains more than 13,500 programs, speeches, and contemporary talk shows on the Catholic faith. These programs focus on Sacred Scripture, magisterial documents, lives of the saints, spiritual classics, and the spirituality and documents of Pope John Paul II. Over 400 leading Church authorities and teachers are featured on the programs. This priceless collection of video classics makes the following ministries possible. (See pages 571–572 and 637–640.)

Family Wisdom Curriculum™

A lifetime learning system for families and parishes utilizing the AFC's tri-media resources (video, audio, and written word) to draw families more deeply into Scripture, the *Catechism of the Catholic Church, Veritatis Splendor*, and Vatican II teachings on the Faith. The *Be Not Afraid Family Hours* represent the VIDEO dimension of the *Family Wisdom Curriculum*. (See pages 546–579 and 614–621.)

Be Not Afraid Family Hours® on video are weekly formation in the Truth for families. These programs are normally conducted in homes first, with the ultimate goal of being run in the parish church on a weekly basis. (See pages 564–579.)

Day of Grace Divine Mercy Sunday Parish Mission™ prepares people for celebrating Mercy Sunday (the first Sunday after Easter), while introducing or revitalizing the weekly *Be Not Afraid Family Hours* in a parish. This program may also be used as a continuing formation program throughout the year. (See pages 584–586.)

First Saturday Cenacles™ honor Our Lady of Fatima's requests for a Communion of Reparation and a meditative Rosary on the First Saturday of each month. Besides the First Saturday video, the day may include presentations on the Rosary, Divine Mercy, or the Holy Family, using approved resources. (See pages 582–583.)

Peace of Heart Forums® utilize videos and books to draw families together for weekly discussions on a particular spiritual topic. These programs introduce adults to daily, meditative reading and build spiritual friendships and spiritual support groups based on learning and sharing the truths of the Catholic Church. They also can be very helpful for hurting and broken families. (See pages 588–613.)

International TV & Radio Ministry

The following programs are broadcast on satellite in North, South, & Central America; Europe; Africa; and Asia (presently reaching over 50 million homes in the USA alone).

- Family Covenant™
- Spirit of John Paul II™
- Be Not Afraid Family Hours®
- First Saturday Cenacles™
- Healing Our Families™
- Family Rosary

Plus Vatican radio broadcasts our programs with Roman Curia Cardinal Francis Arinze.

The Apostolate's Family Catechism™

by Father Lawrence G. Lovasik, S.V.D.

Building Bridges with the Family Catechism!

in the words of Cardinal Sin

✔ **Doctrinal Bridge** – It acts as a doctrinal bridge by which ordinary men, women, and children in homes, communities, and parishes can gradually understand the papally promulgated *Catechism of the Catholic Church*. With its biblical references and quotations from the Second Vatican Council, it allows us to see the link between the Bible, Tradition, and the Magisterium.

✔ **Generational Bridge** – It serves as a bridge between generations because it is readable and accessible to both old and young persons. Its more than 600 pictures makes it attractive to children who are still learning to read.

(Ask about our 7-volume set with over 3000 pictures.)

✔ **Spiritual Bridge** – Finally, it is a spiritual bridge, since it merges doctrine and piety, by addressing not only the head, but, even more so, the heart, through the hundreds of short prayers sown generously in its pages.

Cardinal Ratzinger Endorses The Apostolate's Family Catechism

COMMISSIONE INTERDICASTERIALE
PER IL
CATECHISMO DELLA CHIESA CATTOLICA

l Presidente

Prot. N. ....XII/91 C....

(Si prega citare il numero nella risposta)

00193 Roma   March 4, 1994
Piazza del S. Uffizio. 11

Dear Mr. Coniker:

Thank you for your courtesy in sending a copy of <u>The Apostolate's Family Catechism</u> published by the Apostolate for Family Consecration. The work's publication in this year of the family could not be more timely. It anticipates many of the themes of His Holiness Pope John Paul's Letter to Families of February 2, 1994. The cross-references provided to the <u>Catechism of the Catholic Church</u> will make it an especially helpful instrument to parents and teachers.

With prayerful best wishes for the success of your vital apostolate, I remain

Sincerely yours in Christ,

Joseph Cardinal Ratzinger

Cardinal Trujillo Endorses the Family Catechism

Prot. N. 206/96

Vatican City State
September 17, 1997

Dear Mr. Coniker,

The Apostolate's Family Catechism is an impressive and beautifully presented work. The systematic method, the art, the cross references leading into the *Catechism of the Catholic Church*, all assist the family to become the first school of faith and the virtues. As the Holy Father has pointed out: "Family catechesis precedes, accompanies and enriches all other forms of catechetics". (Catechesi Tradendae, 68).

However, this Catechism is not simply an instrument for the formation in faith of the children. It can become the key to a deepening of the faith of all members of the family. Through the use of this Catechism and the media resources provided by the Apostolate, families may be equipped for their special mission of evangelization that has been proclaimed by the Holy Father Pope John Paul II.

This significant project is surely to be commended.

With every prayerful wish for your work, I remain

Sincerely yours in Christ

A. card. López Trujillo

Alfonso Cardinal López Trujillo
President
Pontifical Council for the Family

The Apostolate's Family Catechism is...

... a living catechism

The *Apostolate's Family Catechism* is a living catechism because it grows by means of the cross-references and the Family Wisdom supplements (catechetical handbooks, teacher's guides, student workbooks, coloring books, flash cards, audiotapes, and more) which are continually being produced to be used in conjunction with it.

... a lifetime catechism

The *Apostolate's Family Catechism* is a lifetime catechism because one set of books will teach all ages. Students can use the same book from first through twelfth grade because the *Teacher's Guides* and *Student Workbooks* systematically draw each grade level more deeply into the subject matter through the cross-referenced resources and texts as the catechism is taught and reviewed each year.

Parents can easily facilitate their children's catechetical study, no matter how many children there are, because of the common textbook. Also, they can easily teach the various grade levels to their children by utilizing the accompanying *Parent's Handbook, Student Workbooks, and Teacher's Guides* for each of the 12 levels. This Catechism can be passed on from generation to generation.

... a teaching tool for parents

The *Apostolate's Family Catechism* enables parents to fulfill their responsibility to be the primary teachers of the Faith to their children. Because of the grace of state in their lives, the Holy Spirit will work through parents in a more powerful way and make up for any lack of professional teaching skills. Pope John Paul II tells us to "Be Not Afraid!"

550

A Over 600 vibrant pictures in the 2-volume set and 3000 pictures in the 7-volume set

B 304 penetrating questions and answers

C Scripture and Vatican Council II texts for the majority of the 304 questions

D Cross-references with the *Catechism of the Catholic Church* and *Veritatis Splendor*

B

Chapter Twenty-Five
Jesus is God — II

Q. 77. Did Jesus say He was God?

Yes, Jesus said He was God. For instance, He said to the Jews: "I and the Father are one" (John 10:30).

"If God were your Father, you would indeed love Me. For from God I proceeded and came. For I came not of Myself, but He sent Me ... And you have not known Him, but I know Him. And if I shall say that I know Him not, I shall be like to you a liar. But I do know Him and do keep His word ... Amen, amen I say to you, before Abraham was made, I Am [i.e. the eternal present]" (John 8:42, 55, 58).

Men come to believe in God because He shows something of Himself to them. Catholics believe in what the Catholic Church teaches about Christ because they have the supernatural gift of Faith. Thus, God the Son revealed Himself in what He said and did, how He lived with others, and by what He revealed of His thoughts and feelings. He revealed more of Himself than we can fully understand. Nevertheless, through faith and the virtue of love, we can understand a great deal about Him.

Jesus is the center of our Catholic faith. Everything that He said and did is important, because in Him we find God our Father and come to believe in Him, Jesus is our Way, our Truth, and our Life (cf. John 14:6).

Sacred Scripture
"And the Word was made flesh and dwelt among us." John 1:14 **C**

Vatican Council II
"The eternal Father, in accordance with the utterly gratuitous

D

See Papally-Promulgated
Catechism of the Catholic Church
Q. 77. See paragraphs: 589-590
See encyclical **Veritatis Splendor**
Q. 77. See sections 2, 21

E Summary prayers at the end of each of the 147 chapters, and at the end of most of the 304 questions and answers

F Family Wisdom Library cross-references for each question opens up a world of truth for your family

includes the complete texts of *Humanae Vitae* and *Veritatis Splendor*.

552

Chapter Summary Prayer

Jesus, in You, the Father has renewed all things and has given us all a share in Your riches. Though Your nature was divine, You stripped Yourself of all glory, and by shedding Your Blood on the Cross, You brought Your peace to the world. Therefore, You are exalted above all creation and have become the source of eternal life to all who serve You. With all the choirs of angels in heaven, we proclaim Your glory and profess our faith in You as Peter did when he said: "You are Christ, the Son of the living God!" (Matthew 16:16). All glory and honor be to You, to the Father, and to the Holy Spirit. Amen.

Family Wisdom Library
Cross-References

Q. 97. What effects did the Passion of Jesus have?

Catechisms/Theology Books

The Teaching of Christ [Second Edition], Lawler, Wuerl, and Lawler, p. 132;
The Catholic Catechism, Hardon, pp. 431-432;
Fundamentals of Catholicism, Baker, Vol. 2, pp. 292-295, 298-301;
Faith for Today, Hogan and LeVoir, pp. 82, 100, 228-229.

Philosophy Books

Transformation in Christ, von Hildebrand, pp. 232-233

Papal Documents

Guardian of the Redeemer, John Paul II, sect 8;
On Reconciliation and Penance, John Paul II, sect. 8;
On the Christian Meaning of Human Suffering, John Paul II, sect. 15;
On the Holy Spirit in the Life of the Church and the World, John Paul II, sect. 30-32, 39-42;
Redeemer of Man, John Paul II, sect. 9, 18.

The Apostolate's Family Catechism is Vatican-Approved!

His Holiness, Pope John Paul II, wrote:

"The faith-filled witness of Christian families is an essential element in the new evangelization to which the Holy Spirit is calling the Church in our time… 'family catechesis precedes, accompanies, and enriches all other forms of catechesis' *(Catechesi Tradendae, 68)*. **I encourage the Apostolate for Family Consecration in its efforts to promote an effective catechesis in homes and parishes.**"

Mario Luigi Cardinal Ciappi,

Pro-Theologian *Emeritus* for Pope Pius XII, Pope John XXIII, Pope Paul VI, Pope John Paul I, and Pope John Paul II, wrote:

"…your family catechism will make it extremely easy for parents and teachers to confidently teach their children and students the Faith, and have easy access to the new *Catechism of the Catholic Church*…

"I am happy to approve the edited and cross-referenced version of *The Apostolate's Family Catechism* and highly recommend it to families and schools as a sure source for authentic Catholic doctrine."

Edouard Cardinal Gagnon,

while President of the Pontifical Council for the Family, wrote:

"It is with great pleasure that I recommend *The Apostolate's Family Catechism*, which is further enhanced by videotaped cassettes for adults and for children. (Also see page 548.)

"Therefore, I would particularly encourage the use of *The Apostolate's Family Catechism* by parents as a helpful means for fulfilling their solemn duty to impart adequate knowledge of the faith to their children and to prepare them properly for receiving the sacraments."

Silvio Cardinal Oddi,

while Prefect of the Sacred Congregation of the Clergy (which has direct responsibility for the teaching of catechetics throughout the world) wrote:

"I am sure that a great tool in this apostolate is the special catechism written by Rev. Lawrence G. Lovasik, S.V.D., approved by the Rev. John A. Hardon, S.J., and with the imprimatur of the Rev. Msgr. John F. Donoghue, Vicar General of the Archdiocese of Washington, D.C.

"We are happy to notice that *The Apostolate's Family Catechism* gives the parents a complete tool to fulfill their obligations as being primary teachers of the Faith to their children, and, at the same time, gives the parents a good refresher course in their Faith."

William Cardinal Baum,

one of the three Roman Curia Cardinals on the Commission for the *Catechism of the Catholic Church*, wrote:

"We believe that *The Apostolate's Family Catechism*, with which the Catechism for the Universal Church will be cross-referenced, will truly be a break through for family formation and for parents, who indeed are the primary educators of their children. This integrated program of teaching the catechism in the home, and then gathering together once a week with other families to hear Cardinal Arinze and others teach on your 'Be Not Afraid' Holy Hours in churches, can be very effective in rebuilding both the domestic church and the parish community."

Family Wisdom Supplements
for Teaching the Apostolate's
Family Catechism

Unites the family with the school!

Administrator's Handbook

The *Administrator's Handbook* includes an overview of the
program and guidelines for parents, faculty, and students
and a description of the materials used. This handbook
also includes tips for organization, achieving goals, and
recommended grading guidelines. From an administrator's perspective, this handbook includes comprehensive
sections pertaining to parents, teachers and students. The
parent section covers topics such as parental participation,
sacramental preparation, and formation available to them.
The faculty section covers spiritual and catechetical forma-

tion, faculty workshops, and teacher evaluations. The student section includes evaluations and topics such as respect and reverence, liturgical life, and discipline. (Resource #380-70)

Teacher's Handbook

The *Teacher's Handbook* includes an overview of the materials and methods used in the classroom. Also included are suggestions on motivation, memorization, understanding, respect, reverence, discipline, prayer, and organization. (Resource #380-69)

Parent's Handbook

The *Parent's Handbook* includes an overview of the discipline, prayer, and materials and program methods which are described in the Administrator's and Teacher's Handbooks. It includes thought provokers for family discussions on each of the topics in the Family Catechism. (Resource #380-71)

Teacher's Guides for Levels 1-12

The *Teacher's Guides* include lesson plans for each of the twelve levels. They are uniquely written and designed to be used with *The Apostolate's Family Catechism* and with the catechism videos featuring Francis Cardinal Arinze for levels 5-8 , and Sister John Vianney for levels 1-4. Levels 1-4 also incorporate the *Life of the Holy Family* audio album. Each year students go more deeply into the 147 chapters of the Vatican-approved *Apostolate's Family Catechism*.

Level 9 reviews the Gospel of St. Mark. It also incorporates Cardinal Francis Arinze's formation videos on the following books and topics: Pope John Paul II's encyclical, *The Splendor of Truth*; and the Sacraments of Penance, Holy Eucharist, Confirmation, and Matrimony as found in the *Catechism of the Catholic Church*.

Level 10 reviews the Gospel of St. Matthew. It also incorporates Cardinal Francis Arinze's formation videos on the following books and topics: Pope John Paul II's encyclical, *Gospel of Life*; and the Sacraments of Matrimony and Holy Orders as found in the *Catechism of the Catholic Church* .

Level 11 reviews the Gospel of St. Luke using the commentaries of Bishop John Magee (former Papal Secretary); Pope John Paul II's letter, *To the Youth of the World*; the *Catechism of the Catholic Church*; and Fr. Peter Lappin's books and videos on the lives of St. John Bosco (*Give Me Souls)* and St. Dominic Savio *(Dominic Savio: Teenage Saint)*.

Level 12 reviews the Gospel of St. John and the following books and videos: *Art of Living*, by Dr. Alice von Hildebrand; *What Does God Want?*, by Fr. Michael Scanlan T.O.R.; and *Purgation & Purgatory*, by St. Catherine of Genoa.

Please specify the item number below when ordering.

Level 1, 380-57	Level 7, 380-63
Level 2, 380-58	Level 8, 380-64
Level 3, 380-59	Level 9, 380-65
Level 4, 380-60	Level 10, 380-66
Level 5, 380-61	Level 11, 380-67
Level 6, 380-62	Level 12, 380-68

Student Workbooks for Levels 1-12

Every student will have a workbook that refers to all the material covered in the *Teacher's Guides*. Levels 1-4 include pictures to color, prayers, crossword puzzles, and catechetical topics. Levels 5-8 include pictures to enhance meditation and other activities. Levels 7 & 8 focus on Sacred Scripture and levels 9-12 focus on the papal documents, books, and video programs referred to in the *Teacher's Guides*.

Please specify item number below when ordering.

Level 1, 380-93	Level 7, 380-99
Level 2, 380-94	Level 8, 380-100
Level 3, 380-95	Level 9, 380-101
Level 4, 380-96	Level 10, 380-102
Level 5, 380-97	Level 11, 380-103
Level 6, 380-98	Level 12, 380-104

By Heart Catechism and Scripture Review*

The *By Heart Catechism and Scripture Review* is a condensed version of the question and answer portion of the *The Apostolate's Family Catechism*. This review book sums up the fundamental teachings of the Catholic Church in simple, easy-to-memorize language. In fewer than 200 questions and answers, students in levels 1-6 master the basics of the Catholic Faith. Levels 7 and 8 emphasize Scripture, giving students the Biblical basis for the key teachings of the Catholic Church in the form of short Bible quotations taken from the *Family Catechism*. (Resource #380-72)

Heroes of Our Faith: The Family Catechism Illuminated by the Lives of Saintly People*

Heroes of Our Faith is a unique series of stories which depict saintly individuals or Bible heroes speaking in the first person. These partially fictional stories illustrate truths contained in the catechism by relating the life experiences of saintly individuals in their particular quest for holiness, encouraging and enlightening us in our own earthly pilgrimage so that we might someday join the Communion of Saints in the Kingdom of Heaven.

Heroes of Our Faith: Francisco of Fatima (a review for levels 1-5) is available in book and audio. (Audio: Resource #115-264AK, 5 audios. Book: Resource #380-82.)

* Items included in the 7-volume edition of the Family Catechism

Flash Cards and Merit Cards

The *Flash Cards* help students memorize the *By Heart Catechism and Scripture Review* lessons. These *Flash Cards* can be used in games and can easily be taken anywhere for quick review.

The *Merit Cards* are designed to help children understand the positive consequences of good behavior and how it impacts not only the individual, but the entire family and the Mystical Body of Christ.

Level 1, 112 cards, 380-92	Level 5, 144 cards, 380-76
Level 2, 136 cards, 380-73	Level 6, 152 cards, 380-77
Level 3, 128 cards, 380-74	Level 7, 136 cards, 380-78
Level 4, 136 cards, 380-75	Level 8, 128 cards, 380-79

"*The Apostolate's Family Catechism* will now enable parents to fulfill their primary obligation in teaching their children. I pray that every parent will use The Apostolate's catechetical program in their neighborhood."

Mother Teresa of Calcutta

Family Catechism on Tape™
Dialogue with Cardinal Arinze
on audio and video

Roman Curia Cardinal Francis Arinze, President of the Pontifical Council for Inter-Religious Dialogue and a member of the executive committee of the Congregation for the Doctrine of the Faith, answers and explains each of the 304 topics found in *The Apostolate's Family Catechism* (Vatican-approved). His dynamic style of teaching inspires people to want to learn more and to share their Faith with others.

Makes family catechetics a reality!

- ✔ Clear and to-the-point
- ✔ Enables you to easily evangelize by sharing these tapes with others
- ✔ Helps you explain the Faith to your children and others with confidence
- ✔ Easy to use in the home or any teaching environment and assures sound doctrine is being taught
- ✔ Used in conjunction with *The Apostolate's Family Catechism*

AFC Catholic Familyland®, Bloomingdale, OH 43910-7903

Topics include: *(Partial List)*

- God and His Perfections
- Sin
- Jesus, the Son of God
- Holy Spirit: Life of Grace
- Virtues and Gifts
- Precepts of the Creed

- Papacy and Bishops
- The Church, Teacher of Truth
- Sacraments
- Prayer
- Communion of Saints
- Blessed Virgin Mary

Resource #115-93AK, 22 audios plus 2 free bonus tapes
Resource #15-93VK, 22 videos plus 2 free bonus tapes
(Ask about Fr. Pablo Straub's Family Catechism commentaries in Spanish.)

For the family and for use in CCD, school, RCIA, and parish-wide formation!

1-800-FOR-MARY • *Fax: (740) 765-5561* • *www.familyland.org*

The Apostolate's

Catechism for Kids on Tape™

with Sr. John Vianney

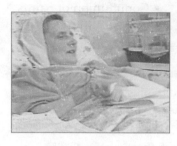

Sr. John Vianney Gorecki was a Notre Dame teaching nun who suffered excruciating pain for over forty years, bedridden with a rare disease; she lived from 1920 to 1990. Her hospital room was frequently filled with children and adults who came from far and near to hear the beautiful truths of the Faith, which she told in a gentle, almost magical way. She was able to especially reach children with her stories — her eyes and smile were so vibrant that the children often forgot that she was even sick. She makes *The Apostolate's Family Catechism* come alive for children.

- ✔ Simple heart-warming stories
- ✔ Captures the imagination of children and adults alike
- ✔ Language that children can understand
- ✔ Answers and explains the 304 questions in *The Apostolate's Family Catechism*

AFC Catholic Familyland®, Bloomingdale, OH 43910-7903

These tapes cover subjects such as:

- Obedience
- Charity
- Creation
- Mass
- Sin & Hell
- Sacraments
- The Creed
- Virtues and Gifts
- Ten Commandments
- The Holy Trinity

- Prayer
- Purity
- Heaven
- Mary

Building Blocks of Faith

"I am particularly pleased to endorse your Apostolate's Family Catechism series, written by Fr. Lawrence Lovasik, supported by your exclusive videotaped programs with Sr. John Vianney... and others."

Mario Luigi Cardinal Ciappi
Official Theologian of the Supreme Pontiff
Sept. 12, 1984

The complete series of *Catechism for Kids on Tape* contains 4 volumes of 7 audios or videos.

Resource #115-180AK, 28 audios. #115-180VK, 28 videos

1-800-FOR-MARY • *Fax: (740) 765-5561* • *www.familyland.org*

Be Not Afraid Family Hours®

on video

Mother Teresa's idea for...

... Stopping Abortion!

... Healing Families!

... Building Parish Community Life!

... Focusing on Confession, our Eucharistic Lord, Mary, and the Papacy!

Mother Teresa embraces AFC co-founder, Gwen Coniker, mother of 13 and grandmother of 35

Be **Not Afraid Family Hours** are one-hour long videotapes produced by the Apostolate for Family Consecration to help families pray, learn, and share their Faith on a continuous basis. They provide a weekly opportunity to evangelize the unchurched and re-evangelize inactive Catholics. Currently there are 72 Family Hours on video, with more in production.

Every Family Hour includes a video faculty member discussing a particular aspect of the Catholic faith, Roman Curia Cardinal Francis Arinze teaching the catechism, inspiring music from contemporary Catholic artists, a beautiful meditative Rosary with vibrant pictures for each Hail Mary and at least one Mystery acted out in movie format, and insights from Pope John Paul II and Mother Teresa.

Wherever possible, Family Hours should immediately be started in the home and prayed into the parish church. Showing the Family Hours in the church helps families to adore Our Lord in the Blessed Sacrament and opens the door for them to receive God's special graces in the Sacrament of Confession. Mother Teresa encouraged Eucharistic devotion and our *Be Not Afraid Family Hours* in churches as a way of repairing for sin, stopping the scourge of abortion, and saving family life.

1-800-FOR-MARY • Fax: (740) 765-5561 • www.familyland.org

*You can immediately start the Be Not Afraid
Family Hours in the home and pray
them into the parish church.*

Be Not Afraid Family Hours...

Facilitate:

- reception of the *Sacrament of Penance*
- reception of the *healing graces* from Jesus' Eucharistic Presence to mend broken hearts and relationships, preparing the way for the era of peace promised at Fatima
- *fervent reception* of the Holy Eucharist at Mass
- *evangelization* and re-evangelization of our families and neighbors in an inviting way
- *deeper understanding* of our Faith

Produce Long-Term Spiritual Fruits by:

- enabling families to *live their baptismal consecrations* with confidence and to become *"families for others,"* in the spirit of Pope John Paul II
- *reaching our youth,* who are the most affected by our "media culture," and reinforcing their Catholic education; preparing them to make enlightened decisions in life
- *lifting up our overburdened priests* and bonding them with the families of the parish through the Sacraments and the evangelizing mission of the Church
- *building a parish community* which is focused on the Eucharist, Our Lady, and the papacy (the guardian of the Truth)
- *increasing adoration of Our Lord* by growth in knowledge of His love, sacrifice, and example, which can lead to perpetual Eucharistic Adoration

Vatican Encouragement to Use Our Videotapes in Churches
With Our Eucharistic Lord
Reserved in the Tabernacle

Cardinal Augustin Mayer, while Prefect of the Sacred Congregation for the Sacraments and Divine Worship, wrote the following letter to the Apostolate for Family Consecration on November 15, 1987.

Dear Mr. Coniker:

I have known about the Apostolate for Family Consecration's "Be Not Afraid" Weekly Eucharistic Holy Hours and First Saturday "Light of the World Cenacle" video programs for showing in the Eucharistic Presence of Our Lord in churches throughout the world.

Pope John Paul II used television in a very powerful way to open up the Marian Year. I believe your videos, which are produced with such taste and tenderness for the Eucharist, can be a very powerful instrument to draw families to His Eucharistic Presence within parish communities. Here they can also be formed in the truth which will make them free and be motivated to go to confession, a sacrament so vital to the spiritual life.

I am happy to give my deepest encouragement for this type of formation and evangelization in the Eucharistic Presence of Our Lord. Properly produced videotape programs offer an entirely new dimension for the Church to communicate the truth.

Yours in the Hearts of Jesus and Mary,

Paul Augustin Card. Mayer O.S.B.

*On a pilgrimage to Rome, Jerry and Gwen Coniker met
with Cardinal Jorge Medina Estevéz, Prefect of the
Sacred Congregation for Divine Worship.*

Jorge A. Cardinal Medina Estevéz enthusi-astically joined The Apostolate's Advisory Council and lent his full support to showing *Be Not Afraid Family Hours* on video in the Eucharistic Presence of Our Lord in parish churches throughout the world.

Cardinal Estevéz encouraged perpetual adoration and frequent confession, and endorsed all of The Apostolate's programs and its work and mission. In fact, His Eminence sent Father Antonio Lessi, S.J., the department head of the Congregation, to the Family Apostolate's temporary television studio in Rome to do an extensive television program on all of the points mentioned above, and on family consecration.

Mother Teresa's Support

May 20, 1989

Dear Jerome and Gwen,

I want to encourage you in your efforts to bring families to church every week for a Holy Hour.

Your weekly "Be Not Afraid Family Hours" [on video] will bring down many graces for the Church and especially for our families.

Prayer is essential if we wish the scourge of abortion to be lifted, and families to be renewed. Eucharistic devotion is the most powerful form of prayer we can participate in, outside of the Holy Sacrifice of the Mass.

Drawing families once a week into the Eucharistic Presence of Our Lord, where the Sacrament of Penance and Reconciliation is being offered while your "Be Not Afraid Family Hour" videotapes are presented, is a great grace for families.

I encourage all families to participate in this powerful devotion, which is calling down the Mercy of God upon all of us. Be assured of my continued prayers for the success of your work.

Give my love to your family and co-workers in the Apostolate for Family Consecration.

God bless you
M. Teresa MC

M. Teresa, M.C.

Because of modern communications, some of the Church's best teachers can now reach the families of the world with the Truth that sets hearts free...

Be Not Afraid Family Hour Teaching Faculty:

His Holiness Pope John Paul II

Cardinal Lopez Trujillo*

Francis Cardinal Arinze*

Anthony Cardinal Bevilacqua

Mario Luigi Cardinal Ciappi†

Edouard Cardinal Gagnon*

Pio Cardinal Laghi*

Adam Cardinal Maida

John Cardinal O'Connor

Jose Cardinal Sanchez*

Jaime Cardinal Sin

Edmund Cardinal Szoka*

J. Francis Cardinal Stafford*

Jozef Cardinal Tomko*

Archbishop Agostino Cacciavillan*

Archbishop John Foley*

1-800-FOR-MARY • Fax: (740) 765-5561 • www.familyland.org

Bishop
Thomas
Daily

Bishop
John
Magee

Bishop
Gilbert
Sheldon

Bishop
Juan F.
Torres

Father
Pablo
Straub

Father
Thomas
Forrest

Father
Benedict
Groeschel

Father
George
Kosicki

Father
Frederick
Miller

Father
Patrick
Peyton†

Father
Frank
Pavone

Father
Michael
Scanlan

Mother
Teresa of
Calcutta†

Sister
Gratia
of Poland

Doctor
Scott
Hahn

Cardinal Christoph Schonborn, O.P.
Cardinal Giovanni Cheli*
Bishop Peter Van Lierde†
Bishop Thomas Welsh
Msgr. Peter Elliott*
Msgr. Roger Foys
Msgr. John McCarthy
Msgr. Josefino Ramirez
Msgr. John Woolsey
Fr. John Bertolucci
Fr. Arthur B. Calkins
Fr. Roger Charest, S.M.M.
Fr. Harold Cohen, S.J.
Fr. Robert J. Dempsey*
Fr. Richard Drabik, M.I.C.
Fr. Thomas Dubay, S.M.

Fr. Gregory Finn, O.S.J.
Fr. Bernard Geiger, O.F.M. Conv.
Fr. John H. Hampsch
Fr. Brian Harrison, S.T.L.
Fr. M. Albert Krapiec, O.P.
Fr. S. Michalenko, M.I.C.
Fr. Bruce Nieli, C.F.R.
Fr. Randall Paine
Fr. Adrian van Kaam, C.S.Sp., Ph.D.
Mother Immaculata, H.M.I.
Dr. Mark Miravalle
Dr. John Haas
Dr. Susan Muto, Ph.D.
Dr. Burns Seeley
Jerry and Gwen Coniker

*Members of the Roman Curia – The Pope's Direct Staff
† Deceased

Family Hour Series Currently there are eight Be Not Afraid Family Hour series (72 Family Hour programs) with more in production. Each series includes 9 one-hour videotapes and 1 Sunday Mass Preview tape.

St. Joseph Series *A model for husbands and fathers*
(also in Spanish) (Resource #133-363VK)

Roman Curia Cardinal Francis Arinze reviews subjects from *The Apostolate's Family Catechism*, selected from questions 1-137.

This series also features Fr. Gregory Finn (Oblates of St. Joseph) and Jerry Coniker.

Topics include: The Key Virtues of St. Joseph, Joys and Sorrows of St. Joseph, St. Joseph the Worker, Humility & Obedience of St. Joseph, The Trust of St. Joseph, and St. Joseph's Way, Silence.

St. Joseph is truly the model for husbands and fathers; he also presents a fatherly role model to families who have no father at home.

Immaculate Conception *Our Lady of Guadalupe*
(also in Spanish) (Resource #133-361VK)

Roman Curia Cardinal Francis Arinze reviews subjects from *The Apostolate's Family Catechism*, selected from questions 138-268.

This series also features Cardinal Edouard Gagnon, Cardinal Pio Laghi, Cardinal Bernard Law, Cardinal Anthony Bevilacqua, Cardinal John O'Connor, Fr. George Kosicki, Fr. Harold Cohen, Fr. Patrick Peyton, Loretta Young, and Jerry Coniker.

Topics include: Mary, Seat of Wisdom; The Marian Multiplier; Mary Reveals Her Name; Mary's Purity; John Paul II's Marian Devotion; Mary's Maternal Love; Mary and the Rosary; and To Jesus Through Mary.

Living Eucharist Series *Our Source*
(also in Spanish) (Resource #133-390VK)

Roman Curia Cardinal Francis Arinze reviews subjects from *The Apostolate's Family Catechism*, selected from questions 269-304, and presents entirely new explanations for subjects relating to questions 1-113.

This series also features Cardinal Jose Sanchez, Cardinal Bernard Law, Bishop John Magee, Bishop Fremiot Torres, Fr. Brian Harrison, Fr. Michael Scanlan, Fr. George Kosicki, and Jerry Coniker.

Topics include: Reverence for the Eucharist, The Eucharistic Heart of Jesus, The Eucharist & John Paul II, and The Eucharist and the Family.

Our Mission is Mercy Series *Divine Mercy Devotion*
(also in Spanish) (Resource #133-410VK)

Each of the one-hour programs includes both the Holy Rosary and the Chaplet of Divine Mercy. Roman Curia Cardinal Francis Arinze reviews different subjects from *The Apostolate's Family Catechism*, selected from questions 114-235.

This series also features Bishop John Magee, Msgr. John McCarthy, Fr. John Bertolucci, Fr. Brian Harrison, Fr. George Kosicki, Fr. Seraphim Michalenko, Fr. Michael Scanlan, and Jerry & Gwen Coniker.

Topics include: Misery and Mercy; Three Levels of Love; The Chaplet of Divine Mercy; The Feast of the Divine Mercy; Mercy and Youth; and Mary, Mother of Mercy.

The Holy Rosary Series *Key to family unity*
(also in Spanish) (Resource #133-430VK)

Roman Curia Cardinal Francis Arinze reviews entirely new material from *The Apostolate's Family Catechism*, selected from questions 236-304, and week 7 starts a new cycle of different catechetical discussions for questions 1-71.

This series also features Cardinal Mario Luigi Ciappi (at the time, papal theologian), Cardinal Anthony Bevilacqua, Msgr. Peter Elliott (Pontifical Council for the Family), Fr. Bernard Geiger, Fr. Patrick Peyton, Mother Immaculata, and Jerry Coniker.

Topics include: Fatima and the Rosary, The Joyful Mysteries, The Agony in the Garden, The Meaning of Suffering, The Cross & Crucifixion, and Mary's Triumph.

Healing Through Consecration Series
According to St. Louis de Montfort (also in Spanish) 133-450VK

Roman Curia Cardinal Francis Arinze reviews entirely new material from *The Apostolate's Family Catechism*, selected from questions 72-189.

This series also features Roman Curia Cardinal Pio Laghi, Roman Curia Archbishop John Foley, Fr. Roger Charest, S.M.M. (de Montfort missionary), Fr. Bernard Geiger, O.F.M., Conv. (an expert on St. Maximilian Kolbe), Mother Immaculata, H.M.C., Loretta Young, and Jerry Coniker.

This series is to be used with St. Louis de Montfort's 33-day *Preparation for Total Consecration* to Jesus through Mary. It focuses on the Marian spirituality of Pope John Paul II, which is based on that of St. Louis de Montfort and St. Maximilian Kolbe. This series will show how, by living consecrated lives and by grounding ourselves in the truths of our Faith, we will be better disposed to receive the graces to repair broken relationships and to heal our families, and thus help to usher in the era of peace promised by Our Lady of Fatima.

The Doctrine of Purgatory Series

Final Preparation for Heaven (Resource #133-530VK)

Roman Curia Cardinal Francis Arinze reviews entirely new material from *The Apostolate's Family Catechism*, selected from questions 198-304.

This series also features Bishop Thomas Welsh, Msgr. Peter Elliott, Fr. Randall Paine, Fr. Frank Pavone, Fr. Michael Scanlan, and Jerry Coniker.

Topics include: The Reality of Purgatory, Justice and Mercy, Purgation from What?, Capacity for Holiness, Purgatory on Earth, Heaven, Hell, Indulgences, and Prayer for the Holy Souls.

Mary, Life, & the Sacraments Series

Solution to Abortion (Resource #133-550VK)

Roman Curia Cardinal Francis Arinze reviews entirely new material from the *Catechism of the Catholic Church* on the sacraments.

This series also features Roman Curia Cardinal Edouard Gagnon, Cardinal John O'Connor, Cardinal Bernard Law, Roman Curia Archbishop J. Francis Stafford, Fr. Frank Pavone, Fr. Michael Scanlan, Fr. Fredrick Miller, and Jerry Coniker.

Topics include: Mary's Life Giving Role; Let it Be Done to Me; Mary's Charity; Mother of God; The Presentation; Healing From the Loss of an Aborted Child; The Church, Defender of Life; and Supporting Life.

Family Hour Media Promo Pack

(Resource #133-560VK)

We made it EASY for you!

You can now become a first-class evangelizer by using the **Family Hour Media Promo Pack** which assists you in properly promoting the *Be Not Afraid Family Hours*.

You can **NOW** promote your *Be Not Afraid Family Hours* using all of the basic materials provided in this package. No previous experience is necessary.

Family Hour Media Promo Pack includes:

- Family Hour Planning & Training Tape: A step-by-step "how-to" video on forming/training a committee, & the details for TV/radio promotion. (160-555V)

- Putting God's Armor On/Family Wisdom Curriculum Video & Audio: Used to generate interest in the Family Hours. Can be shown to committee members for inspiration/training. (120-295VK)

- Family Hour Media Tapes: Professionally produced commercials for TV and radio on ¾" and ½" videos and on an audio master. Includes 30 & 60-second commercials and a 28½ minute TV show.

  - ¾" broadcast quality video for TV stations (133-397MD)

  - ½" video for your own VCR viewing (133-397V)

  - broadcast quality audio for radio stations (133-398AMD)

- Literature Pack: 25 full-color 11" x 17" posters, (317-43K) and glossy artwork booklet for reproduction (313-84).

- Family Hour Step-by-Step Manual (375-97): Includes complete training instructions, along with press releases, ads for newspapers, bulletin inserts and announcements, & clip art.

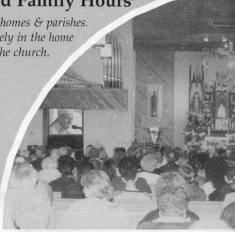
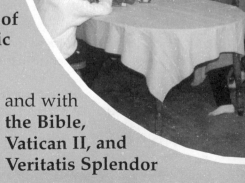

Family Catechism on Tape

Dialogue with Cardinal Arinze

interviewed by Jerry Coniker on 22 audio or video tapes

Dialogue with Fr. Pablo Straub, C.Ss.R. in Spanish

interviewed by Tani Friedrich on 20 audio or video tapes

Catechize with the Vatican-approved
Apostolate's Family Catechism
A Lifetime Catechism!

Includes quotes from Sacred Scripture and Vatican Council II documents and over 600 pictures

Endorsed by Cardinal Ratzinger

Consecration and Enthronement Program

(Resource #133-282VK)

Enthrone the Holy Family in your home

The Sacred Hearts Family Consecration & Enthronement Program contains a video featuring Mother Teresa of Calcutta and five 16" x 20" Holy Family Portraits. *The video is also available in Spanish.*

This one-hour video features Mother Teresa, who witnesses to the healing power which families can experience when they conse-  crate their families to the Sacred Heart of Jesus through the Immaculate Heart of Mary, in union with St. Joseph. (Resource #133-281V)

 The Holy Family Portrait serves as a constant reminder of the peace and unity which is the fruit of giving everything to Jesus through Mary, in union with St. Joseph. Four extra portraits are included so you can share this consecration with four other families. (361-18K)

AFC Catholic Familyland®, Bloomingdale, OH 43910-7903

*A family hangs the Holy Family Portrait
in a prominent place in their home.*

The Pilgrim Virgin Statue is a beautiful 36" high statue, reproduced from a statue in Fatima. We suggest you take this image of Our Lady into the home where the Enthronement of the Sacred Hearts is to take place and leave it there for a week with the Soul of the Rosary video (133-158VK, page 649) or the Be Not Afraid  Family Hour series on the Holy Rosary (133-430VK, page 575). In this way, Mary's presence is brought into the family in a special way as they spiritually prepare themselves for the consecration. Please allow up to 12 weeks for delivery of this beautiful handpainted statue. (Resource #505-29)

First Saturday Cenacles™
on video

**These video devotions will help you live
Our Lady's Fatima message and increase
your love for the Holy Family
and your own family.**

The First Saturday Cenacle video programs are shown on the first Saturday of each month in parish churches or homes. Each First Saturday Collection is made up of 6 one-hour videos

which draw people into churches to fulfill Our Lady's specific request, given to Sr. Lucia, for a Communion of Reparation on the First Saturday of 5 consecutive months. Each one-hour video includes a beautiful, meditative Rosary with 15 extra minutes of pictorial meditation on the mysteries, and a reminder to go to Confession within a reasonable amount of time. Each video features Pope John Paul II, Mother Teresa, and a special guest teacher speaking on topics which will increase devotion to Jesus through His Blessed Mother, while enhancing your knowledge of the Truth.

AFC Catholic Familyland®, Bloomingdale, OH 43910-7903

Our Lady's Promise for Salvation :

"My daughter, look at My Heart surrounded with the thorns with which ungrateful men pierce it at every moment by their blasphemies and ingratitude. You, at least, try to console me, and say that I **promise to assist at the hour of death with all the graces necessary for salvation** all those who, on the first Saturday of five consecutive months, go to Confession and receive Holy Communion, recite five decades of the Rosary and keep me company for a quarter of an hour while meditating on the mysteries of the Rosary, with the intention of making reparation to me."   *(Our Lady to Sr. Lucia)*

First Saturday Collection One

First Saturday Collection One contains 6 one-hour videos. Topics are the Holy Family of Nazareth —School of Love; the Brown Scapular; Holy Eucharist; Mary & Matrimony; Our Lady of Guadalupe; and the Shroud of Turin. (Resource #157-1VK)

First Saturday Collection Two

First Saturday Collection Two contains 6 one-hour videos. Topics are Our Lady of Divine Providence; Divine Mercy; The Church & Mary; St. Joseph & Commitment; Pope John Paul II's Devotion to Mary; and St. Louis de Montfort's Consecration to Jesus through Mary. (Resource #157-2VK)

Roman Curia Cardinal Pio Laghi taught on our first satellite broadcast of our First Saturday Cenacles.

Day of Grace Parish Mission™ Program

Learn about, Prepare for, and Celebrate the Feast of Divine Mercy

The Feast of Divine Mercy is celebrated on the first Sunday after Easter. It is a day set aside by Our Lord Himself. The *Day of Grace Parish Mission* is an enjoyable, yet comprehensive way to prepare for and celebrate the Feast of Divine Mercy in your parish each year. This deeply spiritual video presentation will captivate any congregation.

Our Lord said to Blessed Faustina Kowalska, "I desire that the Feast of Mercy be a refuge and shelter for all souls, and especially for poor sinners." (*Divine Mercy in My Soul Diary*, 699)

The *Day of Grace Parish Mission* reveals the complete message of Divine Mercy and reasons behind this amazing promise. You'll hear from inspiring speakers such as Pope John Paul II, Mother Teresa, Sr. Gratia Kelly (of the same order as Blessed Sr.

Faustina), Fr. George Kosicki, Fr. Seraphim Michalenko, and others.

The *Day of Grace* program can also be shown throughout the year on days of recollection to teach the five dimensions of this devotion, or combined with the First Saturday devotion as a day of recollection.

An inspiring way to celebrate Divine Mercy!

The Day of Grace Parish Mission video program presents all of the facets of the Divine Mercy devotion:

- The Chaplet of Divine Mercy
- Veneration of the Image of Mercy
- The Feast of Mercy
- The Hour of Great Mercy
- Spreading the Message of the Devotion

"On that day the very depths of My tender mercy are open. I pour out a whole ocean of graces upon those souls who approach the fount of My mercy."

Jesus to Blessed Faustina *(Diary, 699)*

Call 1-800-FOR-MARY

The Day of Grace Parish Mission Program includes all of the components necessary to run a successful Day of Grace program…

Pictured above are all of the components of the Day of Grace Parish Mission video program (147-48VK), including 20 videos, 7 audios, and 100 books…

…PLUS all the promotional materials needed to assure a full church.

St. Peter's parish in Kenosha, Wisconsin, on Mercy Sunday — A full church!

A summary video and audio explaining the Day of Grace Program is available (147-57VK).

Chaplet of Divine Mercy
Audio and Video Tape Collection

The Chaplet of Divine Mercy is a powerful prayer with extraordinary promises attached to its recitation:*Whoever will recite it will receive great mercy at the hour of death...Even if there were a sinner most hardened, if he were to recite this chaplet only once, he would receive grace from My infinite mercy."* (Diary, 687)

The Chaplet of Divine Mercy tapes can be prayed in your living room using the video or in the car with the audio tape. Excellent for home, prayer groups, cenacles, or churches.

Audio/Video set: 147-58VK; audio only: 147-58A; video only: 147-58V.

Divine Mercy in My Soul
Sr. Faustina's Diary

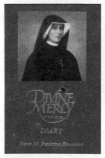

Blessed Sister Faustina, a mystic and a modern day apostle of Divine Mercy, is the recipient of special messages of mercy from Our Lord. This diary reveals the depths of God's mercy and how much He yearns for all of mankind to drink from His Fountain of Mercy. Softcover, 697 pages.

(Resource #522-6)

Peace of Heart Forums®
on audio & video tape

A guide through one book per month. The perfect way to sustain prayer and spiritual reading while fostering lasting friendships.

Peace of Heart Forums:

- ✔ Teach the Faith and develop a spiritual life
- ✔ Deepen spiritual bonds among family and group members
- ✔ Strengthen and heal broken relationships
- ✔ Provide answers for complex problems of today

They also:

- ✔ Inspire people to read and meditate daily on the truths of our Faith
- ✔ Guide people through spiritual books on many different subjects
- ✔ Increase people's understanding of books and provide insights for provocative discussion

AFC Catholic Familyland®, Bloomingdale, OH 43910-7903

Peace of Heart Forum video programs bring spiritual books to life. People gather on a weekly basis in a home or parish to view videos and participate in inspiring discussions based on a particular book they are reading. They learn not to "speed read" but to meditate on the sections that the Holy Spirit moves them to think about. Peace of Heart Forums help to create a community committed to daily spiritual reading, meditation, and weekly gatherings for learning and sharing the Truth.

Forums are easy to run, last from 1-2 hours, include discussion, and feature some of the most spiritual and brilliant minds in the Catholic Church.

Building Community and Support Groups upon the Truth! Peace of Heart Forums are ideal for prayer groups, cenacles, and study groups. These weekly Forums can develop into strong support groups for individuals and families. They draw youth and adults deeper into their Faith to such a degree that they can transform their trials into stepping stones toward a life of union with God.

Topics include:

- Scripture
- Mary
- Youth
- Liturgy
- Philosophy
- Suffering
- Papal Documents
- Lives & Writings of the Saints
- Marriage and Family
- Purgatory
- Catechetics
- Theology

Peace of Heart Forums®
on audio & video tape

Papal Documents

As the Third Millennium Draws Near and On Human Work by Pope John Paul II

Faculty: Roman Curia Cardinal Francis Arinze, interviewed by Jerry Coniker

Companion Books:
As the Third Millennium Draws Near, by Pope John Paul II, 503-73810
On Human Work, by Pope John Paul II, 503-EPO862,

Video set (3 hours), 115-310VK
Audio set (3 hours), 115-310AK

Crossing the Threshold of Hope by Pope John Paul II

Faculty: Roman Curia Cardinal Francis Arinze, interviewed by Jerry Coniker

Companion Book: *Crossing the Threshold of Hope,* by Pope John Paul II, 558-12

Video set (5 hours), 115-290VK
Audio set (5 hours), 115-290AK

Gospel of Life by Pope John Paul II

Faculty: Roman Curia Cardinal Francis Arinze, interviewed by Jerry Coniker

Companion Book: *Gospel of Life,* by Pope John Paul II, 503-3078X

Video set (6 hours), 115-237VK
Audio set (6 hours), 115-237AK

Lay Members of Christ's Faithful People I (Christifideles Laici) by Pope John Paul II

Faculty: Roman Curia Cardinal Francis Arinze; Bishop William D'Mello; Bishop John the Baptist Kakubi; Bishop Albert Ottenweller; Fr. Michael Scanlan, T.O.R.; Fr. George Kosicki, C.S.B.; Dr. Keith Fournier; and Jerry Coniker

Companion Book: *Lay Members of Christ's Faithful People*, by Pope John Paul II, 503-EPO702

Video set (4 hours), 126-3381VK
Audio set (4 hours), 126-3381AK

Lay Members of Christ's Faithful People II (Christifideles Laici) by Pope John Paul II

Faculty: Cardinal Anthony Bevilacqua; Bishop J.B. Kakubi; Fr. Michael Scanlan, T.O.R.; Charles Presberg; Dr. Burns Seeley; and Jerry Coniker

Companion Book: *Lay Members of Christ's Faithful People*, by Pope John Paul II, 503-EPO702

Video set (4 hours), 126-3397VK
Audio set (4 hours), 126-3397AK

Letter to Families by Pope John Paul II

Faculty: Roman Curia Cardinal Francis Arinze, interviewed by Jerry Coniker

Companion Book: *Letter to Families*, by Pope John Paul II, 503-44713

Video set (8 hours), 115-208VK
Audio set (8 hours), 115-208AK

Letter to Women and Letter to Children by Pope John Paul II

Faculty: Roman Curia Cardinal Francis Arinze, interviewed by Jerry Coniker

Companion Books:
Letter to Women, by Pope John Paul II, 503-44799
Letter to Children, by Pope John Paul II, 503-44756

Video set (3 hours), 115-300VK
Audio set (3 hours), 115-300AK

On Evangelization in the Modern World I (Evangelii Nuntiandi) by Pope Paul VI

Faculty: Fr. Michael Scanlan, T.O.R., Jerry Coniker, and the staff of the Franciscan University of Steubenville (Ohio).

Companion Book: *On Evangelization in the Modern World*, by Pope Paul VI, 503-EPO850

Video set (4 hours), 126-1703VK
Audio set (4 hours), 126-1703AK

On Evangelization in the Modern World II (Evangelii Nuntiandi) by Pope Paul VI

Faculty: Bishop John Magee (former Papal Secretary), Msgr. John McCarthy, Dr. Burns Seeley, and Jerry Coniker

Companion Book: *On Evangelization in the Modern World*, by Pope Paul VI, 503-EPO850

Video set (4 hours), 126-1906VK
Audio set (4 hours), 126-1906AK

On Reconciliation and Penance I (Reconciliatio et Paenitentia) by Pope John Paul II

Faculty: Fr. Alfred Kunz, Dr. Burns Seeley, and Jerry Coniker

Companion Book: *On Reconciliation and Penance*, by Pope John Paul II, 503-EPO894

Video set (4 hours), 126-1014VK
Audio set (4 hours), 126-1014AK

On Reconciliation and Penance II (Reconciliatio et Paenitentia) by Pope John Paul II

Faculty: Pope John Paul II, Fr. Timothy Byerley, Dr. Burns Seeley, and Jerry Coniker

Companion Book: *On Reconciliation and Penance*, by Pope John Paul II, 503-EPO894

Video set (4 hours), 126-1839VK
Audio set (4 hours), 126-1839AK

On Reconciliation and Penance III (Reconciliatio et Paenitentia) by Pope John Paul II

Faculty: Charles Presberg, Dr. Damien Fedoryka, Dr. Burns Seeley, and Jerry Coniker

Companion Book: *On Reconciliation and Penance*, by Pope John Paul II, 503-EPO894

Video set (4 hours), 126-3576VK
Audio set (4 hours), 126-3576AK

On Reconciliation and Penance IV (Reconciliatio et Paenitentia) by Pope John Paul II

Faculty: Cardinal Francis Arinze, Dr. Burns Seeley, and Jerry Coniker

Companion Book: *On Reconciliation and Penance*, by Pope John Paul II, 503-EPO894

Video set (4 hours), 126-3678VK
Audio set (4 hours), 126-3678AK

On Reconciliation and Penance V (Reconciliatio et Paenitentia) by Pope John Paul II

Faculty: Fr. Michael Scanlan, T.O.R., Dr. Burns Seeley, and Jerry Coniker

Companion Book: *On Reconciliation and Penance*, by Pope John Paul II, 503-EPO894

Video set (4 hours), 126-3694VK
Audio set (4 hours), 126-3694AK

On the Christian Meaning of Human Suffering (Salvifici Doloris) by Pope John Paul II

Faculty: Sr. John Vianney, S.S.N.D. (suffered for over 40 years in bed), Dr. Burns Seeley, and Jerry Coniker

Companion Book: *On the Christian Meaning of Human Suffering*, by Pope John Paul II, 503-EPO145

Video set (4 hours), 126-1305VK
Audio set (4 hours), 126-1305AK

On the Mercy of God - II (Dives in Misericordia) by Pope John Paul II

Faculty: Fr. George Kosicki, C.S.B., and Jerry Coniker

Companion Book: *The Mercy of God*, by Pope John Paul II, 503-EPO863

Video set (4 hours), 126-3607VK
Audio set (4 hours), 126-3607AK

Rich in Mercy (Dives in Misericordia) by Pope John Paul II; retranslation and outline by Fr. George Kosicki

Faculty: Fr. George Kosicki, C.S.B., and Jerry Coniker

Companion Book: *Rich in Mercy* (in the *Family Consecration Prayer and Meditation Book: Divine Mercy Edition*) 305-14

Video set (4 hours), 126-3853VK
Audio set (4 hours), 126-3853AK

Reflections on Humanae Vitae I by Pope John Paul II

Faculty: Fr. John Hardon, S.J., and Jerry Coniker

Companion Book: *Reflections on Humanae Vitae*, by Pope John Paul II, 503-EPO972

Video set (4 hours), 126-1080VK
Audio set (4 hours), 126-1080AK

Reflections on Humanae Vitae II by Pope John Paul II

Faculty: Pope John Paul II, Cardinal John Krol, Fr. Andrej Szostek, M.I.C. (Lublin University, Poland), Fred Martinez, Dr. Richard Dumont, Dr. Burns Seeley, and Jerry Coniker

Companion Book: *Reflections on Humanae Vitae*, by Pope John Paul II, 503-EPO972

Video set (4 hours), 126-1726VK
Audio set (4 hours), 126-1726AK

To the Youth of the World I by Pope John Paul II

Faculty: Msgr. Peter Elliott (Pontifical Council for the Family), Dr. Burns Seeley, and Jerry Coniker

Companion Book: *To the Youth of the World*, by Pope John Paul II, 305-22

Video set (4 hours), 126-1541VK
Audio set (4 hours), 126-1541AK

To the Youth of the World II by Pope John Paul II

Faculty: Pope John Paul II, Bishop John Donoghue, Msgr. John Woolsey, Dr. Burns Seeley, and Jerry Coniker

Companion Book: *To the Youth of the World*, by Pope John Paul II, 305-22

Video set (4 hours), 126-1667VK
Audio set (4 hours), 126-1667AK

To the Youth of the World III by Pope John Paul II

Faculty: Pope John Paul II, Bishop John Magee (former Papal Secretary), Dr. Burns Seeley, and Jerry Coniker

Companion Book: *To the Youth of the World*, by Pope John Paul II, 305-22

Video set (4 hours), 126-1970VK
Audio set (4 hours), 126-1970AK

The Splendor of Truth (Veritatis Splendor)
by Pope John Paul II

Faculty: Roman Curia Cardinal Francis Arinze, interviewed by Jerry Coniker

Companion Book: *The Splendor of Truth*, by Pope John Paul II, 503-69643

Video set (8 hours), 115-197VK
Audio set (8 hours), 115-197AK

The Role of the Christian Family in the Modern World I (Familiaris Consortio) by Pope John Paul II

Faculty: Msgr. Diarmuid Martin (Pontifical Council for the Family), Fr. John Hardon, S.J., Fr. Richard Talaska, Dr. Burns Seeley, and Jerry Coniker

Companion Book: *The Role of the Christian Family in the Modern World*, by Pope John Paul II, 503-EPO973

Video set (4 hours), 126-960VK
Audio set (4 hours), 126-960AK

The Role of the Christian Family in the Modern World II (Familiaris Consortio) by Pope John Paul II

Faculty: Msgr. Diarmuid Martin (Pontifical Council for the Family), Fr. Alfred Kunz, Sr. John Vianney, S.S.N.D.,

Fr. Stanley Smolenski, Mother Teresa, Sandy Redmond, Dr. Burns Seeley, and Jerry Coniker

Companion Book: *The Role of the Christian Family in the Modern World*, by Pope John Paul II, 503-EPO973

Video set (4 hours), 126-1111VK
Audio set (4 hours), 126-1111AK

The Role of the Christian Family in the Modern World III (Familiaris Consortio) by Pope John Paul II

Faculty: Msgr. John Woolsey, Fr. James Genovesi, Dr. Richard Dumont, Dr. Burns Seeley, and Jerry Coniker

Companion Book: *The Role of the Christian Family in the Modern World*, by Pope John Paul II, 503-EPO973

Video set (4 hours), 126-1466VK
Audio set (4 hours), 126-1466AK

The Role of the Christian Family in the Modern World IV (Familiaris Consortio) by Pope John Paul II

Faculty: Cardinal Edouard Gagnon (when he was President of the Pontifical Council for the Family), Msgr. John Woolsey, Msgr. Peter Elliott, Dr. Richard Dumont, Dr. Burns Seeley, and Jerry Coniker

Companion Book: *The Role of the Christian Family in the Modern World*, by Pope John Paul II, 503-EPO973

Video set (4 hours), 126-1482VK
Audio set (4 hours), 126-1482AK

Vatican II - Decree on the Apostolate of the Laity (Apostolicam Actuositatem)

Faculty: Cardinal Francis Arinze, Dr. Burns Seeley, and Jerry Coniker

Companion Book: *Decree on the Apostolate of the Laity*, promulgated by Pope Paul VI, 503-EP0360

Video set (4 hours), 126-3710VK
Audio set (4 hours), 126-3710AK

Be Not Afraid I: On the interview of Pope John Paul II by André Frossard

Faculty: Fr. Albert Krapiec and Fr. Andrej Szostek (both from Lublin University, Poland, where Pope John Paul II formerly studied and taught), Dr. Richard Dumont, Dr. Burns Seeley, and Jerry Coniker

Companion Book: No book is currently available for this series

Video set (4 hours), 126-1434VK
Audio set (4 hours), 126-1434AK

Sacred Scripture

Meditations on St. Matthew I

Faculty: Bishop William D'Mello; Bishop Thomas Welsh; Fr. Lawrence Lovasik, S.V.D.; Mother Angelica; Mother Immaculata, H.M.I.; Fr. Michael Scanlan, T.O.R.; Mother Teresa; Admiral Jeremiah Denton; Charles Presberg; Peter Mergen; Dr. Burns Seeley; and Jerry Coniker

Companion Book: *Meditations on St. Matthew*, by Dr. Burns K. Seeley, 323-76

Video set (4 hours), 126-114VK
Audio set (4 hours), 126-114AK

Meditations on St. Matthew II

Faculty: Cardinal Anthony Bevilacqua, Charles Presberg, Dr. Burns Seeley, and Jerry Coniker.

599

Companion Book: *Meditations on St. Matthew*, by Dr. Burns K. Seeley, 323-76

Video set (4 hours), 126-589VK
Audio set (4 hours), 126-589AK

Meditations on St. Matthew III

Faculty: Msgr. John McCarthy, Fr. John Hardon, S.J., Dr. Burns Seeley, and Jerry Coniker

Companion Book: *Meditations on St. Matthew*, by Dr. Burns K. Seeley, 323-76

Video set (4 hours), 126-884VK
Audio set (4 hours), 126-884AK

Meditations on St. Mark

Faculty: Fr. John Hardon, S.J., Dr. Burns Seeley, and Jerry Coniker

Companion Book: *The Navarre Bible — St. Mark*, Revised Standard Version and New Vulgate with commentary by the members of the Faculty of Theology of the University of Navarre, 511-43

Video set (4 hours), 126-459VK
Audio set (4 hours), 126-459AK

Meditations on St. Luke

Faculty: Fr. John Hardon, S.J., Dr. Burns Seeley, and Jerry Coniker

Companion Book: *The Navarre Bible — St. Luke*, Revised Standard Version and New Vulgate with commentary by the members of the Faculty of Theology of the University of Navarre, 511-44

Video set (4 hours), 126-477VK
Audio set (4 hours), 126-477AK

Acts of the Apostles

Faculty: Fr. Tom Forrest, C.Ss.R., Dr. Burns Seeley, and Jerry Coniker

Companion Book: *The Navarre Bible — Acts of the Apostles*, Revised Standard Version and New Vulgate with commentary by the members of the Faculty of Theology of the University of Navarre, 511-60

Video set (4 hours), 126-3493VK
Audio set (4 hours), 126-3493AK

Meditations on St. John I

Faculty: Msgr. Alphonse Popek, Fr. William Dorney, Mother Angelica, John Hand, Dr. Richard DeGraff, Laurie Coniker, Dr. Burns Seeley, and Jerry Coniker

Companion Book: *Meditations on St. John*, by Dr. Burns K. Seeley, 323-75, $6.95

Video set (4 hours), 126-102VK
Audio set (4 hours), 126-102AK

Meditations on St. John II

Faculty: Fr. Ralph Skonieczny, Fr. Frederick Heuser, Fr. John Hardon, S.J., Dr. Burns Seeley, and Jerry Coniker

Companion Book: *Meditations on St. John*, by Dr. Burns K. Seeley, 323-75

Video set (4 hours), 126-561VK
Audio set (4 hours), 126-561AK

The Book of Revelation

Faculty: Fr. Randall Paine, Dr. Burns Seeley, and Jerry Coniker

Companion Book: *The Navarre Bible — the Book of Revelation*, Revised Standard Version and New Vulgate with commentary by the members of the Faculty of

Theology of the University of Navarre, 511-59

Video set (4 hours), 126-3839VK
Audio set (4 hours), 126-3839AK

Meditations on St. Paul I: 1 Corinthians, 2 Corinthians, Galatians, Ephesians, & Philippians

Faculty: Fr. John Hardon, S.J., Mother Angelica, Dr. Richard DeGraff, Dr. Burns Seeley, Laurie Coniker, and Jerry Coniker

Companion Book: *Meditations on St. Paul*, by Dr. Burns K. Seeley, 323-77

Video set (4 hours), 126-126VK
Audio set (4 hours), 126-126AK

Meditations on St. Paul II (same Epistles as previous forum)

Faculty: Fr. Alfred Boeddeker, O.F.M.; Fr. Bernard Geiger, O.F.M. Conv., Mother Immaculata, H.M.I., Dr. Burns Seeley, and Jerry Coniker

Companion Book: *Meditations on St. Paul*, by Dr. Burns K. Seeley, 323-77

Video set (4 hours), 126-605VK
Audio set (4 hours), 126-605AK

Meditations on St. Paul III (same Epistles as previous forum)

Faculty: Cardinal Mario Luigi Ciappi, O.P. (Papal Theologian), Msgr. Peter Elliott, Fr. Michael Scanlan, T.O.R., Mother Angelica, Dr. Keith Fournier, Tim Croes, Peter Mergen, Dr. Burns Seeley, and Jerry Coniker

Companion Book: *Meditations on St. Paul*, by Dr. Burns K. Seeley, 323-77

Video set (4 hours), 126-2123VK
Audio set (4 hours), 126-2123AK

Meditations on St. Paul IV (same Epistles as previous forum)

Faculty: Fr. Michael Scanlan, T.O.R., Fr. Randall Paine, O.R.C., Mother Teresa, Robert and Rita Feduccia, Janie and Kerry Casserly, Tim Croes, Dr. Burns Seeley, and Jerry Coniker

Companion Book: *Meditations on St. Paul*, by Dr. Burns K. Seeley, 323-77

Video set (4 hours), 126-2139VK
Audio set (4 hours), 126-2139AK

Reflections on St. Paul II: Colossians, 1 Thes., 2 Thes., 1 Timothy, 2 Timothy, Titus, Philemon, & Hebrews

Faculty: Bishop John Joseph (from Pakistan), Fr. John Hardon, S.J., Dr. Burns Seeley, and Jerry Coniker

Companion Book: *Reflections on St. Paul*, by Dr. Burns K. Seeley, 323-78

Video set (4 hours), 126-626VK
Audio set (4 hours), 126-626AK

Reflections on St. Paul IV (same Epistles as above)

Faculty: Fr. Seraphim Michalenko, M.I.C., Sr. John Vianney, S.S.N.D., Dr. Burns Seeley, and Jerry Coniker

Companion Book: *Reflections on St. Paul*, by Dr. Burns K. Seeley, 323-78

Video set (4 hours), 126-1160VK
Audio set (4 hours), 126-1160A

Mary and Consecration

Immaculate Conception

Faculty: Cardinal Mario Luigi Ciappi, O.P.; Cardinal Bernard Law; Cardinal Silvio Oddi; Bishop John Van Lierde, O.S.A.; Fr. Bernard Geiger, O.F.M. Conv.; Mother Immaculata, H.M.I.; Dr. Burns Seeley; and Jerry Coniker

Companion Book: *The Wonder of Guadalupe*, by Francis Johnston, 510-085

Video set (4 hours), 126-1191VK
Audio set (4 hours), 126-1191AK

Total Consecration by St. Louis de Montfort

Faculty: Cardinal Francis Arinze; Fr. Dominic De Domenico, O.P.; Fr. Bernard Geiger, O.F.M. Conv.; Fr. Michael Scanlan, T.O.R.; Dr. Burns Seeley; and Jerry Coniker

Companion Books:
True Devotion to the Blessed Virgin, by St. Louis de Montfort, 520-25

Preparation For Total Consecration according to St. Louis de Montfort, 520-26.

Video set (6 hours), 126-998VK
Audio set (6 hours), 126-998AK

Immaculate Conception and the Holy Spirit

Faculty: Cardinal Mario Luigi Ciappi, O.P., Msgr. Peter Elliott, Fr. Brian Harrison, O.S., Dr. Burns Seeley, and Jerry Coniker

Companion Book: *Immaculate Conception and the Holy Spirit*, by Fr. H.M. Manteau-Bonamy, O.P., 513-101-20,

Video set (4 hours), 126-1557VK
Audio set (4 hours), 126-1557AK

Consecration in the Spirit of St. Vincent Pallotti

Faculty: Fr. Joseph Mungari, S.A.C., Fr. John Hardon, S.J., Dr. Burns Seeley, and Jerry Coniker

Companion Book: *Yearning of a Soul*, by Fr. Flavin Bonifazi, S.A.C., 503-SPO830

Video set (4 hours), 126-927VK
Audio set (4 hours), 126-927AK

Immaculate Heart of Mary: True Devotion by Fr. Robert Fox

Faculty: Fr. Robert Fox, Dr. Burns Seeley, and Jerry Coniker

Companion Book: *Immaculate Heart of Mary: True Devotion*, by Fr. Robert J. Fox, 502-32

Video set (4 hours), 126-1638VK
Audio set (4 hours), 126-1638AK

First Lady of the World by Fr. Peter Lappin, S.D.B.

Faculty: Cardinal Pio Laghi, Fr. Peter Lappin, S.D.B., Melissa Pierce, Dr. Burns Seeley, and Jerry Coniker

Companion Book: *First Lady of the World*, by Fr. Peter Lappin, S.D.B., 527-091-6

Video set (4 hours), 126-2034VK
Audio set (4 hours), 126-2034AK

Saints and Youth

Give Me Souls — St. John Bosco
by Fr. Peter Lappin, S.D.B.

Faculty: Fr. Peter Lappin, S.D.B., Sandy Redmond, Dr. Burns Seeley, and Jerry Coniker

Companion Book: *Give Me Souls,* by Fr. Peter Lappin, S.D.B., 527-25

Video set (4 hours), 126-2002VK
Audio set (4 hours), 126-2002AK

Bury Me Deep (About Zepherin Namuncura)
by Fr. Peter Lappin, S.D.B.

Faculty: Fr. Peter Lappin, S.D.B., Monica Heithaus, Dr. Burns Seeley, and Jerry Coniker

Companion Book: No book is currently available for this series

Video set (3 hours), 126-2060VK
Audio set (3 hours), 126-2060AK

Blessed Kateri Tekakwitha by Fr. Henri Bechard, S.J.

Faculty: Msgr. Paul Lenz, Fr. Henri Bechard, S.J., Fr. Thomas Egan, S.J., and Jerry Coniker

Companion Book: *Kateri Tekakwitha*, by Fr. F.X. Weiser, S.J., 569-25

Video set (4 hours), 126-1605VK
Audio set (4 hours), 126-1605AK

The Falcon and the Dove — Blessed Laura Vicuña
by Fr. Peter Lappin, S.D.B.

Faculty: Fr. Peter Lappin, S.D.B., Monica Heithaus, Dr. Burns Seeley, and Jerry Coniker

Companion Book: No book is currently available for this series

Video set (3 hours), 126-2047VK
Audio set (3 hours), 126-2047AK

Jérôme Le Royer de la Dauversière: His Friends and Enemies (Founder of Montreal) by Henri Béchard, S.J.

Faculty: Fr. Henri Béchard, S.J., Fr. Thomas Egan, S.J., and Jerry Coniker

Companion Book: *Jérôme Le Royer de la Dauversière: His Friends and Enemies*, by Fr. Henri Béchard, S.J., 323-92-S

Video set (4 hours), 126-1621VK
Audio set (4 hours), 126-1621AK

Dominic Savio, Teenage Saint by Fr. Peter Lappin, S.D.B.

Faculty: Fr. Peter Lappin, S.D.B., Sandy Redmond, Dr. Burns Seeley, and Jerry Coniker

Companion Book: *Dominic Savio: Teenage Saint*, by Fr. Peter Lappin, S.D.B., 305-21

Video set (2 hours), 126-2069VK
Audio set (2 hours), 126-2069AK

Special Urgency of Mercy: Why Sr. Faustina by Fr. George Kosicki

Faculty: Fr. George Kosicki, C.S.B., and Jerry Coniker

Companion Book: *Special Urgency of Mercy: Why Sr. Faustina,* by Fr. George Kosicki, C.S.B., 591-UP136

Video set (4 hours), 126-3528VK
Audio set (4 hours), 126-3528AK

Marriage & Family

Preparation for Marriage by the Pontifical Council for the Family

Faculty: Francis Cardinal Arinze and Jerry Coniker

Companion Book: Book not currently available

Video set (3 hours), 115-320VK
Audio set (3 hours), 115-320AK

Truth & Meaning of Human Sexuality by the Pontifical Council for the Family

Faculty: Francis Cardinal Arinze and Jerry Coniker

Companion Book: *Truth & Meaning of Human Sexuality*, 503-7390X

Video set (8 hours), 115-330VK
Audio set (8 hours), 115-330AK

Today's Parents by Dr. Nino Camardese

Faculty: Dr. Nino Camardese, Fr. Mauro Ventura, Jerry and Gwen Coniker

Companion Book: *Today's Parents*, by Dr. Nino Camardese, 526-25

Video set (4 hours), 126-1938VK
Audio set (4 hours), 126-1938AK

Love and Life Chastity Program

Faculty: Pope John Paul II, the Foxhoven Family, The Foundation for the Family (presenting "The Springtime of Your Life"), Sr. John Vianney, S.S.N.D., Dr. Burns Seeley, and Jerry and Gwen Coniker

Companion Books: *Love and Life Books*, by Coleen Kelly Mast
Student Textbook/Workbook, 582-106-6
Parents' Guide, 582-107-4
Teacher's Manual, 582-108-2
Video set (6 hours), 126-3427VK
Audio set (6 hours), 126-3427AK
Complete set, 3 books & 6 videos, 126-3429VK

St. Joseph: Blessed among Husbands, Blessed among Fathers

Faculty: Fr. Stanley Smolenski, Fr. Francis Filas, S.J., Mother Teresa, Mother Immaculata, H.M.I., Frank Milligan, Pat Spencer, Dr. Burns Seeley, and Jerry Coniker

Companion Book: *Life With Joseph*, by Fr. Paul J. Gorman, 552-26

Video set (4 hours), 126-2185VK
Audio set (4 hours), 126-2185AK

Marriage; the Mystery of Faithful Love by Dr. Dietrich von Hildebrand

Faculty: Dr. Alice von Hildebrand, Dr. Burns Seeley, and Jerry and Gwen Coniker

Companion books:
Marriage: the Mystery of Faithful Love, by Dietrich von Hildebrand, 528-5

By Love Refined: Letters to a Young Bride, by Alice von Hildebrand, 528-2

Video set (4 hours), 126-3790VK
Audio set (4 hours), 126-3790AK

Religious Liberty and Contraception by Fr. Brian Harrison, O.S.

Faculty: Fr. Brian Harrison O.S., Dr. Burns Seeley, and Jerry Coniker

Companion book: *Religious Liberty and Contraception*, by Fr. Brian Harrison, O.S., 525-25

Video set (4 hours), 126-1922VK
Audio set (4 hours), 126-1922AK

Liturgy & Purgatory

Understanding the Mass by Fr. Maynard Kolodziej, O.F.M.

Faculty: Pope John Paul II; Bishop John Magee; Fr. Maynard Kolodziej, O.F.M.; Fr. Joseph Mungari, S.A.C.; Dr. Burns Seeley, and Jerry Coniker

Companion book: *Understanding the Mass*, by Fr. Maynard Kolodziej, O.F.M., 567-25

Video set (5 hours), 126-1858VK
Audio set (5 hours), 126-1858AK

Purgation & Purgatory by St. Catherine of Genoa

Faculty: Bishop Thomas Welsh, Fr. Randall Paine, Dr. Burns Seeley, and Jerry Coniker

Companion book: *Purgation & Purgatory*, by St. Catherine of Genoa, 515-22073

Video set (4 hours), 126-1823VK
Audio set (4 hours), 126-1823AK

Theology, Prayer, & Philosophy

Alone With God by Francis Cardinal Arinze

Faculty: Francis Cardinal Arinze, Jerry Coniker, Bishop William L. D'Mello, and Keith Fournier.

Companion book: *Alone With God* (in the *Family Consecration Prayer and Meditation Book: Divine Mercy Edition*), 305-14

Video set: (4 hours), 126-3365VK
Audio set (4 hours), 126-3365AK

Orthodoxy — A Defense of Truth Against Modern Error by G.K. Chesterton

Faculty: Fr. Randall Paine, Dr. Burns Seeley, and Jerry Coniker

Companion book: *Orthodoxy - The Romance of Faith*, by G.K. Chesterton, 501-01536-4

Video set: (4 hours), 126-1807VK
Audio set (4 hours), 126-1807AK

Spiritual Life in the Modern World by Fr. John Hardon, S.J.

Faculty: Fr. John Hardon, S.J., Dr. Burns Seeley, and Jerry Coniker

Companion book: No book is currently available for this series

Video set (4 hours), 126-975VK
Audio set (4 hours), 126-975AK

Theology of Prayer by Fr. John Hardon, S.J.

Faculty: Fr. John Hardon, S.J., Dr. Burns Seeley, and Jerry Coniker

Companion book: No book is currently available for this series

Video set (4 hours), 126-1402VK
Audio set (4 hours), 126-1402AK

Rejoice in the Lord by Fr. George Kosicki

Faculty: Fr. George Kosicki, C.S.B., and Jerry Coniker

Companion book: *Rejoice in the Lord Always*, by Fr. George Kosicki, 522-RLA

Video set (3 hours), 126-3590VK
Audio set (3 hours), 126-3590AK

The 12 Steps to Holiness and Salvation by St. Alphonsus Liguori

Faculty: Fr. Francis Novak, C.SS.R., Sandy Redmond, Dr. Burns Seeley, and Jerry Coniker

Companion book: *The 12 Steps to Holiness and Salvation*, by St. Alphonsus Liguori, 510-037

Video set (4 hours), 126-3632VK
Audio set (4 hours), 126-3632AK

Transformation in Christ I by Dr. Dietrich von Hildebrand

Faculty: Dr. Alice von Hildebrand, Dr. Burns Seeley, and Jerry Coniker

Companion book: *Transformation in Christ*, by Dietrich von Hildebrand, 528-3

Video set (4 hours), 126-3726VK
Audio set (4 hours), 126-3726AK

Transformation in Christ II by Dr. Dietrich von Hildebrand

Faculty: Dr. Alice von Hildebrand, Dr. Burns Seeley, and Jerry Coniker

Companion book: *Transformation in Christ*, by Dietrich von Hildebrand, 528-3

Video set (4 hours), 126-3822VK
Audio set (4 hours), 126-3822AK

What Does God Want? by Fr. Michael Scanlan, T.O.R.

Faculty: Fr. Michael Scanlan, T.O.R., and Jerry Coniker

Companion Book: *What Does God Want?*, by Fr. Michael Scanlan, 591-190

Video set (3 hours), 115-227VK
Audio set (3 hours), 115-227AK

Suffering

On the Christian Meaning of Human Suffering (Salvifici Doloris) by Pope John Paul II

Faculty: Sr. John Vianney, S.S.N.D. (suffered for over 40 years in bed), Dr. Burns Seeley, and Jerry Coniker

Companion Book: *On the Christian Meaning of Human Suffering*, by Pope John Paul II, 503-EPO145

Video set (4 hours), 126-1305VK
Audio set (4 hours), 126-1305AK

The Good News of Suffering by Fr. George Kosicki

Faculty: Fr. George Kosicki, C.S.B., and Jerry Coniker

Companion book: No book is currently available for this series

Video set (2 hours), 126-3617VK
Audio set (2 hours), 126-3617AK

Friends of the Cross by Saint Louis de Montfort

Faculty: Fr. Ed Wade, Fr. Basil Smith, and Jerry Coniker

Companion book: *Friends of the Cross*, by St. Louis de Montfort (in the *Family Consecration Prayer and Meditation Book: Divine Mercy Edition*), 305-14

Video set: (3 hours), 126-3774VK
Audio set (3 hours), 126-3774AK

Catechetics

Faith for Today by Fr. Richard Hogan & Fr. John LeVoir

Faculty: Fr. Richard Hogan, Fr. John LeVoir, Dr. Burns Seeley, and Jerry Coniker

Companion Book: *Faith For Today* by Fr. Richard Hogan & Fr. John LeVoir, 503-26553

Video set (4 hours), 126-2091VK
Audio set (4 hours), 126-2091AK

Alone With God by Francis Cardinal Arinze

Faculty: Francis Cardinal Arinze, Jerry Coniker, Bishop William L. D'Mello, and Keith Fournier.

Companion book: *Alone With God* (in the *Family Consecration Prayer and Meditation Book: Divine Mercy Edition*), 305-14

Video set (4 hours), 126-3365VK
Audio set (4 hours), 126-3365AK

Family Catechism on Tape: Dialogue with Cardinal Arinze

Faculty: Francis Cardinal Arinze and Jerry Coniker

Companion book: *The Apostolate's Family Catechism*, by Fr. Lawrence Lovasik, S.V.D., 380-18

Video set (22 hours), 115-93VK
Audio set (22 hours), 115-93AK

Catechism for Kids on Tape with Sr. John Vianney

Faculty: Sr. John Vianney, S.S.N.D., Dr. Burns Seeley, Jerry Coniker, and children

Companion book: *The Apostolate's Family Catechism*, by Fr. Lawrence Lovasik, S.V.D., 380-18

Video set: (28 hours), 115-180VK
Audio set (28 hours), 115-180AK

Sacrament Preparation Program

with Francis Cardinal Arinze

(Resource #115-142VK)

15 videotaped "preparation programs" based on the *Catechism of the Catholic Church*

Baptism (two tapes)

- Baptism; Celebration of Baptism; Meaning of the Baptismal Ceremony (115-103V, 1-hour)
- Vocation and Mission of the Baptized; The Graces of Baptism (115-104V, 30-minutes)

Confirmation (one tape)

- The Meaning of Confirmation; The Effects of Confirmation (115-109V, 30-minutes)

Penance (two tapes)

- The Sacrament of Penance — Its Nature; Conversion & Reconciliation; Contrition & Confession (115-113V, 1-hour)
- The Minister and the Effects of the Sacrament (115-114V, 30-minutes)

The Most Holy Eucharist (three tapes)

- The Eucharist and Its Titles; Eucharist: Preparation and Institution; Celebration of the Holy Eucharist (115-119V, 1-hour)
- Parts of the Celebration; Thanksgiving & Memorial; The Presence of Christ (115-120V, 1-hour)
- The Eucharistic Table; Effects of the Eucharist (115-121V, 30-minutes)

Matrimony (four tapes)

- Marriage: God's Plan; Marriage: Under the Sway of Sin; Marriage & the Old Testament (115-126V, 1-hour)

- Marriage & the New Testament; Celebration of Marriage; The Marriage Bond (115-127V, 1-hour)

- Virgins for the Sake of the Kingdom Complement Marriage (115-128V, 30-minutes, includes music)

- Chastity: A Virtue for All; Offenses Against Chastity; Living the Virtue of Purity (115-129V, 1-hour)

Anointing of the Sick (one tape)

- Anointing of the Sick (115-134V, 30-minutes)

Prayer (one tape)

- Origins of Prayer; Prayer in the Old Testament; Prayer of Jesus and Mary (115-138V, 1-hour)

Holy Orders (one tape) (115-136V, 1-hour)

You can learn the Truth about the Sacraments with Cardinal Arinze.

✔ Teaching with the authority and competence of a Roman Curia Cardinal

✔ Teaching from the *Catechism of the Catholic Church*

✔ Dealing with critical issues in the Church that have been clouded by confusion in today's society

---

1-800-FOR-MARY • Fax: (740) 765-5561 • www.familyland.org

Time for Truth

Video Sets & Audio Albums

On the Christian Meaning of Human Suffering

 Learn the joy which comes from discovering the true meaning of suffering, the salvific meaning. Sister John Vianney **reviews the Pope John Paul II's Apostolic Letter,** *On the Christian Meaning of Human Suffering.* Having suffered for over 40 years in bed, Sister brings a wealth of insight into this document.

Resource #126-1305AK, 4 one-hour audios
Resource #126-1305VK, 4 one-hour videos
Companion book: *On the Christian Meaning of Human Suffering* (Resource #503-EPO145)

Life of the Holy Family PLUS

 This spiritual classic is a compendium of works which serves to enrich your faith life. You will learn about the life of the Holy Family of Nazareth in a dynamically narrated series (taken from the Bible and *The Mystical City of God).* Contemporary music and traditional hymns will deepen your family-held values. A dramatization of the Fatima story will touch your family members' imagination with this most challenging prophetic message of our time. Also includes the Family Rosary with the Coniker family. Excellent for the whole family. **A must for young families!**

Resource #121-52AK, 8 one-hour audios

Encounters with Mother Teresa
Insights on Family Life

This series penetrates the depth of Mother Teresa's wisdom. It includes interviews with Jerry and Gwen Coniker, founders of The Apostolate, plus various speeches Mother Teresa has made throughout the world. This collection of tapes reveals Mother Teresa's hidden wisdom as she shares her insights on family life. Also featured is Fr. Sebastian, M.C., superior and co-founder of Mother Teresa's contemplative order of priests and brothers and director of her Lay Missionaries of Charity. When listening to Fr. Sebastian, it's like hearing Mother Teresa—he has truly been formed in her spirit. See pages 618-619 for complete listing.

Resource #164-120AK, 8 one-hour audios
Resource #164-120VK, 8 one-hour videos

What Does God Want?
A Practical Guide to Making Decisions

Jerry Coniker interviews Fr. Michael Scanlan, author of the book, *What Does God Want?*—allowing you to draw deeper insights from this practical book which helps you discern God's will at each crossroad of your life and in daily decisions. This series is ideal for any person in any situation — housewife, career person, student, or priest.

Resource #115-227AK, 3 one-hour audios
Resource #115-227VK, 3 one-hour videos
Companion book: *What Does God Want?* (Resource #591-190)

Pope John Paul II and Cardinal Arinze Collection

Commentaries on Pope John Paul II's works and on recent documents of the Pontifical Council for the Family. In section-by-section dialogues, Roman Curia Cardinal Francis Arinze explains the penetrating messages in these powerful documents in a way which is easily understood.

Gospel of Life *(Evangelium Vitae)*

Taken from the Holy Father's encyclical. Understand your vital role in the struggle between the "culture of life" and the "culture of death" in this timely document on life.

115-237AK, 6 one-hour audios plus free encyclical

115-237VK, 6-one hour videos, plus free encyclical
Companion book: *Gospel of Life* (503-3078X)

The Splendor of Truth *(Veritatis Splendor)*

Learn what the Catholic Church is really teaching and cut through today's moral confusion. Cardinal Arinze explains this treatise on the moral formation of society.

115-197AK, 8 one-hour audios, plus free encyclical

115-197VK, 8 one-hour videos, plus free encyclical
Companion book: *The Splendor of Truth* (503-69643)

Letter to Families

Learn the role of the family in today's society from the Church's perspective.

115-208AK, 8 one-hour audios, plus free encyclical

115-208VK, 8 one-hour videos, plus free encyclical
Companion book: *Letter to Families* (503-44713)

Crossing the Threshold of Hope

The Holy Father authored this book on how to cultivate hope in today's world.

115-290AK, 5 one-hour audios

115-290VK, 5 one-hour videos
Companion book: *Crossing the Threshold of Hope* (558-12)

As the Third Millennium Draws Near *(Tertio Millenio Adviente)* and On Human Work

In-depth commentaries on the Holy Father's preparations for the great Jubilee Year 2000 and on the dignity of work.

115-310AK, 3 one-hour audios

115-310VK, 3 one-hour videos
Companion books: *As the Third Millennium Draws Near* (503-73810); *On Human Work* (503-EPO862)

Letter to Women & Letter to Children

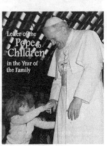

115-300AK, 3 one-hour audios

115-300VK, 3 one-hour videos
Companion books: *Letter to Women* (503-44799); *Letter to Children* (503-44756)

Preparation for Marriage

Commentaries taken from the book issued for the Pope by the Pontifical Council for the Family.

115-320AK, 3 one-hour audios

115-320VK, 3 one-hour videos

Truth & Meaning of Human Sexuality

Cardinal Arinze reviews this vital and timely document issued by the Pontifical Council for the Family. Includes guidelines for sex education.

115-330AK, 8 audios • 115-330VK, 8 videos
Companion book: *Truth & Meaning of Human Sexuality* (503-7390X)

Encounters With Mother Teresa

Exclusive Mother Teresa Interviews on Tape

Presented by the
Apostolate for Family Consecration®

Catholic Familyland®
3375 County Road 36
Bloomingdale, OH 43910-7903 (740) 765-
4301 or 1-800-FOR-MARY
www.familyland.org

Insights
into
Family
Life

Also featuring Fr. Sebastian, M.C., Superior and co-founder with Mother Teresa of her contemplative order of priests and brothers, and director of her "Lay Missionaries of Charity." When you listen to Fr. Sebastian, it's like listening to Mother Teresa.

Encounters with Mother Teresa: Insights into Family Life

Audio Album (164-120AK) *or Video Set* (164-120VK)

Tape		
1	**Her Spiritual Depth/Year of the Family**	
	Mother Teresa and Jerry Coniker	
	The Holy Family & Unconditional Surrender	
164-112A	*Fr. Sebastian*	

Tape 1
Her Spiritual Depth/Year of the Family
Mother Teresa and Jerry Coniker
The Holy Family & Unconditional Surrender
164-112A *Fr. Sebastian*

Tape 2
Consecration to the Sacred Heart & Prayer
Mother Teresa, Panel, and Fr. Sebastian
Mary/Parental Unity
164-113A *Mother Teresa, Panel, and Fr. Sebastian*

Tape 3
St. Joseph and Unity in Marriage
Mother Teresa, Panel, and Fr. Sebastian
The Holy Family As Our Model
164-114A *Mother Teresa, Panel, and Fr. Sebastian*

Tape 4
Dignity of Women and Humility of Mary
Mother Teresa
Depth of God's Mercy/A Way of Life
164-115A *Fr. Sebastian, Mother Teresa, and Jerry Coniker*

Tape 5
The Joy of Loving and Being Loved
Mother Teresa
Spiritual Hunger Worse Than Physical Hunger
164-116A *Mother Teresa, Fr. Hardon, and Jerry & Gwen Coniker*

Tape 6
Family Hours Can Stop Abortion
Mother Teresa and Jerry & Gwen Coniker
Role of Women in the Church
Encounter with Priests
164-117A *Mother Teresa*

Tape 7
Consecration Can Protect Families
Mother Teresa and Jerry & Gwen Coniker
Who Is Our Neighbor?
164-118A *Mother Teresa and Jerry & Gwen Coniker*

Tape 8
Hunger for God Filled By Priests
Mother Teresa
Need for Holy Priests/Family Prayer
164-119A *Mother Teresa and Jerry & Gwen Coniker*

Also includes the audio and video re-presentation of the famous "Prayer Breakfast Address" to Congress (120-278A/V).

The Apostolate's Catholic Corps™

The Catholic Corps works to spread the mission of the AFC, which is committed to spreading the spirituality of **Pope John Paul II** to the four corners of the earth.

Modern communications allow us to teach the Truth without limit, amplifying the voice of the Holy Father and other qualified speakers, such as Mother Teresa and Cardinal Francis Arinze.

In view of this awesome plan of God for the establishment of the public reign of Christ and His Mother, we are looking with hope toward the **Third Millennium** to be the era of saints!

Go out to the whole world; proclaim the Good News to all creation. —MARK 16:15

Be not afraid! —ACTS. 18:9

Follow me and I will make you fishers of men. —MATT. 4:19

If you desire to follow the call of the Holy Father to the youth of the world, and be a foot soldier of Our Lady in the battle for souls, come and see our Apostolate's Catholic Corps in action, at Catholic Familyland in Bloomingdale, Ohio, USA, or the St. Joseph Center in Manila, Philippines. Entering age 18-35. Call or write for more information. Phone: 1-800-FOR-MARY

The Apostolate's Catholic Corps Vocations

P R A Y E R

The Catholic Corps are young consecrated singles who serve the Church by serving in the work of the Apostolate for Family Consecration.

We make private commitments of poverty, chastity, and obedience.

We seek to serve the Lord with an undivided heart and mind.

Our spirituality is that of **Pope John Paul II**, which is firmly rooted in the **Holy Eucharist** and consecration to Jesus through the **Immaculate Mother of God**.

Over three hours of prayer each day strengthens us for our intense work of saving souls for God.

The Apostolate's Catholic Corps Vocations

W O R K

Our day-to-day work involves the latest technology in the multi-media fields. Our television studio, graphic arts, publishing, leadership, conferences, and many other departments keep us busy all year round.

We look at our work with joy, knowing that we are serving the Holy Family, renewing family life, and building the "civilization of love."

During our Holy Family Fests in the summer, we work directly with families. We serve the families in the music ministry, children's program, horse trail crew, youth ministry, and many other areas.

The Apostolate's Catholic Corps Vocations

C O M M U N I T Y

We find much strength in community. We know that wherever two or more are gathered in His Name, He is there in the midst. We know that with the encouragement of our sisters and brothers in Christ, it is much easier to stand firm in our Faith.

We live, work, and pray together, helping each other to become one with God.

If you desire to serve the Holy Family by saving families around the world…

If you desire to give the gift of your youth to the Church as the Holy Father is asking us to do…

If you desire to save souls for God…

…please call us and ask about our men's or women's Catholic Corps communities.

The Apostolate's Catholic Corps Vocations

M I S S I O N S

Consecrating the poor in the truth through *The Apostolate's Family Catechism* and the Lay Ecclesial Evangelization Teams.

Ministering to families in the Philippines

Be Not Afraid Family Hours for churches and Peace of Heart Forums on video harness the media for evangelizing our media culture of today.

The AFC St. Joseph Center studio located in Las Piñas City, Philippines

The Apostolate's Catholic Corps are apostolic celibates who bring the spirituality of Pope John Paul II to the families of the world through modern communications.

Praying or Suffering Sacri-State Members

Mother Teresa of Calcutta with Jerry and Gwen Coniker.

In 1976, Mother Teresa joined The Apostolate's Advisory Council and told Jerry and Gwen Coniker that The Family Apostolate would touch many more families if it gathered an army of suffering souls to support its active members.

Sacri-State members of the Apostolate for Family Consecration are those who offer up their prayers or physical sufferings to God, through Mary, for active members and for The Apostolate's mission of renewing families and parishes.

Sacri-State members are channels of spiritual power for The Family Apostolate's mission. They bear with love all of the crosses that God, in His infinite wisdom, chooses to send them. Sacri-State members are remembered in a special way in The Apostolate's daily prayers and are spiritually united with other associations.

To receive a Sacri-State member application, write: The Family Apostolate, Bloomingdale, OH 43910-7903.

Sister John Vianney, S.S.N.D., the AFC's first Sacri-State Associate, suffered for over 40 years in bed, and yet taught the Faith to children from her bedside.

Holy Family Fests

A Week of Family Fun for Everyone!

A chance for the entire family to experience Catholic community! Pray, work, and play together for **seven days**, while learning to use a Vatican-approved, multi-media parish evangelization program.

Concerts
Family banners
200 ft. water slide
Sing-along campfires
Trail rides on horseback
Hiking through the woods
St. John Bosco Pool
Family prayer & catechesis
Family sports
Sacrament of Reconciliation
...and much more!

LEARN the Family Catechism

GROW in the Sacraments of
Reconciliation and Holy Eucharist

LEARN how to implement The Apostolate's Lay
Ecclesial Team Evangelization System
in your parish

SHARE joyfully with other families and bring
your family closer to God
and to one another

AFC Catholic Familyland®, Bloomingdale, OH 43910-7903

Experience Catholic community life for a whole week! Learn the Eucharistic and Marian formula to heal families and usher in the era of peace that Our Lady of Fatima promised once enough of us make and live our consecrations.

Pro-God, Pro-Life, Pro-Family

Families praying, working, and playing together!

Come join us for a Holy Family Fest.
For more information call **1-800-FOR-MARY**.

1-800-FOR-MARY • Fax: (740) 765-5561 • *www.familyland.org*

Marriage "Get-Away" Weekends

Get away with your spouse for three unforget-table days. You and your beloved will experience:

- insights from our Faith to live by
- the wisdom of others for inspiration
- strength from the Sacraments
- laughter to lift your heart
- a few tears of gratitude and healing
- the grace of God to send you forth with renewed commitment for Christ and one another
- plus valuable tips on parenting and spousal communication

Evangelization & Catechetical Workshops

We are training parents and parish and association leaders to be part of a Lay Ecclesial Team, to bring about "the civilization of love" in the spirit of Pope John Paul II – an achievable goal if we plan and act now!

Come join us. For more information call

1-800-FOR-MARY

AFC Catholic Familyland®, Bloomingdale, OH 43910-7903

Conceptual Chart of The Apostolate's Gifts to the Church

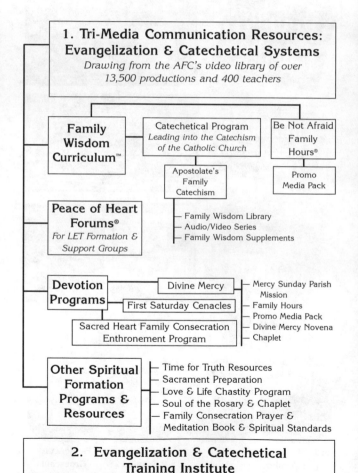

1. Tri-Media Communication Resources: Evangelization & Catechetical Systems

Drawing from the AFC's video library of over 13,500 productions and 400 teachers

Family Wisdom Curriculum™

Catechetical Program
Leading into the Catechism of the Catholic Church

Be Not Afraid Family Hours®

Apostolate's Family Catechism

Promo Media Pack

— Family Wisdom Library
— Audio/Video Series
— Family Wisdom Supplements

Peace of Heart Forums®
For LET Formation & Support Groups

Devotion Programs

Divine Mercy

First Saturday Cenacles

Sacred Heart Family Consecration Enthronement Program

— Mercy Sunday Parish Mission
— Family Hours
— Promo Media Pack
— Divine Mercy Novena
— Chaplet

Other Spiritual Formation Programs & Resources

— Time for Truth Resources
— Sacrament Preparation
— Love & Life Chastity Program
— Soul of the Rosary & Chaplet
— Family Consecration Prayer & Meditation Book & Spiritual Standards

2. Evangelization & Catechetical Training Institute

AFC Catholic Familyland®, Bloomingdale, OH 43910-7903

3. Lay Ecclesial Team Evangelization System™

Serving Families, Pastors, & Bishops; Open to Members of Other Movements

- Evangelization Outreach
- Family Hours
- Home & Parish Catechesis
- Perpetual Adoration
- Devotions
- Right-to-Life
- Teen Chastity & Evangelization
- Marriage Preparation
- Feeding & Housing the Hungry
- Single Parent Support Group
- Chemical Dependent Support Group
- and more

4. Support Ministries

International TV & Radio Ministry

- Daily Family Covenant Series
- Daily Holy Rosary
- Daily Chaplet of Divine Mercy
- Weekly Spirit of John Paul II Series
- Weekly Healing Our Family Series
- Weekly Holy Family Fest Series
- Weekly Be Not Afraid Family Hour Series
- Same as above except in Spanish
- Weekly Family Catechism Series (with Cardinal Arinze)
- Same as above except in Spanish (with Fr. Pablo Straub)
- Weekly Catholic Corps Christ Calls Series
- Monthly First Saturday Cenacles

Catholic Familyland
950 acres set apart

- Conferences
- Holy Family Fests
- Marriage Get-Away Weekends
- Youth Retreats
- Theme Retreats
- Pilgrimages
- Evangelization & Catechetical Training Institute

Membership: First, Second, Third Degree and Life

- Sacri-State Suffering & Praying Members
- Cooperator Members
- Disciple Ecclesial Team Members
- Apostle Married Full-Time Staff
- Catholic Corps — Consecrated Single Full-Time Staff
- Mystical Rose — Consecrated Widow Full-Time Staff
- Tower of David — Consecrated Widower Full-Time Staff

© MCMXCVII

APOSTOLATE for family consecration®
Helping you nourish families through the Catholic Faith

A "fail-safe" way of igniting the sleeping giant of the laity for the New Evangelization in the Catholic Church for the third millennium.

The Apostolate's Lay Ecclesial Team Evangelization System™

using theologically-approved tri-media resources to simultaneously renew the family & the parish

Area Coordinator
in cooperation with the hierarchy

Neighborhood Core of up to 12 Lay
Ecclesial Teams using approved tri-media resources

Each Ecclesial Team has specific evangelization outreach assignments using approved tri-media resources. Examples from more than 40 outreach ministries are given below.

Spiritual Works of Mercy

Ecclesial Team 1	**Ecclesial Team 2**	**Ecclesial Team 3**
Evangelizes with Weekly Be Not Afraid Family Hours on video B20	Catechesis, Home Visitation, & Consecration and/or CCD C20 or C25	Catechesis, Home Visitation, & Consecration and/or Schools C20 or C30

Ecclesial Team 4	**Ecclesial Team 5**	**Ecclesial Team 6**
Adult Convert Catechetics & Consecration and/or RCIA Program C35	Perpetual Eucharistic Adoration P20	First Saturday Days of Recollection & Divine Mercy Parish Missions F20 or D20

Corporal Works of Mercy

Ecclesial Team 7	**Ecclesial Team 8**	**Ecclesial Team 9**
Youth Programs: Home Visitation for Right to Life, Teen Chastity, and PHF Y30	Marriage Preparation & Enhancement Peace of Heart Forums M25	Peace of Heart Forum Support Groups, includes Single Parent Women S30

Ecclesial Team 10	**Ecclesial Team 11**	**Ecclesial Team 12**
PHF Support Groups, includes those Healing from Abortion H20	Feeding, Clothing, & Housing the Poor, includes Peace of Heart Forums H25, H30, H35	Peace of Heart Forums, includes Chemical Dependents C55

- Up to 12 Ecclesial Teams per Neighborhood Core, each with up to approximately 24 members per Team.

- Ecclesial Team members only need to be first degree members of the Apostolate for Family Consecration, meaning they use AFC tri-media resources and programs, which are loyal to the teaching authority of the Catholic Church, **but they need _not_ necessarily follow the spirituality of the AFC.** See section 850 on page 532.

- **Ecclesial Teams may also consist of other associations** loyal to the Magisterium and teaching authority of the Church, such as the Legion of Mary, Knights of Columbus, Serra Club, Opus Dei, Focolare, Couples for Christ, CFM, DMI, Marriage Encounter, Nurturing Network, Rachael's Vineyard, Cursillo, Holy Name Society, St. Vincent de Paul Society, Perpetual Eucharistic Adoration, Natural Family Planning, Right-to-Life, various Third Order communities, etc. The formation which team members receive through this system will enable them to grow more deeply in their faith and expand their ministries. Loyalty to the Magisterial Teaching of the Church, specifically to the CCC, is a prerequisite.

- Each Ecclesial Team conducts weekly 2-hour meetings. **The first part of the meeting is focused on formation and support of its members, the second part on evangelization reporting & planning.** For formation, team members use **The Apostolate's tri-media, theologically-approved "Peace of Heart Forums," which are formation programs** based upon the Vatican-approved "Apostolate's Family Catechism," Sacred Scripture, the "Catechism of the Catholic Church," papal documents, Total Consecration, and other treasures of Catholic spirituality. (See pages 590–621.)

- Each Team conducts at least one outreach program, requiring a minimum commitment of 2 hours per week for each team member. In addition, every Ecclesial Team member should attend the weekly "Be Not Afraid Family Hour" (with their family) or other outreaches, and the weekly Ecclesial Team formation and evangelization planning meeting mentioned above. The Ecclesial Team Coordinators and trainers meet monthly with their Neighborhood Core Leader, who is a Second Degree or above member of the AFC.

- Cardinal Ciappi, O.P., Papal Theologian Emeritus, assured bishops and pastors when he wrote the AFC on Oct. 9, 1994: "Your use of the social communications and the way in which you are using audio and video tape is a **'fail-safe method' of teaching** and will allow families of today's media culture, which the Holy Father frequently mentions, to become powerful instruments of the Immaculata to bring about the era of peace she promised at Fatima." Cardinal Ciappi was the Primary Theological Advisor to The Apostolate from 1979 until his death on April 17, 1996.

Apostolate for Family Consecration's

Video Faculty, Authors, and Advisory Council

Administration

Jerome and Gwen Coniker* ** ***
President/Founders
Rev. Kevin S. Barrett* ** ***
Chaplain
Rory D. Freiermuth*
Vice-President
Patricia R. Hauber*
Secretary
Carolyn E. Stegmann*
Treasurer

Theological Auditors

Fr. Ronald D. Lawler, O.F.M., Cap., Ph.D.*
Dr. Regis Martin, S.T.D.*

Primary Theological & Spiritual Advisors

Francis Cardinal Arinze* ** ***
Mario Luigi Cardinal Ciappi, O.P.†* ** ***
John J. Cardinal O'Connor*
Jaime Cardinal Sin (Philippines)*
J. Francis Cardinal Stafford* ***
Alfonso Cardinal Lopez Trujillo* ***
Archbishop Agostino Cacciavillan*
Bishop John J. Magee (Ireland)* ** ***
Bishop Gilbert I. Sheldon*
Bishop Juan F. Torres (Puerto Rico)* ***
Rev. Msgr. Roger J. Foys*
Rev. Msgr. Josefino Ramirez* ***
Rev. Msgr. Dennis M. Schnurr
Rev. Msgr. John G. Woolsey* ***
Fr. Roger Charest, S.M.M.* ***
Fr. Bernard Geiger, O.F.M.Conv.* ** ***
Fr. Michael Scanlan, T.O.R.* ***
Fr. Timothy M. Sparks, O.P.* **

---

*AFC Video Faculty Member
**Members who have written for our work
***Members featured on multiple videos
†Deceased members

Fr. Pablo Straub, C.Ss.R.* ***
Mother Teresa of Calcutta†* ***

Advisory Council Members of the Roman Curia
William Cardinal Baum
Giovanni Cardinal Cheli*
Jorge A. Cardinal Medina Estevéz
Edouard Cardinal Gagnon, P.S.S.* ***
Pio Cardinal Laghi* ***
Augustine Cardinal Mayer, O.S.B.
Silvio Cardinal Oddi* ***
Eduardo Cardinal Pironio†
Agnelo Cardinal Rossi†
Opilio Cardinal Rossi
Jose Cardinal Sanchez* ***
Edmund Cardinal Szoka* ***
Jozef Cardinal Tomko*
Archbishop Paul Cordes*
Archbishop John P. Foley* ***
Archbishop Sergio Sebastiani
Bishop Peter Canisius J. Van Lierde†* ***
Rev. Msgr. Francesco Di Felice*
Rev. Msgr. Peter Elliott* ** ***
Fr. Robert J. Dempsey* ***
Fr. Frank Pavone* ***

International Episcopal Advisory Council Members
Anthony Cardinal Bevilacqua* ***
John Joseph Cardinal Carberry
Norberto Cardinal Rivera Carrera
Terence Cardinal Cooke†
William Cardinal Keeler
Adam Cardinal Maida*
Humberto Cardinal Medeiros†
Christoph Cardinal Schonborn (Austria)*
Archbishop John F. Donoghue*
Archbishop Patrick F. Flores
Archbishop Gaudencio B. Rosales (Philippines)*
Bishop Paul Andreotti, O.P. (Pakistan)†*
Bishop Ramon C. Arguelles (Philippines)* ***
Bishop Ayo-Maria Atoyebi, O.P. (Nigeria)*
Bishop Teodoro Bacani (Philippines)
Bishop Warren L. Boudreaux†*
Bishop Fabian W. Bruskewitz
Bishop Leo Brust†*

Bishop Ignatius A. Catanello
Bishop Thomas V. Daily*
Bishop William L. D'Mello (India)*
Bishop Joseph A. Galante
Bishop John Joseph (Pakistan)*
Bishop J.B. Kakubi (Uganda)* ***
Bishop Angel N. Lagdameo (Philippines)
Bishop Joseph J. Madera (Military Archdiocese)* ***
Bishop John J. Myers*
Bishop Bernard Martin Ngaviliau, C.S.Sp. (E. Africa)
Bishop Lawrence J. Riley
Bishop Augustine M. Shao, C.S.Sp. (Tanzania)
Bishop James S. Sullivan
Bishop Martin Igwe Uzoukwu (Nigeria)*
Bishop Thomas J. Welsh* ***

Advisory Council Members and Video Faculty

Abbot Edmund McCaffrey, O.S.B.*
Rev. Msgr. P. Luciano Guerra (Portugal)*
Rev. Msgr. Paul A. Lenz* ***
Rev. Msgr. John McCarthy, J.C.D., S.T.D.* ***
Rev. Msgr. Eugene Pack†*
Rev. Msgr. Alphonse S. Popek†* ***
Rev. Msgr. Michael J. Wrenn*
Fr. Henri Bechard, S.J.†* ** ***
Fr. Alfred Boeddeker†* ***
Fr. Timothy Byerley* ***
Fr. Gabriel Calvo
Fr. Harold Cohen, S.J.* ***
Fr. Dominic De Domenico, O.P.* ***
Fr. William Dorney†* ***
Fr. Thomas F. Egan, S.J.* ***
Fr. Francis Filas, S.J.†*
Fr. Tom Forrest, C.Ss.R.* ***
Fr. Lambert Greenan, O.P.†* ***
Fr. Benedict Groeshel, C.F.R.*
Fr. John Hardon, S.J.* ** ***
Fr. Brian Harrison, S.T.L.* ** ***
Fr. Richard M. Hogan, Ph.D.* ***
Fr. M. Albert Krapiec, O.P. (Poland)* ***
Fr. Maynard Kolodziej, O.F.M.* ***
Fr. George Kosicki, C.S.B.* ** ***
Fr. Alfred J. Kunz* ***
Fr. Peter Lappin, S.D.B.* ** ***
Fr. Francis Larkin†

Fr. John LeVoir* ***
Fr. Lawrence Lovasik, S.V.D.†* ** ***
Fr. Seraphim Michalenko, M.I.C.* ***
Fr. Thomas Morrison, O.P.**
Fr. Joseph Mungari, S.A.C.* ***
Fr. Bruce Nieli, C.F.R*
Fr. Francis Novak, C.Ss.R.* ***
Fr. Randall Paine* ***
Fr. Gabriel Pausback, O.Carm†*
Fr. Howard Rafferty, O.Carm†*
Fr. Charles F. Shelby, C.M.* ***
Fr. Stanley Smolenski* ** ***
Fr. Andrej Szostek, M.I.C. (Poland)* ***
Fr. Edmundo Ortega Tirado (Mexico)
Sr. Concetta, F.S.P.
Mother M. Dolorosa, H.P.B.
Mother M. Immaculata, H.M.I.* ** ***
Sr. John Vianney, S.S.N.D.†* ** ***
Mrs. Patricia Balskus†**
Dr. Warren Carroll, Ph.D.*
Dr. N.M. Camardese, M.D.* ***
Mr. Raymond E. Cross*
Ambassador Howard Dee*
Dr. Richard DeGraff* ***
Hon. Jeremiah Denton* ***
Dr. Richard Dumont* ** ***
Dr. Damien Fedoryka* ***
Mr. Frank Flick†
Mr. Dale Francis†* ** ***
John and Eleanor Hand*
Mr. Frederick W. Hill*
Mr. Carl Karcher*
Mr. August Mauge†
Allen & Marlene McCauley*
Mr. Frank J. Milligan, Jr.†*
Mr. Thomas Monaghan*
Dr. Anthony N. Paruta* ***
Dr. Wanda Poltawska*
Dr. Herbert Ratner, M.D.†
Mr. Anthony F. Sansone, Sr.
Mr. Charles F. Scholl
Dr. Alice von Hildebrand* ***
Dr. Charles Wahlig†* ** ***
Dr. and Mrs. Paul Whelan* ***

[Partial List]

INDEX

Note: The numbers in parenthesis refer to specific prayer and section numbers.

642

644

648

Mother Teresa Speaks to Families

A videotape presentation of Mother Teresa's message for families from the Apostolate for Family Consecration. This one-hour video highlights the extensive footage of Mother Teresa's interviews and speeches. And it's all primarily addressed to you...*the family.*

Mother Teresa speaks out on:
- **Prayer in the family**
- **The evils of abortion**
- **Our Lady**

Also includes her last videotaped message to the world, <u>PLUS</u>, a free audio-tape of the re-presentation of Mother Teresa's famous Prayer Breakfast Speech to Congress. (Resource #120-283V)

Soul of the Rosary
Pray-Along Videos and Audios for the Entire Family

The Soul of the Rosary combines the benefits of a spoken Rosary with beautiful Scriptural images for each Hail Mary. These full-color pictures hold the attention of young and old alike, making the Rosary come alive for the entire family and enriching your meditation on each mystery. The audio format can be prayed in the car while commuting or traveling. Available on audio (133-158AK), or video (133-158VK).

The family that prays together stays together!

AFC Catholic Familyland®, Bloomingdale, OH 43910-7903

Family Consecration Prayer & Meditation Book
Divine Mercy Edition

*If you love Divine Mercy, here's the most complete
devotional book on Divine Mercy in the world.*

It's both a "family consecration" prayer book and an in-depth meditation book
which will help you to be "in tune" with the richness of God's Mercy every day.

• A complete presentation of the five dimensions of
the Divine Mercy Devotion: the Image, the Chaplet,
the Novena (includes illustrated Stations of the
Cross), the Feast Day (Mercy Sunday), and the
Spreading of the Message

• Pope John Paul II's Encyclical on Divine Mercy —
with Fr. George Kosicki's commentaries

• In-depth Examination of Conscience exercises

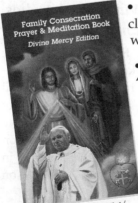

Resource #305-14

• Cardinal Arinze's spiritual
classic for our times, "Alone
with God"

• St. Louis de Montfort's
"Friends of the Cross" treatise

• PLUS many other prayers,
meditations, and commen-
taries that will bring down
the mercy of God. Over 250
pictures and 650 pages!

1-800-FOR-MARY

Reply Section

❏ Please place this petition at the foot of the altar in your St. John Vianney Chapel at Catholic Familyland, and include it in all of the Masses offered for the needs of your petitioners throughout the coming week.

_____

_____

_____

_____

❏ I promise to pray that God will use The Apostolate to inspire people to live the Eucharistic and Marian Spirit of Pope John Paul II.

❏ I am physically suffering from _____ and would like to offer my suffering for your work.

❏ I am a priest and will include the intentions of The Apostolate and all of those who are asking for your prayers in my available Masses, particularly on Fridays.

❏ Enclosed is my best for God—my seed-Charity donation for the vital work of The Apostolate. _____

❏ I am not on your mailing list; please add my name.

❏ Please send me information about your tri-media Vatican-Approved Family Catechism for families, CCD, and schools.

❏ I would like to receive more information about conducting your Be Not Afraid Family Hours on video.

❏ I would like to receive more information about starting or joining a Lay Ecclesial Evangelization Team in my area.

❑ Please send me _____ copies of this *Family Consecration Prayer and Meditation Book–Divine Mercy Edition* (#305-14) for $10.00 each in the U.S.A., plus shipping & handling.

Quantity Prices

1-14	$10.00	50-99	$8.00	500-999	$6.50
15-24	$ 9.50	100-249	$7.50	1000	$6.00
25-49	$ 8.50	250-499	$7.00	**(call for larger quantity prices)**	

Regular Shipping and Handling Rates	
Up to $9.99 add $2.00	$60.00 - $119.99 add $6.50
$10.00 - $24.99 add $3.50	$120.00 - $239.99 add $8.50
$25.00 - $59.99 add $4.50	$240.00 and up add 7% of value

Canada & Other Countries: Payments must be an international money order or a bank check payable in "U.S. Funds" at any bank in the U.S. (Address of the U.S. bank must be printed on the money order or check.) Please double shipping rates for Mexico and Canada; triple the shipping rates for other countries.

Please Print

Name: _____

Address: _____

City/State _____

Zip _____

Phone: (____) _____

In the U.S.A. mail to:

Apostolate for Family Consecration
Catholic Familyland, 3375 County Rd. 36
Bloomingdale, OH 43910-7903 USA
Phone: (740) 765-4301 or 1-800-FOR-MARY
Fax: (740) 765-5561 • www.familyland.org
email: info@familyland.org   **U.S.A.**

In the Philippines contact:

St. Joseph Center, P.O. Box 0026
Las Piñas City, Philippines
Phil. Phone: (632) 800-4440 or 800-4439
Fax: (632) 800-4438 • email: st_paul@mozcom.com